BRUMBACK LIBRARY
3 3045 00129 2735

P9-DBI-253

FLOWERING GARDENS

FLOWERING SHRUBS

CUTTING GARDENS

ORNAMENTAL TREES

FLOWERING GARDENS

FLOWERING SHRUBS
by **Ken Druse**

CUTTING GARDENS
by **Chet Davis**

ORNAMENTAL TREES
by **Charles O. Cresson**

SMITHMARK

Burpee Flowering Gardens was originally published in three volumes.

This edition published in 1997 by SMITHMARK Publishers, a division of
U.S. Media Holdings, Inc., 115 W. 18th St., New York, NY 10011.

SMITHMARK books are available for bulk purchase for sales promotion and premium use. For details call or write the manager of special sales, SMITHMARK Publishers, 115 W. 18th St., New York, NY 10011; (212) 519 1300.

This edition published by special arrangement with Simon & Schuster, Inc. and W.S. Konecky Associates.

ISBN: 0-7651-9329-9

Manufactured in the U.S.A.

10 9 8 7 6 5 4 3 2 1

1998

CONTENTS

FLOWERING SHRUBS

CUTTING GARDENS

ORNAMENTAL TREES

FLOWERING GARDENS

Flowering Shrubs, Cutting Gardens and Ornamental Trees

This three-part volume is filled with ideas and information that will help you create a more beautiful home and garden. It describes hundreds of plants and tells you how to grow them successfully and keep them healthy. You'll learn how to feature trees and shrubs as prominent specimens in a garden, and how to produce a bountiful supply of cut flowers for indoor arrangements. Throughout the book, lovely color photographs show you what all the plants and flowers look like and supplement the detailed descriptions.

Flowering Shrubs

Varied and versatile, shrubs are the most useful plants in a garden. They make the hedges or screens that enclose an area, define its limits, and provide privacy. A foundation planting of clipped evergreen shrubs makes a quiet, dignified frame for a traditional house, while a mixture of unpruned evergreen and deciduous shrubs creates a natural-looking setting for a contemporary home. A large, broad, flowering shrub is the classic centerpiece for a lawn. Smaller shrubs combine well with perennials in a mixed flower border. Low-growing shrubs serve as groundcovers.

Shrubs are relatively inexpensive, fast-growing, and easy to care for. The main challenge is choosing from the many wonderful varieties available. *Flowering Shrubs* recommends the best selections of popular, well-known shrubs such as lilac, camellia, butterflybush, azalea, and rhododendron, and introduces many less-familiar shrubs such as spicebush, tamarix, and chaste tree. Adding some of these uncommon shrubs will make your garden more interesting and distinguish it from your neighbor's.

Cutting Gardens

Making bouquets of flowers brings the beauty of the garden into the house. Arrangers who want a generous supply of flowers often designate a special area for growing them. *Cutting Gardens* tells how to plant and tend a garden of annuals, perennials, and bulbs whose flowers last well in arrangements, such as asters, cosmos, sweet peas, dahlias, and lilies. It gives detailed advice on how to pick and prepare the flowers so they will stay fresh as long as possible. It also tells how to pick roses, lilacs, forsythia, apple blossoms, and other flowers from shrubs and trees and use them for indoor arrangements.

Ornamental Trees

Trees dominate a garden. They are the largest plants, they live the longest, and they set the stage for everything else you grow. Their lower limbs make an outdoor "ceiling" that gives a garden a sheltered feeling, at the same time as their upper boughs lead your eyes to the sky. Trees provide cool shade in summer, create privacy and screening, and accommodate songbirds.

If, like most properties, your lot already has some trees growing on it, you need to know how to prune, train, mulch, fertilizer, and water them, and how to protect them from insects and diseases. *Ornamental Trees* gives both general guidelines and specific advice on caring for particular kinds of trees.

If you have space to plant a new tree, this section will help you choose one. There are many factors to take into account: your climate and soil, the tree's size and shape at maturity, how fast it grows, whether it needs any special care or is susceptible to damage from common problems, as well as how it looks throughout the year. Because trees are a long-term investment, it's worth taking time to make a thoughtful decision. Read here about dogwoods, magnolias, crabapples, and many other kinds of trees that are adaptable, carefree, neat, and shapely, and have one or more ornamental features—fresh flowers in spring, vivid fall foliage, bright-colored berries, or attractive bark.

FLOWERING SHRUBS

Ken Druse

1

THE FLOWERING SHRUB PLANNER

NATURE'S HAND

Nature abhors a vacuum. Open land if left, even for a little while, begins to change. First the opportunistic plants, what we might call weeds or maybe wildflowers and meadow grasses, take hold. In a year or so, woody plants brought to this place as seeds by birds or borne on the wind, sprout. These are the shrubs and trees.

These seedlings continue to grow, and in a few more years, the open land is covered with good-size shrubs and small trees. In time, the trees grow up and shade out much of the underplantings. Some shade-tolerant shrubs exist in the shadows cast by the taller trees. Along the edge of open land or by rivers, lakes and streams, the shrubs of the understory flourish in great variety. Some hydrangeas, sweet pepperbushes, rhododendron, mountain laurels and shrub dogwood grow there. In hot, dry climates or in places with poor, rocky soil, the trees may never get a good foothold, and the sun-loving, low woody shrubs remain. Rockroses, brooms and California lilacs are among those that continue to eke out an existence in this moisture- and nutrient-starved environment. These persistent plants, the flowering shrubs, are the progenitors of the ornamental shrubs for our home gardens.

USES OF SHRUBS IN THE LANDSCAPE

Not only does nature supply these shrubs, it also provides suggestions on how to use them in the landscape. Inspiration for informal shrub designs comes from this model. Under tall trees in a shady garden shrubs can be planted. Such shrubs as the oak-leafed hydrangea, Carolina allspice, fothergilla, redvein enkianthus and Virginia sweet spire populate middle-layer plantings above ferns and shade-loving wildflowers.

If you live by the edge of a wooded area, then the shrubs that populate those transitional areas, the ones that "introduce" the forest, would offer recommendations for you. Viburnums in variety, witch hazels and sweet bay magnolia could be included. If space allows, a nearly wild area could be developed for the outside boundaries of your property. A selection of trees to include some of those that live in the wild places around you as well as similar ones from other parts of the world could be garnered for your collection. In front of these, masses of shrubs would provide a transition from the maintained areas of your yard, the lawn or flower plantings, to simulate the forest understory and add interest in a space too often left barren.

A deep screen could be developed for a large property by planting a variety of large shrubs that bloom in turn along the edge. Not only do these shrubs hide a view but they also dampen traffic noise and reduce the effects of wind—all while adding the visual interest of their forms

Just as shrubs in nature line the woodland edge, so too will they form a perfect transition from lawn to tall trees. The meeting of horizontal lawn to vertical trees is softened by this flowering shrub mediator.

The colorful coral blossoms of a deciduous azalea highlight the base of a city gardener's staircase. A decorative flower pot atop a classical column punctuates this formal statement.

and beautiful flowers. Shrubs can actually cool the environment by adding shade and reducing glare and reflected and radiant heat. Their leaves transpire, cooling the air with evaporating moisture. In a situation like this, a screen of shrubs that bloom sequentially, you could select from an enormous variety of shrubs. The only limitation would be that they all had similar requirements as to soil, light and moisture. Here in an informal screen, a shrub such as the mock orange would be welcome. It has the scale and form and leaf surface to do the job. But, because it blooms for a relatively short time and adds little in the way of foliage color or texture, fall or winter interest, berries or fruit, it might not do for small gardens. There, we demand more from our shrubs—they have to perform during at least two seasons, or bloom for several weeks.

Out-of-the-way places present chances to use some wonderful specimens that may or may not offer long-season color. These are occasionally viewed spots where little else will grow, or waste areas where you want some color and texture, but you will not be able to supply extra water, or other maintenance needs. Perhaps along the roadside, behind the garage, in a low, moist spot, or among the rocks of a natural outcrop, such plants as slender deutzia, Australian bottlebrush, buckeye and bush honeysuckle could fit the bill. Security hedges can be made from flowering shrubs, too. For places where meticulous, high-maintenance evergreen hedges or nonliving, chain-link fence might not be the best choices, flowering quince or, better still, the hardy trifoliate orange, with its razor-sharp thorns, could be more useful than barbed wire and infinitely more beautiful.

Many shrubs are also low groundcovers, and some can hold an embankment. These plants are perfect for "streetscapes" or steep slopes that tumble down to the road and climb up across the street. Even dwarf forsythia varieties such as *Forsythia* ×*intermedia* 'Arnold Dwarf' could be pressed into service. Aaron's-beard St.-John's-wort with large, yellow flowers all summer long is a cover just greater than 1 foot tall. Vines can be allowed to climb up through the shrubs to add color from flowers when the shrubs themselves may not be in bloom. Clematis varieties would work well, as would variegated porcelain berry or magnolia vine with red berries that form even in the shade of dense shrubs. The prerequisite for selecting shrubs for the "out back" is that they be perfectly situated. Place moisture lovers in a wet area, sun lovers to bask in the solar rays, shade lovers in the shadows, drought-tolerant candidates in fast-draining sites. This is one of the keys to growing any plant successfully.

Formality is also enhanced by repeating two similar elements. These cerise Camellia japonica *shrubs flank the gateway to the formal rose garden at Filoli in northern California.*

These suggestions for using

flowering shrubs in informal settings don't exclude their use in the formal garden or formal spaces around your home. Usually the areas around the house and the utility places, walkways, access to outdoor meters and storage areas, for example, are paved to some degree. The flowering shrubs can be worked into schemes there as well. However, much care must be exercised as to selection. These shrubs should be chosen for long interest, even if that just means evergreen foliage. And they should also stay in bounds with as little pruning as possible. Small-leafed evergreen rhododendron, usually called "azaleas," can be used to good advantage next to brick paving and around the patio edge. The new 'Robin Hill' hybrids with enormous white or pink flowers in late spring and well into summer are alternatives to the familiar suburban magenta and hot orange spring kinds. These plants have flowers more like petunias than the minitrumpet-flowered Kurume azaleas. Glossy abelia could be another choice. It is semievergreen and blooms for months, from late spring often into fall, in sun or partial shade. The shiny bronze-green foliage is also useful. Pruning will be needed from time to time if they spread and become obstructive.

Repeating symmetrical elements always imparts an air of formality, whether that's with a pair of urns or twin daphnes flanking the steps to the front door. Rows of shrubs on either side of a front walk can also be elegant. Even large shrubs could be used. Imagine rows of camellias in a shaded area on either side of a straight, or even a winding, path. These midsize shrubs bloom winter to spring, by variety, and have glossy evergreen leaves year 'round.

A flowering-shrub collection is the perfect foil for ornamental plantings. The traditional perennial border is nearly always backed by a wall or, more often, by a screen of shrubs. Flowering shrubs would do more than, say, a needle evergreen hedge—they would produce flowers that would contribute to the colorful effects through the season. A narrow access path, hidden behind the tallest plantings at the back of the border, could separate the flower planting from the flowering-shrub tableau; it would give access to both the back of the herbaceous border and the front of the flowering-shrub planting—yet be invisible to visitors who see this planting from the front only.

Large shrubs can be used to define spaces in the garden or landscape. These "walls" create "rooms" for flower plantings, or better, to furnish with more flowering shrubs. Tall lilacs, viburnums, rose of Sharons or even pussy willows could make the framework. For the rooms' "interiors," one could assemble variegated *Daphne ×Burkwoodii* 'Carol Mackie', purple smoke bush or *Kerria*

A single flowering shrub in the lawn can in itself be an arresting formal element. Isolated a bit from the crowd, this spike winter hazel has a grand and elegant presence.

Big-leafed hydrangeas and mature evergreens gracefully direct visitors to an elegant stairway. A sudden level change becomes an opportunity to create a garden masterpiece.

The complementary colors of common lilac and creamy yellow 'Lady Bank's' rose create a spectacular spring picture which, however fleeting, makes an unforgettable memory and a lasting impression on the landscape.

Flowering shrubs can be beautiful landscape problem-solvers, too. This naturalized planting of assorted azaleas forms a river of color where grass lawn would be difficult to mow.

species along with a decorative iron bench or table and chairs.

A single, grand specimen in the lawns is perhaps the most effective living formal element. One terrific flowering shrub, perhaps a peegee hydrangea, bottlebrush buckeye, tree lilac or fringe tree, would make a spectacular addition to the front yard, even where space is limited. Just take precautions to keep lawn mowers and "weed wackers" away from the base of the shrubs. A simple solution is a circle of mulch around the base of the plants, or a more formal mowing strip. This is a line of paving, usually brick, designed for the mower wheel to ride on, that keeps the mower away from the plant's trunk.

The top of a masonry retaining wall might be the place for a cascading bridal wreath whose arching stems, covered in spring with white, buttonlike flower clusters, would soften the wall's hard architecture without destroying its formal presence. Shrubby cinquefoil would be the choice for a curbside in sun. Poolside plantings of larger evergreen rhododendron and hydrangeas can hide the fences that are required by law in most municipalities.

Shrubs can be used to direct traffic as well. Arranged shrubs can tell the meter reader which way to turn to find the object of his or her mission. A line of shrubs broken in the center can keep people from walking across the lawn and let them know from a distance where the entry path begins. Massed shrubs in corners can direct visitors while creating a spectacular display in an otherwise unused spot. And a fragrant shrub should always be placed in an unavoidable spot. Imagine turning a corner in the path to come right up next to a lilac. A pink-flowered sweet pepperbush would be a good choice for a spot frequented in summer.

All of these shrubs represent more than the fleeting color of their flowers or the short-lived beauty of, say, annuals. These are permanent additions to the landscape. They may require an investment at first, but they will pay off in the long run by increasing your property value, and along the way they will continue to pay dividends in the form of lovely flowers, ornamental fruits, foliage textures, autumn colors and winter interest from bark and branches forming tracery patterns against the sky and sketching shadowy etchings in the snow.

A large planting bed of mixed shrubs, trees and herbaceous perennials is highlighted in spring by a flowering Fothergilla gardenii *(right). Soft fuzzy tufts grow from the tips of the branches in partial shade or sun (you might even try it in shade if there is bright light). Fabulous fall foliage color is a bonus of this handsome plant.*

Natural Shrub Shapes

The flowering shrubs, especially the deciduous ones, have wonderful natural shapes. They do not need to be pruned, except for the removal of dead wood. If they are well sited they will not outgrow their spaces to cover the walk or obscure a window. However, that is the case in a perfect world without inherited foundation plantings, or ice storms that split a shrub in two. When pruning, or planning, it is helpful to know something about the natural shapes of shrubs. You may have to restore the natural shape of a shrub that has, through some twist of environmental fate, gone off course.

Fastigiate, *or columnar, shrubs are upright and slim—taller than they are wide. Rose of Sharon, sweet pepperbush and buckthorn are more upright than horizontal growing in general, but the true cylindrical shrubs are usually cultivars bred to maintain this shape.*

Globe-shaped *shrubs form controlled mounds that are very round and compact in their natural state. Evergreen azaleas and most rhododendron are globe shaped.*

Vase-shaped *shrubs have the form of feather dusters. They are gathered at the base and shoot up and out toward the sky. Weigela is an example.*

Weeping *shrubs are shaped like fountains, with many stems shooting up and cascading down like water droplets. Examples are bridal wreath (*Spiraea × Vanhouttei*) and larger forsythia varieties.*

Spreading, *or prostrate, are those low shrubs that can be used for the front of a planting or as groundcovers. Rockrose (*Cistus *species), Aaron's-beard St.-John's-wort (*Hypericum calycinum*) and shrubby cinquefoil (*Potentilla fruticosa*) are examples.*

Rounded *shrubs are shaped like trees but emanate from several trunks or from one trunk that branches at the base. See* Magnolia *species, fringe tree (*Chionanthus virginicus*) and peegee hydrangea for examples.*

Rambling *shrubs are taller than the low spreaders but they, too, flow in every direction. Japanese kerria (*Kerria japonica*), and blue mist spirea (*Caryopteris *species) are ramblers.*

Colonizers *spread to naturalize over an entire area. See false spirea* Sorbaria sorbifolia.

Pyramidal, *or conical, shrubs look like Christmas trees. These are needled evergreens, for the most part.*

At California's Blake Gardens, Nandina domestica *(center) blooms happily in USDA Zone 9. This elegant scene belies the tenacity of the tropical-looking "heavenly bamboo." Not a true bamboo, but undeniably celestial. This sturdy plant will grow well in USDA Zone 7, and with protection, in Zone 6. Flowers, fruit and fall foliage color are added enticements.*

THE PLANTINGS

It is unusual to see a single shrub growing on its own in the wild, and when there are several shrubs, they are rarely of different species. To effect the most natural, or better, aesthetically pleasing creation include several of each shrub, just as you would have several of each perennial in a border. Then your schemes look more like drifts that interweave in the landscape.

The line of shrubs for a screen planting or at the edge of the property should include selections with varied texture, size and flower color, if this area is to be more than just a demarcation of the boundary. For example, on a smaller property, this kind of planting becomes a shrub border. It is planned and scaled just as if it were a herbaceous perennial border, only in this case, made up of woody, flowering shrubs. Evergreen shrubs should be included for winter interest, but also for their texture. That's especially the case with needled evergreens not known for their flowers.

Now you've learned a lot about the flowering shrubs and can't wait to apply this knowledge. But resist the temptation of choosing every glorious flowering shrub that money can buy. Pause and ponder. What can the flowering shrubs do for you and your property? The thoughtful, well-planned use of these exquisite plants is the mark of the truly artful landscape designers. Sharing nature's bounty and making one of its greatest gifts work for you is the test of your horticultural know-how.

2

DESIGNING WITH FLOWERING SHRUBS

SELECTION

Let's get specific. Is the shrub evergreen, semievergreen or deciduous? For the most part, evergreen shrubs are used for hedges and screens and for their solid forms in winter. The deciduous kinds are most often those grown for flowers, and they usually do have more and showier blossoms. Some shrubs are semievergreen. Glossy abelia loses some of its leaves in cold climates, nearly none in warm spots. Some other "evergreens" have leaves that last two years. They are constantly replacing the two-year-old leaves with new ones, but no one really notices this—the plant seems to always be clothed in green leaves. Small-leafed, evergreen rhododendron, the ones we call "azaleas," often have leaves that last one or two years. One set is produced in spring and another set is produced midseason. They last until new leaves push them off the plant, so the effect is the same as it would be if the plant were totally evergreen.

Deciduous shrubs lose their leaves every autumn and remain bare through the winter, just like the deciduous trees. Plan to include some that produce brilliant fall color such as fothergilla. Some of these deciduous shrubs may behave like herbaceous perennials in cold climates. Butterfly bush, for example, may die to the ground in severe winters and sprout new "woody" growth right from the hardy roots. Semiwoody shrubs such as butterfly bush and *Vitex* produce flower buds on new growth; otherwise the winter kill would result in a leafy plant with no blossoms at all. Late winter- and spring-blooming shrubs have flowers that sprout on the growth produced the previous growing season. For that reason, we don't prune them until just after flowering; otherwise we would be removing the flowering mechanisms for the following season. If we wait too long to prune, we might remove next year's developing flower buds.

Needled evergreen shrubs, such as pines, yews and junipers, are not what we're about here. We want to concentrate on the ornamental ones that bloom, and bloom quite a bit. Selecting shrubs for your landscape takes forethought. You have to decide what the purpose of the shrub will be, what conditions you have, what color flowers you want and when you want them and the other aesthetic effects, such as winter interest, foliage texture and possibly, fall color and fruit.

Selecting Shrubs

The considerations for selecting shrubs begin with knowledge of the conditions *in situ*. Climate is first and foremost. Can the shrub you want grow in your climate? You'll have a pretty good chance with shrubs bought at the local garden center, or better still, from a nearby grower. But I have seen shrubs offered at the nursery in flower that really could not be grown locally. A plant that is not damaged by frost is said to be *hardy*, one that cannot stand frost is *tender*. Hardiness refers to a plant's ability to withstand temperatures in your area. Shoppers often ask nursery personnel, "Is this plant hardy?" They may be asking about a tropical houseplant. And the answer is invariably yes. Hardy has come to mean tough and resilient.

Large-leafed evergreen rhododendron make a perfect background foil for this elegant sculpture —in and out of flower. Thoughtful siting is a mark of garden mastery.

A weeping bridal wreath (Spiraea × Vanhouttei) *chases a garden nymph through a colonized planting of flowering shrubs at Magnolia Plantations in Charleston, South Carolina.*

Winterthur's famous azaleas carpet the understory of the edited woodland where light filters through the tree-top canopy to provide the partial shade that suits them best.

What you want to know is whether the plant is frost hardy, able to withstand minimum temperatures in your area.

The U.S. Department of Agriculture has made a map of hardiness zones in the United States (pages 90–91). These tell us what the minimum temperature in any area is expected to be. Learn your zone number. For example, if you live in an area where the temperature generally goes down to between 0° and 10°F, then you live in Zone 7, and you know that most shrubs listed as appropriate for Zones 5 to 8 will do well in your area. The zone reference, unfortunately, does not consider heat. A plant that is happy in Zone 5 will certainly survive the Zone 7 winter, but the summer might prove too hot for it and, in some cases, too humid. You'll have to learn by observation and find a nursery person you can rely on, or call your Cooperative Extension Service agent, usually listed in the telephone book, for recommendations.

Plants listed for Zone 7 generally will survive in that zone, but there can be winters with exceptionally low temperatures as well as extenuating environmental circumstances, such as drought or flooding, that affect success. Your own property has pockets of warmth or cold, called "micro-climates." Cold air may pour down a hillside and pool in a low spot that can actually stay colder than the rest of your lot. A place against a south-facing wall can be much warmer than other parts of the property. Learn about your yard's micro-climates, and use them to your advantage. You might select a shrub that is especially hardy or late-spring blooming for the cold spot and grow a marginally hardy specimen in the warm place.

Locations near large bodies of water tend to have less drastic fluctuations of temperature because the water takes longer to heat up and longer to cool off than those areas without water, and that affects the air around it. Even proximity to the ocean can affect climate temperatures. Long Island, N.Y., tends to have warmer winters than areas inland at the same latitude, but spring comes later to this area because the water holds the cold temperature longer in spring.

Sun and shade are obvious environmental factors. Full sun is most often considered to be six or more hours of direct sunshine in the summer. Partial shade is about three hours of sun. Shade is less than three hours and as little as none; but there is often good light from above or reflected off a building. Many of the flowering shrubs we want to grow can take full sun. Some of these same shrubs will also bloom in partial shade. A rhododendron may have more flowers in sun, but in a shadier, protected spot, although flowers will be fewer in number, they will probably be larger, last longer, and colors will not fade. The overall effect can be greater for the landscape as a whole.

Shade limits selections. For a start, find shrubs that grow naturally in the woodland. Broadleafed evergreens generally can take shade. They have leaves all year 'round to absorb the sun's rays. The larger the leaves, the more light they absorb, Shrubs for partial shade to shade include such evergreens as camellia, mountain laurel, Oregon holly grape, Japanese andromeda, rhododendron and such deciduous shrubs as sweet pepperbush, winter sweet, winter hazel, red-twig dogwood and witch hazel.

The desiccating effects of wind must be considered, too. Most plants set in the direct path of constant winds won't be able to put up with such abuse. You will have to select ones that come from areas where wind is a problem; mountainside plants or ones with succulent leaves that can store water would be appropriate. As a rule, plants that have some water-storing capacity or wind tolerance will have either thick, leathery leaves or devices such as hairs, or coverings like wax or powder, to help keep water in the leaf tissues. These plants often appear to have gray leaves because their pale coverings reflect light. Blue mist spirea is an example. Consider bush honeysuckle, rockrose and cinquefoil. Seaside areas present special problems, and there you'll need to collect plants that come from similar sites in similar zones from around the world for your conditions. Tamarisk, sand cherry and beach plum are some of my favorites for the seaside garden.

Newly planted shrubs may need some protection in rigorous situations. A screen can be constructed with stakes and burlap to block the wind until the shrubs become established. These screens could be left in place for the first year, longer in particularly difficult sites. You will have to know something about the moisture in the soil as well. If the site is wet for most of the year, moisture-tolerant shrubs should be selected. Swamp azalea, Carolina sweet shrub, chokeberry, serviceberry, Virginia sweet spire and, of course, the pussy willow are good for wet soil. Dry, sandy soil is a problem, too. This condition can be altered, though, and more easily than a constantly wet area. Of course, you can irrigate constantly, but we've come to realize that water is a very precious resource, not to be wasted. Improvements should be made by adding mositure-retentive humus in the form of leaf mold, compost or peat moss to the soil. Best of all, select shrubs that can tolerate dry conditions, among them St.-John's-wort, blue mist spirea and California lilac.

The ultimate height of a shrub must be considered. Nothing is worse than having to remove a

Landscape architect Bill Wallis realizes the importance of bringing lightness to dark corners of the garden. In a border of shrubs and small trees, the variegated dogwood, Cornus sibirica 'Alba', *brightens the spot. A window (right) has been treated with a reflective coating so that it acts like a mirror adding more "light" to the scene.*

The tamed wild garden is the perfect spot for flowering shrubs in a mixed planting of perennials and bulbs, such as the Japanese andromeda (Pieris japonica), *center right, with its drooping lily-of-the-valley-like flowers.*

Flowering Shrubs for Wet and Dry Locations

Selecting the right plants for certain situations is often the key to success in the landscape. Obviously a succulent cactus, for example, would perish in the dark rain forest, and a lush-leafed jungle dweller, philodendron, would fry in the Arizona sun. These are extremes. However, around your property there are moist spaces and dry ones. Ask your nursery person, check the "Plant Portraits" chapter of this book and refer to the list below for suggestions.

FLOWERING SHRUBS FOR MOIST SOIL

Amelanchier (shadblow)
Aronia arbutifolia (red chokeberry)
Clethra alnifolia (summer sweet)
Cornus alba (Tatarian dogwood)
Kalmia angustifolia (sheep laurel)
Kalmia latifolia (mountain laurel)
Magnolia virginiana (sweet bay)
Rhododendron arborescens (sweet azalea)
Rhododendron viscosum (swamp azalea)
Rubus odoratus (flowering raspberry)
Salix discolor (pussy willow)
Virburnum alnifolium (hobblebush)
Viburnum trilobum (American highbush cranberry)

FLOWERING SHRUBS FOR DRY SOIL

Aronia species (chokeberry)
Budddleia Davidii (butterfly bush)
Caryopteris species (blue mist shrub)
Ceanothus species (California lilac)
Cistus species (rockrose)
Cotinus Coggygria (smoke bush)
Cytisus species (broom)
Hamamelis virginiana (witch hazel)
Hibiscus syriacus (rose of Sharon)
Hypericum species (St.-John's-wort)
Lonicera species (shrub honeysuckle)
Potentilla fruticosa (cinquefoil)
Prunus Besseyi (sand cherry)
Prunus maritima (beach plum)
Spiraea species (spirea)
Tamarix species (tamarisk)
Viburnum Lantana (wayfaring tree)
Vitex Agnus-castus (vitex)

shrub because it has outgrown its intended home. This happens all too often with foundation plantings that grow up to obscure views from the window. (Dwarf shrubs are particularly useful for these situations.) Another aspect to shrub selection is to find plants, especially for vital areas of the property and for small landscapes, that will have more than a few weeks of interest and, maybe, more than a single season of interest. There are many.

About the best way to learn about shrubs is to observe them, fully grown, in your area. You can discover height and circumference in books, but the best thing to do is to take a trip to a local botanical garden or arboretum to see mature shrubs in their finest condition. Or, note the shrubs in your neighborhood that look good and are doing well. If you do this frequently, you'll be able to observe flowering habits and fall color. Your local Cooperative Extension or botanical garden may publish lists of multiple-season shrubs for your particular area.

Taking Stock

Examine your property. Give yourself a guided tour of your yard. You might even consider asking a friend or family member to accompany you on your journey. When you think of adding shrubs to the landscape, your first impulse might be to go to the garden center. There you'll find many beautiful shrubs blooming their heads off. The "kid in the candy store" syndrome tends to take over, and you'll buy some wonderful specimens only to find later that there is no place for them, or worse, you'll install them in the wrong place and have to prune them constantly, move or remove them altogether. If you just bought a house with its own landscape history, it's best to observe for at least a season. You never know what jewels lie sleeping in the landscape. Shrubs especially may look nearly worthless, until they burst into bloom. Start taking notes, and consider making maps of the property to include its assets and liabilities.

If you have a surveyor's map of your property, that will be the place to start. Make a tracing and have some copies made so that you can sketch areas that can be developed with shrub plantings. If you don't have one, borrow a 100-foot tape measure to create your own "base plan," on which you will install all your landscape dreams. Make the drawing on graph paper. Depending on the size of your property, you could make each ¼-inch square on the graph paper equal to 4 feet (10 feet for a large property).

Begin a list of what, in landscape parlance, is called the "program"—what's required from the landscape by the people who use it. If yours is a brand-new home, you'll probably be starting from scratch and need a whole range of amenities. Note utility lines, plumbing features, etc. You will want to screen some from view with shrub plants. Interview family members, too, and write down their thoughts on the landscape.

Incurable collectors (such as myself) don't always make the

best use of the shrubs. We want to possess every possible plant. But a garden of many one-of-a-kind plants rarely looks like a garden at all. It's either a hodgepodge of polka dots, or a catalog of nature's diversity. Plan before you plant: Do you need evergreens and deciduous shrubs for a foundation planting? Will you need to screen unsightly views or enhance desirable vistas? Do you want flowers for cutting and for fragrance? Is your goal season-long color? Do you want to attract birds, butterflies and other wildlife? Do you want to develop a woodland setting, hold a hillside in the sun or fill an area with low-maintenance naturalizers?

One of the things we do most with shrubs is define space. Shrubs surrounding an area of lawn define it as a place for recreation or relaxation, or just to gaze on. Shrubs can alter architecture. A tall shrub by a corner of the house can make a sharp edge seem more relaxed and graceful, subtle instead of abrupt. The look of a house can be modified or enhanced. A modern, single-level house could be smashing with low, jagged shrubs adding abstract "sculpture" to the exterior. An asymmetrical arrangement of shrubs or even a design with an Asian influence might also be perfect for the modern exterior. The shadow pattern of a shrub or group of shrubs should also be used. Imagine a long shadow cast against a wall. Silhouettes too can affect design. A Spanish-style house would look great with some pseudotropical foliage and flowers. A rose of Sharon's flowers conjure memories of warmer climates, and the crape myrtle's colors are riotously tropical. The feeling of a Tudor house might be reinforced with a staid and formal shape of a certain shrub or row of shrubs, camellias or rhododendron, perhaps.

Attracting Birds and Butterflies

Many flowering shrubs attract wildlife. Here are shrubs birds and butterflies visit for food—berries for birds, nectar for butterflies.

BIRD ATTRACTORS

Amelanchier species (serviceberry, shadblow)
Aronia species (chokeberry)
Callicarpa species (beauty-berry)
Chionanthus virginicus (fringe tree)
Cornus species (shrub dogwood)
Lonicera species (bush honeysuckle)
Mahonia species (Oregon holly grape)
Prunus species (cherry)
Ribes species (currant)
Rubus species (blackberry)
Viburnum species (viburnum)

BUTTERFLY ATTRACTORS

Buddleia species (butterfly bush)
Caryopteris species (blue mist spirea)
Ceanothus species (California lilac, New Jersey tea)
Cephalanthus occidentalis (buttonbush)
Clethra alnifolia (sweet pepperbush)
Lindera Benzoin (spicebush)
Rhododendron species (deciduous azalea)
Salix species (pussy willow)
Syringa species (lilac)

THE BORDERLINE

A border of shrubs should have certain components that are principal to all one-sided plantings. Scale is primary: tall plants at the back, small shrubs in front. However, the depth of the planting is up to you. It really can be as deep and as long as you want, perhaps 10 feet deep and 30 feet long for a property-line planting. That's a substantial planting, and although you may employ easy-care flowering shrubs, you still should think about how much can easily be managed. Make allowances for watering, feeding, pruning and mulching. And create an access way behind the planting. You should also make a utility path, perhaps with stepping-stones, to allow you to get to each plant without compacting soil too much from foot traffic. This path will be virtually invisible when the shrubs have matured. The shrub border doesn't have to be a straight, rectangular construction. It can have an undulating front boundary. The border can pour into the landscape and ebb back toward the rear.

Draw on paper first. You can also lay a length of rope or a garden hose out on the lawn to plan the front line, or drive wooden stakes into the ground and connect them with string for a more stable line that can be observed over a longer period of time. Be sure to look at this line from all parts of the landscape, from indoors and, if you can, from a ladder and upper story windows. When you think your design is getting to look the way you want it, then draw on the lawn or ground with horticultural-grade, ground limestone—ordinarily used for raising the alkalinity of soil for lawns, and easily erased with a

The simplest shrub borders can feature an all-of-a-kind massing of spring azaleas. Here, a clear line of demarcation is formed by the shrubs fronted by scilla bulbs.

broom or rake or washed away with the hose, if you want to alter the line. It will not hurt the garden.

When you're ready, cut the front line with a sharp spade and begin to turn over the planting bed. This is a great time to add humus to the soil in the form of compost, well-rotted manure, leaf mold or peat moss. One pound of humus, organic matter, can hold up to three pounds of water. This one ingredient is the cure-all for poor-draining clay soil and too fast-draining sandy soil. The humus improves the moisture retention of the sandy soil and opens up the clay soil so that there is adequate drainage and air (so roots don't suffocate). Make the most of your chance to improve the home where a new shrub can stretch its roots.

Shrubs can simply be members of a garden repertory's varied cast of foliage and flowering characters. White viburnum and azaleas star with Japanese primroses in this season's production and are secondary players in the next.

Planning in Three Dimensions

The "large plants to the rear, small plants to the front" concept is only the starting point. Arrange plants so the new border undulates up and down as well as along the single dimension—the line of the border's edge—or the two dimensions—the shape of the bed, its width and depth on the ground. Create a rhythm of movement that carries your eye through the planting, like waves rolling to the beach, crashing, spilling, tumbling and then gently receding, and starting all over again. The contours viewed as your eye moves along the varying heights of the shrubs will give the planting enormous impact. Color, too, will help sustain this interest. And although we are using flowering shrubs, some of the color should come from the countless shades of green-, silver- and many times, purple-leafed plants.

Consider a shrub such as the purple smoke bush. If it were planted in the center of the border, it would certainly become a focal point, but that would be at the expense of the entire planting. Try repeating the smoke bush three times through the planting. Your eye will drift from purple point of color to purple again, and be carried through the border. Never sacrifice the planting for one overwhelming point of interest, unless you are creating an enclosure for a sculpture or other ornamental feature. (In that case, you would be creating a background screen and not a running border planting at all.)

FLOWERING SHRUBS WITH FALL FOLIAGE COLOR

Amelanchier species (shadblow, serviceberry)

Chionanthus virginicus (fringe tree)

Cornus alba 'Siberica' (red-twig dogwood)

Cornus mas (Cornelian cherry)

Cotinus Coggygria purpureus (purple smoke bush)

Enkianthus species (enkianthus)

Fothergilla species (fothergilla)

Hamamelis species (witch hazel)

Hydrangea quercifolia (oak-leafed hydrangea)

Magnolia stellata (star magnolia)

Mahonia species (Oregon holly grape)

Rhododendron Schlippenbachii (royal azalea)

Rhododendron Vaseyi (pinkshell azalea)

Viburnum species (viburnum)

WINTER INTEREST FROM BARK

Amelanchier species (serviceberry, shadblow)

Cornus alba 'Siberica' (red-twig dogwood)

Corylus avellana 'Contorta' (Harry Lauder's walking stick)

Cytisus species (broom)

Hydrangea anomala petiolaris (climbing hydrangea)

Hydrangea quercifolia (oak-leafed hydrangea)

Kerria japonica (Japanese kerria)

Kolkwitzia amabilis (beautybush)

Sculptured Plantings in Three Dimensions

The transition of foliage scale can be used to great advantage. Large leaves can lead to progressively smaller leaves and then back to large again. Large ones can accentuate depth by being set in front of shrubs with small leaves. A wall of small leaves in the background would make this foil seem farther away and be a fine-textured, uninterrupted screen for foreground plantings, which would seem to come forward.

Consider perspective at this time. You may want to accentuate the length of the property when viewed from one point. Mirror-image borders that exaggerate a diminishing perspective by actually coming closer together in the distance can make the garden appear longer. In another situation, plants can become progressively shorter.

In the first example, the planting that plays with perspective, color can be brought into play. Subtler shades of foliage and flowers, especially toward the blue end of the spectrum, seem farther away from the viewer. Bright red and white flowers are best in the foreground—they always stand out, and jump into view.

The shape of shrubs, of course, is also a major consideration when building a border. A shrub that has a tidy mounding shape, such as an evergreen azalea, might be perfect next to a fountain-shaped bridal wreath with its cascading flower-covered branches. There are many varieties of familiar shrubs called "fastigiate," or columnar. These grow straight and tall. A few tall columns of foliage could be punctuated perfectly with balls of Hidcote St.-John's-wort. This is the place to integrate needle evergreens and foliage plants not selected for flowers. Mounds of boxwoods and spires of juniper 'Skyrocket' would impose form and structure to the planting for 12 months of the year.

Forcing Branches Indoors

Branches of many flowering shrubs can be forced into bloom weeks or even months before they bloom outside. Professional growers and suppliers to the flower markets around the world use arduous tactics to trick plants into thinking that it's time to unfurl their floral bounty. Some branches are easy to force with a lot less expertise (not to mention without room-size refrigerators or hothouses that resemble the Superdome).

Keep in mind that the easiest branches to push into bloom are the early flowering ones that blossom before their leaves sprout. Forsythia and pussy willows top the list. The closer to the actual blooming time outdoors, the faster the buds will open and the simpler it will be to force them to do so. You can just cut stems two weeks before they bloom outdoors and place them in a vase indoors and mist the buds—they'll open in short order. But in order to have flowers earlier, say, January for forsythia, or to force some of the more difficult branches, follow these guidelines.

Cut long stems from late-winter to early spring flowering shrubs. Choose ones that have the most flower buds, the chubby round ones (leaf buds, on the other hand, are usually pointed). With a sharp chef's knife on a cutting board slice the bottom 3 to 4 inches of the stem lengthwise twice with perpendicular cuts—the bottom of the stem will be cut into four strips, which will expose more branch area to water. Place the branches in warm water in a tall container, so that as much as possible of the stems are submerged, in a room away from sun, radiators or hot-air registers. After 24 hours, replace the water and move the branches to a cool space, perhaps the garage or an unheated guest room—where the temperature is around 60° to 65° F. After a few days, bring them inside and cut about an inch off the bottoms and change the water. Soon the buds will begin to open.

You can speed up the process or slow it down to have flowers for a special occasion by controlling the temperature. To hasten the process, place the branches in tepid water (110°F) in a warm room, but still away from direct sunlight or heating ducts. Mist the branches at least once a day so that they are dripping wet. When the buds are completely swollen and beginning to open, place them in your arrangements. To delay opening, keep them in the cool space. Try this a few times and you'll get the hang of it.

SOME BRANCHES FOR INDOOR FORCING

Abeliophyllum distichum (white forsythia)

Chaenomeles species (flowering quince)

Cornus mas (Cornelian cherry)

Corylopsis species (winter hazel)

Forsythia species (forsythia)

Hamamelis species (witch hazel; late-winter, early spring varieties)

Lindera species (spicebush)

Magnolia species (magnolia)

Prunus species (flowering cherry, almond, etc.)

Salix (pussy willow)

A mixed planting featuring Spiraea × Bumalda *(center, right) packs mounds of interest from foliage texture and plant scale within the limited span of a garden path.*

The Fourth Dimension is Time

The balance of the planting is important, but we are creating landscape art in the fourth dimension. There is line and form on the ground, height and depth in the planting and then there is time—the fourth dimension. The planting will never be static, never stand still. The flowers will come and go, there will be new grass-green growth in spring, rich summer foliage colors and autumn color from many plants. In winter, bark texture and color and berries will punctuate the plantings and spark the always-present evergreens. In late winter, it all begins anew. With each year the shrubs will become larger, and the border will as well.

Consider bloom times of, for example, the various hydrangeas. The oak-leafed hydrangea blossoms start in early summer, Annabelle hydrangeas bloom soon after, then the mop-top and lacecap big-leafed hydrangeas and, finally, the peegee, which is almost tree size, with blossoms in white fading to pink and bronze. Planning color is one of the greatest challenges to the

FLOWERING SHRUBS WITH ORNAMENTAL FRUITS

- *Amelanchier* species (shadblow, serviceberry)
- *Aronia* species (chokeberry)
- *Callicarpa* species (beauty-berry)
- *Chaenomeles* species (flowering quince)
- *Chionanthus virginicus* (fringe tree)
- *Clerodendron trichotomum* (harlequin glory bower)
- *Cornus mas* (Cornelian cherry)
- *Cotinus Coggygria purpureus* (purple smoke bush)
- *Daphne* species (daphne)
- *Kolkwitzia amabilis* (beauty bush)
- *Lonicera* species (bush honeysuckle)
- *Magnolia stellata* (star magnolia)
- *Mahonia* species (Oregon holly grape)
- *Pieris japonica* (Japanese andromeda)
- *Prunus* species (cherry, plum)
- *Viburnum* species (viburnum)

artist who works in this living medium.

You might want an all-of-one-color scheme, one of the easiest to develop. An all-white-flower border would be spectacular, and there are many white-flowered shrubs from which to choose: fothergilla in midspring, followed by white-flowered rhododendron and azalea, then deutzia, mock orange, viburnum and lilac, glossy abelia through it all, Annabelle hydrangea, big-leafed hydrangea, butterfly bush, glory bower and the peegee hydrangea for early fall. A "hot" border would contain harmonious colors from the orange-to-deep-red spectrum. A complementary scheme includes flowers in colors from opposite sides of the color wheel, for example, violet flowers next to yellow ones. Blue, pink and violet flowers would create a calm border planting that could be sparked by the occasional pale yellow-flowered shrub. You will have to select several different shrubs with similar colors that blossom at various times to maintain your desired scheme through the season.

The Mixed Border

Keeping the color constant by using only shrubs is hard. In an important area of the garden, you may want more color, and be willing to do some more work maintaining the planting, including pruning, planting and deadheading faded flowers. In this case you could include herbaceous perennials in the border and even annuals to fill in with long-season blooms. This describes another use of the flowering shrubs, in a garden art form that blends the perennial border and the shrub border into what the English named the "mixed border." Here, the imagination runs free. Color can come from any plant, and forms and shapes evolve.

The shrubs for the mixed border provide a near-permanent framework for the plantings. In the background, evergreens and deciduous shrubs form a wall to contain the planting and act as a foil for the colorful goings-on inside the mixed planting. The blooms of flowering shrubs are as attention getting as the herbaceous perennials' blossoms. Massive shrubs anchor the border, define space and highlight perennials by creating a frame for the color-play between them. In autumn, the turning leaf colors of deciduous shrubs add a dimension to the mixed border when most of the flowers have long since passed. Some of these can be massed in small areas so that even when all of the herbaceous color fades, there will be plenty to look at in the occasional groupings. Shrubs such as serviceberry, heavenly bamboo, deciduous viburnum, witch hazel and smoke bush are known for their autumnal colors. (Drying ornamental grasses look fantastic with their metallic fall colors.)

When leaves drop and herbaceous foliage dissolves, berries and bark join the evergreen "bones" of the planting to sparkle with color through the winter months. Red and black chokeberries, dogwood, jetbead, viburnum, mahonia and heavenly

A range of textures produces nearly infinite variety in a mixed border that fascinates even when out of bloom with evergreen and deciduous shrub leaves contrasted by succulent herbaceous foliage.

bamboo have arresting berry effects. *Poncirus* and flowering quince have larger fruits. Besides the colorful bark of shrubs like crape myrtle and oak-leafed hydrangea, there is the effect of the varied silhouettes of deciduous shrubs seen in the winter months.

In the mixed border, bulbs and trees, vines and biennials also join the mélange. The mixed border has much more dimension than the perennial equivalent. An incredible variety of plants adds textures and foliage colors to the usual floral points of interest. Rhythm is the concept. Groundcovers, even shrubby ones, lead to higher plants; bulbs push up through the shrub cover and ivy may grow in among it as well. Colorful herbs such as sage and gold-leafed marjoram add foliage color in the foreground. Summer bulbs, such as garden lilies, push up through the arrangement to add huge colorful blossoms in their season. Mounds of shrub forms and spikes of herbaceous perennials make the planting undulate. Even dwarf trees can be included for their vertical lines.

There will be more for the gardener to do in this kind of planting than in the all-shrub border, but perhaps less than in the herbaceous perennials border. Much of the fussing is the kind of "work" gardeners love—moving perennials about, for example, or adding annuals and bulbs. And parts of this border may have to be redone from time to time as some non-woody plants outgrow their intended spaces. This can be especially true if you dare to include trees in the planting. Dividing some clumps of one kind of perennial or another will be a task during spring and fall. And there will always be the compulsion to add new and unusual finds to the collection. Interestingly enough, this homogeneous community tends to have fewer pest and disease problems than the all-perennial border. The diversity of plants means that susceptible plants are isolated and problems can't spread as easily. Be sure to read *Burpee American Gardening Series: Perennials* by Suzanne Frutig Bales.

With visions of flowers from spring to fall dancing in our heads, armed with plan on paper, we still have to acquire the living colors of the planter's palette. Then we have to learn how to "install" them. Methods for preparing the planting hole, mixing the precise medium and watering practices can be learned. So much of gardening is common sense with just a bit of scientific know-how. Learning to cope with all eventualities will come in time. I can tell you all about the mechanics of our craft, but some things can be acquired only through hands-on experience. But don't worry; if at first you don't succeed, you're bound to be a great gardener.

Flowering Shrubs with More Than One Season of Interest

It is wonderful to find an extra dimension to the shrubs that we collect for flowers. Of course, all of these shrubs have leaves through spring and summer that affect placement and design, but there may also be fall foliage color from some, ornamental fruits from others and showy winter twig and bark from others. In limited spaces, plants that can perform double or even triple duty are most welcome. The Cornelian cherry, for example, has early spring flowers, ornamental (and edible) fruits and fall foliage color. Seek out some of these versatile shrubs.

3

THE SHRUB PLANTING AND GROWING GUIDE

PLANTING SHRUBS

A gardener's resilience is tested with regularity by such realities as aberrant temperatures, insect invasions and too much or too little rain. But perhaps the supreme test comes in springtime, when the local garden-center yard is packed with all those plastic pots of flowering shrubs.

Unlike the experience of buying seeds, which requires imagination to visualize full-grown plants, or herbaceous perennials, most of which are mere crowns or tufts of emerging foliage in the plant-buying frenzy of earliest spring, the selection of shrubs presents a real test of will. Not only are they already of considerable size but the early bloomers will have burst into flower, and be standing there in their pots or burlapped root balls, tugging at the hearts of the shoppers with their distinctive forms, color and even the almost irresistible lure of fragrance.

No surprise, then, that so many American yards are bright with nearly identical mounds of azaleas and forsythia—big blasts of bright color bought in bloom and carried home to create an instant spring. To select only these harbingers is to miss a lot, though. The landscape will peak far too early, when in fact many of the best things are yet to come into (or in the case of the witch hazels, fothergilla and others, already past) their peak form. It is well to be prepared, then, to become an educated consumer before setting out to shop.

Foremost, there is no more important consideration than the reality of your garden. Is it sunny or shaded, and at what time of day? Is the soil mostly clay and positively soggy, or is it, thankfully, high in organic matter and therefore moisture retentive? Or perhaps it is too quick draining, sandy or otherwise dry in character? Fighting the site by bringing home the wrong kinds of plants will simply result in a waste of time and money. Plants grown against their will are fish out of water— doomed. Soil can be amended (read on in this chapter), and light patterns can be changed somewhat, too, by pruning or removal of trees, but sometimes this requires professional assistance or the use of heavy equipment that can be quite costly.

Never set out for the garden center—or even dare to pore over the stack of springtime mail-order catalogs—without making at least a tentative garden plan (see chapter 2 for help incorporating flowering shrubs into your garden design). Before shopping for shrubs, have the sites planned, maybe even the holes fully prepared or be ready to care for your nursery stock carefully until it is safely in the ground, which means daily watering and protection from extremes like direct sun and drying winds.

How Shrubs are Sold

First, it is important to know that there is more than one way to buy a shrub. As with virtually

Shrubs can be a welcome addition to the city landscape. Here a Poncirus *brightens up a city stoop.*

every aspect of horticulture, there is disagreement on which way is best.

CONTAINER STOCK, that is, plants that have been grown for most or all of their lives in some kind of pot, usually made of molded plastic, is probably the most common and easiest-to-handle form. Because container plants are grown not in garden soil but in lightweight potting mixes, the roots develop easily. Container plants can become pot-bound, a tangled, solid mass of roots in the shape of the pot. This mass will need to be scored around the circumference like pie wedges. Make vertical slices with a sharp knife about an inch deep around the entire root ball. If the roots have formed a very tight mass at the bottom of the container (and you discover this only upon getting the plant home), pull the entangled roots apart before planting, cut a disk about ¾ inch thick off the entire base. Otherwise, the roots may not grow out into the surrounding soil and the plant will die after a year or two. In severe cases, some gardeners actually slice up through the root ball in the center and "butterfly" the root mass and spread it apart in half in the planting hole over a cone of soil.

Some of the plants sold at the local garden center in containers are not really container grown at all. Instead, they were shipped a month or two earlier in dormant, bare-root form, that is, dug up from nursery beds and cleaned of traces of earth, to save on trucking of heavy soil. The local nursery pots them up and brings them out of dormancy before putting them out for sale. This is a common practice with fruit trees, roses and some small shrubs.

Conventional wisdom once suggested tying a young shrub to a stake. The more modern approach counters this. If you prepare the soil correctly and plant the shrub in well, then it will stand up on its own. A stake will protect the shrub from wind damage, but protect it too well. Recent research shows that a plant not tied to a stake grows stronger because of having to put up with wind, and that a weak, staked shrub may actually be more vulnerable to wind damage as it grows and the stake is removed.

Recycle Plastic Containers

Plastic containers revolutionized the growing industry, but unfortunately have left an unpleasant legacy—one that might be around nearly as long as the plants themselves. I find nothing more horrible than the sight of piles and piles of plastic gallon to five-gallon containers stacked by the garbage at the garden center. When using shrubs purchased in such containers, be sure to recycle all empty plastic containers. Return them to the garden center for reuse, or deposit them at your local solid-waste center if your community takes this kind of plastic material. Perhaps you can suggest that your local nursery impose a deposit on these valuable containers, or better still, offer discounts to those who bring them back.

When to Shop, What to Look For

When possible, acquire new plants early in spring, before the arrival of sustained bouts of heat that might threaten successful transplanting. Or, plant in late summer or early fall, when temperatures begin to decline again. Also, spring and fall are usually the most rainy seasons, something transplants appreciate in getting adjusted, and this will help minimize watering duties.

Even the best, most experienced gardeners fall prey to occasional impulse buying, such as in midsummer sales, or to buying more plants than they can set out in the garden before hot weather or winter approaches. Two techniques requiring minimal effort, called "heeling-in" and "plunging," can protect plants until their permanent home is prepared.

HEELING-IN is a way to cope with dormant, bare-root plants that are delivered too early in spring or too late in fall to plant in the garden. This technique can also be used if your plant arrives just before you're about to leave town for a week or two. Dig a narrow trench on an angle and lay the plants in it so that their roots and the lower portion of their trunks are underground. Close the trench by replacing the soil. If the plants must stay this way over winter, then mulch the whole plant after the ground freezes with up to 4 to 6 inches of a coarse mulch such as chopped fir bark and cover the rest of the plant with evergreen boughs or straw. This technique also protects the upper portions of the plants from the drying effects of wind.

PLUNGING can save container-grown shrubs with root systems that would otherwise roast or freeze if the pots were left above ground in extremes of summer or winter. The earth acts as insulation for the roots, and the plants don't dry out as frequently below ground, either. Simply dig a hole big enough to accommodate the pot and plunge the container in the hole. Refill any crevices with soil and mulch the soil surface. Some gardeners who like to shop the late-summer sales keep an out-of-the-way area prepared for plunging and keep plants there until the next good planting time arrives.

When shopping, plan to select a diverse group of shrubs. This not only extends the season of bloom, berries and other ornamental interests in your garden but also helps avoid the kind of mass planting of a single species, called "monoculture," which invites disease and pests to settle in for a real feast.

Generally speaking, don't buy woody plants after they have reached more than half their mature size, and don't buy them too small, either. Mature specimens are hard to transplant successfully, and once out of the pot and sunk into the ground, small plants suddenly become extra small in appearance. Because shrubs form much of the backbone of the garden, buying good-size ones is worth the extra investment whenever possible.

Evaluate each potential purchase according to its structure; view it from every side and from every angle. Don't be afraid to ask a nursery employee to slide a container-grown shrub out of the pot so you can see its root system. Is it very pot-bound? Perhaps it has been in the container too long. Do balled-and-burlapped specimens have soil balls of adequate size, or were they poorly dug, having had their life-support systems hacked off? Are they wilted? Is the soil ball firm and solid? Look closely at flower buds—are they alive? Is the bark healthy, or are there cankers or fissures evident that may indicate disease? If you have any doubts as to whether a plant in the garden or at the garden center is dormant or actually alive, you can scrape a little bark with your thumbnail. Living tissue should scratch off easily and be green below the surface. A dead twig will either be brown, or too dry to scratch at all. A living twig will bend when pulled down gently, a dead one will snap (still, perhaps this isn't the best thing to do—go around snapping twigs at the garden center). Avoid overgrown shrubs whose branches are clumped closely together; they will never be graceful or well shaped. And remember, there are few real "bargains" in the garden world.

Soil Preparation

When planting shrubs, as with trees, soil preparation is especially critical. These long-lived plants are seldom moved, nor are they dug up to be divided the way herbaceous plants are every couple of years. Also, unlike the ever-improving soil of a vegetable garden or an annual flower bed, the soil of the shrub border cannot be cultivated and amended each year. Make the first preparation count.

The importance of organic matter in the soil cannot be stressed enough. Organic additives like leaf mold (partly to mostly decomposed leaves, available free from many municipal composting sites and a great all-purpose amendment), peat moss (expensive and acidic in nature, but available at every garden center and great for lightening clay soils and increasing moisture-retention in sandy ones) and compost (a blend of decomposed garden wastes like grass clippings, leaves, spent annuals, stable bedding, manure and even vegetable scraps from the kitchen) can make all the difference in soil health, tilth and drainage.

Do not skimp on the investment of labor at this stage, or on the ingredients. Too often, it is not the soil *chemistry* that is wrong for a particular plant, but the physical *condition* of the soil. Construction, for instance, or even heavy foot traffic, can badly damage soil, compacting it so much that plants' roots will suffocate from lack of oxygen. Resist the temptation to rely on chemical fertilizers to get plants up and growing, and instead create a healthy soil where roots will be able to get enough nutrients, air and water to sustain the shrub over a lifetime. Most of all, do not do *anything* to change your soil chemistry—that is, making it more acidic with something like aluminum sulfate because you plan to grow rhododendron, or adding lime to grow daphne or lilac—until you have a soil test, which can be performed by the Cooperative Extension for a small fee.

Organic Mulches for the Shrub Border

Leaves and leaf mold: *Make your own lightweight mulch by shredding raked leaves with your lawn mower or a shredder and spread them on garden beds. Oak leaves are slow to decompose and more acidic than the leaves of most other deciduous trees. Leaves gradually break down into the top layer of the soil, contributing organic material, humus —another benefit.*

Straw: *Not hay but oat straw is a good all-purpose mulch, one that is widely available. It changes color from tan to gray as it ages and breaks down in several seasons. Salt marsh hay, available to gardeners on the East Coast, is an excellent mulch, and because it needs a salty environment for seeds to sprout, it does not contribute weeds to a planting. But environmentalists are concerned about the supply of this material, because it is only collected from the wild where it is a habitat for wildlife. It is best to leave this mulching material for the birds.*

Wood or bark chips: *Available bagged at garden centers or in bulk from mills (a less expensive source). The bark may be from pine or fir trees. It comes in various sizes. Large, chopped bark can be used in interiors of plantings where it will not be seen. It lasts the longest, because of its size, but it is not very natural looking. Shredded bark looks best for the front of a planting.*

Cocoa or buckwheat hulls: *These are elegant, and expensive, mulching materials. Cocoa hulls are bagged in Hershey, Pennsylvania, and distributed all over the country. The shells smell great, although the fragrance fades. The only problem with this mulch is that it may mold if it is applied thickly. Adding sawdust or sand to the mulch helps. Buckwheat hulls are tiny, and a very attractive mulch, especially for small plantings. It is excellent, but it can blow away in exposed sites and become untidy or lost altogether.*

Better-quality home soil-testing kits have become increasingly available, but a professional evaluation is best for the first property analysis because it will come back to you with complete recommendations, eliminating guesswork. Then, and only then, use organic ingredients like cottonseed meal, rotted oak leaves, peat moss or pine needles (to acidify soil) or domolitic limestone or bone meal (to sweeten it). Do not expect miracles, though; even heroic measures won't allow you to grow rhododendron in the desert.

Everyone has heard the aphorism, "plant a dollar tree in a $5 hole." A similar wisdom holds true with shrubs. Dig a hole two or three times as wide as the root ball. The depth is not that important because the roots of most woody plants tend to be in the top foot or so of soil. Slightly deeper than the existing ball is sufficient. Using the soil you have excavated and 25 to 50 percent humus-rich amendments like peat moss, compost, well-rotted manure or rotted leaves (best of all, a blend of these ingredients), prepare the medium you will use to back-fill the planting hole. Spread a layer of this mixture in the bottom of the hole and tamp down.

Always lift a woody plant by the root ball, not by the stem. Cut apart and untangle the root ball (container stock) or slit open the burlap (B & B shrubs—if the ball breaks apart, that's fine, new roots will form) and position the roots so that they are reaching outward and the shrub is standing straight up. Plant a little bit high, because the shrub will sink as the newly mixed-up soil compresses. Half-fill the hole with water, and let it soak in. Then begin to back-fill with the improved medium gradually, watering in between loads of soil. Tamp down and mulch.

Don't fertilize shrubs at planting time, and use fertilizers minimally at other times, too. The U.S. National Arboretum recommends fertilizing established shrubs lightly once a year, after the first hard frost for early bloomers and in earliest spring for all others. Use a slow-release fertilizer formula that is at least 50 percent organic and whose formulation corresponds to the plant's needs. Learn to think more in terms of conserving moisture instead of watering. Realities of drought have threatened areas of the country and groundwater supplies are limited resources that must be cherished. Underground soaker hoses or drip irrigation systems get the water where it's needed with minimal loss to evaporation. Newly planted specimens may require water the first summer or two, while they get well established, but after that water only in times of infrequent rain or drought. Water deeply when watering is required. Shallow watering is not beneficial to plants, and is simply wasteful.

Organic mulches help keep the moisture in the soil, suppress weeds and also prevent soil compaction. Don't pile mulch on more than 3 inches deep, and don't place it right up against the trunk, either, or you will invite problems like rodents eating bark in winter, root suffocation or rot.

Balled and burlapped *is the traditional way that woody plants are moved. When you see a shrub whose root ball is in burlap, it implies that the plant was field grown, then dug up and wrapped for transport. Large specimens are often available only in this form, acquired from sites of new development, for instance, where they were to be bulldozed, or from nurseries that specialize in mature plants. Balled-and-burlapped shrubs can be hard for the home gardener to handle; unlike small, sturdy containers of lightweight potting mix, these tend to be large bags of somewhat wobbly, very heavy garden soil.*

When transplanting "B & B" stock, as it is called, be sure to remove all of the burlap that you can after the shrub is settled in its hole. Even if it is real, biodegradable burlap (much of what's used today is anything but biodegradable), any left above soil can wick water away from the roots of the plant.

Bare-root stock, *the most common condition in which young woody plants are shipped through the mail, is a good, low-cost way to buy dormant fruit trees, roses and many other woody plants like forsythia and pussy willow, but it is not as successful with older specimens of flowering shrubs that have grown to less "whiplike" forms. Shipping bare root allows faraway mail-order nurseries to reach more clients, though, and if that's the only source you can find for something special, try it, because most guarantee safe arrival.*

Immediately on receiving bare-root shrubs, soak them in tepid water for half a day or overnight (a five-gallon bucket is perfect for this). Bare-root shrubs take a little more patience to position in their planting holes than container-grown or B & B plants because their roots are not already spread out in a fashion that supports the branches above. Arrange the roots over a cone of amended soil in the planting hole. Water gently but very well, adding more medium as necessary so that the fibrous roots all come in contact with the soil particles.

Cut the top growth of the woody stems above the crown (where the trunk meets the roots) down by at least one-third. This may seem drastic, but you must compensate to some degree for the roots lost when the plant was dug up and cleaned of soil, when tiny roots were broken. (Fast-growing shrubs—roses, for example—are often cut down drastically.) The pruned-back top growth will produce less leaf area to dry out, so fewer roots support it. The cut back stimulates root production and gives the plants a better start as well. You will end up with a larger, stronger shrub in the long run. If the root system seemed small compared to the size of the plant, more severe pruning, up to two-thirds, might be necessary. If roots are hefty and there doesn't seem to be have been much loss, use your judgment; you might not have to remove much top growth.

When you prune at this time, follow the line of the branch down until you find an out-facing bud. That is a leaf node with a dormant bud on the outside of the plant, away from the center. The new branch will follow the lead of this bud and help to create the open form that is best for all shrubs, instead of a tangled mass of twigs. First remove any dead wood. Then remove any branches that cross or touch each other. Control the direction of the new ones with the bud choice.

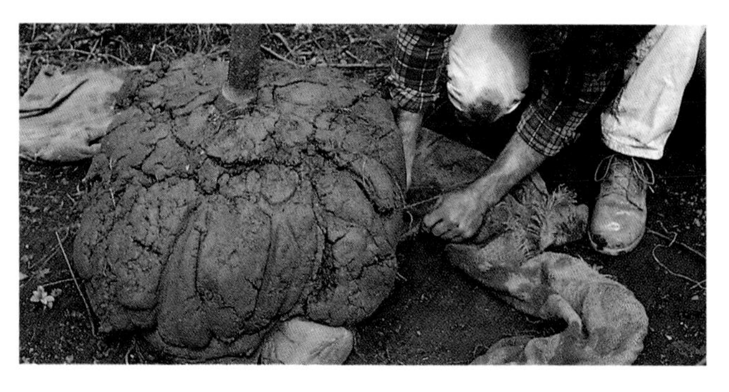

Shrubs and trees can be purchased in containers, as bare-root stock, or balled and burlapped. It is a good idea to remove the fabric covering of balled and burlapped trees' and shrubs' roots.

Pruning Primer: The Kindest Cuts of All

Flowering shrubs are an undemanding lot when it comes to pruning, because many of them have graceful, natural shapes that are best left alone. Who could improve on the weeping character of a bridal wreath spirea, which will cascade over a wall of its own accord, or the upright vase shape of a weigela?

Sometimes, shrubs will need our attention, and it is important before taking shears to shrub to keep these basic tenets in mind: To avoid losing next year's flower buds in the pruning process, prune flowering plants that bloom on the current year's growth (like peegee hydrangea, rose of Sharon and crape myrtle) before the new growth pushes out, in late winter or earliest spring. Flowering plants that bloom on last year's wood (lilacs and forsythia, for instance) should be pruned just after the flowers fade, before any new flower buds are set.

Here are some further pruning imperatives:

- *When pruning to limit the size of a plant, do so in summer, after active growth has ceased for the season.*
- *Always remove dead wood. Leaving it on the plant is an invitation to disease.*
- *In general, never remove more than a third of a plant's live wood in a growing season, to avoid shocking it to death. (Exceptions to this rule may include some very old specimens, which may require more drastic measures.)*
- *Cut large branches back just to the collar or ring of bark tissue at which the branch joins the trunk. Don't cut into this collar, or below it; never cut flush with the trunk. (The old-style flush cut has been shown to allow disease to enter the wood.)*
- *When clipping small branches and twigs, cut on a diagonal of about 45 degrees about 1/8 inch above an outward-facing leaf bud. When the new branch sprouts, it will follow the direction of the diagonal and help to hide the cut.*
- *Pruning cuts should not be painted or otherwise sealed with wax, tar or other material. Let the plant use its natural resources to heal.*
- *Avoid early fall pruning, because woody plants tend to heal most slowly at this time.*

Angle the cut up and away from an outward facing bud. The example on the far left is correct. The remaining examples show cuts made at the wrong angle, one too far and one too close to the bud.

COMPOST MAKING

Making compost is simple; nature has been doing it for millions of years. The basic materials include food, somebody to chew it up and pass it through, fertilizer and air. This translates quite simply into organic material such as leaves, straw, kitchen vegetable waste (don't include meat, bones or eggs); oxygen (collect twigs to place on the bottom of the pile, to keep spaces open for air circulation); nitrogen from such sources as grass clippings (free of pesticides or herbicides), manure (my choice) or perhaps liquified seaweed and microorganisms—these animals do the work. Microorganisms live in the soil all around you. Use garden soil to inoculate the compost pile with the critters that turn your organic materials into compost.

You can make a compost pile or two in an out-of-the-way area, behind the garage, perhaps. If you make more than one pile, you'll have one "cooking" while another is available to receive more material, and perhaps, a third is ready to use. A more presentable pile can be made by using a container. A 4-foot-square box of 2 × 4 lumber with chicken wire will work. Snow fence can be made into a cylinder and placed directly on the ground, or you can buy a container designed for this purpose. Such containers are expensive, and they don't hold very much material, certainly not all the clippings and prunings from the average property, but they would be useful in small gardens, rooftops or places where the process goes on in full view. A more permanent enclosure can be built with cinder blocks forming walls on three sides with the front open for loading and unloading and turning the pile. Leave spaces in the block construction for air.

Assemble the materials before you start. For the fastest compost, shred all the organic material by running over it with a lawn mower or putting it through a chipper-shredder, which can be purchased or rented. Layer the materials in your pile or composter. Start with a loose bed of twigs, so air enters from the bottom. This should be about 3 inches high. Now begin layering: add a 3- to 6-inch layer of organic material, then spread one or two shovelsful of soil over that layer, and finally your nitrogen source. The microorganisms need nitrogen while they do the work of breaking down the material. Continue layering until the pile reaches about 4 feet in height. That seems high, but the mass will settle. The mélange must be moist but not soggy (too wet, and there are no air spaces). In periods of very wet weather, cover the pile with plastic to keep rain out (but much of the moisture in). The well-made compost heap doesn't smell or attract vermin.

The interior of the pile will heat up as the microorganisms process the contents. It can even reach 150°F. The heat will kill most weed seeds. If you have the strength and time, turn the compost regularly. This really hastens the process. Turn it over and under with a garden fork as often as twice a month. Plunge the fork deep into the pile and try to bring the bottom material to the top. The time it takes to break down the material can be as long as two years.

Don't worry if you can't use the stuff fast enough (a very unlikely occurrence). If you leave the compost too long in the bin, there is no danger that it will turn into coal, or worse, diamonds.

LEAVES, WELL ENOUGH ALONE

You probably fondly remember the smell of burning leaves every fall when you were growing up. Well, the children of today won't have such memories (but they may be able to breathe easier for it). Ever since leaf burning has been banned, municipal leaf dumps have been started all over the country. This is a great source of material for your compost pile. These places give the stuff away for free. Just think, nearly 20 percent of all garbage picked up in the United States is garden waste! Some communities have started charging landscaping companies a fee for dumping garden refuse. When ecology becomes economy, composting becomes chic.

Be sure to compost the leaves that come from the dump. There will be weed seeds in there too, so this will not be the best ready-made mulching material, unlike the leaves you rake, collect and shred yourself. The heat of the compost pile kills most pathogens and weed roots and seeds.

4

PLANT PORTRAITS

The flowering shrubs are among the easiest plants to grow in the garden. Unlike herbaceous perennials, there isn't a lot of coddling through the summer or fall cleanup. As long as these plants are properly selected and sited, most prefer to be just left on their own. More than 65 flowering shrubs are discussed in this chapter. They are presented with their Latin names and also cross-referenced by common name.

There is a bit of a problem when it comes to common names. They vary by region and, sometimes, one grower will adopt one name for a plant whereas another chooses a different name. But the generic, or Latin, name is the same in Pittsburgh, Shanghai, Berlin, Montreal and Mexico City. "Carolina allspice" may be the same as "sweet shrub," but a *Calycanthus* is a *Calycanthus* is a *Calycanthus*. That's the main reason for including the scientific name, but there's another. One of the best ways to improve your skill as a gardener is to treat plants as individuals. When you learn the Latin name of a flowering shrub, it no longer is just a bush. It becomes elevated to something special, something about which you are knowledgeable.

The first word of the Latin name for a plant tells you which genus it belongs to; the second identifies the species. *Syringa vulgaris*, for example, tells you that the genus is *Syringa* and the species is *vulgaris*. This plant, a lilac, is not vulgar, but it is familiar or *common*—that's what *vulgaris* means. You might be surprised to discover that you know something about these species names already. For example, *gigantes* means giant, *minimea* means small, *grandiflora* means large flowers, *multiflora* means many flowers, *purpurea* means purple, *sulphurea* means sulfur colored—a shade of yellow. There is reason, if not rhyme.

Of course, common names are useful, too. They're often very descriptive; sweet shrub tells you something, lilac tells you less. Unfortunately, hybrid names are not always as helpful. Often the cultivated varieties of plants, written as proper names in single quotes, are obscure, say, references to the discoverer's sister's husband's dog. Worse, these can be a marketing-person's idea of a sales booster. Names like 'Hot Pants' leave me cold. But whatever the name may be, having the correct name will ensure you get the plant you're after, and that you find out what you need to know from the profiles that follow. A *Rhododendron* by any other name may smell as sweet, but it might be the wrong color, or worse, not a *Rhododendron* at all.

Syringa *is planted as much for its glorious scent as for its visual beauty.*

PLANT PORTRAIT KEY

Here is a guide to the symbols and terms used throughout this section.

Latin name of the shrub is boldface italic.

Phonetic pronunciation of the Latin name is in parentheses.

Common name of the shrub is in boldface type.

Native American identifies those shrubs growing in North America at the time of its colonization.

Season of bloom: SP = spring, SU = summer, F = fall, W = winter; E = early, L = late, i.e., ESP = early spring

The average hours of sun needed per day is indicated by symbols. The first symbol is what the shrub prefers, but it is adaptable to all conditions listed. In general we think of light in terms of the following:

○ *Sun*—Six hours or longer of direct sunlight per day.

◐ *Part Shade*—Three to six hours of direct sunlight per day.

● *Shade*—Two hours or less of direct sunlight per day.

✱ —Fragrant blooms or foliage

Forceability: Cut branches that can be forced to bloom indoors, are indicated by a + for yes, and a – for no.

Zones: Check the USDA Plant Hardiness Map (pages 90–91), based on average annual temperatures for each area—or zone—of the United States to see what zone you live in. Every plant portrait lists the zones best for that shrub.

Height: Flowering shrubs come in all shapes and sizes, and we have supplied a guide to their heights so that you can judge placement of any given entry. The size stated is an approximation for the shrub after 10 years in the landscape (providing, of course, that the shrub was a fairly young specimen to begin with). For some shrubs, that is maturity. Of course, climate, moisture, exposure and other environmental factors affect size. Note, this is a general guide.

Cultural Information: All recommendations for light, hardiness, height and care are made in general terms. There is a lot of science in horticulture, but there is also a lot of art and firsthand experience. Because shrubs are living things, there aren't any precise recipes for success. We can't just recommend, "water once a week," because we don't know how large the plant in question is, where it lives, whether there has been rain this week or not, how much moisture the soil retains, the age of the plant, the season of the year and so on. Consider the cultural information your point of departure. Common sense and this book will make you a good shrub gardener.

Recommended Varieties: Whenever possible, we have highlighted certain varieties of the species listed for their wonderful form, floral color or habit of growth. We couldn't include every variety under the sun, but have noted many of the most available kinds and listed their distinctive attributes.

Aaron's-beard St. John's-wort; see ***Hypericum***

Abelia ×*grandiflora*

(a-BEL-ee-a) × (gran-di-FLO-ra) **glossy abelia,** LSP, SU, EF. ○ ◐ –

Zones: 5 to 9
Height: 3 to 5 feet
Colors: White, blushed pink
Characteristics: This is a useful shrub, all too often overlooked. White bell-shaped flowers flare at the ends and are suffused with pink. Best of all, they bloom for a very long time—most of the summer and into fall. Very shiny, bronze-green leaves are semievergreen, persistent in mild winters and southern climates. The plants are graceful, and although rather twiggy, this fountain-shaped habit complements the foliage and flowers.

The glossy abelia can be pruned but it's not necessary. These plants can be used alone as specimen plantings, along a low wall, or in a mixed border with herbaceous perennials. The delicate flowers would be welcome in a cottage-garden planting, along with summer flowers and even herbs. Abelia could be used for an informal hedge in an out-of-the-way place, because of its unfussy appearance and low maintenance requirements. The dense twigs might also keep small animals out (or in).
Cultural Information: One of the best traits of the glossy abelia is its adaptability to various locations, from sun to partial shade. It isn't fussy about soil or moisture. Average, well-drained soil, even somewhat on the lean side, will suit. If any pruning is necessary to keep the plant in bounds or restore the shape, it should be done in late winter or early spring.

Abelia ×grandiflora

Abeliophyllum distichum

(a-bel-ee-o-FIL-lum DIS-tik-um) **white forsythia,** LW. ○ ◐ ● ✱ +

Zones: 5 to 8
Height: 3 to 5 feet
Colors: Pink to white
Characteristics: The white forsythia's common name is misleading. The flowers are pinkish, especially in bud, and in shade, where the plants do fairly well, they stay pink. It is not an enormously handsome foliage shrub, and should be grown for its flowers. Because of the flowers' early arrival in late winter to spring, and perfume, white forsythia might be worth growing by the edge of the path or walk. The buds last for weeks, swelling to become larger and larger until the small flowers, shaped just like those of true forsythia, finally open. They are borne all along the stems of last season's wood.
Cultural Information: Average soil suits this plant. It will need pruning if you care about its untidy habit. This should be done immediately after flowering.

Abeliophyllum distichum

Aesculus parviflora

Aesculus parviflora (ES-kew-lus par-vi-FLO-ra) **bottlebrush buckeye, buckeye**, Native American, SU..○ ◐ ✱ –

Zones: 4 to 8

Height: 8 to 12 feet

Color: White

Characteristics: The bottlebrush buckeye is a specimen plant for a large space. A mammoth among shrubs, it often grows wider than it is tall. In summer, fuzzy cylindrical spikes grow up from the ends of the new growth. They look a lot like horse chestnut flowers, a close relative. The flowers are white with pink stamens and are fragrant. The leaves of these deciduous shrubs are also of a gargantuan scale and will have to be raked in the fall. A good way to use these plants is on their own in the middle of the lawn or to screen passing cars from view.

Cultural Information: These shrubs are not finicky as to their soil or moisture needs. They tolerate heat and some drought, and do not require pruning. Irrigation in the early days after planting is a good idea until the shrubs become established.

Amelanchier lamarckii

Amelanchier (a-me-LAN-kee-er) **shadblow, serviceberry,** Native American, ESP. ○ ◐ –

Zones: 4 to 9

Height: To 20 feet

Color: White

Characteristics: There are several Native American shadblows. This common name derives from the fact that the plants flower in early spring when the shad are running. Clouds of small white flowers bloom before the

foliage sprouts. Other ornamental qualities of these deciduous plants are red fruits in summer and brilliant fall foliage color of yellow or red. In winter the attractive stems are grayish white.
Cultural Information: These medium to large shrubs are useful in a naturalistic planting, but may not be best for general landscape use, because they are susceptible to various pests. No pruning is necessary, but shrubs can be trained into tree shapes or standards. The species *Amelanchier stolonifera*, can be easily rooted from underground stems or stolons. The fruits can be used to make jelly or pie.

Aronia (a-RO-nee-a) **chokeberry,** Native American, SP. ◐ –
Zones: 4 to 9
Height: 4 to 8 feet by species
Color: White
Characteristics: The wild chokeberry, species and cultivars bloom in May in fuzzy dense clusters, white with contrasting black anthers. The fruits, as you might imagine, are ornamental, either red or black, by species: *Aronia arbutifolia*, red, *A. melanocarpa*, black. This is another plant for an informal shrub border or woodland edge.
Cultural Information: These deciduous shrubs are easy to grow and easy to propagate from seeds, stems or by layering. Some of the dense kinds can also be divided at ground level with a sharp spade. They are tolerant of a wide variety of soil types and have few pests.

Australian bottlebrush; see ***Callistemon***

Azalea; see ***Rhododendron***

Beauty-berry; see ***Callicarpa***

Beautybush; see ***Kolkwitzia***

Blackberry, ornamental; see ***Rubus***

Blue mist spirea; see ***Caryopteris***

Bottlebrush, Australian; see ***Callistemon***

Bottlebrush buckeye; see ***Aesculus***

Broom; see ***Cytisus***

Buckeye; see ***Aesculus***

Buddleia Davidii (BUD-lee-a da-VID-ee-eye) **butterfly bush,** SU. ○ –
Zones: 5 to 9

Aronia arbutifolia

Height: 4 to 6 feet
Colors: White to violet-pink, lilac, lavender, orange, reddish
Characteristics: The butterfly bush, also called "summer lilac," is one of the most fragrant flowering shrubs. The aroma resembles a heliotrope's, sort of cherry

Buddleia Davidii

Callicarpa americana

Callicarpa americana

baby powder. The shrubs are not special in and of themselves, although gray-green leaves add interest. We grow them for the tiny flower that completely cover spikes up to 18 inches long.

In colder areas, the shrubs die back by half, and sometimes, all the way to the ground. Fortunately, the flowers are borne on the season's new growth. Because of this die back, *Buddleia* can be used like herbaceous perennials. In fact, they are great choices for the back of a sunny flower border where arching stems can bend toward the front for close inspection. As the common name implies, they are seldom seen without the accompaniment of colorful butterflies. *B. alternifolia* is a more wild looking species to look for, along with its cultivars. *Cultural Information:* In spring, cut back all the dead, dried brown stems, to green, live wood. This is one of the few instances when an additive that is higher in nitrogen, such as cow manure, could be recommended. You'll want to encourage vegetative (foliage and twig), fresh growth early in the season. Top-dress in early spring with well-rotted cow manure or use manure tea or liquid seaweed. If you fertilize later in the growing year, switch to a high-phosphorus fertilizer.

Burkwood's daphne; see ***Daphne***

Butterfly bush; see ***Buddleia***

Buttonbush; see ***Cephalanthus***

California lilac; see ***Ceanothus***

Callicarpa (KAL-li-kar-pa)
Beauty-berry, F. ○ ◐ –
Zones: 5 to 8
Height: 4 feet
Colors: White to purple berries
Characteristics: Beauty-berry is a deciduous shrub that has elliptical leaves with serrated edges and pink flowers in summer. But these are not the big attraction of these plants. It's the berries, which are so colorful that they elevate this shrub to the category of the finest flowering ornamental shrubs. In fall, purple or magenta berries line the stems. Interesting species, including *Callicarpa dichotoma*, *C. americana* and *C. japonica*, all have berries and there are cultivars with fruit in shades of white, blue and red. *C. japonica*

Callistemon citrinus

'Leucocarpa', with white fruits, is frequently found in mail-order catalogs.
Cultural Information: Not much has to be done to the beautyberry, but it will not become a handsome specimen without some pruning to give shape. Because the fruit forms along the stems from summer flowers, it can be pruned in early spring. Some gardeners, eager to encourage as much fruit growth as possible, prune the shrub back hard, even to the ground. It *is* a good idea to at least cut back winter-killed growth each spring.

Callistemon citrinus (kal-is-TEE-mon si-TREE-nus) **Australian bottlebrush**, SP, SU. ○ –
Zones: 9 (8 with protection)
Height: 10 feet
Color: Red
Characteristics: This is one of the most familiar shrubs along the streets of California. What more could you want besides handsome, broad, spear-shaped evergreen foliage on an upright, dense shrub? Flowers? That's the beauty of the Australian bottlebrush. From late winter through summer, it produces upright, perfect flower spikes covered with stamens that make it look exactly like its namesake. Unfortunately for many of us, it is not very hardy. It is a good, large shrub for along the street in climates it accepts. It can even be grown as a tub plant for the cool greenhouse throughout the country.
Cultural Information: Callistemon is very easy to grow in nearly any soil condition as long as the earth is not overly alkaline. They are very tolerant of various moisture levels, and especially useful for their ability to withstand drought. Pruning can be done at any time, and every few years, the woody plants appreciate a thorough clipping in late winter to encourage soft new growth and ultimately more flower spikes.

Calycanthus floridus (kal-ee-KAN-thus FLO-ri-dus) **Carolina allspice, sweet shrub**, Native American, SP, SU. ◐ ○ –
Zones: 4 to 9
Height: 5 feet
Colors: Reddish brown, chartreuse
Characteristics: Catalogs describe the fragrance of Carolina allspice flowers as strawberry-like, but I think the fragrance is actually more like the inside of an old whiskey barrel: deep, heady, not unpleasant. The deciduous leaves are quite large, about 6 inches long and somewhat puckered. The flowers are curious: small knobs with upward-facing, spiky petals start in spring and continue sporadically into summer. The color is really unusual—they are reddish brown. These odd disclaimers should not be off-putting. These are terrific plants, notably for a shaded spot. And they are a must for anyone with a naturalistic garden where they really look at home. The cultivar 'Athens', selected by Dr. Michael Dirr of the University of Georgia, has chartreuse flowers.
Cultural Information: Sweet shrub will do something in nearly any location in almost any soil, but it performs best in rich, well-drained, moist soil. Sometimes, new plants can be grown from the suckers that form around the base of the plant after five years or so.

Calycanthus floridus

Camellia japonica (ka-MEE-lee-a ja-PON-i-ka) · **camellia**, W, LSP. ◐ –
Zones: 8 to 10
Height: 15 feet
Colors: White, pink, red
Characteristics: If the camellias were hardier, they would be even more popular shrubs than they are. Still, these broad-leafed evergreens are suited to partially shaded spots in much of the South and along the West

Camellia japonica

Camellia japonica

Camellia japonica

Camellia Sasanqua

Coast. They are, arguably, more handsome landscape plants than even the rhododendron, because of the glossy, stiff leaves that cover them from top to bottom.

Camellias are closely related to the plant whose leaves are the source of tea, but these are grown for flowers. They start to bloom in winter, some varieties as early as December (*Camellia japonica Sasanqua* blooms in fall). Flawless roselike, double blossoms unfurl from pointed buds. They can be white, pink or red and often are striped in bicolor combinations. Some varieties have semidouble flowers with two rows of petals arranged around colorful stamens. There are hundreds of hybrids available from southern and western nurseries. 'Debutante' is a pink-flowered variety with 3-inch-wide flowers. 'Herme' is a bicolor that is a bit fragrant. 'Alba Plena' is an easy-to-find white-flowered double, and 'Gloire de Nantes' is a very large (4 inches in diameter) red-flowered one. The flowers can be cut with stems; stemless, individual blooms can be floated in a bowl of water or the flowers can be made into corsages.

There are other species of camellia. The hardiest might be the fall-blooming *C. Sasanqua*. These plants have 2-inch-long leaves, as opposed to *C. japanica*'s 4-inch ones. Many varieties of this species are on the market, and hybridizers are constantly selecting more and more hardy types for introduction to northern gardens.

Cultural Information: Camellias need a situation similar to the rhododendron: partial shade and acidic, moist soil. The soil should be covered with a coarse-textured mulch such as chopped fir bark. Fine particles in mulches such as peat moss, although acidic, may encourage roots to grow up into the material and be more exposed to cold and drought damage. Plants are usually bought container grown. Break up the root ball when planting, especially if the plant is pot-bound, as they all too often are. Some insects visit the camellias and usually group along the bark, in the case of scale, and in branch and stem crotches, as with mealy bug. Safer's Insecticidal Soap is effective with repeated applications. Blossoms are susceptible to a blight that causes edges of petals to brown, especially in wet weather. Sulfur, or another fungicide that has low toxicity, can be used, but it's better to select resistant varieties.

Carolina allspice; see ***Calycanthus***

Caryopteris* × *clandonensis (carry-OP-ter-is) × (klan-don-EN-sis) **blue mist spirea**, SU. ○ –

Zones: 5 to 8

Height: 2 feet

Color: Blue

Characteristics: These low shrubs resemble the Mediterranean "sub-shrubs"—herbs such as lavender—because of their bushy, twiggy habits and small, elliptical, silver leaves. In late summer the plants are covered with clear blue flowers that make it important for both color as well as season of bloom. They can be a useful plants for a spot by paved walkways and might be as successful for edging a flower border in sun and heat. The species are not well known, but the hybrid *C.* × *clandonensis* has produced a few spectacular cultivars including 'Blue Mist', by far the best. The leaves and wood are aromatic when crushed.

Cultural Information: The drought tolerance of *Caryopteris* is well-known. They are happy in any soil, even nutritionally poor soil, as long as there is good drainage so the earth is never soggy. These plants can put up with a windy site, even by the seaside. Cut them back hard in early spring. They bloom on new wood and benefit from this treatment.

Ceanothus (see-a-NO-thus) **California lilac,** Native American, SP, SU by species. ○ ✹ –

Zones: 8 to 9 (except where noted)

Height: 2 to 15 feet by species

Colors: Blue, white

Characteristics: Ceanothus is a large group of native shrubs that includes low groundcovers, such as Carmel creeper (*Ceanothus griseus* 'Horizontalis'); such plants of middling height as the 8-inch-tall Siskiyou mat *(C. pumilus)* and giant shrubs, San Diego ceanothus *(C. cyaneus)*, at 12 feet, and feltleaf ceanothus *(C. arboreus)*, which tops out at 20 feet. There is an East Coast species, *C. americanus* (Zones 4 to 8), called "New Jersey tea," which is a good choice for the wild garden; its leaves were used as a tea substitute during the Revolutionary War. But most of the genus live in warm climates and are typified by the spectacular, true blue flowers in upright clusters like small, fuzzy lilacs, in spring. There are evergreen and deciduous

examples. The leaves are small, thick, often leathery, sometimes woolly with deep veins.
Cultural Information: These plants are excellent for hillsides where they will help to stabilize the earth. The plants are drought tolerant and enjoy good drainage. The West Coast kinds need sun. Many will tolerate sea spray and wind.

Cephalanthus occidentalis

(sef-a-LAN-thus ox-i-den-TAL-is) **buttonbush,** Native American, SU. ◐ –
Zones: 5 to 10
Height: 6 to 8 feet
Color: White
Characteristics: One of the most extraordinary things about this native shrub, which ranges from Nova Scotia to Mexico, is that it is not grown in more American gardens. The other unusual aspect is the floral clusters. Little tubular flowers are arranged in perfect, 1-inch balls all over the woody plant. The pompons are favorites of butterflies, too. Excluding its interesting flowers and tolerance of overly moist soil, it may not be a choice for a small yard—there are better plants for limited spaces. But in a wild, marshy garden setting, it is a must.
Cultural Information: This shrub will grow in just about any soil and will do well in wet soil. In fact, this is the perfect choice for the edge of a bog garden.

Chaenomeles japonica

(kee-NOM-e-lees ja-PON-i-ka) **Japanese flowering quince**, ESP. ○ ◐ +
Zones: 4 to 9
Height: 4 feet
Color: Red
Characteristics: These are a brilliant deciduous shrubs whose flowers appear before the foliage in early spring. The species has semidouble flowers in a deep wine color, about 1½ inches across. The foliage, green to bronze, is also attractive. Add to these features the very spiky twigs that make this plant useful as a dense security hedge, and you have an excellent landscape subject. Branches can be cut in late winter for forcing indoors, and flowers left on the plant may produce yellow, edible, applelike fruits used for making jelly. The hybrid *Chaenomeles ×superba* adds colors of white, orange and pink, by variety, to the red species.
Cultural Information: Quinces are not hard to grow. They are accepting of a wide variety of soil conditions. They can, and should, be pruned; however, they will not take to hard pruning. If you do choose to use them for hedges, be sure to leave room, because they can only be lightly sheared, and not cut back severely.

Chaste tree; see ***Vitex***

Chimonanthus praecox

(KY-mo-nan-thus prie-KOKS) **winter sweet**, W. ○ ✽ +
Zones: 6 to 9
Height: 10 feet
Color: Yellow
Characteristics: This winter-blooming shrub is grown for fragrance. Place it where you'll be sure to encounter it, perhaps by the path to the garage. The

Caryopteris ×clandonensis

Ceanothus thyrsiflorus

Cephalanthus occidentalis

Chaenomeles speciosa *'Toyo Nishiki'*

Chaenomeles speciosa *'Simonii'*

Chimonanthus praecox

flowers are borne along the stems and are little downward-facing cups, yellow with red stripes inside.
Cultural Information: Winter sweets are not fussy about soils as long as there is good drainage.

Chionanthus virginicus

(ki-o-NAN-thus vir-JIN-i-kus) **fringe tree,** Native American, SP. ○ ✽ –
Zones: 3 to 9
Height: 25 feet
Color: White
Characteristics: Fringe tree is actually a large, multibranched, deciduous shrub. Huge, foamy clusters of fragrant flowers form at the ends of old wood. The individual flowers are like fringe. Sometimes extremely ornamental, egg-shaped blue fruits form but they are quickly snatched by birds. Only the female forms fruit, so you must have both sexes to get them. The flowers on the male plant are larger than the female's, however.
Cultural Information: Fringe tree is another large shrub to use as a specimen in the lawn, where it can be appreciated alone or with a twin of the opposite sex, one on either side of the main walk. Soil should be moist and slightly acidic; otherwise, cultural needs are not demanding.

Chionanthus virginicus

Chionanthus virginicus

Choisya ternata

Choisya ternata

(SHAW-si-a ter-NAH-ta) **Mexican orange,** SP. ○ ◐ ✽ –
Zones: 8 to 10
Height: 4 to 6 feet
Color: White
Characteristics: This evergreen shrub for warm climates produces flowers that have the appearance and fragrance of orange blossoms. It's an excellent plant for the foundation, perhaps under the porch railing, where the fragrance can be appreciated.
Cultural Information: Prune this plant after flowering to produce the desired shape, form and size. Sometimes they are bothered by insects, aphids and red spiders among them.

Chokeberry; see ***Aronia***

Cinquefoil; see ***Potentilla***

Cistus

(SIS-tus) **rockrose,** SU. ○ –
Zones: 8 to 10
Height: 2 to 4 feet by variety
Colors: White, yellow, purple, with contrasting "eye"
Characteristics: Cistus species and hybrids are plants originally from the Mediterranean regions, where they hug rocky cliff faces, so they are very tolerant of heat and dry soil and will also grow well on an embankment. The flowers are large, up to 4 inches across by variety. They do resemble single roses or giant apple blossoms. There are several pastel colors available. View varieties in bloom at local nurseries.
Cultural Information: These plants are excellent for hot climates, mostly in Zone 8 southward. The soil should have very good drainage and be alkaline. They cannot stand wet areas. They are fairly fast growing, and it is best to start with small plants. This is an excellent choice to naturalize on a slope in full sun.

Clerodendrum trichotomum

(kler-o-DEN-drum tri-KO-to-mum) **harlequin glory bower,** SU. ◐ ✽ –
Zones: 6 to 8 (5 with protection)
Height: 10 feet
Color: White with pink
Characteristics: Most *Clerodendrum* are vines and, for the most part, tropical and subtropical. There is one that is a large shrub and quite hardy. It has dull, felted leaves that have an unpleasant odor if crushed. However, the flowers are among the most fragrant of any shrub, always covered with butterflies and other nectar-loving creatures. The white flowers have

showy pink bracts and interesting protruding stamens and pistils. After the flowers fade, very decorative fruits form that are lustrous blue encased in a rich red calyx.
Cultural Information: Give the big harlequin glory bower room to grow. It's not too particular about soils but in a moist one, it will tolerate full sun. However, it does beautifully at the edge of the woodland, on the north side of a tree, or even under a high-limbed one. This plant is very rare, but not because it is hard to grow, just because it is unknown to gardeners and seldom in commerce. Keep your eye out for it if you like to watch the winged creatures.

Clethra alnifolia (KLETH-ra al-ni-FO-lee-a) **summer sweet, sweet pepperbush,** Native American, SU. ○ ◐ ✱ –
Zones: 3 to 9
Height: 5 to 8 feet
Colors: White to pink
Characteristics: Clethras are excellent native shrubs for a marshy area, but will grow in an average garden setting if there is enough moisture and slightly acidic soil. In summer, fragrant white spires grow from terminal buds, and in the evening, these look like 5-inch-tall candles shining in the dark. There are exquisite pink-flowered varieties that even outdo the species 'Pink Spires' and 'Rosea'. These shrubs look good just about anywhere.
Cultural Information: Summer sweet are easy to grow in moist, acidic soil. They can be pruned in very early spring to keep in bounds, but the natural shape is handsome, and no pruning (except for removal of dead wood or faded flower spires) is necessary. However, the shrubs send up side shoots to form substantive colonies, and they can be propagated by dividing these with a sharp spade. Cut back top growth on new divisions by one-third.

Cistus ×purpureus

Cistus ×cyprius

Clerodendrum trichotomum

Clerodendrum trichotomum

Clerodendrum trichotomum *(showing fruit)*

Coralberry; see ***Symphoricarpes***

Cornus alba (KOR-nus AL-ba) **Tartarian dogwood, red-twig dogwood**, Native American, SP, SU. ○ ◐ ● –
Zones: 2 to 8
Height: 4 to 6 feet
Color: White
Characteristics: The red-twig dogwoods are useful shrubs with long canes. In late spring, flat umbels (clusters) are covered with flowers, and later, blue-black berries form. However, it is the twigs, turning bright red in winter, for which these shrubs are known. There are wonderful variegated-leaf forms that can light a dark area. They are vigorous shrubs and can be cut back in late winter to produce succulent long shoots for more winter color. There are other *Cornus* shrubs for interest in winter. Our native *C. sericea* is the yellow-twig dogwood. Native Cornelian cherry (*C. mas*), isn't known for its winter twigs, but late winter fragrant flowers, reminiscent of the witch hazels, and then edible cherrylike fruits in the fall that are as ornamental as the flowers.
Cultural Information: Any good garden soil will suit these plants, and with sufficient moisture, sun can be tolerated. They are most useful at the edge of the woodland in partial shade.

Clethra alnifolia *'Rosea'*

Cornus alba *'Sibirica'*

Cornus mas

Cornus alba
'Sibirica'

Corylopsis glabrescens (kor-ril-LOP-sis gla-BRES-enz) **winter hazel**, ESP. ◐ ✱ –
Zones: 5 to 8
Height: 8 feet
Color: Yellow
Characteristics: The lovely, open, vase shape of this deciduous shrub is enough to recommend it, but the real interest occurs during the blooming period. Full, pendant clusters of pale yellow flowers form in late winter to early spring. They are fragrant. If you have space, include this Asian species. It really isn't well known or included in plantings enough, considering how special the flowers are.
Cultural Information: Sandy, well-drained soil on the acidic side is appreciated. This one is the hardiest of the genus, but still, in some winters, flower buds are killed by late frosts. Plant in front of a wall or tall evergreens so that the plants are a bit protected and so that flowers show up well.

Corylopsis sinensis

Corylus Avellana
'Contorta'

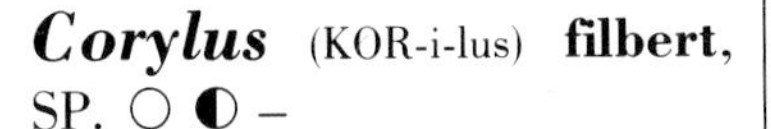

Corylus (KOR-i-lus) **filbert**, SP. ○ ◐ –
Zones: 4 to 9
Height: 10 feet
Color: Brown
Characteristics: These are ornamental versions of the edible hazelnut. *Corylus Avellana* is a European weeping plant with oval, coarse, ribbed leaves. The twigs in winter are ornamental, especially from the cultivar 'Contorta', commonly called "Harry Lauder's walking stick," which is twisted with spiraling growth, and unparalleled among the deciduous shrubs for winter twig interest. The flowers are long, stringy clusters that hang down in spring before the leaves sprout. They resemble birch catkins—in fact, a close relative. *C. maxima*, a less hardy giant (Zones 5 to 9), comes in a wonderful variety, 'Purpurea', with dark burgundy leaves through the season. A few can be used in a mixed border, repeating their unusual color to bring a long planting together.
Cultural Information: Well-drained soil in sun or partial shade suits the filberts. They grow every which way, so pruning is necessary. You'll want to gather the dormant twigs for flower arrangements in winter, and so they can be pruned and cut for indoors at the same time.

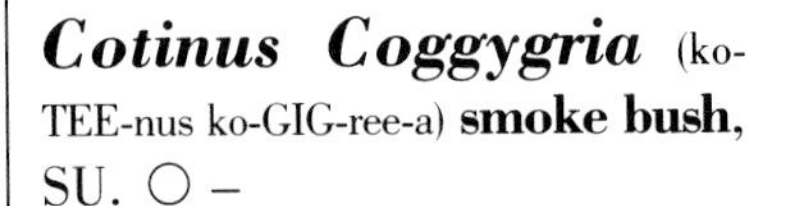

Cotinus Coggygria (ko-TEE-nus ko-GIG-ree-a) **smoke bush**, SU. ○ –
Zones: 5 to 8 (4 with protection)
Height: 8 to 10 feet
Colors: Green, light purple
Characteristics: The original smoke bush is an old-fashioned shrub that was popular years ago and grown in many gardens. Today, the variety purple smoke bush (*C. Coggygria* 'Purpureus') is grown much more often than the species because it has the bonus of wonderful foliage color. The leaves are like coins and incredibly ornamental. The flower clusters do look like billowing smoke, and a mature specimen in bloom is a sight never forgotten. This plant is a worthwhile investment. The purple one can be grown in a mixed border or shrub planting and pruned in early spring to keep it in bounds. But if space allows, grow either one as a specimen on its own. The ultimate width will be equal to its height, about 10 feet.
Cultural Information: Ordinary soil (not too wet, not too dry, not too rich) will suit smoke bushes. Pruning is necessary for shrubs included in flower-border plantings. Although you might be inclined to try these plants in partial shade or shade, where the purple leaves would be wonderful, don't; the plants will languish. They grow so tall and

wide that it would seem to be a mistake to grow them by a walkway, but if you are a diligent pruner, they can be grown on either side of the walk and a tunnel or arch can be carved out of them as they grow up—an incredible effect.

Crape myrtle; see ***Lagerstroemia***

Currant, Indian; see ***Symphoricarpes***

Cytisus (SIGH-ti-sus) **broom**, SP. ○ –

Zones: 5 to 9
Height: up to 10 feet
Colors: Yellow, purple
Characteristics: These plants exemplify the legumes, of which the pea is the most familiar member, and the flowers of the broom are like small sweet peas. These are useful, easy-to-grow shrubs for various climates throughout America. Unfortunately, some of them have escaped into the wild, and in California, they have supplanted the wild plants completely, coming up from seeds everywhere. Although they *are* beautiful in spring when the wispy, tall shrubs are covered with yellow flowers, one escapee, called "French broom," has become one of the worst weed problems along the roadside and throughout the hillsides above San Francisco. The most familiar garden brooms are the Scotch broom *(Cytisus scoparius)*, hardy to Zone 5, and Warminster broom (*C.* ×*praecox*), not quite as hardy, but a valuable landscape plant growing to 10 feet (this broom is fine for poor soil that is dry).
Cultural Information: Their success in the wild should give you a tip as to their tenacity. The plants reach mature height quickly and then tend to decline. Either keep young plants cut back or rip the old ones out and start over. The various species and varieties differ as to hardiness. Many kinds are available in flowers at garden centers and nurseries. Give them space (unless they are dwarf varieties).

Daphne ×*Burkwoodii*

(DAF-nee) × (burk-WUD-ee-eye) **Burkwood's daphne**, ESP. ○ ☀ –

Zones: 4 to 8
Height: 4 feet
Colors: White, pink
Characteristics: There are many daphnes for various garden conditions in different parts of the country, but some are difficult to grow and known well for slow growth and precise requirements. A few, such as *D.* ×*Burkwoodii*, are rather easy. *D* × *B.* 'Carol Mackie' is a popular cultivar that deserves a place in every garden. It is semievergreen and has variegated, small, elliptical leaves. In early spring, pink buds form that slowly open into tubes, then open into wide stars that are extremely fragrant. Fragrant daphne (*D. odora*) is an evergreen species with winter flowers for the West Coast and southern climates; there are also variegated cultivars.
Cultural Information: Daphnes don't need pruning. *D.* ×*Burkwoodii* forms a perfectly rounded mound. Sandy soil that is neutral to slightly alkaline suits daphne well.

Cotinus Coggygria

Cytisus ×praecox

Daphne ×Burkwoodii
'Carol Mackie' (right)

Deutzia gracilis

Deutzia gracilis

Enkianthus campanulatus

Deutzia gracilis (DOOTZ-ee-a gra-SIL-lis) **slender deutzia,** SP. ◐ –
Zones: 4 to 8
Height: 4 feet
Color: White
Characteristics: What happened to the deutzias? These wonderful shrubs were popular at one time, but are rarely grown today. There doesn't seem to be any reason for this, except perhaps that the shrubs aren't interesting except when in bloom. They are excellent shrubs, however, for almost any site. They can be terrific planted with *Cornus* species, flowering dogwoods that bloom about the same time. Deutzias are related to the mock oranges. The flowers are about ½ inch long, are white with yellow centers and point to the ground. This species is especially elegant, with long arching branches that cascade like a fountain of white bloom in spring. *Deutzia scabra* 'Pride of Rochester' is a taller species with long-lasting, double, 1-inch flowers with a pink blush. Less common, it is very desirable in bloom, but because it is larger and will take up more space, it is a good choice for filling in a screen between property lines. The cultivar 'Nikko' has interesting, rich burgundy fall foliage and reaches a height of 2 feet.
Cultural Information: Grow these plants just about anywhere in ordinary soil. They can be wonderful by the street at the entrance to the driveway. In rural areas, plant them along the roadside for the enjoyment of neighbors and visitors. The plants easily root from soft wood cuttings and can even be divided. Rarely expensive, it pays to grow many.

Dogwood, red-twig; see ***Cornus***

Dogwood, Tartarian; see ***Cornus***

Enkianthus campanulatus (en-ki-AN-thus kam-pan-ew-LAH-tus) **redvein enkianthus,** LSP. ◐ –
Zones: 4 to 7
Height: 15 feet
Color: Cream, striped with red
Characteristics: The lovely, delicate nodding bells of enkianthus are a delight, but they must be viewed close up to be really appreciated. Because the shrub itself is rather undistinguished, this easy plant may be hard to use. It would be terrific as an understory plant along a walk through the woods. It might be useful for a border of mixed deciduous shrubs for a large property.
Cultural Information: Pruning may consist of limbing the plant up to get branches out of the way of the path, so that as the plant matures, its dangling flowers can hang over the walk and be viewed from below. They like a similar soil to the rhododendron, woodsy and acidic.

False spirea; see ***Sorbaria***

Filbert; see ***Corylus***

Flowering-almond; see ***Prunus***

Flowering-cherry; see ***Prunus***

Flowering currant; see ***Ribes***

Flowering-plum; see ***Prunus***

Flowering quince, Japanese; see ***Chaenomeles***

Forsythia, white; see ***Abeliophyllum distichum***

Forsythia × *intermedia*

(FOR-SYTH-i-a) × (IN-TER-mee-de-a) **forsythia**, LW, ESP. ○ ◐ ● +
Zones: 5 to 8
Height: 6 to 8 feet
Color: Yellow
Characteristics: These might be the best-known deciduous shrubs in the United States, and they are one of the earliest to bloom. They are overused—all too often, used poorly. Nothing looks worse than a tightly pruned bowling ball or bright yellow tombstone carved out of a shrub that naturally has a wonderful, spreading fountain shape in its unpruned form. When it must be pruned, the way to do it is to pick long stems for indoor forcing from January on. They are about the easiest shrub to bring into bloom indoors. Although many flowers will form in full sun, forsythia can be grown as a foliage plant in deep shade.

The bright yellow flowers of varieties such as 'Lynwood Gold' are a little too loud for every situation. Seek out varieties with more subtle color, if you can. 'Spring Glory' has lemon-yellow flowers on an otherwise typical *F.* × *intermedia* shrub.
Cultural Information: Can forsythias be killed? They'll take just about any treatment, but do best in rich, well-drained soil in full sun. Prune after flowering and top-dress with well-rotted manure. Flowering is best on year-old wood, and older plants may need to be "opened up" and rejuvenated. Cut one-third of the growth back to the ground every few years, and always remove any dead wood. Sometimes forsythias are host to insects, such as aphids or spider mites, in dry locations. Use a garden hose to spray foliage with water as a control. In severe cases, try repeated applications of Safer's Insecticidal Soap.

Fothergilla major

(foth-er-GIL-la MAY-jor) **fothergilla**, Native American, SP. ○ ◐ ● –
Zones: 4 to 8
Height: 6 to 10 feet
Color: White
Characteristics: This native member of the witch hazel group has fuzzy white flowers in early spring. There are no petals, just prominent stamens. They appear before the foliage, but may persist when leaves unfurl. This deciduous shrub with round, hairy, 4-inch-long leaves is another find for an informal garden space. Autumn foliage color is presented as the sensational crescendo to the fothergillas' season. Look for the *F. gardenii* species and cultivars as well, especially *F. gardenii* 'Blue Mist', which has a blue cast to its leaves.
Cultural Information: Well-drained loam that is slightly acidic is the place for fothergillas. They are usually pest-free.

Fremontodendron californicum

(free-mon-to-DEN-dron KAL-i-forn-i-KUM) **fremontodendron, leatherwood**, Native American, SP. ○ –
Zones: 8 to 9
Height: 10 to 20 feet
Color: Yellow
Characteristics: For an uncommon plant, *Fremontodendron* has a host of common names in addition to its generic name: flannel bush, leatherwood, mountain leatherwood and slippery elm. Felted green and brown leaves

Forsythia ×intermedia

Fothergilla gardenii

Fremontodendron californicum

cover these tall evergreen shrubs. Wonderful, large, bright yellow flowers, sometimes touched with red appear through spring. It is often cited as California's native shrub (and that state is practically the only place that it is grown). However, it could be a good choice for other places that enjoy warm, dry weather.
Cultural Information: These plants are extremely drought tolerant, and they can stand heat, too. They need very good drainage and plenty of sun.

Fringe tree; see ***Chionanthus***

Glossy abelia; see ***Abelia***

Hamamelis mollis

Hamamelis *'Arnold Promise'*

Hamamelis (ha-ma-MELL-is) **witch hazel**, some Native American, F, W by species. ○ ◐ +
Zones: Varies
Height: 6 to 20 feet
Colors: Yellow, red, white
Characteristics: Witch hazels comes from Asia and North America. Our native species *Hamamelis virginiana* (Zones 3 to 8) blooms in fall. The most popular Asian, *H. mollis* (Zones 5 to 8), from China, flowers by variety from mid- to late winter. Both have ribbonlike flowers that are wonderfully fragrant. The large shrubs have an open shape that is rather handsome and requires no pruning. The fragrance of these species is one of their great attractions, along with the fact that they bloom at such unusual times: in late fall, after everything else has long since passed, and in midwinter, before anything else in the garden is stirring. The winter-blooming *H. mollis* flowers last for months and brighten the otherwise bleak landscape. The leaves that follow in spring are large and coarse, but not unattractive. They have wonderful fall foliage color. A cross between *H. mollis* and *H. japonica*, *H. ×intermedia*, is becoming very popular and adds many cultivars to the aforementioned species. 'Arnold Promise' is bright yellow and blooms in early spring. 'Jelena' and 'Diana' have coppery red flowers. Not as familiar is the American native *H. vernalis*, hardy to Zone 4. It is one of the first to bloom, often in January in Zone 6.

Witch hazels can be used in the landscape as specimen plants or for a background to finer-textured shrubs or perennials. They can be grown as understory plants beneath high-limbed trees.
Cultural Information: The witch hazels are all very easy to grow in any soil that is moist. Not surprisingly, woodland conditions are best—light and open, slightly acidic material high in humus content, such as leaf mold.

Hardy orange; see ***Poncirus***

Harlequin glory bower; see ***Clerodendrum***

Hawthorn, Indian; see ***Raphiolepis***

Heavenly bamboo; see ***Nandina***

Hibiscus syriacus (hy-BIS-kus see-REE-ah-KUS) **rose of Sharon**, SU, F. ○ ◐ –
Zones: 5 to 8
Height: 8 to 12 feet
Colors: White, rose, lavender-blue, pink
Characteristics: The rose of Sharons are shrubs with lovely flaring flowers typical of this enormous genus but smaller than those of the tropical *Hibiscus Rosa-sinensis*. They can be white, pink or lavender, often with a contrasting eye, and can be single or double. There are positive and negative things to say about these Jack-of-all-shrubs (or Jill?). On the minus side: They are not self-cleaning—they have to be dead-headed, or else flower size diminishes throughout their blooming season; the faded flowers hang on to the branches as they dry and look unsightly; the fruits are heavy and can bend branches;

they self-sow like crazy, sometimes hybridizing into interesting color combinations, other times reverting to a rather dull lavender; they leaf-out very late in spring, and you might think they had died over winter.

The good side to these plants counters every negative: They bloom late when little else is happening among the shrubs. They can be pruned hard, which not only does not damage them, but produces vigorous new growth, and the cut-back, stocky shrubs look terrific without leaves among the bulbs and other flowers that are in full bloom before the rose of Sharon sprouts leaves. The once-heavy seedpods split, dry and are ornamental through winter and for cutting for arrangements indoors. All in all, these are rather worthwhile plants for home gardens, but I think it pays to seek out some of the newer hybrids, which will add a considerable dimension to your collection. The wonderful variety 'Blue Bird' has a near-blue color that elevates it above the all-too-common kinds. The new hybrid 'Diana' is said to be self-cleaning, dropping flowers as they fade, and forming few seedpods. There are double white and pink varieties and white flowers streaked with red.

Cultural Information: Hibiscus syriacus does self-sow, but it also is very easy to grow from cuttings. This is one to plant in spring; they need time to become established and harden their woody growth to survive winters in the colder parts of their range. If you want a particular variety from a cutting of a friend's plant, mark it in late summer when it is blooming and go back to take a 6- to 10-inch cutting the following spring. They are fast growing, so starting from cuttings is realistic. A 6-inch plant will become a 5-foot-tall, well-branched shrub in about five years. You can prune them hard anytime but to avoid losing the present year's flowers, prune before June. If you dead-head them, you'll have flowers into fall. Feed with an all-purpose, organic fertilizer in spring.

Hibiscus syriacus
'Blue Bird'

Honeysuckle; see *Lonicera*

Hydrangea (hy-DRAN-jee-a)

some Native American, SU. ○ ◐ ● –

Zones: Varies
Height: 3 to 8 feet by species
Colors: White, pink, blue
Characteristics: There are hydrangeas for nearly every situation and every taste. Some are among the easiest and most reliable shrubs (and even vines). Others have several pest problems. One of the best, *Hydrangea quercifolia* (Zones 5 to 9), the American native oak-leafed hydrangea, has very few and may be one of the best all-around shrubs of all. With very large, lobed leaves, these plants will produce flowers in shade or sun, if there is enough moisture, except in the South where it must have shade. In early summer, conical flower heads form that have fertile interior buds surrounded by large, flat, sterile "bee landing pads." And this is one of the most fragrant hydrangeas. It smells of honey. The white flowers fade to pink and finally to brown and they will last well into winter. In most years, the plants' leaves, which turn remarkable colors of burgundy and bronze, will last into winter, too, sometimes until the new leaves of spring push the old ones to the ground.

H. arborescens (Zones 3 to 9) is not very common in gardens. For some reason, these plants has been named "tree hydrangea," odd because they often behave like a herbaceous perennial. They can be cut down to the ground in early spring and they will produce tall new growth. The flower clusters are borne on new wood formed during the season. The flowers are white, ripening to green by fall. The most widely available cultivar is 'Annabelle' and gives the plant another common name, Annabelle hydrangea.

The *H. macrophylla*, called "big-leafed hydrangeas," include the large mop-top hydrangeas and the delicate lace caps. These certainly are beautiful, but they are easily damaged through the season by fluctuating weather. Buds are formed on the former year's growth—there's the rub. If there is a warming period in winter, buds

Hydrangea quercifolia

Hydrangea macrophylla

Hydrangea aborescens
'Annabelle'

Hydrangea paniculata
'Grandiflora' (peegee)

will begin to swell, and they can be damaged by a late frost. For this reason, these plants do well near bodies of water that moderate temperatures so extremes are less likely. In fact, these plants are rather tolerant of seaside locations, despite their large leaves, which you might suspect would wilt in sun (they often do) and be shredded by wind. In Zones 7 southward, they can be grown to flower reliably. Farther North, try one in a protected spot, and see what you think.

H. paniculata and its cultivated variety 'Grandiflora' are old-fashioned shrubs familiar to everyone. These have conical buds in late summer and into fall. The white flowers turn pink on the plants and finally green and brown. They can be cut for indoors and dried, but there is a trick. Cut the stems and arrange them in a vase—without water—that's the way to preserve them. They will last for years, but their wonderful colors will be evident for only about a year. *H. paniculata* (Zones 3 to 8) is a nice plant with a blend of sterile and fertile flowers, but it has virtually disappeared from commerce in America, having been replaced by the popular cultivar nicknamed peegee hydrangea, which has a greater proportion of sterile flowers, although the heads are a bit smaller.

Cultural Information: Hydrangeas likes moist soils and acid. *H. macrophylla* will "blue-up" in acidic soil and turn pink in alkaline soil. As mentioned, the big-leafed variety's problem is bud hardiness, and unfortunately, the plants most people think of when they imagine hydrangeas are the most trouble to grow. These plants also have some pests, and that should be considered. *H. macrophylla* is completely hardy in Zone 6, but after about the fourth year in a row without blossoms, even the most patient gardener begins to think about editing the landscape. Prune out two-year-old canes after flowering, all the way down to the ground. Another reason for no flowers is that some gardeners prune them in spring, which removes the flowering mechanism.

Hypericum (hy-PER-i-cum) **St.-John's-wort**, some Native American, SU, SP by species. ○ ◐ –
Zones: Varies
Height: 1 to 6 feet by species
Color: Yellow
Characteristics: This is a varied group of plants that includes many herbaceous perennials and shrubs. Some are low groundcovers and others are large woody specimens. All of them have yellow flowers with fuzzy stamens in the centers. For the most part, the herbaceous ones are more ornamental and have larger blossoms. The shrubs are evergreen or semievergreen. Some are subshrubs, low scruffy plants such as Aaron's-beard St.-John's-wort (*H. calycinum*, Zones 5 to 8) the best groundcover, especially for sandy soil. The flowers are up to 3 inches across. The leaves are large for the genus, too, up to 4 inches long. If the plant becomes scraggly, it can be cut back to the ground, and in severe winters it may act as if it were herbaceous. Kalm St.-John's-wort (*H. kalmianums*, Zones 4 to 8) is one of the hardiest, and taller (to 3 feet), with 2-inch flowers. *H. patulum* 'Hidcote' is a very ornamental cultivar that stays low, about 18 inches. It has smaller, 2-inch flowers that are fragrant. It is hardy only to Zone 7, and in colder areas, it is grown as an herbaceous perennial. All bloom in summer. Shrubby St.-John's-wort (*H. prolificum*, Zones 3 to 8) is a spirited native. It is not evergreen

but it has rather ornamental, shiny brown twigs in winter, with shaggy, exfoliating bark. The flowers are small, about ¾ inch, in terminal clusters. The leaves are lustrous green with glowing spots.
Cultural Information: These plants are quite vigorous, and most varieties are drought tolerant. They like fast-draining, sandy soil. Some are good choices for partial shade. As noted, rank growth can be reclaimed by sharp pruning in early summer.

Indian currant; see ***Symphoricarpos***

Indian hawthorn; see ***Raphiolepis***

Itea virginica (IT-ee-a vir-JIN-i-ka) **Virginia sweet spire,** Native American, SU. ○ ◐ ● ✱ –
Zones: 5 to 9
Height: 5 feet
Color: White
Characteristics: Virginia sweet spire is a shrub with a lot of interest, but it is rare in American gardens. This is unfortunate, because one of the best species, *Itea virginica*, is native to the East. In early summer, 2- to 6-inch-tall foamy candles rise above the foliage. The leaves add exquisite fall color. It is wonderful in a naturalized stand under small-leafed trees.
Cultural Information: Itea virginica grows in moist, well-drained soil. It can be grown in sun, partial shade and even shade. This is also a good plant for container gardening in Zones 6 to 9.

Japanese andromeda; see ***Pieris***

Japanese flowering quince; see ***Chaenomeles***

Japanese kerria; see ***Kerria***

Japanese pieris; see ***Pieris***

Jetbead; see ***Rhodotypos***

Kalmia latifolia (KAL-mee-a la-ti-FO-lee-a) **mountain laurel,** Native American, LSP. ○ ◐ ● –
Zones: 4 to 9
Height: 15 feet
Colors: White, pink, red
Characteristics: Mountain laurel is one of our nation's great contributions to the botanical world. These evergreens make handsome shrubs for almost any location in the landscape. If beautiful, shiny, deep green foliage were not enough, luscious flowers bloom in late spring. The clusters, or corymbs, are made up of many little cupped flowers with frilly edges, which start out as red buds and open pink or white.

There is quite a bit of hybridizing going on now, and new flower colors and plant forms are being introduced. Most of them have various shades of red flowers, such as 'Olympic Fire', and some are dwarf in stature, 'Elf', for example. Sheep laurel (*Kalmia angustifolia*) is a little-known, diminutive cousin of the mountain laurel, and it is gaining popularity as a landscape plant because it is easy to grow and very versatile. Also native, this plant has handsome rose-colored flowers in spring.
Cultural Information: They tolerate sun if there is plenty of moisture and the root area is cool, but partial shade is better, and shade will do. Being a member of the heath family, which includes rhododendron, they want an acidic soil. The addition of plenty of peat moss is suggested when planting.

Hypericum calycinum

Itea virginica

Kalmia latifolia

Kalmia latifolia

Kerria japonica *'Pleniflora'*

Kolkwitzia amabalis

Lagerstroemia indica

Kerria japonica (KER-ree-a ja-PON-i-ka) **Japanese kerria,** SP. ○ ◐ ● +
Zones: 4 to 9
Height: 4 to 8 feet
Color: Yellow
Characteristics: Kerrias are terrific plants with several seasons of appeal. The species has wing-shaped, quilted leaves on weeping green stems. The stem color seems to intensify after frost and remains grass-green through the winter. The single flowers, more than 1 inch across, resemble blackberry or strawberry blossoms or single roses (the plant is related to all three), but they are butter-yellow. There are several variegated varieties. The real show stopper, however, is *Kerria japonica* 'Pleniflora'. Its egg-yolk-yellow flowers are fully double and cover the plant, even in partial shade. After their explosion of color, which comes along with the daffodils, the kerrias have sporadic blossoms through the summer. Buy this plant!
Cultural Information: Because they bloom on new and old wood, pruning pretty much puts an end to the cycle for a while, and is best after the first floral flush. The species has a flowing, spreading shape, and requires only clipping if it gets in the way, or dips to the ground, which it might do in shade. Remove dead branches from time to time. The cultivar 'Pleniflora', on the other hand, has strong, tall canes that shoot up from the ground, and pruning for it might mean division of the clump, which can be done at nearly any time of the year. Push a spade into the ground in the middle of the shrub. Lift a section for transplanting elsewhere, and cut its canes back by two-thirds. In a year or so, strong new canes will shoot up next to the replanted clump. The original clump left in the ground will regenerate at once. Little or no feeding is necessary, but high phosphorus fertilizer is appreciated.

Kolkwitzia amabilis (kolk-WIT-zee-a a-MAH-bi-lis) **beautybush,** LSP–ESU. ○ ◐ +
Zones: 4 to 8
Height: 8 to 12 feet
Color: Pink
Characteristics: Beautybush is the single species of an Asian plant that is well named. Lovely pink bells with yellow throats bloom in profusion on flat masses, 2 to 3 inches across. Later, fuzzy fruits are also ornamental. The large shrub has a vase shape without pruning. This plant is quite tolerant of heat and drought and is a good choice up against a windowless wall where reflected heat won't be a problem. A position next to a sunny wall will also allow it to grow safely in the northern parts of Zone 4.
Cultural Information: Any soil will do, even nutrition-poor soil, as long as it isn't waterlogged. Top-dress with well-rotted manure in spring. Beautybush will grow in partial shade, but flowers are best in full sun.

Lagerstroemia indica (lay-ger-STREEM-ia in-DI-ka) **crape myrtle**, SU. ○ –
Zones: 7 to 9
Height: 4 to 25 feet
Colors: Pink, red, orange
Characteristics: Crape myrtles are ubiquitous in southern

Virginia and down to northern Florida. In late summer, southern towns explode with some of the most magnificent, brightly colored, frilly flowers of any large shrub. New leaves are bronze-red. The bark is cinnamon-colored, smooth and attractive, and the plants also have fall foliage color. If well sited, these shrubs grow into trees, up to 60 feet high. In the South, they are usually confined by pruning.

North of maritime Cape May County, New Jersey, however, it's a different story. Crape myrtles *can* be grown, but they are sometimes killed to the ground by cold weather. Still, they are root-hardy through Zone 7 and bloom on new wood as herbaceous "shrubs" that grow to 4 feet tall. New varieties are being made available that are more hardy.

Cultural Information: The crape myrtles need full sun, and in the North, in such places as Long Island, they would do well in a corner where the house meets the garage, perhaps, and with southern exposure. The soil should be acidic. No special feeding is necessary, but a yearly spring feeding is savored—a high phosphorous preparation in the South and a balanced formula with nitrogen in the North. In the South, prune in early spring to encourage new growth for flowering. Keep the shrub in bounds and create the shape and scale you want. Crape myrtles don't have many pests, although they may be visited by Japanese beetles. Powdery mildew can be a late-summer problem. Use a fungicide, such as sulfur, weekly in wet years.

Leatherleaf mahonia; see ***Mahonia***

Leatherwood; see ***Fremontodendron***

Lilac; see ***Syringa***

Lilac, California; see ***Ceanothus***

Lily-of-the-valley shrub; see ***Pieris***

Lindera Benzoin (lin-DER-a BEN-zo-in) **spicebush**, Native American, ESP. ◐ ✱ +
Zones: 4 to 9
Height: 8 feet
Color: Yellow
Characteristics: Spicebushes come from North America. There are many species in the wild, but this vase-shaped one is perhaps best adapted to home gardens. The oval leaves turn yellow in the fall. In early spring, tiny, fragrant flowers cover the stems; then, bright red berries form. Although plants from the marshlands and woods, they tolerate drought.
Cultural Information: This is a plant-it-and-forget-it shrub. It is happiest in partial shade in the open woodland, but will grow in a wider variety of locations. Pruning is unnecessary.

Lindera Benzoin

Lonicera tatarica

Lonicera (lon-ISS-er-ra) **honeysuckle**, W, SP by species. ○ ◐ ✱ –
Zones: Varies
Height: 5 to 10 feet
Colors: Green, white, pink, red by variety
Characteristics: When you think of honeysuckles, you think of fragrant vines that scamper across the back fence. However there are many honeysuckle shrubs of the forest understory. Most are large, twiggy masses. They flower in spring, some are fragrant, and most have berries. Some of the species are above the norm and worthwhile for certain home gardens with room for shrubs that are a bit on the wild side.

Starting in late winter, winter honeysuckle *(Lonicera fragrantissima*, Zones 4 to 8) produces tiny greenish white flowers for months that are intensely fragrant. In milder climates, this hardy plant will be evergreen. Tatarian honeysuckle (*L. tatarica*, Zones 3 to 8) is exceptional for its neat appearance and for rapid growth that makes it useful as a quick screen or hedge. *L. tatarica* has many fragrant cultivars with various flower colors including white (*L. t.* 'Alba'), deep rose and pink (*L. t.* 'Rosea') and deep red (*L. t.* 'Arnold Red' and 'Zabelii'). Fruits are equally ornamental and colorful. *L. t.* 'Lutea' has yellow fruits and *L. t.* 'Morden Orange' has pale pink flowers and translucent orange fruits.

Cultural Information: As long as there is fairly good drainage, the honeysuckles will stand almost any soil quality. They need no fertilizer, but do look better when given an occasional feeding. Also, pruning, although unnecessary, will improve the appearance of the shrubs. After a rainy spring, powdery mildew might show up in late summer. In years when tent caterpillars are prevalent, they may chew up a bit of the honeysuckles, but this and other pests such as aphids and leaf rollers are never fatal. Prune off damaged wood, and spray with a garden hose for light infestations of aphids.

Magnolia stellata
cultivars

Magnolia virginiana

Magnolia (mag-NO-lee-a) some Native American, ESP. ○ ◐ ✱ +

Zones: 5 to 9
Height: 6 to 8 feet
Colors: White, pink

Characteristics: Magnolias are primarily thought of as trees, including the familiar native southern magnolia (*Magnolia grandiflora*). But many branch low and may be considered shrubs. After years, these shrubby ones can reach the size of small trees—up to 30 feet high. One native, sweetbay magnolia (*M. virginiana*, Zones 5 to 9), has waxy, light green leaves and greenish white flowers. It is unexcelled as a specimen plant when subtlety is desired. The flowers and leaves are out on the plant at the same time, and although most flowers are in spring, there can be sporadic blossoming through the summer. The star magnolia (*M. stellata*, Zones 3 to 8) and many similar hybrids (such as *M.* ×*Loebneri* 'Merrill') are showy, early-blooming landscape specimens. They have many-rayed, strappy blossoms at daffodil time, when the familiar Asian saucer magnolias bloom. These star magnolias star in the landscape—on their own or in an all-magnolia border where similar varieties in various shades from white to dark pink can be interplanted for a stunning effect.

Cultural Information: Magnolias want a rich soil full of organic material that will hold moisture. When young, the plants should be watered, but as they become established, you'll need to irrigate only in periods of extreme drought. They are relatively free of disease and pests. Sometimes magnolia scale can show up on stems. Oil sprays when the plants are dormant are the best cure. For any fungal disease, sulfur and copper-based wettable fungicides may be used judiciously.

Mahonia (ma-HO-nee-a) **Oregon holly grape,** Native American, **leatherleaf mahonia,** ESP. ◐ ● –

Zones: Varies
Height: 2 to 12 feet by species
Color: Yellow

Characteristics: In early spring, 4- to 6-inch-tall stems covered with delicate lemon-yellow flowers sprout from the ends of the last year's growth. By season's end, blue or black fruits cover every inch of the former cluster's stalks, and these are also ornamental. But the mahonias are coarse shrubs with large leaves that resemble those of English holly, only bigger. The flowers *are* beautiful; the bronzy green leaves may leave something to be desired. I have mixed emotions about these plants. Although they are evergreen and easy to grow, they are not the easiest plants to integrate into the landscape. It takes some special thought to find just the right place for these unique, shade-tolerant evergreens. On the floor of the woodland, the native Oregon holly grape (*Mahonia Aquifolium*, Zones 5 to 9) can be attractive. The larger Asians, such as leatherleaf mahonia (*M. Bealei*, Zones 6 to 10), can become massive screens between properties or be planted with other broad-leafed evergreens such as rhododendron.

Cultural Information: The mahonias want a woodsy soil that is organically rich and friable. They should have moisture, often present in shaded woodland. One of the problems with these plants as landscaping candidates is that they very often exhibit damage from winter burning by sun or wind. This results in unsightly brown spots that persist through the year, so consider this when locating them. The Oregon holly grapes can become leggy if they get too tall, but a simple cutting back after flowering will remedy this condition.

Mexican orange; see ***Choisya***

Mock orange; see ***Philadelphus***

Mountain laurel; see ***Kalmia***

Nandina domestica (nan-DEE-na do-MES-ti-ka) **heavenly bamboo**, SP, F. ◐ ● –

Zones: 7 to 9 (6 with protection)
Height: 2 to 6 feet
Colors: White, pink
Characteristics: Arguably, the foliage is the greatest attraction of this shrub. It is not a bamboo, but that's what it resembles. Evergreen, palmlike fronds grow on a shapely shrub. New growth is red, as is fall color. In spring, tall flower clusters form. Buds open from deep pink to white, and it is common to have flowering throughout the summer and into fall along with the ornamental red berries that grow from it. This shrub is ideal for humid areas in warm climates, but it is worth trying it at the northern reaches of Zone 7. If it is grown between buildings or in other protected sites, it will be able to grow in Zone 6. In the North, though, it won't reach 6 feet in height; it will die back.

Cultural Information: Prune off any winter-killed growth. Soil moisture is important: Mulch to keep the moisture in the soil and also provide a coarse winter mulch in the North. If there is a severe winter, the plant may die to the ground, but roots carry over and new growth will come from below the soil if mulched.

Nerium Oleander (NEER-i-um o-lee-AN-der) **oleander**, SU. ○ ✹ –

Zones: 8 to 10
Height: 8 to 20 feet
Colors: Pink, red, orange, cream, white, mauve
Characteristics: The oleanders are very useful shrubs for hedges

Mahonia Aquifolium

Mahonia Aquifolium

Nandina domestica

Nerium Oleander

Paeonia suffruticosa
hybrid

and screens in windy, dry or seaside situations in warm climates. In full sun, they flower their heads off. The long, lanceolate (elliptical, pointed at the ends) leaves are tough and leathery, gray-green in color. Flowers are sometimes fragrant and reminiscent of the tropical plumeria and hibiscus colors: peach, pink, red, cream and mauve.
Cultural Information: Oleanders love it hot and sunny. They are extremely drought resistant. They can be pruned at any time, but spring is best, and care should be taken with the disposal of the clippings; they should be thrown away, not burned, and never used for plant stakes. Every reference to oleanders makes mention of the fact that these plants are poisonous. It's true; they are not poisonous to the touch, but wash hands before handling food. I recently saw a television commercial for a hotel in which the doorman picks an oleander flower for an appreciative guest; she would be well advised to seek lodging elsewhere. Many plants have various degrees of toxicity, but oleander should probably not be planted where small children play. If they already are there, instruct the children that they should look but not touch—good gardening advice in general, I think.

Oleander; see ***Nerium***

Oregon holly grape; see ***Mahonia***

Ornamental blackberry; see ***Rubus***

Paeonia suffruticosa

(PEE-o-nia suf-froo-ti-KO-sa) **tree peony**, SP. ○ ◐ –
Zones: 4 to 8
Height: 4 feet
Colors: Yellow, pink, white, orange, lavender, red
Characteristics: Tree peonies are true deciduous shrubs, varieties and hybrids of a few species of the familiar herbaceous peonies. They have woody stems that do not die to the ground in the fall. The flowers are larger and come in some unusual colors, including clear apricot, pale yellow shades and rich lavender. The floral texture is also special, somewhat like crepe paper, and the size of the flowers is astounding, up to 6 inches across. They can be single or double, and some of the frilly ones have elaborate centers with yellow anthers. Like their herbaceous cousins, these peonies will live a very long time and should be placed where they will not have to be moved—for a century or so. All the varieties available are hybrids, most of which are grafted to *Paeonia lactiflora* root stock. The hybrids result from crosses of *P. suffruticosa* and *P. lutea*. Some of them are Japanese and others are European concoctions bred from Chinese ancestors. Among the best Japanese ones are 'Kamada-fuji', a spectacular near blue, and 'Uba–tama', an iridescent crimson. Hybrids include 'Reine Elizabeth', deep rose-pink and fully double; 'Fragrans Maxima Plena', a fragrant salmon-colored double; and 'Godaishu', pure white. Among the *P. lutea,* yellow-flowered cultivars are 'Canary', single yellow, and 'Age of Gold', a subtle golden double.
Cultural Information: Plan before you plant; these shrubs must not be disturbed. The planting hole should be prepared for the long haul. Good drainage and plenty of humus in the form of compost, well-rotted manure or peat moss should be incorporated into a hole at least 18 inches deep and about as wide. As with other peonies, planting is best in the fall, after the shrubs have lost their leaves and are dormant.

These plants can be hit by botrytis, which can result in rotting blossoms and damaged new growth and leaves. Use a fungicide such as sulfur, following package directions. These peonies like sun, but only in the early morning and late afternoon. They should be protected from noontime rays that can fade flower color and burn leaves. To avoid this, they can be placed in a bed on the north side of a tall, high-limbed tree, for example.

Peony, tree; see ***Paeonia***

Philadelphus (fil-a-DEL-fus) **mock orange**, some Native American, LSP. ○ ◐ –
Zones: 4 to 8
Height: 5 to 10 feet by species or variety
Color: White
Characteristics: In a way, the mock oranges are extremely typical of the flowering shrubs. They are a woody deciduous plants that usually grow to about 10 feet (although there are smaller cultivated varieties available). Single or double flowers form along with the roses in late spring to early summer. They are white, with nectar-filled centers, and yellow anthers showing on the singles, obscured by frilly petals on the doubles. They last a short time, only about two weeks. For the rest of the season, fresh green leaves cover the large shrubs. They are invaluable for creating property screens where they do not require pruning, except for the removal of dead wood, if you get around to it. They would be good along the driveway if it is against the property line, as so many driveways are. There are about 50 available varieties from which to choose at nurseries and through mail-order sources. *Philadelphus coronarius*, the common mock orange, a familiar species, is still available. Seek out new varieties of single or doubles, as they are often superior to older hybrids. Try the double *P.* ×*virginalis*, for example, which itself comes in varieties such as 'Albâtre' and 'Argentine'. The double-flowered kinds hold their petals longer than the singles. Some of the best cultivars include *P.* ×*lemoinei* 'Boule d'Argent', large double flowers and somewhat fragrant; *P.* ×*cymosus* 'Conquête', one of the most fragrant of the singles; *P.* ×*lemoinei* 'Innocence', with slightly smaller flowers but in ample clusters is also intensely fragrant; 'Frosty Morn', perhaps the most hardy and *P. coronarius* 'Aureus', a cultivar whose new foliage is bright golden green.
Cultural Information: These shrubs are easy to grow. They are not particular as to soil. Because they bloom on new wood, they could be sheared just after flowering. Some of the varieties are arching, almost fountain shaped. These will need pruning to keep them in shape.

Philadelphus coronarius

Pieris japonica (PY-eer-is ja-PON-i-ka) **Japanese andromeda, Japanese pieris, lily-of-the-valley shrub**, ESP. ◐ –
Zones: 5 to 8 (4 with protection)
Height: 4 to 8 feet
Colors: White, pink
Characteristics: Japanese pieris would be known as an ornamental evergreen for hedges and

Pieris japonica *'Valley Rose'*

Pittosporum Tobira *'Variegata'*

screens only, if but for the beautiful flowers. In early spring, long drooping clusters of bell-like flowers cover this plant. The flowers are usually white with golden bracts, but there are cultivars, such as 'Valley Rose', 'Flamingo' and 'Wada', with pink flowers. These plants are hardy, but a protected spot might be advisable in northern climates, because the flower buds can be damaged by a surprise late frost. The new growth on some cultivars is vivid red, 'Forest Flame' and 'Mountain Fire', for example. This effect is interesting, but not too subtle, and the fact that these varieties will stand out from the crowd should be noted. Dwarf varieties can be used in a rock garden. All are slow growing and would be suitable for an entry planting. There are other species, including a native, mountain pieris, or mountain andromeda (*P. floribunda*).

Cultural Information: Heath plants, *Pieris* species want acidic soil that is moist with lots of organic material. The shrub will stand sun, but if the atmosphere and soil are dry, red spider mites may visit. They can be controlled with Safer's Insecticidal Soap in repeated applications, but it is far better to provide an environment that is more favorable to the shrubs and less to the liking of the mites.

Pittosporum Tobira (pit-TOSS-por-um to-BI-ra) **pittosporum**, SP. ○ ◐ ✸ –

Zones: 8 to 10

Height: 6 feet

Color: White

Characteristics: Pittosporums are evergreen woody shrubs with 2- to 3-inch-long elliptical leaves with a distinct midrib. They have a wonderful, mounding shape with little or no pruning, and there is a variegated variety, *Pittosporum Tobira* 'Variegata', with gray-green leaves marked with white. They would be noted only as evergreens except for the flowers. Substantial clusters of white stars that fade to gold cover all the tips of last season's growth. They are intensely fragrant. This plant is not very hardy, but in areas where it can be grown, it should be.

Cultural Information: This imported shrub from Japan is easy to grow. Hot, sandy sites are fine, even when soil conditions are dry. It can be grown by the seaside in Bermuda, but is equally at home in a protected spot, away from sun, in Seattle. It also makes an excellent tub plant for a cool room or greenhouse, in which case, it would love to spend the summer in its pot in a sheltered spot outdoors.

Poncirus trifoliata (pon-SEER-us try-fo-lee-AH-ta) **trifoliate orange, hardy orange**, SP. ○ ◐ ✸ –

Zones: 6 to 9

Height: 10 feet

Color: White

Characteristics: The hardy trifoliate orange is actually a citrus that produces real fruits in cold climates. Rich, dark green, three-part leaves grow all over these deciduous shrubs. They have 1-inch single flowers in spring that are fragrant but don't challenge subtropical varieties. The fruits are wonderfully ornamental in fall, fuzzy, like peaches, and about 1½ inches in diameter. They can be used for marmalade or as a garnish for drinks but are too sour to eat fresh off the shrub.

This may be one of the best plants to use as a security hedge—it has 1-inch-long thorns. The spear-covered branches will go all the way to the ground if unpruned, or on sheared specimens, but *Poncirus* can also be limbed up as it grows to make a magnificent "standard," a lollipop- or tree-shaped topiary. It has lovely striped bark.

Cultural Information: Well-drained, acidic soil is all that is needed for these shrubs that can, but infrequently do, reach 20 feet in height. These plants are rarely offered in nurseries. Some mail-order companies offer small plants. But if you know where one grows, you can collect fruits, because it is simple to grow these shrubs from seeds. Store fruits in the refrigerator for a few months and then cut open to remove seeds, which can be sown in any houseplant medium in a sunny window. Fruits that drop and remain on the ground through the winter may also be a source for "stratified" seeds—those exposed to chilling and warming. (In order to germinate, some seeds of hardy plants need a period of chilling to break the seeds' dormancy.)

Poncirus trifoliata

Potentilla fruticosa (po-ten-TILL-a froo-ti-KO-sa) **cinquefoil**, some Native American, SU. ○ –

Zones: 2 to 7

Height: 1 to 5 feet

Color: Yellow

Characteristics: This is a large group of shrubby plants. Some run along the ground, others are herbaceous. The ones that we want to learn about are, of course, medium-size woody shrubs. *Potentilla fruticosa* is one of the few species found all over the northern hemisphere. They are small, 1 to 5 feet high, and twiggy with small leaves and numerous yellow, single-roselike flowers in clusters. There are about 40 varieties with varying pale colors. They are principally used for low hedges

Potentilla *'Gold Drop'*

or as groundcovers and look well along a low wall or as a curbside planting.
Cultural Information: Cinquefoils would be good next to the lawn, because they need similar conditions: full sun, clayey but well-drained soil, and alkalinity. Sometimes older shrubs tend to flop open, leaving a dead area in the center. Severe pruning, back by one-third, will rejuvenate older plants.

Prunus glandulosa

Prunus (PROO-nus) **flowering-cherry, -almond, -plum**, SP. ○ ◐ ✱ +
Zones: Varies
Height: Varies
Colors: Pink, white
Characteristics: Cherries, peaches, almonds, plums, all are members of the *Prunus* genus. Some are ornamental shrubs, such as the dwarf flowering almond, *P. glandulosa*, hardy in Zones 4 to 8. Numerous pink or white flowers cover the stems before the foliage sprouts. The sand cherry (*P. Besseyi*) is a medium-size shrub up to 6 feet that is hardy to Zone 4. Small flowers bloom in clusters in spring, and it produces small black, edible, sweet fruits that are often used for jelly. *P.* ×*cistena* is the purple-leaf sand cherry. It adds colorful foliage to the same qualities as the preceding ornamental, and it is hardy in Zones 2 to 8. The cherry laurel, *P. Laurocerasus*, isn't as hardy (Zone 7; 6 with protection), but it is evergreen. It is extremely ornamental and there are several cultivars. This plant tolerates partial shade, and some of the varieties, 'Otto Luyken', for example, can grow in shade.
Cultural Information: Except where noted, these flowering plants are deciduous and need full sun. They all like very well drained soil. Some insect infestations may occur. Prune out and destroy damaged wood. Try Safer's Insecticidal Soap.

Pussy willow; see *Salix*

Quince, Japanese flowering; see *Chaenomeles*

Raphiolepis indica (ra-fi-OL-ep-is IN-di-ka) **Indian hawthorn**, SP. ○ ◐ –
Zones: 8 to 10
Height: 4 feet
Color: Pink
Characteristics: Indian hawthorn is not the hardiest plant, but it is rather forgiving in the zones that it likes. It makes an excellent city shrub, even along a busy street or highway. It won't need watering there, either. It is evergreen, with interesting small leaves, but the flowers are the best part. Full clusters of rich pink flowers cover the shrubs through most of spring.
Cultural Information: Easily grown in most soils. Best flowering occurs in sun, but it will do quite well in partial shade.

Red-twig dogwood; see *Cornus*

Redvein enkianthus; see *Enkianthus*

Rhododendron (ro-do-DEN-dron) **rhododendron, azalea, rose bay**, ESP, SP, SU by species. ○ ◐ ● ✱ –
Zones: Varies
Height: 1 to 20 feet by species
Colors: All except true blue
Characteristics: One could easily write a book on *Rhododendron* alone, and many authors have. Included in this group are large, tropical evergreens with enormous leaves, the familiar large evergreens, deciduous woody specimens often called azaleas, and tiny-leafed evergreen azaleas that grow in nearly every suburban landscape

in the United States. Most of the ones known best as rhododendron have large, flat, bell-shaped flowers. The azaleas have flowers that are more funnel or trumpet shaped. Some individuals in each of these groups are fragrant, a few are not. Some bloom in late winter to early spring, and one Native American, *Rhododendron prunifolium*, blooms mid- to late summer. It would be impossible to name all of the hundreds of species and varieties here, but some of the best are worth noting individually.

Of the large-leafed evergreens, *R. catawbiense* (Zones 4 to 8) and its hybrids are about the most reliable. They are very hardy and even somewhat drought tolerant—unusual for these moisture lovers. This late–spring-blooming plant is also native. The species has unpretentious, dull lilac flowers, but lots of them. They should be deadheaded for the most bloom the following year. This native is from the American southeast. Rose bay rhododendron (*R. maximum*, Zones 4 to 8) is another southeastern American native. It flowers from late spring to early summer. In cultivation since 1736, it is popular because it adapts better to deeper shade than most.

To keep in moisture, the leaves have an unusual self-preservation device. When the temperature drops below freezing, the leaves curl. You can almost tell the temperature by looking out your window at the "rhodies." When it's really cold, the shrubs look as if they're covered with cigars.

One of the earliest spring bloomers is the P.J.M. hybrid, an evergreen variety that is a rich purple, named for the developer, Peter John Mezitt of Weston Nurseries in Hopkinton, Massachusetts. P.J.M. doesn't set seed often, so it directs its energy toward flower bud production and is a profuse bloomer. There is also a white one due on the market soon. These were developed from the native Carolina rhododendron (*R. carolinianum*, crossed with *R. dauricum sempervirens*), which comes from the Blue Ridge Mountains. It is very compact and floriferous. At maturity it forms a perfect mound 6 feet high and 7 feet wide in Zones 4 to 8.

Among the best of the Asian members of the genus is *R. Fortunei*. Its hybrids are magnificent for flower lovers. The individual flowers can be up to 3½ inches wide in trusses (compact flower clusters) of up to 12. The flowers are usually pink to lilac, sometimes with streaks of white or yellow. The species likes warmth. Floridian gardeners take heart, this is one of the best for Zones 8 and 9. Nevertheless, it does just fine north to Zone 6, and the hybrids are often hardier. Perhaps the most wonderful is 'Scintillation', which has a veritable sunset of colors in its flowers. It is a dependable and hardy subject, available each spring at nearly every garden center and nursery.

A somewhat recently introduced Asian species, *R. yakusimanum* (Zone 5), is being used to develop hybrids that will be introduced over the next few decades. This is always one of the stars of the collector's garden. Very shiny green leaves are covered on the undersides

Raphiolepis indica

Rhododendron *hybrids*

Rhododendron *Kurume hybrids*

Rhododendron

with thick brown or white hairs that feel like felt. Large bunches of bell-shaped pink or white flowers bloom in spring. The small, mounded shrubs grow only to about 3 feet by 3 feet after 10 years.

Many of the deciduous rhododendron, usually called azaleas, come from North America. Yellow shades and tints are not uncommon in these plants—from flame orange to chrome yellow to pale primrose. Consider these species and look for some of the hundreds of hybrids with incredible floral colors. Many have fall foliage color as well.

R. arborescens is called sweet azalea (Zones 4 to 8) and is native to moist areas from Pennsylvania south to Georgia. Another common name for this plant is tree azalea, which should tell you to give this plant ample room to grow. From Kentucky southeast to Georgia comes *R. Bakeri* (Zones 5 to 7). It and its hybrids are particularly good in shade. After the plants have leafed-out, red, orange or yellow flowers with a yellow-orange blotch appear. Flame azalea (*R. calendulaceum*, Zones 5 to 8) blooms late, and it was one of the plants for the Ghent and Exbury hybrids.

R. periclymenoides, called pinxterbloom or wild honeysuckle (Zones 3 to 8), can tolerate dry locations with sandy soil. The flowers are purple to pale pink and have very long stamens. It grows from the coast of Maine down to South Carolina and Tennessee. It also parented some of the Ghent hybrids, and the common name comes from what the Dutch call *Pingsterbloem*. *R. prinophyllum* (Zones 3 to 8) resembles the former, but the undersides of the leaves are hairy and the flowers lily- and spice-scented. It leafs-out and blooms early for azaleas; in fall, their foliage turns scarlet. The flowers bloom in a full range of pink shades. This plant is indigenous from Quebec to Oklahoma.

R. Vaseyi is the pinkshell azalea (Zones 4 to 8) from North Carolina swamps; it is remarkably adaptable, even to a dry location. Deep green, 5-inch-long leaves turn crimson in fall. In midspring, before the foliage appears, unscented gossamer blossoms of pale pink to rose with sienna speckles bloom.

The spicy fragrance of the swamp azalea (*R. viscosum*, Zones 3 to 9) is wonderful. Trumpet flowers in the palest pink to white come in early summer—July in Zone 6, the middle of its Zone 3 to 9 range. This native shrub has a very fragile, lacy pattern of growth that complements its pale flower clusters.

The royal azalea (*R. Schlippenbachii*), a native of Manchuria, Korea and Japan, looks at home everywhere (Zones 4 to 7). This is one of the most popular deciduous azaleas and should top the list of those new to these plants.

When you go to the garden center in spring, don't snatch up the first tiny-leaf evergreen azaleas in bright orange and magenta. These are easy to grow and dependable, but you'll just end up with a mirror-image landscape that is no different from your neighbors' to the left or right. Seek out instead some of these incredibly varied and spectacular species and hybrids, and many more that cannot be covered in any space limited to under 2,000 pages. Look also to the color catalogs for pictures of plants such as: *R.* ×*gandavense*, Knap Hill and Exbury hybrids and *R.* ×*Kosteranum* (Zones 5 to 7).

Cultural Information: The evergreen rhododendron make good shrub choices for city gardens. Their shiny leaves wash clean in rain storms, and they are tolerant of air pollution. Because of their shallow roots, they transplant well. They benefit from being placed among other plants, as long as there is little root competition. Mulch is a must, however, and it should be a coarse-textured one, such as shredded pine bark.

Most available rhododendron are field grown, that is, they are planted and grown in the open sun and heavily irrigated. This is unfortunate, for you will buy a very compact, densely branched specimen that will not end up looking like that in the shaded garden. Also, it tends to be a shock to the young plants when you set them into the garden. And they will take some time to come back—sometimes years before they go back into the flowering mode. Have patience and you will be rewarded.

When planting the "rhodie," be sure to incorporate a good deal of organic matter, especially into the top foot of soil, because that is where much of the root system will live. Dig a hole about twice as deep and twice as wide as the container or burlap-covered root ball. Enrich the excavated soil with compost, well-rotted cow manure, leaf mold or the ever-available peat moss.

Rhododendron prunifolium

Rhododendron maximum

Rhodotypos scandens

(ro-do-TY-pus skan-DENZ) **jetbead,** SP. ○ ◐ ● –

Zones: 4 to 8
Height: 4 to 6 feet
Color: White

Characteristics: Jetbead is a little-known plant that should be grown more often. It has 2-inch, single white flowers similar to those of a rose. The white flowers and general habit also resemble kerria. Later, black, cherrylike fruits hang from the stems.

Cultural Information: Jetbead is a very natural-looking plant and would be nice for a wild garden. It is, nevertheless, very tolerant of pollution and harsh city conditions and is just as at home in the concrete jungle as in the wild country. Sun and dense shade are both acceptable.

Rhodotypos scandens

Ribes sanguineum (Ribes *calyx after petal drop*)

Ribes sanguineum *'China Rose'*

Ribes sanguineum (REE-beez sang-GWIN-ee-um) **flowering currant**, Native American, SP. ○ ◐ ●
Zones: 6 to 8
Height: 5 to 10 feet
Color: Red
Characteristics: The flowering currant is related to the gooseberry and edible red and black currants. They have beautiful hanging flowers in early spring and lovely green ribbed, felted leaves. Although this was at one time a very popular landscape plant, you don't see it very often today. The only possible reason is that currants in general have been banished because some of them are the alternate host of white pine disease. This is not the case with this ornamental. In Europe, you'll find this plant and various cultivars widely grown, and there it is an import from the West Coast. It does produce ornamental fruit in late summer that is blue-black and glaucus—covered with a powdery bloom like an Italian plum.
Cultural Information: Ribes is easy to grow and usually presents few problems. It can be attacked by aphids and Japanese beetles, and some of the other predators that go after fruiting crops. But it will grow in sun or shade, and is worth trying when you find it at the nursery or in mail-order catalogs.

Rockrose; see **_Cistus_**

Rose bay; see **_Rhododendron_**

Rose of Sharon; see **_Hibiscus_**

Rubus (ROO-bus) **ornamental blackberry,** some Native American, LSP. ○ ◐ –
Zones: Varies
Height: 5 feet
Colors: White, pink
Characteristics: These are ornamental relatives of the raspberries and blackberries, and although they are common in European gardens, they are not often grown in America. However, being also related to roses, they have lovely flowers. *Rubus odoratus* is a North American native, hardy to Zone 3. This one is an upright shrub with raspberry red to purple flowers from late spring to summer. It has practically no thorns, but does have fruits, although they are inedible. *R.* ×*tridel* 'Benenden', hardy to Zone 6, is the one that is most popular in Europe. It is often grown in an

all-white-flowered border among roses, lilacs and iris.
Cultural Information: These plants are easy to grow; just cut out dead wood. *R.* ×*tridel* 'Benenden' seems to grow in a similar way to the canning fruits to which it is related, that is, the 2-year-old wood blooms and then dies, and these canes should be removed in the spring once you can determine that they have died and dried, turning brown. It is quite easy to tell the faded wood from new and second-year growth.

Rubus odoratus

St.-John's-wort; see ***Hypericum***

Salix (SAY-licks) **pussy willow**, LW. ◐ –
Zones: Varies
Height: 10 feet
Color: Gray
Characteristics: There are willows from all over the world. More than 300 species are known. There are tiny shrubs that hug rocky cliff faces in the wild and many more from marshlands in the cooler parts of the temperate world. We grow the ones that produce ornamental catkins, the pussies. The most familiar is the common pussy willow (*Salix discolor*). It has long canes that are wonderful to cut and bring indoors in midwinter to force into bloom. The more you cut it, the nicer the canes will be; in fact, cut it down near the ground every so often. One of the most hardy, it grows to Zone 3. *S. discolor* 'Melanostchys' is the black pussy willow, hardy to Zone 5. Its catkins are truly black. Rosegold pussy willow

Salix gracilistyla

Salix gracilistyla

(*S. gracilistyla*) has the most elegant catkins in a wonderful feline gray color. The male catkins of this shrub, which can grow to Zone 6, show pink to rose as they grow. Many are produced and they are large. *S. sachalinensis* 'Sekka' from Japan has twisted, flat branches as it matures. The branches are fantastic cut for indoors. Its contorted twigs form on a plant that has a rather nice vase shape. It is hardy to Zone 5.

Cultural Information: Pussy willows like a very moist location, but will thrive anywhere within their zone, and they are among the easiest shrubs to grow. They are very rewarding plants for beginners, although they can grow out of bounds in the landscape. Cut stems will root readily in water, and in fact, the willow water possesses properties that induce rooting in other plants. Place cuttings of ivy or other water-rooting plantings in willow water, and they will sprout roots faster.

Serviceberry; see ***Amelanchier***

Shadblow; see ***Amelanchier***

Slender deutzia; see ***Deutzia***

Smoke bush; see ***Cotinus***

Snowberry; see ***Symphoricarpos***

Sorbaria sorbifolia (sor-BAIR-ee-a sor-bi-FO-lee-a) **false spirea**, SU. ◐ –

Zones: 2 to 7

Height: 6 feet

Color: White

Characteristics: False spirea is a plant for the waste places, and in fact, can often be seen naturalizing along the highways and roadsides. Still and all, this might be a good choice for summer bloom in just such situations, perhaps for the unpaved road to a second home in a rural setting. In a wild garden, it does have a place.

Cultural Information: These plants need space, and they do spread. They like rich, moist soil, but as you might imagine, will put up with just about anything.

Spicebush; see ***Lindera***

Spirea, false; see ***Sorbaria***

Sorbaria sorbifolia

Spiraea (spy-REE-a) **spirea**, SP, SU. ○ ◐ ● –
Zones: 3 to 8
Height: 3 to 5 feet
Colors: White, pink, red
Characteristics: This is an enormously useful group of deciduous ornamental, flowering shrubs, from spring's bridal wreath with its arching stems covered with white flower tufts (*Spiraea* ×*Vanhouttei*), to summer's *S.* ×*Bumalda* with flat clusters of rose-pink flowers. And there are dwarf species as well. *S. albiflora* (Zones 4 to 8) is the Japanese white spirea—only 18 inches tall. Look for the chartreuse-colored leaves of *S.* ×*Bulmalda*, 'Gold Flame'; *S.* ×*Bulmalda* 'Shibori', has white and rose-pink flowers on the same plant. The most common variety is *S.* ×*Bulmalda* 'Anthony Waterer'. Most of the other spireas have white flowers in a usual button form. There is a dwarf bridal wreath, 'Swan Lake', for example.
Cultural Information: Ordinary garden soil suits. Nearly all of these plants can be pruned. The arching stems of the spring-blooming whites should be pruned just after flowering. Some of the summer-blooming, rose-red kinds and ones with interesting foliage benefit from being almost sheared in late winter. New growth will be vigorous and leaves, lush. Cut them back to about 10 inches from the ground.

Spirea; see ***Spiraea***

Summer sweet; see ***Clethra***

Sweet pepperbush; see ***Clethra***

Sweet shrub; see ***Calycanthus***

Spiraea prunifolia

Spiraea ×Bumalda *'Gold Flame'*

Spiraea ×Bumalda

Symphoricarpos albus

Sweet spire, Virginia; see ***Itea***

Symphoricarpos (sim-for-i-KAR-pos) **snowberry, Indian currant, coralberry**, SP, SU.
◐ –
Zones: 3 to 7
Height: 4 feet
Colors: White, pink
Characteristics: Symphoricarpos shrubs are not grown for their flowers at all, although they are related to the honeysuckles. They have incredibly ornamental fruits. These oddities are wonderful for wild gardens, but be sure to place the arching stems where the fruit, which is usually carried on the ends of the branches, can be viewed up close and touched. Snowberry (*S. albus*) have fruits that are about the size of marbles and pure white. They are squishy and unfortunately don't dry, but are good cut for fresh arrangements. The gray leaves are moderately attractive, but the plant's habit is not special. Indian currant or coralberry (*S. orbiculatus*) has long-lasting red fruits and fall foliage interest as well. The cultivar 'Leucocarpus' has yellow flowers and white fruits. This is also a plant for the wild garden.
Cultural Information: Poor soil and partial shade are fine for snowberry. Very hardy (to Zone 3), these are good plants for the Midwest and will even stand Chicago winters and summers easily.

Syringa (sir-RING-a) **lilac,** SP.
○ ✱ –
Zones: Varies
Height: 5 to 20 feet by species
Colors: White, pink, lavender, red, blue

Syringa vulgaris Hybrid

Syringa vulgaris Hybrid

Syringa Meyeri

Characteristics: If rhododendron are America's favorite evergreen shrubs, then lilacs are the favorite deciduous ones. They certainly are among the most nostalgic. Their fragrance brings back memories of courting on the porch swing or of stealing fragrant bunches of flowers from a neighbor's yard, and often, they remind one of Mom, perhaps because they bloom around Mother's Day in many parts of the country.

When we think of the lilacs, we picture the common lilac (*Syringa vulgaris*, Zones 3 to 7). These are the lilac-purple or white (*S. v. alba*) flowers born in terminal stems and filled with fragrance. But there are many others, including hundreds of hybrids of this plant alone (more than 400, actually). At one extreme is *S. v.* 'President Lincoln', one that is true blue, and 'Primrose', a creamy white that is too often listed in catalogs as "yellow." There are also many kinds with double flowers.

An unusual and very hardy lilac grows into a tree with glossy, waxy leaves. Japanese tree lilac (*S. reticulata*, Zones 3 to 7) makes an impressive landscape plant, especially in pairs flanking the walkway. It is very hardy (Zone 4) and grows to 30 feet. Late lilac (*S. villosa*) is even hardier, Zones 2 to 7. It blooms last of all the lilacs, into early summer. *S. patula* 'Miss Kim' (Zones 3 to 8) is a small shrub that is becoming more and more popular. It is sometimes called Korean or Manchurian lilac. Lilac-colored flowers become lighter as they fade.

The Persian lilac (*S.* ×*persica*, Zones 3 to 8) is a compact plant with fragrant flowers. *S. laciniata* has interesting lobed leaves that give rise to its common name "cut-leaf lilac" and to a different perfume. Hardy from Zones 4 to 8, it is one of the best lilacs to try for nostalgic northerners who relocate in Texas or Georgia. Meyer lilac (*S. Meyeri*, Zones 3 to 7) is known for its high flower-to-plant ratio. The flowers are violet and panicles shorter, about 4 inches long.

Cultural Information: Lilacs can grow in just about any garden soil—neutral to slightly acid is best; if it is too acidic, there may be no flowers. They should be fertilized every other year or so with a high phosphorus preparation—never an acidic shrub fertilizer. The plants will not bloom the first year after planting, but take a few years to settle in. Plants may have to be rejuvenated after several years. Go inside and remove the oldest wood and any spindly water sprouts or suckers that grow up straight from the base of the plant—up to one-third of the growth—at ground level. A cutback shrub will have fewer flowers the next year, but by the third year, will be producing more flowers than it did when it was in decline.

Flowers are produced on the last year's vigorous growth, so never prune until after or during flowering—you *must* cut these flowers and bring them in for the table and, especially, the nightstand. Dead-head if any seeds form, and don't feel guilty about cutting the neighbor's flowers all those years ago—it only led to more flowers the next year.

Tamarix ramosissima

Tamarisk; see ***Tamarix***

Tamarix ramosissima

(TAM-a-ricks rah-mo-SI-si-ma) **tamarisk,** ESU. ○ –
Zones: 2 to 9
Height: 10 feet
Colors: Pink to lavender
Characteristics: This is a rarely seen shrub that is really easy to grow, and it can stand some pretty awful locations—for example, right by the seaside. Feathery, airy blossoms in warm pink are produced in early summer. The foliage is purple-green, and the growth is shaggy. Try to see this plant at a botanical garden or nursery. It might be for you, perhaps to grow at the rear of the sunny flower border.
Cultural Information: Well-drained, even sandy, soil is best. Prune in early spring.

Tartarian dogwood; see ***Cornus***

Tree peony; see ***Paeonia***

Trifoliate orange; see ***Poncirus***

Tamarix ramosissima

Viburnum

(vy-BUR-num) many Native Americans, SP, SU. ○ ◐ ● ✱ –
Zones: Varies
Height: 4 to 15 feet by species and variety
Colors: White, pink
Characteristics: Vying for first place among the shrub genera for sheer scope and variety are the viburnums. Some are deciduous giants, others are evergreen dwarfs. All of them flower—mostly in umbels (flat flower clusters) of white or pinkish white sterile or fertile flowers.

Some have tubular flowers that end in stars, somewhat like those of the daphne. Often these types, such as Koreanspice viburnum (*Viburnum Carlesii*, Zones 4 to 7), are intensely fragrant. Others have flat umbels with sterile flowers surrounding fertile ones, like a lace-cap hydrangea, and those often lead to extremely ornamental fruits, such as the highbush cranberry (*V. trilobum*) and its European counterpart *V. Opulus* (Zones 3 to 8). These two have bright green, maplelike leaves and are deciduous. *V. Opulus* 'Sterile' is the snowball bush, which has only sterile flowers in perfect 2-inch to 3-inch balls, first green and then bright white. *V. plicatum tomentosum* is the double file viburnum whose flowers resemble a dogwood's showy bracts. Semievergreen leatherleaf viburnum (*V. rhytidophyllum*, Zones 5 to 8) is as well known for its leaves as for its flowers and fruit. They are long and puckered. These plants are related to the honeysuckles, a fact that can be recognized by the fruits. Many are beautiful and often in colors of orange or red. Some fruits are translucent and some persist until the following spring. Generally, these are tall shrubs for the landscape. They can be grouped into a collection or featured as specimens for almost any situation.

Cultural Information: These popular shrubs owe some of their fame to their ease of culture. They will accept various climates and soil conditions, but for the most part, they want a moist, slightly acidic medium. They also are not too picky about sunlight, and many varieties do well in partial shade, some in shade.

Prune away any dead wood after flowering. And watch out for water sprouts on some varieties— tall whips that shoot up from the soil level, or low on the trunk. These can be cut down at the ground or cut back to a place where other shoots branch. They too will branch and blend in. Also this will produce more branches on which flowers can develop.

Virginia sweet spire; see ***Itea***

Viburnum opulus var. sterile

Viburnum sieboldii

Vitex Agnus-castus

Vitex Agnus-castus (VY-tex AN-yus-KAS-tus) **chaste tree, vitex**, SU. ○ ◐ ✱ –
Zones: 7 to 9
Height: 6 feet
Colors: Violet, blue
Characteristics: The chaste tree has fragrant lilac-blue flowers in summer for a very long period of time. The bark and leaves are fragrant too, when crushed or bruised or even brushed as you pass by. Not familiar to many gardeners, this is a long-cultivated plant.
Cultural Information: In many areas, the chaste tree can be treated like a buddleia, that is, it can be cut down to about 1 foot high in early spring. Don't be alarmed if the plant looks dead: Vitex rarely sprouts leaves before June, but by July, it is in flower. For this reason, it might be best to blend it with herbaceous perennials, or even roses, where its dormant twigs can be hidden from view. It is an excellent flowering shrub in its zone range.

Weigela florida

Weigela florida (wy-GEE-la FLO-ri-da) **weigela**, ESU. ○ ◐ –
Zones: 5 to 8
Height: 8 feet
Colors: Red, pink, white
Characteristics: Sometimes, one wonders why so many people fuss about crab apple cultivars, or some esoteric shrub newcomer, when some of the tried-and-true, old-fashioned ones are just about perfect and bloom for such a long period. Weigela have trumpets of deep and light pink that completely cover the shrubs for more than a month from late spring to early summer. It creates a large fan shape that can get a bit out of hand, but can be pruned with impunity after the main burst of flowering ceases. There will be sporadic blooms throughout the summer.

Grow the weigela alone, with other shrubs or even at the back of the perennial border. Try growing a clematis up through the weigela, one that blooms in a complementary or harmonious shade at the same time, for a most wonderful effect. There are cultivars with white flowers or darker pink, and there is a variegated one that is not as vigorous as the species. *Weigela florida* 'Eva Supreme' is a dwarf with red flowers. *W. f.* 'Bristol Ruby' is also red flowered, but a giant, up to 10 feet tall.
Cultural Information: Plant it and forget it. This is terrifically

easy in ordinary garden soil. Often, you'll inherit this plant along with a "new" old house. If it is woody and misshapen, it can be severely pruned to bring it back. Take out some of the old growth right at ground level and trim away any spindly, wispy branches. Feeding with a fertilizer high in phosphorus and top-dressing with well-rotted cow manure will be appreciated then. Sometimes long branches will touch the ground. Anchor the stems about 10 inches from the end with a rock, and next year, you'll be able to cut off a new plant to give to a friend or to plant in another part of the garden.

White forsythia; see ***Abeliophyllum***

Winter hazel; see ***Corylopsis***

Winter sweet; see ***Chimonanthus***

Witch hazel; see ***Hamamelis***

5

PESTS AND DISEASES

A drive through one of America's older communities quickly illustrates the inherent sturdiness of many of our flowering shrubs. Like the solid prewar homes they surround, the forsythia and lilac, weigela and *Kolkwitzia*, quince and spirea proved tough enough to stick around for the next generation of homeowners to enjoy, too.

Even many of the more finicky subjects can be grown without great difficulty in the home landscape, provided they are planted in the right site and given the care they require. As discussed in chapter 3, a disregard for a plant's basic needs and preferences is just plain wasteful and an invitation to disaster. The best policy of all is to plant the right plant in the right place. A true shade lover will be weakened by the rigors of full sun; a sun lover banished to life in a dark corner will never be vigorous. Diseases and pests will have their way with these weaklings first, and dispatch them most easily. When shopping for plants, look for disease-resistant strains like the new crape myrtles developed by Donald Egolf and introduced to the nursery trade by the U.S. National Arboretum, including 'Catawba', 'Powhatan' and 'Seminole'. Among the honeysuckles, for example, *Lonicera tatarica* 'Arnold Red' is more resistant to aphids than many others. Plant breeding programs worldwide will continue to place major focus on incorporating improved resistance into new varieties; ask your county Cooperative Extension for updated lists of such strains before shopping for new additions to the garden.

Recently, new interest in native species for plants has emerged, and a growing number of nurseries are propagating these old-timers. Proponents believe that natives are inclined to possess inherent tolerance to local climate conditions, having evolved along with the particular habitat. Natives also ask less in the way of water and fertilizer than many hybrids, so they are said to be more environmentally sound choices for the landscape.

Sometimes, even when a good-quality plant is planted in a proper site and well cared for, it does become sick. When this happens, there is no substitute for proper, and immediate, diagnosis. If a shrub is droopy, don't just water it automatically, assuming it's thirsty without checking other indications. The droopiness may be a result of *too much* water or of a bacterial wilt or other disease, such as a fungal canker or root rot. Don't jump to conclusions; ask for help in confirming your suspicions *before* you act.

Describe the symptoms of the affected plant to the horticulturist at your local nursery, botanical garden or Cooperative Extension; better yet, take a sample in to the Extension for evaluation and diagnosis, which is usually available at a small fee or no charge. Many outbreaks of pests and diseases are related to weather conditions. These local experts are in tune with what's out there and can help you pinpoint and solve your problem fast, minimizing guesswork that could otherwise prove costly or even fatal to the ailing shrub.

As with health problems in people, the end result of many plant problems can be moderated by preventative care and early diagnosis. Stay in touch with your garden by checking plants carefully each week, including the undersides of leaves and the bark of trunks and branches. Before a few aphids on the viburnum swell to a horde of sufficient force to overtake the whole garden, you can spray them away with a strong blast from the garden hose or an application of insecticidal soap and water. Likewise, it is better to cut out a portion of a forsythia's wood that is affected with nodular lumps called "galls" than to have the disease spread to the whole plant.

A KINDER, GENTLER APPROACH

Over the last decade, there has emerged an increasing awareness of the environmental impact of traditional agricultural methods. Too many of the chemicals touted as miracles in the postwar era proved to be poisonous. In response, federal and state agencies have put substantial money into developing large-scale pest-management strategies that rely less on chemicals for their effectiveness.

A new, still-emerging era of organic farming has been born from this research, but for the small-scale home gardener with a honeysuckle full of aphids or a rhododendron beset with borers, there were still many questions left unanswered. Were there alternatives to the traditional chemical controls for these problems? Fortunately, in the last several years, enterprising and environmentally concerned companies like Safer and Ringers have begun to introduce natural pest- and disease-control products geared specifically to home-garden use.

The staff at Burpee is encouraged that the healthy garden, healthy environment movement continues to build momentum. In the last year, the USDA's network of land-grant universities (the ones that administer each state's county-by-county system of Cooperative Extensions) have begun to recommend nonchemical methods to eradicate insects and disease, whenever such an alternative is available, before advising gardeners to resort to traditional chemical controls. This least toxic approach is part of a system called Integrated Pest Management (see pages 82–83) that has already made great changes in the way the nation farms and gardens, and holds great promise for the future of the earth.

As simplistic as it may sound, good housekeeping is the cornerstone to maintaining a healthy garden. Although there are a few pests capable of traveling great distances, most begin and end their life cycle within a relatively small area, leaving the next generation poised to repeat the chain again. Often, they hide under debris such as fallen foliage, which is best carted away to decay in the compost pile, where it will become next year's natural fertilizer. Don't put parts of diseased plants in the pile, though; put them in the trash. Watering practices, if incorrect, can sometimes do more harm than good, inviting fungal pathogens like mildew, leaf spot and root rot to have a field day. Drip-irrigation systems, soaker hoses, or other underground and on-the-ground watering devices eliminate the problem of wet leaves caused by overhead sprinkling.

Sometimes, shrubs are victims of other gardening practices, such as the way we care for our lawns. Bark injuries inflicted by mowers and string trimmers can spell death for shrubs. Keep these hazards well clear of woody plants.

Besides being potentially harmful to the environment and ourselves, herbicides, fast-release fertilizers and other lawn-care chemicals are often too much for shrubs to handle. In what is like a slow death by poisoning, small doses administered on the nearby grassy areas season after season leach into the shrubs' root zones and finally become lethal. If you must fertilize the grass, switch to a slow-release formula of at last 50 percent organic ingredients. Instead of toxic herbicides, consider old-fashioned mechanical removal: Dig out the weeds.

On a similarly old-fashioned note, why not invite the birds back into your garden? By minimizing use of chemicals, installing even a small water source like a birdbath or small pool, providing nesting sites and some shrubby cover areas and planting berry- and seed-producing food sources, you will attract your own organic bug patrol. A few bedraggled leaves are no longer sufficient incentive for the use of chemicals. Gardeners who care about the environment must learn to tolerate some of these signs of nature at work and cease to try to interrupt and dominate the cycle.

Pollution-tolerant Flowering Shrubs

City gardeners are always looking for colorful additions to plain green yews, small Asian hollies and evergreen rhododendron. It's true that those shiny, green plants are good for urban gardens. Their leaves wash clean in every rain storm. But there are some of our flowering shrubs that have proved to be tolerant to one of the city backyard's worst problems, and also the problem of the urban and suburban front yard: pollution. Areas along the suburban roadway may be subjected to more pollution than many an urban backyard.

- *Amelanchier* species (serviceberry, shadblow)
- *Camellia* species (camellia)
- *Chaenomeles* species (flowering quince)
- *Cornus alba* 'Siberica' (red-twig dogwood)
- *Deutzia* species (deutzia)
- *Forsythia* species (forsythia)
- *Hydrangea* species (hydrangea)
- *Hypericum* species (St.-John's-wort)
- *Kerria japonica* (Japanese kerria)
- *Mahonia Aquifolium* species (Oregon holly grape)
- *Mahonia Bealei*
- *Philadelphus* species (mock orange)
- *Prunus* species (flowering cherry, plum, etc.)
- *Rhododendron* species (evergreen rhododendron)
- *Ribes* species (flowering currant)
- *Spiraea* ×*Bumalda* (spirea)
- *Viburnum* species (viburnum)

Relatively Trouble-free Shrubs

- *Aronia arbutifolia* (red chokeberry)
- *Aronia prunifolia* (black chokeberry)
- *Calycanthus floridus* (Carolina sweet shrub)
- *Caryopteris* ×*clandonensis* (blue mist)
- *Ceanothus americanus* (New Jersey tea)
- *Cephalanthus occidentalis* (buttonbush)
- *Clethra alnifolia* (sweet pepperbush)
- *Cornus mas* (Cornelian cherry)
- *Corylopsis* species (winter hazel)
- *Forsythia* ×*intermedia* (Forsythia hybrids)
- *Forsythia* species (Forsythia)
- *Hamamelis* species (witch hazel)
- *Hydrangea paniculata* 'Grandiflora' (peegee hydrangea)
- *Kolkwitzia amabilis* (beautybush)
- *Lindera Benzoin* (spicebush)
- *Lonicera* species (bush honeysuckle)
- *Nandina domestica* (heavenly bamboo)
- *Pieris floribunda* (mountain andromeda)
- *Potentilla fruticosa* (shrubby cinquefoil)
- *Prunus triloba* (flowering almond)
- *Rhododendron maxima* (rose bay rhododendron)
- *Spiraea* ×*Vanhouttei* (bridal wreath)
- *Symphoricarpos* species (snowberry)
- *Viburnum* species (viburnum)

Leaves damaged by the following pests, from left: beetles, flea beetles, caterpillars, aphids, and leafhoppers.

Diseases

LEAF SPOT: A common fungal disease, particularly in wet or humid weather. Spots develop on leaves, which may eventually drop. Prune out diseased parts of plants. Allowing for good air circulation when planting can help minimize this problem. An organic fungicide may help check spread.

CROWN GALLS: Nodular growths near the soil line, caused by soil-borne bacteria, that can cause shrubs to weaken and die. Galls may be present on branches, too. Check nursery stock carefully. In the garden, remove infected plants and burn or discard in the trash.

FIRE BLIGHT: Bacterial disease that causes leaves to look as if they were exposed to fire. Remove diseased wood, disinfecting shears between cuts with rubbing alcohol.

POWDERY MILDEW: Powdery white buildup on leaves, especially of lilacs, common in humid weather or where air circulation is poor. More ugly than dangerous, but may damage flower buds. An organic fungicide may help prevent severe infestation.

ROOT ROT: Fungal or bacterial ailment encouraged by overwatering or excess rain, especially in areas of poor drainage. Dig out and destroy sick plants. Improve drainage by adding organic matter to the area. In the case of foundation-planted rhododendron that are yellowing, for instance, you should suspect a fungal root rot, common to these shrubs when incorrectly planted in the wet, hot alkaline soil of such spots.

RUST: Leaves and sometimes stems have rusty orange patches caused by a fungus. Leaves may drop. Good sanitation—removal of infected plant parts—is essential.

IPM: A Kinder, Gentler Way

Chemicals were hailed as miracles when they came into widespread use in the postwar years. Now many of these substances are better known as the unwitting culprits in the case of our failing environment, and each year more and more of them are going the way of DDT, banned from commercial or individual use. Not so far in the future, the garden center shelves will look less like a pharmacy.

Whereas once, and not so long ago, it was widely held as good cultural practice to treat lawns, shrubs and trees routinely to prevent outbreaks of pests and diseases, a new consciousness is spreading in the worlds of agriculture and gardening. It has been spawned by the advent of Integrated Pest Management (IPM), a philosophy that employs a series of decision-making steps to arrive at the least toxic approch to each outbreak of trouble. IPM is not an organic approach, strictly speaking, because it does allow for the use of chemicals when, and only when, all else fails. But what has been demonstrated on farms, at land-grant universities doing IPM research and in botanical gardens (more and more of which have begun to try the principles of IPM the last few years) is that the application of chemicals can be reduced by 90 percent by following this approach, compared to the amount used with the old blanket-spray, prophylactic use.

IPM employs a combination of tactics to help gardeners make the decision of how to cope with problems. The most important is monitoring: assessing the actual presence of pests instead of just assuming they're present, in a particular month on a particular plant—the old blanket-spray approach.

As it applies to growing ornamental plants like the flowering shrubs, IPM asks us to think about our aesthetic threshold of damage. Does the presence of a few chewed-up leaves warrant spraying a whole stand of "rhodies?" Can we learn to live with a little imperfection, with nature's way? Is the problem serious enough to warrant chemical intervention?

Before anyone practicing IPM resorts to chemicals, a number of safer alternatives must be exhausted. Can the pests or diseases be eliminated mechanically—picked off, cut out or dislodged with a stiff spray from the garden hose? Can other cultural techniques such as pruning to improve air circulation, altered watering practices, quarantine of a sick plant or better garden sanitation eradicate the problem? Can the offending insects be trapped with the use of a pheremone (sex lure) or some other mechanical trap? Is a nontoxic spray such as one of the Safer brand products a possibility? Are there any predatory insects that can be called in to reduce the bad bug population or is there some other form of biological control, like a parasite or pathogen, that can be used? If spraying turns out to be the only answer,

Pests

APHIDS: Soft-bodied, pear-shaped insects that suck plant juices. Look for curled leaves, traces of secretion called "honeydew" or for licelike insects, particularly underneath leaves. Aphids probably won't kill a shrub, but can transmit viruses that can be dangerous or lethal. A stiff spray of water from the hose or application of solution of insecticidal soap or horticultural oil will smother them.

BORERS AND MINERS: Difficult pests that can devastate shrubs by boring into wood (e.g., rhododendron borer) or mining between surfaces of leaves (such as in Tatarian dogwood). Among the hardest pests to control at present without chemicals; remove infested plant parts and destroy.

WEEVILS: Insects that chew notches into leaves, especially in azaleas and other *Rhododendron.* Won't kill the plants unless infestation is allowed to go unchecked.

SCALES: Soft-bodied insects with hard shells, usually shiny

IPM suggests that it be done in a pinpoint manner, not a blanket spray at all, to focus simply on the affected plant part or parts. And IPM also recommends using the least toxic spray that will fit the bill.

IPM recommendations are being updated regularly as entomolgists continue to study the insect kingdom to devise ways to thwart costly outbreaks of pests. Meanwhile, though, the basic step-by-step strategy for arriving at the least toxic answer to each problem can be adopted by each and every gardener. Think before you act, it asks, especially when the subject is chemicals.

and brown, sometimes white. These insects suck at sap of leaves and stems. Can be smothered with a coating of oil applied (sprayed) to plants when they are dormant. Read and follow all package directions.

CATERPILLARS: Perhaps the most familiar of all leaf-eating pests. Best to handpick most them, but only if you are certain that they are a harmful species, because all of our butterflies and moths go through a caterpillar stage. Spray of a nontoxic biological control like Bt (*Bacillus thuringiensis*), a kind of "germ warfare" against caterpillars is very effective.

BEETLES: Leaf-eating insects. Handpick and kill Japanese beetles or use traps with scented lures placed away from the garden.

MITES: Like the tiniest of spiders, and often reddish in color, these creatures—not insects—congregate and suck on undersides of leaves. A strong spray of cold water may do the trick.

LEAF ROLLERS: These are the larvae of the common *Torticid* moth. The caterpillars cut leaves and roll them up, sometimes fastening them shut; and then they feed while protected inside the roll. They can defoliate entire shrubs.

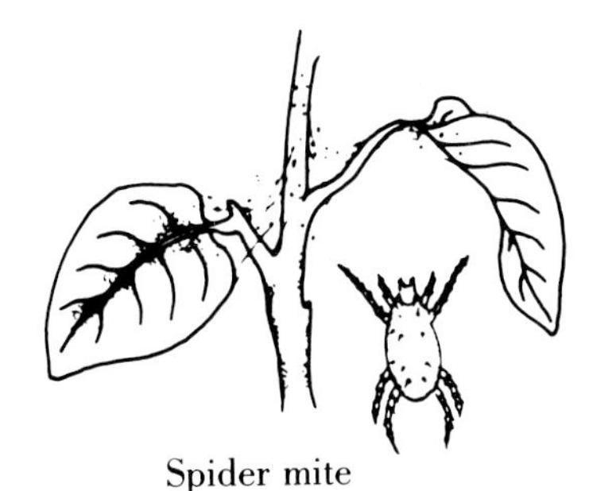

Spider mite

Red spider mite

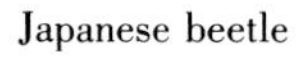

Japanese beetle

Beetle

Aphids

The ladies in Burpee's customer service department answering mail at the turn of the century.

6

GARDENERS' MOST-ASKED QUESTIONS

DESIGNING WITH SHRUBS

Q: Which shrubs are best for growing in a shady spot?
A: Glossy abelia (*Abelia ×grandiflora*), azalea, hydrangea, witch hazel, some viburnum varieties, Carolina allspice (*Calycanthus floridus*), summer sweet, Japanese andromeda and mountain laurel.

Q: How can shrubs be used in a perennial border?
A: Shrubs can act as focal points in a flower border, providing height, winter interest and flowers. Choose shrubs in proportion to the bed, and place it/them off-center for a more aesthetically pleasing, natural look.

Q: What flowering shrubs make good hedges?
A: Shrub roses, spirea, hydrangea, forsythia, bush honeysuckle, some viburnum and lilac.

Q: Which shrubs have the fewest pest and disease problems?
A: Native shrubs tend to have fewer pest and disease problems because they have adapted to the conditions in which they grow. Care must be taken, however, in selecting native species; choose shrubs appropriate to the kind of location where you intend to plant them. Rhododendron, viburnum, fothergilla, witch hazel, *Itea*, summer sweet, fringe tree, bayberry, dogwood, and many azaleas are especially satisfactory.

Q: Which shrubs bloom in summer?
A: Summer sweet, butterfly bush, some rhododendron, some viburnum and hydrangeas.

Q: Do any shrubs bloom in fall?
A: *Abelia ×grandiflora, Camellia sasanqua, Hamamelis virginiana* and rose of Sharon all bloom in fall.

Q: Which shrubs are appropriate for growing in containers?
A: Some azalea varieties, camellias, *Pieris, Deutzia gracilis* and small spirea varieties.

Q: What kinds of shrubs work well for bonsai?
A: Azalea, forsythia and flowering quince all are charming.

Q: What kinds of shrubs work well espaliered?
A: *Forsythia ×intermedia*, flowering quince and viburnum.

Q: What shrubs grow in acid soils?
A: Azalea, rhododendron, mountain laurel, *Pieris* and *Hydrangea*.

Q: What shrubs grow in wet locations?
A: Viburnum, summer sweet, sweet shrub and *Rhododendron viscosum*.

Q: What shrubs attract birds to the garden?
A: *Viburnum dentatum, Viburnum trilobum* and bush honeysuckle

are just a few. See page 21 for more suggestions.

Q: Which shrubs produce fragrant flowers?
A: Witch hazel, many viburnums, some azalea and rhododendron, summer sweet, lilac, rose, *Mahonia* and *Daphne.*

Q: Which shrubs have attractive berries?
A: *Viburnum dilitatum, Mahonia,* beauty-berry, fringe tree and snowberry produce exceptionally handsome berries.

Q: Which flowering shrubs work well as foundation plantings?
A: Try azalea, *Pieris,* deutzia, *Mahonia* and rhododendron.

PRUNING SHRUBS

Q: Can I prune shrubs to keep them the size I want?
A: Most shrubs can be pruned, but it is better to plant shrubs that will grow to the size you want rather than to keep pruning back those that naturally grow larger than you want them.

Q: Which shrubs are best pruned in spring, and which in summer? Does it make a difference?
A: Spring-blooming shrubs, forsythia and lilac for example, are best pruned right after they flower. They bloom on wood that grew the previous year and take all summer to form flower buds. Pruning at any other time would risk cutting off the flower buds. Summer-blooming shrubs such as rose of Sharon, for example, bloom on new growth and should be pruned in spring.

Q: Can hedges be pruned at any time?
A: Keeping the bloom times in mind, hedge plants can be pruned throughout the season.

Q: What is the best way to prune shrubs for a natural look?
A: Rather than shearing all the branches to the same height, for a more natural look prune back to an outward-facing bud or branch and remove the taller branches. Continue removing the taller branches until the hedge reaches the desired height.

Q: Is it important to prune shrubs?
A: Many shrubs, forsythia and butterfly bush among them, are rejuvenated when pruned yearly. Some benefit from being pruned every couple of years—lilac and azalea, for example. Some shrubs flower better when spent flower heads are removed; this is the case with rhododendron. It prevents seed formation and allows the shrub to use its strength for vegetative growth, and will benefit next year's flowering.

PESTS AND DISEASES

Q: How can I control Japanese beetles?
A: Japanese beetles can be a problem on many shrubs, especially crape myrtle and roses. They can be controlled in the long term by applying milky spore disease to the soil. Try to interest neighbors, too, in using milky spore. Milky spore takes a few years to become established, but will work for 20 years. It builds up in the soil over several years and paralyzes the digestive tracts of Japanese beetle grubs. The grubs die, never growing into beetles. Japanese beetle lures are also available, although they can actually attract beetles to your, or your neighbor's, garden. They can also be hand picked and dropped into a can of alcohol.

Q: How can I control scale?
A: Ladybugs attack scale in the crawler stage. Increase your ladybug population by ordering some to release in your garden from time to time. Safer's Soap is effective at this stage, too. Once scale attach to the branch, though, they are difficult to control. Dormant oil can be applied while the shrub is still dormant. Check with your Cooperative Extension agent to learn when the crawler stage occurs in your area.

Q: How can I control powdery mildew? Do I have to?
A: Powdery mildew commonly attacks lilacs during August's humid weather. There are few safe chemical treatments for powdery mildew. However, you can try sulfur-based sprays or dusts. The disease rarely kills plants, but it makes them unsightly and limits their ability to photosynthesize and make food. The disease is worse when plants are overcrowded and air circulation is poor. Keep your shrubs healthy and pruned for a more open shape and the problem should be lessened.

Q: Will the powdery mildew on my lilac spread to my roses?
A: No, powdery mildew diseases are host-specific.. This means that the powdery mildew that attacks lilacs attacks lilacs only, and not roses. The powdery mildew that attacks roses can be more damaging to roses than the lilac disease is to lilacs, because it can destroy rose blossoms.

Q: My azaleas are dying, but I can't see any insects. Could the problem be in the soil?
A: Your plants may be affected by a soil disease known as phytophthora root rot disease. Unfortunately there aren't effective controls for this disease. If you think this may be the problem, have a soil sample tested for the pathogen by your Cooperative Extension Service. Remove any diseased plants and avoid planting related species in the same area. The disease can be more of a problem in poorly drained sites.

Q: My rhododendron have comma-shaped holes on the sides of their leaves. What causes this?
A: It sounds as though your rhododendron are being attacked by black vine weevils. These insects live in the soil and come out at night, so you may never see them. If you do see them, they will be identifiable by the long snout characteristic of weevils. The only controls are to spray the bugs when you see them with Safer's Soap, or use a chemical soil drench recommended by your Cooperative Extension Service.

GENERAL PROBLEMS

Q: My fringe trees don't produce berries. What's wrong?
A: Fringe trees and some other fruiting shrubs are dioecious, meaning there are male plants and female plants. Both sexes are necessary in the garden for fruit production. If you have healthy plants that produce flowers but neither berries nor fruit, your plants are probably the same sex.

Q: I bought an azalea in full bloom last year, planted and watered it, and it grew well. It didn't bloom this year. What happened?
A: Newly planted shrubs may not bloom for a year or more after transplanting because they spend their energy trying to get established in their new locations. Give them a couple of years and they will bloom if the location is favorable.

Q: My hydrangeas aren't blooming. What's wrong?
A: 'French Blue' or big-leaf hydrangeas are hardy in Zones 7 to 9 and flower buds are often killed in more northern areas. Not all blue hydrangeas are 'French Blue', and some varieties are hardier. Check to find out what variety your neighbors are growing if you live in an area cooler than Zone 7. Also, remember these varieties bloom on old wood and should be pruned after bloom. Remove two-year-old canes at or near ground level.

Q: My lilac isn't blooming. What's wrong?
A: When did you prune it? Lilacs bloom on old wood and so should be pruned after bloom. Young lilacs can take a few years to bloom, and old lilacs may become too overcrowded to bloom. Rejuvenate lilacs by removing the older stems every year or every couple of years. Sometimes breaking up the soil around the base of the plant encourages bloom because it stimulates root growth. Try working lime into the soil around the plant. Lilacs require six or more hours of sun.

Q: My Exbury azaleas don't bloom. Why?
A: Exbury azaleas prefer more sun than other azalea varieties and don't bloom well in shade. Prune them after they bloom, and avoid high-nitrogen fertilizers. They can take a couple of years to bloom after planting, as can most azaleas.

Q: Why isn't my shrub honeysuckle fragrant?
A: Not all honeysuckles are fragrant. Check that your variety was supposed to be fragrant. If so, it may be that your soil is lacking in certain trace elements. Have your soil tested for nutrient content and make sure the pH is within the range desirable for the plant.

Q: Why haven't my butterfly bushes bloomed yet? I have had them for three years.
A: Butterfly bush can take three years to bloom after planting, so yours is probably just on the verge. Don't prune in summer as this plant blooms on new wood.

Q: My rhododendron are brown and dying back. What's wrong?
A: This may be due to winter kill, especially if your rhododendron are in a sunny exposure in winter. Prune out dead areas, and consider moving the plants to a more protected location.

PLANTING

Q: Is fall better than early spring for planting shrubs?
A: As long as the plants are dormant, either season is fine. Fall planting is fine for many shrubs. It allows the shrub to develop some roots before the soil freezes, and gives it a headstart for spring growth. The next best time is in early spring, before the shrub breaks dormancy. Avoid planting shrubs when they have leafed-out, as it is more stressful for the plants to develop roots and foliage at the same time.

Q: Which is preferable, bare-root planting or container planting?
A: Bare-root planting allows the plant to establish a more vigorous root system in a well-prepared soil. Sometimes shrubs can become root-bound in containers, and it may cost them time and effort to adapt to your soil. Container-grown plants are easier to hold before planting; plant roots must be kept moist, and bare-root plants dry out more easily.

Q: I just received my shrubs and they look dead. What should I do?
A: Dormant plants can look very much like dead plants—just look at your garden in winter! Burpee tries to send dormant plants early enough for spring planting so that they can grow vigorous roots before they have to leaf-out. If you order late in spring, however, the rest of your garden may already be breaking dormancy. For fall planting, Burpee sends shrubs after they have gone dormant. The roots will continue to grow in the fall until the soil temperature drops to 40°F. Don't compare your established plants to the new dormant plants; they were kept in cold storage until shipping. Even in warmer weather, dormant plants may break dormancy slowly, as root establishment is a priority. Garden centers tend to sell container-grown shrubs that have broken dormancy, because they are seductively eye-catching. Mail-order companies send dormant plants because they ship better—as they can be shipped in cooler weather and can be sent at the best planting time. If you want to know if the shrubs are still alive, try scratching the newer growth with your fingernail. If the bark scrapes away easily to reveal fresh growth, you know your plant is still alive.

Q: My neighbor's shrubs are already in bloom and mine are still dormant. Why are they so slow?
A: Newly planted plants need to develop feeder roots before they can take up enough water and nutrients to support foliage and flowers. Be patient with newly planted plants! Your patience will be rewarded with healthier specimens.

Q: I planted three shrubs at the same time. Two have broken

dormancy but not the other. Is it dead?
A: If you can see green on the stem when you scratch it with your fingernail, it isn't dead. Individual plants will break dormancy at their own rate. If conditions are good and the roots can grow, water your plants and be patient.

Q: How can I hold my bare-root nursery stock until it is time to plant? It is still cold here and we don't plant until after Memorial Day.
A: Bare-root nursery stock should be planted before the last frost. The Memorial Day planting date is usually taken to identify a time when all danger of frost is past, and is really later than you want to plant in most parts of the country. If you have to hold the plants for a week or two because you are unable to plant them, keep the roots moist and in a dark, cool location until you can plant. Check the roots every so often to make sure they are moist.

Q: Do fall-planted shrubs require winter protection?
A: If they are marginally hardy for your area it is a good idea to mulch the roots after the ground freezes. If you are planting a broad-leaf evergreen in a windy location, a screen can be constructed on the north and west sides by stapling burlap to wooden stakes driven into the ground. Or, you can spray an antidescecant, following the manufacturers' directions.

Q: How should I prepare a planting hole for my newly ordered shrubs?
A: Most shrubs arrive with planting instructions. However, in general, a hole is dug twice as deep and twice as wide as the root system; 18 x 18 inches is usually adequate. Mix organic matter such as peat moss with the soil before filling in the hole around the shrub's roots. See page 32.

Q: Should I cut my shrubs back by one-third when I plant them?
A: This is not necessary when planting container-grown shrubs. When you are transplanting shrubs from one part of your garden to another, on the other hand, you will lose some roots when you dig them up. (Bare-root shrubs probably lost some roots when they were dug as well.) To compensate for this loss, cut back some of the top growth (not more than one-third). This will make it easier for the plant's roots to supply water and food to the rest of the plant and enable the plant to become better established in the new location and more quickly.

MISCELLANEOUS

Q: Why does it take so long for some young shrubs to bloom?
A: Shrubs are longer lived than annuals and most perennials, and they take longer to mature. Some take longer than others; lilacs can take quite a long time. Plant annuals near your young shrubs to give your garden flowers until they are mature enough to bloom.

Q: Is it better to buy larger rather than smaller shrubs?
A: If you are willing to wait longer for flowers, it is generally better to plant smaller (but healthy) shrubs that can develop most of their root systems in your garden environment rather than that of the nursery. It is more difficult to transplant large shrubs than small shrubs, because more roots are lost in digging them up.

Q: Can shrubs be grown from seed?
A: Most shrubs, as is the case with most woody plants, are difficult for the home gardener to grow from seed. They can take more than a year to sprout, and they may require conditions for germination too complex for the home gardener to provide. Woody plants are more slow growing than herbaceous plants. It is easier for most people to purchase shrubs that are several years old.

Please write or call for a free Burpee catalog:

W. Atlee Burpee & Company
300 Park Avenue
Warminster, PA 18974
215-674-9633

CUTTING GARDENS

Chet Davis

INTRODUCTION

Flowers in the home are one of those little niceties we can provide for ourselves. The accent of color and scent do much to lift the spirits when avid gardeners find themselves indoors. A flower arrangement need be neither large nor elaborate to be wonderfully effective. I hope to share the enjoyment of the cutting garden experience and to discourage the floral enthusiast from getting bogged down in the virtually endless list of floral design rules and regulations with which we seem to have been burdened since Queen Victoria first started tightening her corset laces. These rules are like rules in cooking, painting or any other hobby; they help the novice learn the basics, but after that, it's best to relax and enjoy creating beauty.

Plants suitable for cutting represent all the major groups of ornamental plants: herbaceous annuals, perennials, biennials, woody trees, shrubs, vines and groundcovers. But why stop there? Stretch the imagination and use wildflowers, weeds, culinary and aromatic herbs and vegetables to create delightfully unique decorations. This book is designed to lead you through the process of creating a cutting garden suitable for your landscape, and to help you plant, grow and harvest (yes, harvest!) materials suitable for a variety of arrangements. For many, the cutting of flowers for arrangements offers a feeling of accomplishment similar to that we may get when harvesting peas, tomatoes and other edibles. A sense of well-being, bounty and—let's not forget—cost savings. Flowers harvested from the garden are as fresh as you will ever find, and they allow you to express yourself in colors, textures and fragrances of your choosing. They let you bring the outdoors in.

The avid horticulturist will learn from the cutting garden. For example, nuances of color in the petals will become more evident when seen from the perspective of the dining table or desktop, and plants successfully combined in the vase may later be similarly grouped in the garden bed. In this way the vase can become a sort of laboratory for the garden. The wily gardener need not laboriously move plants around in the garden to try variations of textures, colors and forms. The cutting garden and flower arrangement become tools you can use to learn more about plants and your garden. This book offers pointers on design. The elements of good design, involving color, texture, balance, rhythm and proportion, are all easily practiced in the vase.

Over the years the cutting gardens at Mohonk Mountain House, where I garden, have provided me with great pleasure. There, tremendous numbers of cut flowers nurtured by dedicated gardeners are harvested and beautifully arranged by talented florists. Flower bouquets on a grand scale grace the hallways of this historic, venerable mountaintop retreat. Displays of this sort have impressed generations of guests seeking to revive their spirits.

All garden endeavors require some study and planning. The chapters that follow will help you create a basic garden plan that will yield cut flowers and greens for your arrangements. More than a paint-by-numbers approach, my advice aims to broaden your horizons by helping you look at a plant's flowers and leaves in a new light. Novice gardeners will learn the essentials of planting as well as how to nurture and harvest the bounty of their labors; old-timers may pick up some tips to improve the use of their landscapes, and I hope they will be introduced to some new plants and techniques along the way.

A word for the faint at heart: Frequently when cutting flowers from the garden, I will hear a low groan—not from the plant being cut, but from an onlooker. Some people seem to harbor a sensitivity to "hurting" the plants. In fact, most plants benefit from cutting. The plants frequently produce more blossoms or succulent shoots, becoming denser and stronger for their sacrifice. Nor is cutting from the garden a sacrifice of blooms. Plant materials harvested and properly handled will frequently outlast their garden counterparts as they are not exposed to wind, rain, insects and disease. Once in the vase, the flowers and greens can successfully live out their lives in regal splendor.

Daffodils harvested from a naturalized planting find a home in a crockery vase. Buds of Amelachier, *and hemlock and hosta foliage complete the composition.*

1

THE CUTTING GARDEN PLANNER

CHOOSING PLANTS FOR THE CUTTING GARDEN

The plants you choose will have to be harvested to be enjoyed in the house. They must be able to last when placed in water. The plant portraits (page 45) recommend those varieties best for cutting. Quite simply, those that don't last in water are not suitable for cutting, although they may be enjoyed in many other ways, including for their garden beauty and fragrance, in potpourri or garden crafts, as edible flowers and as pretty garnishes.

Ages ago, some brilliant person created order in the garden by classifying plants in groups, each group planted in a different part of the garden. Over the years these artificial plant groupings have been maintained as if written in stone. Therefore, we have perennial borders, annual borders, herb gardens, vegetable gardens and shrubbery borders. Later you'll see I'm not averse to anarchy in the garden; we'll overthrow these artificial plant groupings and create gardens to serve a specific purpose.

Plants are grouped by botanical type; thus we speak of annuals, biennials, herbaceous perennials and woody perennials. Within these categories we find our familiar friends: flowers, trees, shrubs, herbs, vegetables and so on. Annuals, frequently grown from seed, complete their life cycle in one year. However, in the annual group of plants, some perennials and biennials are often included. Confused? For practical reasons some perennials native to warm areas and unable to survive cold winter climates are treated as annuals. In a warmer climate, they may be content in the garden for many years. An example of a tropical perennial is the familiar coleus; another, the common horticultural geranium (*Pelargonium* spp.). Other annuals are called "half-hardy" or weak perennials. These are plants capable of surviving the winter under the right conditions but not likely to do so and, therefore, are not reliable. Two garden favorites that are true perennials, though not very reliable, are dusty miller (*Senecio* spp.) and snapdragon (*Antirrhinum* spp.). Biennials ordinarily take two years to produce blossoms. However, some can bloom the first year from seed if they are started early indoors, or if sown in late summer or early fall. A garden favorite is the pansy (*Viola* spp.). Tropical perennials, weak perennials and some biennials are best treated as annuals. Grow them from seed, and discard them at the end of the growing season, to start with fresh seed and new young plants the following year. Annuals are great additions to the cutting garden as they are inexpensive, frequently easy to grow and respond well to cutting, providing blossoms for cutting from summer until frost.

Late summer provides the textures and colors of approaching autumn. An old bronze vase holds rich mahogany and brown sunflowers with apricot dahlias and creamy white roses. Zinnias and phlox contrast nicely with the larger flowers. Bells of Ireland, with their bright green, flowerlike bracts that loop over the edge of the container, provide textural interest.

These commercially grown snapdragons will soon be cut and sent to the flower markets. On a smaller scale, beautiful flowers such as these are easily grown and, when harvested, will provide long-lasting beauty and bright color in a vase or arrangement.

Biennials take two years to complete their life cycle. During the first year they grow vegetatively (leaves, roots and stems); they produce flowers the second season. At the end of the flowering period the biennial frequently sets seed and dies. Many biennials become permanent residents in the garden if a number of flowers are allowed to set seed and self-sow each year, allowing for continuation of the species and making impressive naturalized stands. The common foxglove (*Digitalis* spp.) is one of my favorite biennials.

Perennials are often overlooked in planning the cutting garden. Perennials live for two years or longer. Many perennials can come back year after year, and some will improve with age, producing more beautiful blooms with each passing year. Peonies (*Paeonia* spp.) and wormwood (*Artemisia* spp.) are two hardy perennials that improve with age, providing ever more materials for cutting as the years go by. Too frequently, perennials are linked with low-maintenance landscaping. Perennial plantings may save some aspects of garden maintenance, but don't think perennials are to be planted and left on their own. Like all plants, perennials respond best to good horticultural practices.

Woody plants are the ones that make up the permanent background of the garden. The trunks and branches form a lacy backdrop during the winter months and can provide shade and wind breaks, or form a pattern in the landscape that directs the eye; they can screen unpleasant views, too. Woody perennials are an excellent source of material for bouquets. The blossoms, of course, provide color, scent and texture; the foliage can fill a vase or help to cover the mechanics of an arrangement; and the bare twigs can add line and drama to an arrangement. Many trees and shrubs also provide fruit, a dramatic addition to a flower arrangement.

THE FORMAL CUTTING GARDEN

To some, a cutting garden means neat, orderly rows of flowers. To others it means long beds of flowers with verdant grassy strips dividing them. In some cases a separate area for cutting is fenced or hedged off from other garden features. The formal cutting garden can be any of these and more. I consider the formal cutting garden to be any garden in which the components are in place only for the production of cut flowers, and any aesthetic gain is of secondary value. In fact, a cutting garden can be downright ugly (though you may have to really work at making it so). The formal cutting garden is a utilitarian area that just happens to grow beauty.

The location of the cutting garden is important and will affect the success of your gardening venture and the variety of plants that can be grown. The best location for any cutting garden is in full sun, which benefits the widest variety of plants; although some cutting garden varieties might prefer partial shade, they can be satisfied by planting around trees, creating arbors and so forth. For the formal cutting garden a large rectangular area is ideal because it allows for the development of rows. There is no minimum or maximum size for a cutting garden; this is determined by the amount of land available and the quantity of flowers wanted. A 6-by-12-foot site planted largely with annuals is capable of producing enough blossoms and foliage to provide modest flower displays to decorate an average home. For gardeners with greater ambition, developing a larger garden will allow for greater diversity of cutting materials, larger bouquets and more of them. An extremely ambitious gardener may wish to expand the cutting garden to provide flowers for drying and including in everlasting bouquets, petals for potpourri and sachets and fresh blossoms for private use and gift giving. The scale of your site, your home and your needs will determine the type and size of cutting garden best for you.

Enclosing the cutting garden may be a wise step, for a number of reasons. Enclosure provides protection from animals; the white-tailed deer is our particular bane where I garden. Hedges, walls and fences all offer protection from damaging winds and can screen unsightly components of the landscape—yours or your neighbor's! (Such features as compost piles, utilitarian mulches and plant supports are essential to today's gardens but aren't the best-looking part of any landscape.) Formal or informal hedging is nice in larger gardens where there is enough room to ensure the hedge doesn't create problems with root and light competition. In smaller situations a fence or wall may be the more desirable alternative. Fences and walls may be used as plant supports for vining crops such as bittersweet, gourds, sweet peas, trumpet creeper and clematis.

The materials chosen to enclose a garden should be decided with consideration for the need and economics of the job. I have always fantasized about growing flowers within a brick wall, but as brick doesn't complement my home, landscape or checkbook, a wooden fence provides the landscape definition I seek. No matter what form of enclosure you may choose to employ, it is important to remember that you are raising flowers for cutting and that you don't want to hinder plant growth or your ability to work well in your garden. Plan adequate width for gates or other passways in and out of the garden so you can carry the necessary tools and equipment back and forth without skinning your knuckles.

The cutting garden should be handy. The landscape is more than just a bunch of pretty plants around a home; it should have purpose. Utilitarian areas such as vegetable gardens, herb gardens and cutting gardens should be located so that it is easy to run outdoors and pick a few blossoms before dinner or snip a rose to adorn your desk at work without making a major safari into the wilds of the landscape. An added benefit of keeping the cutting garden close to the home is that it is close to the center of all garden activities: water, tools, equipment and you!

The cutting garden at Mohonk Mountain House provides flowers for cutting and arranging fresh and some blooms for drying, for use in dried bouquets and potpourri. A mulch of wheat straw helps conserve moisture, keeps down weeds and provides a mud-free walkway for Mohonk florists.

A well-dressed cutting garden attractively fenced and softened with plantings. This handsomely designed cutting garden would be a delightful addition to any landscape. The paved path and wide gate provide easy access for florist and gardener alike.

Within the garden the planting rows or beds should run east to west. This allows all plants to benefit from maximum sun exposure. Arranging the shortest plants in the southernmost rows and the tallest plants as a backdrop on the northern edge will prevent taller plants from shading their neighbors.

Formal Cutting Garden Plan

PLANT LIST FOR A FORMAL CUTTING GARDEN (SUITABLE FOR USDA ZONE 5)

Perennials and Hardy Bulbs

1. *Gypsophila paniculata* 'Bristol Fairy', baby's breath (1); underplant with *Allium giganteum* (8), 6 inches apart
2. *Miscanthus sinensis* (1)
3. *Delphinium elatum* 'Pacific Hybrids' (12), 12 inches apart
4. *Phlox paniculata,* garden phlox (9), 12 inches apart
5. *Astilbe* spp., assorted astilbe (7), 12 inches apart; underplant with mixed tulips (25)
6. *Heuchera sanguinea* 'Bressingham Hybrids', coral bells (3), 8 inches apart; underplant with mixed narcissuses (10)
7. *Aquilegia* × *hybrida* 'McKana Hybrids', columbine (5), 8 inches apart; underplant with mixed narcissuses (25)
8. *Digitalis purpurea,* foxglove (12), 6 inches apart
9. *Lilium* × 'Connecticut Lemonglow', hybrid lily (12), 6 inches apart; underplant with *Myosotis sylvatica,* forget-me-nots
10. *Lilium* × 'Sterling Star', hybrid lily (12), 6 inches apart; interplant with *Allium sphaerocephalum,* drumstick allium (16), 4 inches apart
11. *Rudbeckia hirta* 'Gloriosa Daisy' (6), 8 inches apart
12. *Helianthus annuus* 'Italian White', sunflower (5), 9 inches apart
13. *Lysimachia clethroides,* gooseneck lysimachia (12), 8 inches apart
14. *Achillea* 'Summer Pastels' (12), 6 inches apart
15. *Chrysanthemum maximum,* shasta daisy (12), 8 inches apart
16. *Rosa* × 'Sunbright', hybrid tea rose (1); underplant with *Convallaria majalis,* lily of the valley (18)
17. *Lathyrus odoratus,* sweet pea (20), 6 inches apart; train to climb fencing
18. *Veronica spicata,* spike veronica (9), 4 inches apart
19. *Chrysanthemum* × *morifolium,* hardy garden chrysanthemum (8), 9 inches apart
20. *Hosta* × 'Royal Standard' (3), 8 inches apart
21. *Lychnis coronaria* 'Angel Blush' (6), 6 inches apart
22. *Coreopsis grandiflora* 'Early Sunrise' (6), 6 inches apart
23. *Rosa* × 'Garden Party', hybrid tea rose (1); underplant with *Viola tricolor,* Johnny-jump-ups
24. *Aconitum napellus,* monkshood (4), 9 inches apart
25. *Campanula persicifolia,* peach-leaved bellflower (8), 6 inches apart
26. *Monarda didyma,* bee balm, assorted colors (6), 12 inches apart
27. *Achillea* × 'Coronation Gold' (8), 9 inches apart
28. *Liatris spicata,* gayfeather (24), 4 inches apart
29. *Paeonia lactifolia,* assorted peony (3), 18 inches apart
30. *Artemisia ludoviciana albula* 'Silver King' (5), 9 inches apart

Annuals and Tender Bulbs

31. *Cleome hasslerana* 'Queen Mix', spider flower (6), 12 inches apart
32. *Cosmos bipinnatus* 'Sensation Mixed' (6), 12 inches apart
33. *Antirrhinum majus* 'Rocket Mixed', snapdragon (24), 6 inches apart
34. *Consolida orientalis* 'Imperial Mix', larkspur (24), 6 inches apart
35. *Zinnia elegans* 'State Fair Mix' (12), 9 inches apart
36. *Scabiosa atropurpurea* 'Imperial Mix', pincushion flower (18), 6 inches apart
37. *Celosia plumosa* 'Flamingo Feather' (6), 6 inches apart
38. *Amaranthus caudatus,* love-lies-bleeding (6), 8 inches apart
39. *Gladiolus,* assorted gladiola (12), 6 inches apart
40. *Zinnia elegans* 'Cut and Come Again' (9), 6 inches apart
41. *Ageratum houstonianum* 'Blue Horizon' (9), 6 inches apart
42. *Gomphrena globosa,* globe

amaranth (24), 6 inches apart

43. *Callistephus orientalis* 'Bouquet Mixed', aster (12), 8 inches apart
44. *Trachelium caeruleum*, purple umbrella (6), 6 inches apart
45. *Salvia farinacea* 'Blue Bedder' (6), 6 inches apart
46. *Tagetes signata* 'Lemon Gem,' signet marigold (9), 6 inches apart
47. *Xeranthemum annuum*, immortelle (6), 6 inches apart
48. *Acidanthera bicolor* (9), 4 inches apart

Allow enough space between rows or beds for ease in maintaining and harvesting the plants. Wider spacing may be a good idea on some rows to provide access for hoses, wheel barrows of compost and to permit you to pass through the garden without damaging plants.

An alternative to parallel rows or beds is a more formal and ornamental planting with geometrically arranged planting beds. This format is more reminiscent of a formal English or herb garden. The cutting garden diagrams at left and on page 15 show two designs, in the row and geometric styles. Each will produce enough material so vases of leftovers can be given away. When planting the formal cutting garden, it is best to place annuals in beds with annuals, and segregate perennials and biennials to their own area where they can't be disturbed by tilling or spading. The cutting garden is the perfect place for a nursery row. The nursery row is a space dedicated to growing or holding plants for later inclusion in the ornamental garden. Grow biennials such as *Campanula* from seed in the fall to transplant in the garden the following spring.

Carefully arranged to catch all the available sunlight and for easy maintenance, this cutting garden provides a wide variety of blooms from matricaria to cosmos and dahlias to salvia. The tall, fragrant Buddleia *is an inspired addition to the background of this hedged cutting garden.*

The curvilinear border of flowers softens the hedge in this landscape. Well-designed and-cared for, this border will provide loads of flowers and foliage for enjoying indoors in arrangements.

THE INTEGRATED GARDEN

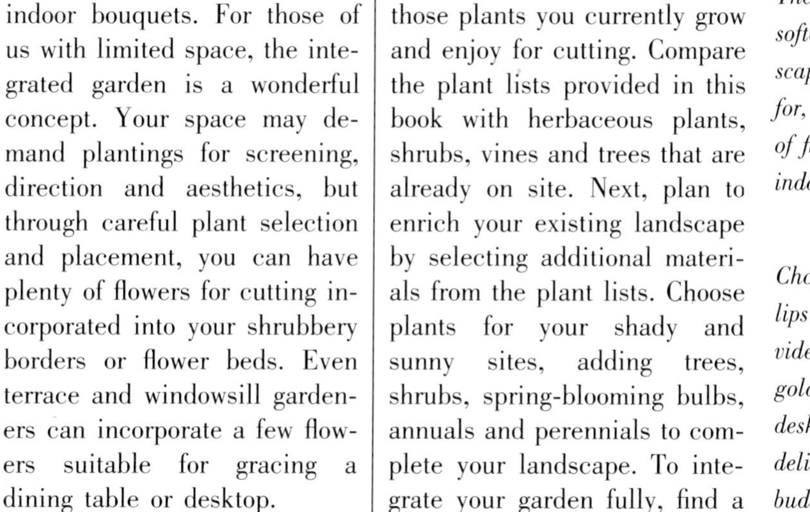

Not everyone has the space for a garden with the sole purpose to provide cutting materials for indoor bouquets. For those of us with limited space, the integrated garden is a wonderful concept. Your space may demand plantings for screening, direction and aesthetics, but through careful plant selection and placement, you can have plenty of flowers for cutting incorporated into your shrubbery borders or flower beds. Even terrace and windowsill gardeners can incorporate a few flowers suitable for gracing a dining table or desktop.

The basis of integrated landscaping is to start with careful site analysis. Study the existing landscape and take note of those plants you currently grow and enjoy for cutting. Compare the plant lists provided in this book with herbaceous plants, shrubs, vines and trees that are already on site. Next, plan to enrich your existing landscape by selecting additional materials from the plant lists. Choose plants for your shady and sunny sites, adding trees, shrubs, spring-blooming bulbs, annuals and perennials to complete your landscape. To integrate your garden fully, find a niche for some culinary herbs,

Chosen with care, a few yellow tulips with a delicate rose blush provide warmth and complement the golden tones of an antique oak desk. The deep red bowl and the delicately blushed Amalanchier *buds provide contrasting texture and help to unify color.*

This old, glazed crock holds a rich array of summer colors. Even in tones of black, gray and white, though, the composition would be a study in textural contrasts: smooth against rough, fine against coarse.

The glory of autumn foliage and feathery plumes collected from the garden and byways.

some vegetables and some fruiting trees and shrubs. Not only will your landscape be beautiful but it will be useful as well, a pleasure for all the senses.

This book isn't meant to be a tutorial on landscape design, but I will occasionally use this space to introduce some of the design elements useful for both the landscape and the vase. Perhaps the most important element of design is function. The landscape must serve a need: to improve or hide a view; to direct the eye or garden visitor; or to provide a harvest of flowers, vegetables or herbs. Flowers arranged in a vase also have function: to decorate a dining table, to accentuate a specific architectural feature or to cover an unsightly flaw; the form the flowers will take in the vase is determined by the function of that arrangement.

Other facets of design are scale, or proportion. Scale is a function of size relationships. The larger the space, the larger the plants can be to fill that space. When dealing with flowers in vases, scale is easily understood. Large flowers placed in tiny vases look silly and give the impression of being top heavy. A tiny vase of flowers centered in the middle of a large dining table looks insignificant and is dwarfed by the expanse of its surroundings.

Texture in the visual sense is the appearance of materials, whether in the landscape or in a vase. Playing a variety of textures off each other heightens the visual excitement of the composition. I liken this to rubbing first sandpaper and then velvet; the velvet feels all the softer after the fingers have experienced coarse sandpaper. In the garden try combining astilbe and hosta, for example. The soft, feathery plumes of astilbe seem to appear even more fluffy when viewed next to the smooth texture of the large hosta leaves.

Perhaps the design element that receives the most attention is color. Color can seem cool, as in the case of blue, lavender and green, or hot, as in the case of orange, red and bright pink. Combinations of color can be subtle, bold, monochromatic or multicolored. Careful use of color in the landscape can create interest, attract attention to specific areas, make portions of the garden seem to recede in the landscape or magically bring the farthest corner of the garden closer. Dark colors recede in a shady nook, for example, whereas bright colors such as yellow and white bring the farthest corners closer. Color preference is a personal matter. We all have favorite colors that appear in our home decor or our wardrobe. Color in the integrated cutting garden will reappear in the home when flowers are harvested and brought indoors.

Rhythm as it applies to design always reminds me of the old roadside Burma Shave signs of a generation ago. They were situated to flow in sequence at a natural pace as one drove along. In the garden or vase, of course, rhythm isn't a matter of spacing a few signs. Rather, it is placing elements in a natural way so the eye can appreciate them without interruption in its natural flow. Some guidelines for rhythm will be helpful to the novice designer. An odd number of elements is invariably more successful than an even number. I don't actually count numbers of flowers when I start to arrange, and one can make dynamite arrangements using even numbers of flowers, but threes, fives and sevens tend to create a natural rhythm without forming stiff, easily recognized lines or boxes. Unlike some commercially grown flowers, garden flowers grow in a variety of sizes and shapes; even blossoms cut from the same plant may be of different sizes. When trying to achieve balance, proportion and rhythm in an arrangement, it is a good idea to place the smaller, individual flowers toward the outside. This means the higher an element is placed in an arrangement, the smaller it should be.

Rhythm in the garden is affected by plant placement. Remember, when placing plants in the landscape, smaller plants musn't be shaded by larger plants. Short plants deserve a place in the foreground of the border, whereas larger specimens will be more appreciated at the back of the border where they won't cover their more diminutive neighbors.

The best effect is gained by planting in multiples, and when the plants mature they will appear as a single grouping. This is as true of many trees and shrubs as it is of annuals and perennials. Planting multiples will prevent a busy look, and

PLANT LIST FOR AN INTEGRATED CUTTING GARDEN (SUITABLE FOR USDA ZONE 5)

WOODY PLANTS

1. *Malus* spp., crabapple (1)
2. *Oxydendron arborescens,* sorrel tree (1)
3. *Tsuga canadensis,* Canadian hemlock (1)
4. *Thuja occidentalis,* arborvitae (1)
5. *Deutzia gracillis,* slender deutzia (3)
6. *Kalmia latifolia,* mountain laurel (1)
7. *Rosa* spp., climbing rose (1)
8. *Rhododendron* spp., azalea (2)

HERBACEOUS PLANTS

9. *Hosta* × 'Royal Standard', perennial (24); underplant with daffodils and narcissuses (48)
10. *Hosta* × 'So Sweet', perennial (24)
11. *Convallaria majus,* lily of the valley, perennial (36)
12. *Nicotiana alata* 'Fragrant Cloud', annual (12); allow to self-sow
13. *Miscanthus sinensis* 'Zebrinus', perennial (1)
14. *Delphinium elatum* 'Pacific Hybrids', perennial (8)
15. *Digitalis purpurea,* foxglove, biennial (12); allow to self-sow
16. *Paeonia lactifolia,* peony, perennial (6)
17. *Gypsophila paniculata* 'Bristol Fairy', baby's breath, perennial (1); underplant with giant alliums (8)
18. *Achillea* × 'Coronation Gold', yarrow, perennial (6)
19. *Artemisia ludoviciana albula* 'Silver King', perennial (5)
20. *Aquilegia* × *hybrida* 'McKana Hybrids', columbine, perennial (6)
21. *Cosmos bipinnatus* 'Sensation Mixed', annual (12)
22. *Zinnia elegans* 'Cut and Come Again', annual (12); underplant with mixed tulips (24)
23. *Antirrhinum majus* 'Rocket Mixed', snapdragon, annual (36); underplant with tulips (36)
24. *Molucella laevis,* bells of Ireland, annual (6)
25. *Tagetes signata* 'Lemon Gem', signet marigold, annual (18); underplant with tulips (24)

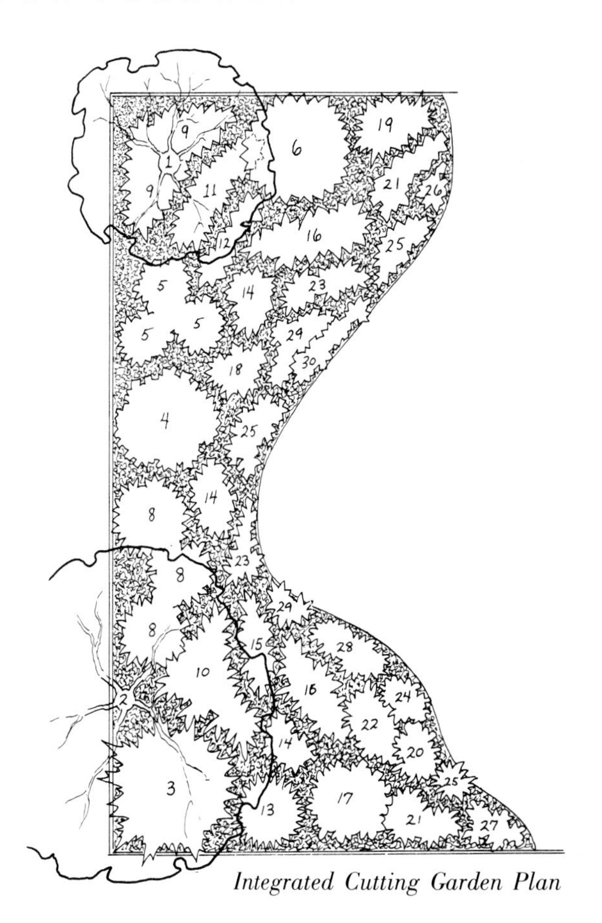

Integrated Cutting Garden Plan

26. *Reseda odorata,* mignonette, annual (12)
27. *Amaranthus caudatus,* love-lies-bleeding, annual (6)
28. *Callistephus chinensis* 'Powder Puff Bouquet', aster, annual (8)
29. *Scabiosa atropurpurea* 'Imperial Mixed', pincushion flower, annual (12)
30. *Tropaeolum majus* 'Glorious Glean', nasturtium, annual (12)

help bring the garden picture together. Repeating clusters of certain plants, colors, textures or lines will create rhythm and add to the unified effect.

The integrated cutting garden shown in the plan above is designed to be both beautiful in the landscape and provide a generous source of materials for cutting. This garden plan considers the elements of design: color, texture, line, function, scale and rhythm. Notice the intentional creation of shade using small trees suitable for cutting and year-'round interest in the landscape, and the selection of plants with seasonal fruits, berries or pods and interesting bark or twig configuration. When harvesting materials from the integrated cutting garden, remember that the integrated garden has several functions. You may harvest several stems of peony blooms, but you must remember this will detract slightly from the overall landscape effect. With this in mind, plant enough of each variety for both cutting and landscape display.

2

THE CUTTING GARDEN PLANTING AND GROWING GUIDE

No matter what style of garden you have the time, energy and land to support, success in the cutting garden relies on plant selection, site preparation and planting. Take the time to do the job right in the beginning, and the payback will be healthier plants with greater production of cutable flowers and larger and more perfect blooms. Choose the right plant for the site. This is a basic axiom of good horticulture. Trying to grow plants under less-than-favorable conditions will invariably be an invitation to trouble. Plants grown in inadequate light will be leggy as they stretch to reach the sun. Flower stems may be weak and production will be diminished. When planning for an area not in full sun, choose plants that do well in shade or dappled sunlight such as astilbe, hosta and nicotiana (see "Flowers for the Shady Cutting Garden," page 88). Similarly, don't expect hosta or other shade lovers to thrive in full sun.

Take the time to become acquainted with your garden. Some areas offer light shade but will support such plants as snapdragons, which thrive in full sun and require cool conditions. Drainage patterns and soil types can affect the success of your garden ventures.

If bread is the staff of life for the body, then soil is the staff of life for the garden. All plants require water, nutrients and air to grow, and these are supplied by the soil. Most of us garden in less-than-desirable soils. Sometimes we joke that our gardens yield more rock than soil, or that we might just as well be growing plants at the beach. The best soil for the greatest variety of plants is a rich, well-draining garden loam. *Loam* describes soil texture; typically it is an equal mix of sand, silt and clay particles. A loam soil will hold its shape (remember dirt bombs?) when compressed in a fist into a ball but will not show the details of the hand print. Heavier or more claylike soils will also form a ball when compressed, but on close inspection, you will be able to identify details of the hand print (the ultimate dirt bomb). Clay soils tend to drain poorly and can become very hard—like concrete, if not carefully handled. Sandy soils will not easily form a ball when compressed and collapse when the fist is relaxed. Sandy soils usually drain too well and offer plants poor nutrition, as water moves quickly through the sand, carrying the nutrients away into the subsoil. Most of us garden on some mixture of the three soil types, and any garden soil, somewhere be-

A cutting garden, planted in the wide-row style. Asters, bachelor buttons, signet marigolds, cirsium and pansies provide abundant flowers for bouquets.

Clay soil compressed in the hand will form a dense "dirt bomb," showing details of the handprint.

Sandy soil compressed in the hand will not hold together and crumbles easily when pressure is released.

Loamy soil will form a loose "dirt bomb" when compressed, but will not show the details of the handprint, and will crumble easily.

tween pure sand and pure clay, offers good garden potential.

If your soil is less than adequate, what can you do? The answer to most soil problems is organic matter in any of a number of forms: compost, leaf mold, peat moss, well-rotted manure or green manure crops. (Green manure refers to particular plants that are seeded, grown briefly and then turned into the soil, where the tender young shoots quickly break down and become part of the organic portion of the soil.) Organic matter added to any soil benefits that soil. The bulk of organic matter will lighten a heavy or claylike soil, increasing the space between soil particles and allowing for faster drainage and more air around the roots to stimulate root growth. In addition, organic matter helps bind tiny soil particles together into aggregate particles. In a sandy soil, organic matter will help increase water-holding capacity and hold some nutrients that are easily washed away by water traveling through the soil. I liken organic matter to fiber in the human diet; it's essential to keep everything working as it should. It isn't enough to have one dose of dietary fiber during a lifetime, it is likewise essential to add organic matter to the garden continuously to keep soil happy and healthy.

Prepare the site for your cutting garden well in advance of planting time. Outline your beds and determine the location of rows and borders. Begin incorporating organic matter in as many forms as possible—it is difficult to overindulge your soil in organic matter. Adding a total of 4 to 6 inches of organic matter is a good start. Mix the soil well. For woody plants or long-lived perennials, this is your one opportunity to enrich the soil thoroughly.

Have the pH of your soil tested. PH is the measure of acidity/alkalinity. Tests for pH are simple and often done at no cost at local cooperative extension headquarters and even some garden centers. Is it necessary to add topsoil to your existing soil? *Topsoil* is a term frequently misused. People generally envision topsoil as a wonderfully dark, rich loam soil ideal for plant growth. Unfortunately, there are no regulations for topsoil, and the quality varies greatly with the purveyor and source. In fact, buying topsoil can sometimes do more harm than good. Buy topsoil only if you need to change the grade of your property. Examine the soil before delivery and make sure it doesn't come from land treated with herbicides.

When you are ready to prepare the soil, choose a day when it is moist but not soggy. If you can hear squishing as you walk or can squeeze water from a handful of soil, or if soil clings overmuch to tools or shoes, it is probably too wet to work without destroying soil texture. Wet soils tend to lose structure when worked or when they receive too much foot or vehicular traffic. It is a good idea to perform other garden duties when soils are wet. If soils are too dry and powdery, it is a good idea to wait until after a rain, or water the site a day or two before working the soil, so that it will have a nice, moist texture.

Some of the best gardens are double dug. Double digging is a method by which you loosen and enrich the soil to a depth of 16 to 18 inches. Double digging benefits the garden for years to come. After the initial garden preparation, add the soil amendments. These can be mixed into the soil using the more traditional garden turning method or with a rotary tiller. I love to work with soil and find the creation of rich, well-prepared soil a warming, fulfilling experience. There is nothing more satisfying than a well-prepared planting bed.

If you have done your soil preparation in advance of planting, perhaps in the fall before a spring planting, I recommend the use of a cover crop such as winter rye or winter wheat that will grow over the winter and then be turned under in the spring. This will hold the soil in place and discourage weeds. For areas of a few square feet, it may be more practical to mulch this area well with shredded leaves, compost, straw or pine needles to protect the soil from exposure to washing rains and blowing wind. Nature almost never leaves bare soil unprotected.

When it comes to planting, always choose plants that can be expected to do well in your environment; don't impose your environment on plants that won't be happy there. Plants purchased for inclusion in your cutting garden should come from a reputable dealer. Choose varieties with care, as some breeders have worked to develop varieties that are short and may not be good for cutting. The plant portraits (page 45) recommend specific varieties to ask for. Look for plants that are strong and actively growing in the spring. Yellowed foliage or faded flowers in the pot or the plant pack suggest they have been neglected, exposed to extreme conditions or should have been transplanted already.

Dig a hole a little larger than the root system of each plant to be sure the roots are not crowded. Leave enough room so that the plant can mature without crowding its neighbors. The mature spacing depends on the plant, but generally speaking, tall plants need more space than the more petite ones. Carefully remove the plant from its container (plants slip out of their pots or cells much more readily when wet). On very root-bound specimens it is always a good idea to slice through the root system in two or three locations from the top of the root ball to the bottom to encourage new roots to branch out into the soil.

Place the plants in the garden at the same depth they were at in the pots or cells. Firm the soil around the base of the plant, and water in well with a watering can or breaker (see Watering in the Garden, page 21) to settle the soil around the root ball. Until young plants are thoroughly established in their new location it may be necessary to water frequently so that plants will not be stressed as they develop new supporting root systems.

Note: Plants benefit from a second application of fertilizer in midseason. This "side-dress" fertilizer dosage is applied in a band around each plant. Avoid direct contact between plant stems and fertilizer, as the fertilizer may burn.

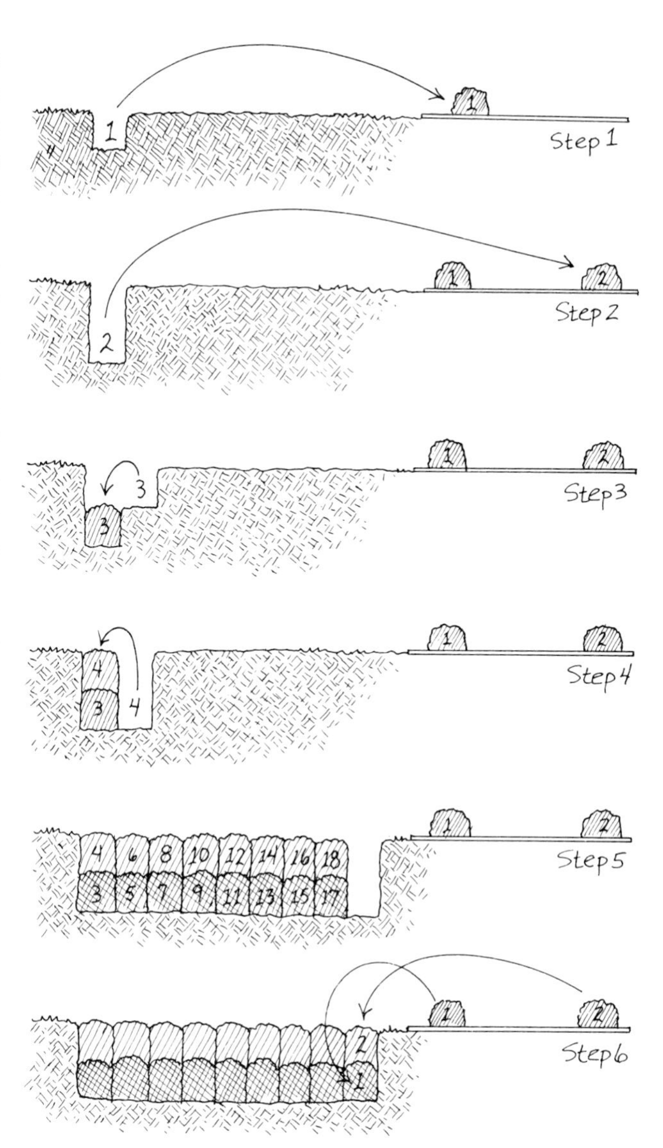

Double digging is the best way to prepare flower beds for planting.

WIDE-ROW PLANTING IN THE CUTTING GARDEN

In the cutting garden, wide-row plantings are more practical than single rows. A row of plants one plant wide (single row) requires more space for the "aisles" between rows; the plants are more exposed to wind and compacted soils. Wide rows may be from 18 to 36 inches wide and as long as the garden. Each row is basically a bed of plants. Plants grown in wide rows are surrounded by other plants, not by the hard, compacted soil of walkways. Plants grown side by side in wide rows will shade out weeds that compete for nutrients and water. Each plant is supported by its neighbors. This way you have less staking to do and can frequently provide plant support for a whole

Well-prepared soil is healthy soil, and healthy soil yields healthy plants. The lush growth and heavy bloom on this Brugmansia *(angel's trumpet) in the Mohonk Gardens is an indication of a well-tended garden soil. Copious amounts of organic matter added each year ensure good results.*

Asters for cutting have long, straight stems and are borne on tall plants. Many dwarf strains of aster are sold for bedding as well. Be sure the varieties you choose for inclusion in your cutting garden will produce cutting stems.

Plants staked for protection from summer rains and winds are grown in a cutting garden at Mohonk Mountain House. The sturdy bamboo stakes are placed next to plants at the beginning of the growing season.

block of plants rather than individuals. Perhaps the biggest advantage to wide-row planting is the space savings. Space is at a premium in any garden. A garden located near a water source in full sun, and soil that has been enriched and is ready for planting are valuable commodities. Use those enriched soil areas as growing spaces, not for paths between rows of plants.

For wide-row plantings some support may be necessary, but the single-stake method may not be suitable. Corner supports can hold weave-wire fencing horizontally about 1 foot over the row. Plants can grow through the wire and get the support they need. Another useful method of supporting plants grown in rows is to provide sturdy support at each end of the row and stretch tiers of heavy twine or wire along the length of the row, trellis style. Plants can be secured to the wire or allowed to lean against the trellis.

In the integrated cutting garden, support should be more discrete. Many plant supports are sold in garden shops and from mail-order houses. They provide a neat, finished look when incorporated in the garden, and are frequently designed to last for many seasons. For generations, European gardeners have used twiggy branches of shrubs or trees to stake plants in the garden. Choose a branch of suitable height and firmly implant it in the ground at the base of the young plants (but not so near as to damage their roots). As the plants grow up through the twigs, they gain support without being "tied to the stake" and cover the branch at the same time. If using bamboo, choose stakes dyed green as they will blend discretely with foliage.

No matter what staking method you choose, it should support the plant throughout the season. Be careful to tie plants to supports with twine or covered-wire twisters that won't cut into tender stems. Some gardeners use strips of cloth. Allow a generous space between stake, stem and plant tie to avoid cutting into and girdling tender stems. Girdled stems are less efficient and result in stunted plant growth, or may kill the plant outright. Improper plant support can damage stems, weakening them and making them more prone to breakage. Nothing is more frustrating than nurturing a plant to the brink of flower production only to have it damaged as a result of poor staking or no staking!

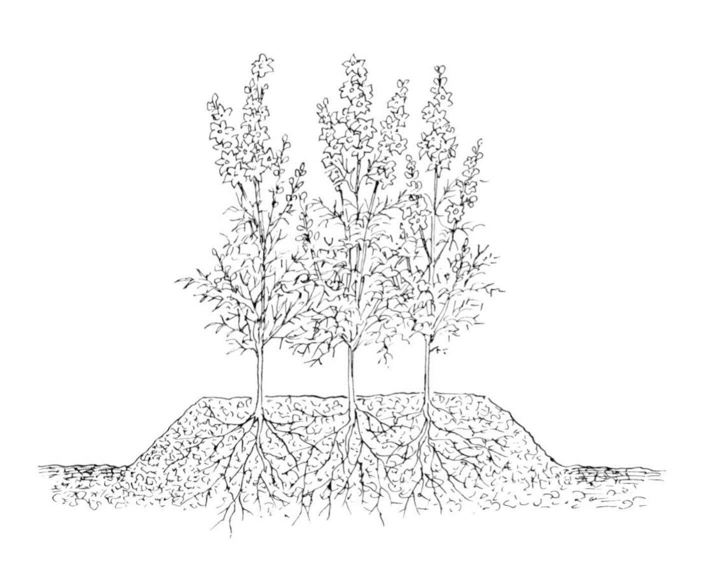

Wide-row planting, as with this planting of larkspur, creates orderly plant communities. Among the benefits are root support and decreased weed growth.

Watering in the Garden

In the garden, water ensures good plant growth and is essential for new plants to establish themselves. All too frequently I see people spraying their plants with hoses and the kind of nozzles designed for washing cars. Delicate misty sprays are great for young seedlings, but more mature plants need larger amounts of water aimed at the roots. Invest in an old-fashioned watering can, good for watering a few plants, and a breaker with an extension handle for supplying a generous amount of water around the plants' roots. Water breakers look very much like shower heads and behave in the same way, dividing a steady stream of water into numerous, more gentle streams. The quantity of water is not altered, but the force is "broken" and the effectiveness is improved.

PEST CONTROL

Pest control in the garden begins in the planning stage. Pests in the garden are a nuisance, but never is an aphid infestation or botrytis outbreak more disheartening than when you find it has made flowers that appear passable in the garden unsuitable for harvesting and using indoors in arrangements. The sight of a string of aphids marching boldly across the dining table in search of new marigolds to explore is beyond compare. A pest control program need not be expensive, time-consuming or injurious to the environment. Success in controlling pests is nothing more than good garden practices.

When it comes to winning the battle against pests, careful attention to site selection and bed preparation are critical to success. Choose plants that will perform well in your garden, for they will be best equipped to fend off attacks by pests and disease. Every garden has microclimates that offer nuances of sunlight, heat, drainage and so forth. Learn about the microclimates in your garden and use them to maximize your cutting garden's growing capacity.

Carefully study the varieties available from your favorite seed source or garden center, and choose those varieties that offer disease resistance or tolerance. Inbred disease resistance isn't a feature of every variety, but it is a necessity for some plants—asters, for example. The key words are *resistance* and *tolerance.* These mean exactly what they say. A plant resistant to a disease will be less likely to get the disease; still, when that plant's resistance is weakened by poor growing conditions or constant bombardment with disease spores, the inbred resistance

Wide-row planting provides beds 24 inches wide with 18-inch rows between. Mulched paths reduce soil compaction and improve water conservation and weed reduction. The plants in the rows are planted four or five across. They help support each other and create a dense canopy that further inhibits weed growth.

may become ineffective. *Tolerance* is a term that means that a plant may "carry" the disease without showing symptoms or effect. Diseases may become symptomatic even on tolerant plants, if they are weakened by poor growing conditions.

Once plants have been selected, don't skimp on planting or care. A wise gardener once told me that you should dig a $10 hole for a $2 plant; in other words, take the time to plant your living investment well. Seeds, seedlings, nursery-grown perennials and woody plants all need some nursing and special care during the first weeks of life in your garden. The first few days or weeks are critical. Remember, water is the important element during this time. Like humans, plants can live for a long time without "food," but life is snuffed out remarkably quickly without water. The key to successful pest control is to keep plants healthy and stress free. Healthy growth requires adequate nutrition.

So, you've done everything right and still have insect and disease problems. Time to go to the sprayer and chemical arsenal, right? Wrong! Keep trying to maintain plant vigor and health through good gardening practices such as proper watering and fertility. Don't neglect weeding! I've always looked on weeding as a great mind release—my own style of meditation. Weeds crowd plants and can encourage diseases by stifling air flow around them; stagnant, damp air can encourage disease. Weeds are also great competitors for water and nutrients. Use mulches to control weeds and help maintain constant soil moisture levels.

Good gardening means going into the garden with eyes wide open and on the look-out for discolored leaves, the first Japanese beetle or a wilting seedling. Often these are the first indications of trouble brewing. What to do when you see that first beetle? Kill it—that's right, kill it! Just pick it up and squish it. It's as simple as that. In the amount of time it takes to apply a pesticide, you can hand-pick and destroy all sorts of pests before they have a chance to multiply and populate your entire garden. Diseased leaves can also be picked, a good means of control if symptoms are noticed early. Once a disease has spread, you may do more damage than good if you hand-pick diseased leaves to the point of defoliating plants. If only one plant of many shows symptoms, consider roguing the entire plant. If leaves are falling off the plant due to disease, gather them and remove them from the garden. Don't add these harbingers of disease to your compost heap; you will just invite trouble later on. Insects that are too small to hand-pick are sometimes easy to spray off with the water hose. Hand-picking, bug squishing and aphid washing are all examples of cultural controls. Repeat cultural controls as necessary. Cultural controls were the mainstay of garden pest control

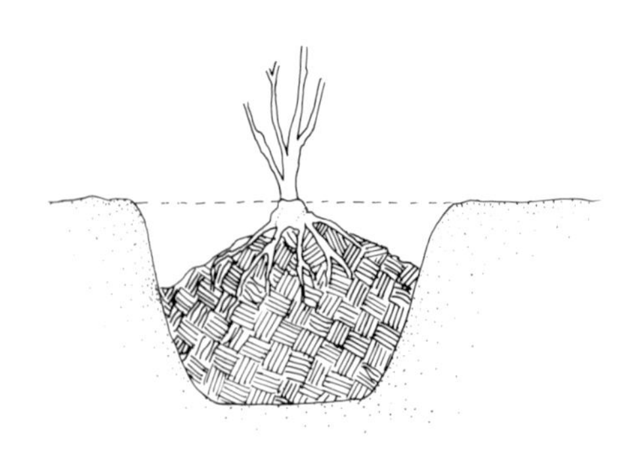

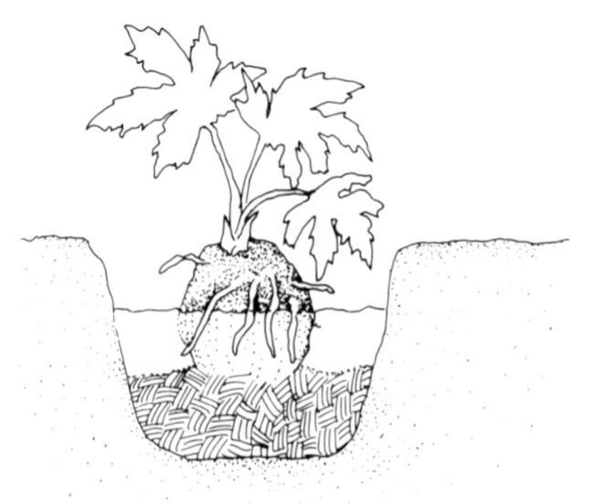

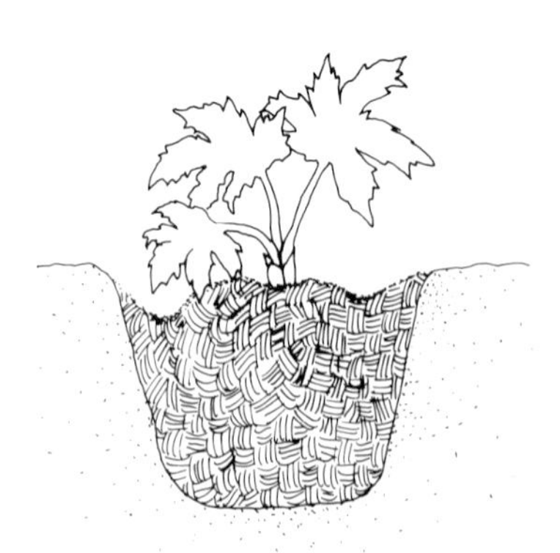

When planting nursery-grown plants, always create a hole larger than the existing root ball. Arrange the soil depth so that the plant will be at the same depth as it was in the nursery. Then backfill with soil that has been amended with organic matter. Tamp the soil carefully to eliminate air pockets before watering in well.

programs before the days of chemical pesticides, the inaccurately named "wonder drugs" of the plant world.

If all else fails, and sometimes it does, it may become necessary to introduce a pesticide into the landscape to control an insect or disease. Pesticides need not be dangerous chemicals. A few drops of liquid detergent in water has some insecticidal action. With environmental concerns in mind, pesticide manufacturers are looking for products that do the job of eliminating unwanted populations with minimal hazard to the environment and user. Many new products are biological or botanical pesticides. Your local cooperative extension agent can advise you as to which products are safest to use.

As the gardening season draws to a close, the garden still needs attention. Annuals in the cutting garden are often still going strong until hit by frost. A killing frost will damage the tender annuals first, leaving some such as snapdragons to continue producing until late in the season. Some plants such as *Echinacea, Rudbeckia, Nigella* and *Scabiosa* provide interesting seed heads for dried arrangements. Healthy annuals damaged by frost can be added to compost heaps where they will break down and provide lots of valuable organic matter.

Carefully lift and store tender roots for next year. Dig the tubers of the most successful dahlias, favorite gladiolas and *Acidanthera.* Clean off excess garden soil and remove damaged roots. Allow them to dry for several days in a shaded, frost-free location. Pack in slightly damp sand, peat moss or wood shavings and store in a cool, frost-free place until spring. Be sure to examine these roots at every step of the overwintering process for signs of insects or disease, and discard any that show signs of infestation.

Labels are critical, as memory often fades with the bright autumn foliage. Be as explicit as possible. Although names are important, you'll save time if you also provide your own description: "My favorite apricot dahlia, three feet tall, best cutting stems!" Organize labels, stakes and pots, not only to protect them from winter weather but to give you a head start in spring. Make notes in a notebook. Your end-of-season notes will reward you ten-fold next spring.

The first killing frost marks the official end of the gardening season—or does it? The autumn garden is full of cutting opportunities. Brightening fall foliage deserves a place indoors. Fall-blooming asters and chrysanthemums last for weeks and look refreshed when arranged with bright scarlet and yellow leaves. The cutting garden continues to yield berries, interesting twig shapes and bark textures as well as dried flowers and seedpods until the snow flies.

The approach of winter indicates the need for protection for tender plantings, exposed broad-leaved evergreen shrubs and newly planted perennials and bulbs. Winter protection may consist of snow fencing; burlap wind breaks; or branches of pine, spruce or fir placed against tender evergreen shrubs. Pine straw, evergreen boughs and straw also provide good insulating cover for bulbs and tender and evergreen perennials. Snow is the best insulating cover, but in areas where snow cover may be suspect, 3 to 6 inches of lightweight mulch will do the job. The concept of winter mulch is not to keep the soil warm. Applied after the ground has started to freeze, a winter mulch will help keep the soil uniformly frozen, and then will help prevent damage from frost heaving due to freezing, thawing and refreezing of soils.

When preparing garden plants for winter, avoid tightly wrapping plants, especially with clear or dark plastics. Light-colored, "breathable" fabrics may be used to protect, but in wrapping plants tightly, you run the risk of heat buildup on sunny days that may cause winter buds to break dormancy or encourage an outbreak of fungal organisms.

Maintaining healthy plants in the garden is a combination of proper cultural techniques and good plant selection. Matricaria *(fever few),* Artemisia *and* Nepeta *(cat mint) are usually free from insects and disease when grown under ideal circumstances.*

3

HARVESTING THE CUTTING GARDEN

Harvesting flowers and greens from the cutting garden is wonderfully rewarding. Picking flowers is a pastime we enjoy from childhood. The term *picking* brings to mind small, pudgy, childish fingers grasping delicate flower stems and wrestling tattered blossoms from the parent plants to be presented in a woeful, endearing bouquet.

Cutting flowers from the home garden has an advantage to using the commercial florist; we have the ability to choose specific blooms with the size and shape we need. Always look for flowers that are still maturing and developing, and free of insects and disease. Flowers that are starting to fade should be harvested and discarded before the plant sets seed, as you would in deadheading any garden. Older flowers will not last as long in a bouquet as younger blooms. An occasional damaged petal may be carefully removed from most flowers without altering the overall beauty of the blossom.

Success in harvesting flowers depends on three factors: sharp cuts, clean water and containers, and proper pruning or cutting. Let's look at the act of cutting flowers. Flowers are attached to the plants with stems. Sometimes individual flowers are attached closely together along the stem, as in snapdragons. In other instances, single blossoms may be found at the end of a stem, as in asters. If you consider harvesting stems instead of blossoms, the harvesting of flowers is basically the same. An understanding of the basics of pruning and plant structure will help you get the most from each cut in the garden. With most plants, both vegetative (leaves and stems) and reproductive (flowers) growth starts out as buds. Buds are found along the stems of plants, and usually it is easy to tell vegetative buds from flower buds. Flower buds are plump and rounded. Vegetative

Cutting stems of flowers is an act of pruning. Care should be taken to balance stem length with foliage loss which will affect plant health.

Mohonk Flower Girl, circa 1901. Courtesy of the Mohonk Mountain House Archives. Gathering flowers for a bouquet from the garden is still a rewarding experience today.

The Knife Myth

Almost every flower-arranging book I have read over the years states unequivocally that you must make cuts with a sharp knife. Few of them actually tell you how it is done without damaging plants and drawing blood from straining fingers. Many professional florists do use a knife as they find it less cumbersome to use. By grasping the knife handle between the pad of the thumb and the ring and pinkie fingers, you can work with thumb, first and middle fingers to handle flowers. The technique is to hold the knife stationary in the hand and hold the flower stem at an angle between knife and thumb. Hold the flower stem in the left hand and pull the knife back with the right hand while holding it tightly against the stem. The blade will cut the stem and not move against the thumb. This technique takes time to perfect and works best with a relatively short, straight-bladed knife. Your knife, like other tools, must be kept clean and sharp. A dull knife will make you work harder and strain with the blade, and it is when you are straining that the knife may slip and cause injury.

There is no reason why you can't achieve excellent results when using good, clean, sharp pruning tools. If the cut is clean and the tool is clean, the stem will function well in a vase of water.

buds are frequently found in the axils of leaves where leaves join stems. When cutting, if you make a sharp cut back to a vegetative bud you will encourage a new stem from that bud. All cuts should be made with a clean pruner or utility shears. Cut close to the bud, leaving about ¼ inch above the bud. Whether cutting flowers or pruning, you can control the shape of the plant and the direction of new growth by cutting to buds that face away from the center of the plant. Outward-facing buds will produce new stem growth in the direction they are facing. By pruning this way, you encourage new growth that will receive maximum sun and allow for open branching, which is less prone to disease.

Some plants don't produce lateral buds and will not branch when cut, among them many of the bulbous plants such as tulips, lilies and gladioluses. Bulbous plants need to produce as much foliage as possible to maintain bulb health and vigor. When harvesting tulips and their like, take only as much stem length as necessary for your design. Leave as much foliage as possible to strengthen the bulb. To

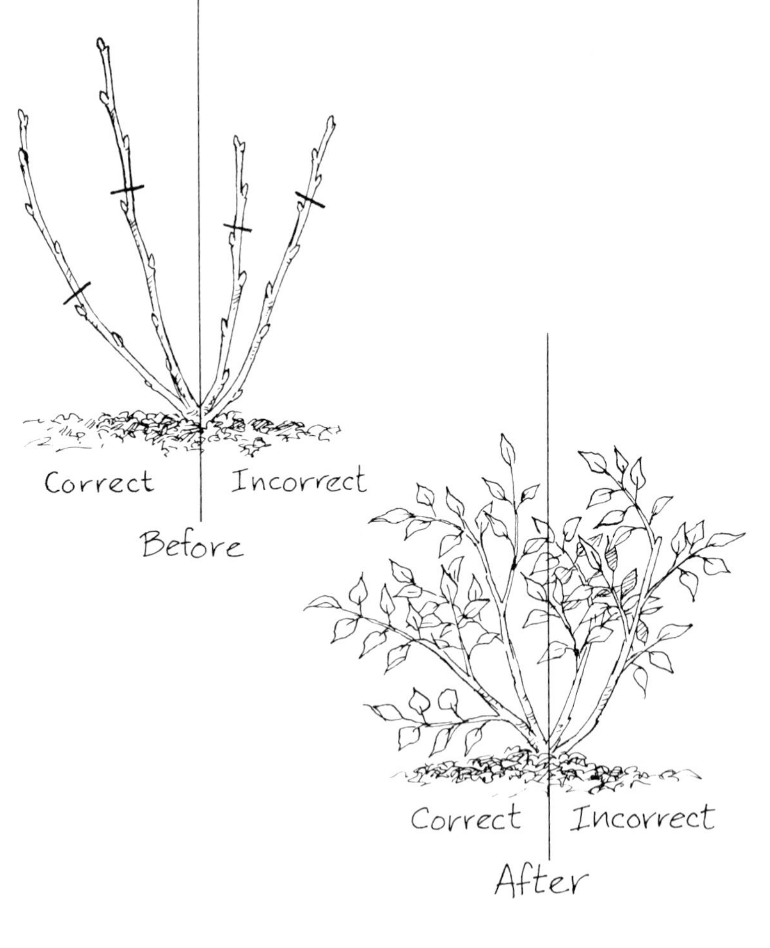

Harvesting flower stems from woody plants not only affects the shape of the plant, but will affect its health, as well. Carefully make cuts that will "open up" the center of the plant and eliminate problems in the future.

When used properly, a sharp knife will cut the stem and not the hand!

maximize stem length, professional cut-flower growers will uproot an entire plant and cut off the bulb at the base of the stem. You may choose to take this extreme measure with some plants, but be forewarned the bulb will probably never produce again.

Trees and shrubs offer many wonderful cut flowers, fresh greens and attractive, seasonal fruits. Forcing flowers in the winter months is greatly rewarding and easy to do (see page 33). Winter cutting should only be done when air temperatures are above freezing. Be very careful when cutting from woody plants because the woody structure is permanent. The basic pruning rules still apply. When cutting from trees and shrubs, cut stems flush with a branch or cut back to an outward-facing bud or budded branch.

A wide variety of cutting tools is available from mail-order catalogs, garden centers, nurseries and hardware stores. The tool should be clean and sharp. I prefer lightweight utility shears for work with most herbaceous materials. When you have to strain to use the lightweight shears, it means the tool can't handle the job. Trying to cut too heavy a stem with lightweight tools may damage the shears, the stem or both. Ragged cuts on the stem will have a more difficult time absorbing water. Ragged cuts left on the plant invite disease and insect infestations. For heavy or woody stems up to ½ inch in diameter, a hand pruner is the tool of choice. I recommend a shear-type pruner (my favorite has replaceable parts, including springs and blades). When stems exceed ½ inch it may be necessary to bring out the lopping shears. Lightweight loppers appear to have the blade mechanism of the hand pruner with extended handles to increase leverage. Not only do loppers increase cutting potential but they provide added reach, handy when working with large shrubs or small trees.

You may want a flowering or fruiting branch that is clearly out of reach. Though ladders are an option, they are unstable in most garden situations. A pole pruner with an extension handle will provide cutting ability at heights of 10 or more feet. Choose the right tool for the job. The investment in a few extra moments to go and get the lopper will save time, strain, extend the life of your hand pruner and give you the quality cut needed to extend the life of the cut stem and ensure continued health of the tree or shrub in the garden.

Woody stems of mountain laurel and Polygonum *require time to condition. For best results, pick flowers in the evening the day before they are to be used, and condition them overnight in a cool location.*

WHEN TO HARVEST

With care, flowers can be successfully harvested at any time of the day. For the most successful arrangements, I recommend that you cut in the cool of the evening and let your fresh-cut flowers condition in water in a cool place overnight. Experience and a hectic lifestyle prove, however, that we don't always have the time to harvest under ideal conditions. We must "cut when the knife is sharp," to quote my mentor, Ruth Smiley, guardian angel of the Mohonk Mountain House Gardens for more than 50 years. And so we find ourselves picking flowers under the noonday sun and by flashlight or in the rain. As the seasons change, the ideal picking time varies somewhat. As August passes to September it is good to pick during the warmer afternoon hours when the plants have started to draw water from their roots. Plants that thrive in hot weather really appreciate the midafternoon heat.

CONDITIONING

Many flowers are happy to go from garden to vase and will last very nicely without special treatment. However, I've found that the life expectancy of cut flowers and greens will greatly increase when cut flowers and greens are "conditioned" before finding a home in a vase of water. This is even more important when designing flowers in floral foam such as Oasis or when using devises such as pin holders or marbles. During the conditioning process, flowers and greens absorb water unimpeded until all the plant parts are completely pumped with water and turgid.

When flowers are cut in the garden they are not quite ready to plunge into water. Careful preparation of cut materials is another step. After coming in

Artemisia *and* Xeranthemum *dry easily when suspended upside down in a warm, dry, dark place.*

Large-petaled daisy flowers such as Rudbeckia *can be difficult to condition successfully. For successful arrangements, take the time to condition them properly.*

Temperature Requirements of Common Garden Cut Flowers and Foliage

Cool (room) temperatures are best for spring-flowering herbaceous plants such as violets, forget-me-nots, spring-flowering bulbs such as tulips and the tender foliage of ferns.

Warm temperatures (100 to 120 degrees Fahrenheit) will condition the widest variety of flowers and foliage. When conditioning an unfamiliar species, try warm water first; chances are it will give excellent results.

Hot water (about 150 degrees Fahrenheit) is best for cuttings from trees and shrubs. On tender plants hot water may actually cause tender stems to break down and impede their success. Hot water is best for roses, hydrangea, lilacs, crabapples and flowering cherries.

Consult the plant portraits (page 45) for the recommended conditioning temperatures for plants included in this book.

from the garden, take the time to remove carefully most of the foliage from each flower stem. The more foliage is removed, the better the blossom will last in the vase. It is essential to remove any foliage that will be under water during the conditioning process and later in the vase. With some plants it is effective to grasp the stem loosely above the set of leaves you wish to remove and pull downward toward the base of the stem. Tools sold as stem "strippers" will also do the job, but I feel that most of them do unnecessary damage to tender stems. Discard healthy foliage into a basket for incorporation in the compost heap. The occasional stem may resist stripping and you may find it necessary to use a knife or snips to remove foliage. Now is the time to remove thorns that may interfere with handling later on. Thorns and stubs left on the stems may cause difficulty during arranging as they tend to grasp other stems and make moving them in the vase more difficult.

When foliage and thorns have been removed, recut the stems at an angle, making sure the cut is clean with no ragged edges, and plunge the stems in clean, fresh water up to the lowest set of leaves. Almost any container may be used to condition flowers as long as it is clean and will hold water. If you are a recycler, be wary of containers that formerly held household cleaning products; the residue may be toxic. Cleanliness cannot be stressed enough! Between each use and the next, take the time to clean the container thoroughly. Dirt is the death knell of cut flowers and greens. Residue left in conditioning buckets and in vases breed bacteria, and bacteria clog the cut stems of flowers and foliage, reducing water uptake. Use a disinfectant solution such as chlorine bleach to clean and disinfect containers between each use.

Woody plants are handled in a different fashion. The foliage is stripped as for other cuts; be sure to do a thorough job of it. Some flowering shrubs such as lilacs do best when all the leaves have been removed and so the water absorbed by the stem goes only to the flower. After you have stripped off foliage, make two 1-inch-long cuts into the cut end of the stem using a proper or snips. These cuts should be made along the length of the stem and in effect will quarter the stem. This will increase the woody stem's ability to take up water. Some sources have recommended using a hammer to crush the stems to increase water absorption. I have always felt that the crushed stems will be less able to draw water and are sites that will be susceptible to bacterial growth.

One school of thought insists on cutting all stems under water to prevent exposure to air, which may enter and move up the stem, blocking the passage of water. The logistical challenge of accomplishing this feat when handling a lot of flowers and foliage is daunting. In my experience, success is achievable without cutting stems under water or using specially designed cutters that do the job for you. Properly prepared stems that have been conditioned will be just fine without being cut under water, as long as the cutting tool is sharp and the water and container are clean.

Water temperature is another critical factor in successful conditioning. Most plants prefer one of three water temperature categories: cool water (room temperature), warm or tepid (100 to 120 degrees Fahrenheit) and hot water (about 150 degrees Fahrenheit). Some plants, especially woody plants, require water that is almost boiling to condition or rescue them. When bringing in difficult woody plants such as mock orange (or sometimes even roses), place them in about ½ inch of boiling hot water (don't attempt to keep the water boiling). When the water cools to warm, place the prepared stems into a deep container of hot water and condition overnight. During the conditioning process, containers of prepared flowers are best stored in a cool place away from the sun. Allow the water temperature to cool naturally and in the morning the flowers will be fully turgid and ready for designing.

Several agents to add to the conditioning or vase water have been suggested over the years. Some are based on fact, others on speculation or myth. "Flower food" or floral preservative is sold in flower shops and garden centers. Floral preservative is typically a combination of sugars and antibacterial agents. The professional florist community is divided as to whether benefit is derived from preservatives. I have heard recommendations ranging from aspirin to lemon-lime soda. The commercially prepared preservatives seem to be of value but can be expensive and difficult to find. By far the best way is to start with *clean* containers and to keep that water clean and fresh by adding two to three drops of household chlorine bleach to one gallon of water. This very dilute bleach solution keeps the bacterial population in check—simply and affordably. Use it for conditioning, arranging in vases and other containers and filling the containers after the bouquet is arranged to keep it fresh.

For Sparkling Vases

Clean vases are the key to long-lasting cut-flower arrangements. The best way to keep vases clean is to change the water in the vase frequently to avoid bacteria buildup. Too often we allow the water in a vase of fresh flowers to die along with the flowers. In discarding a vase of dead flowers, you will frequently see murky green, malodorous liquid. The liquid was water but is now a bacterial slurry that has coated the interior of the vase. Simple glass bowls and wide-neck containers are relatively easy to access with sponge and scrubby. Over time, though, the more intricately molded pieces will develop a buildup of bacterial and hard-water deposits. In glass containers this makes for ugly stains that not only taint water and shorten vase life of flowers but ruin the aesthetic effectiveness of the vase. Simple cleaning may start with a bottle brush and elbow grease, but be prepared to add strong chlorine bleach solutions as found in liquid automatic dishwasher products. To reach all the nooks and crannies, try adding a small amount of coarse sand, fish gravel or fired clay kitty litter. Agitating a mixture of cleaning solution and gritty particles will clean dirt from all the crevices. Rinsed well, the container will be ready to use.

COLLECTING FLOWERS AND GREENS

Cutting from the garden offers some logistical problems. It can be difficult to bring containers of water right into the garden. In fact, doing so may slow you down, leaving the cut flowers sitting in strong sunlight. Even though they are in water, strong sunlight does more harm than the water good. I recommend bringing a small, nonbreakable container to the garden when collecting only a few flowers or greens and make a number of quick trips. Several sources offer easily transportable containers with convenient handles. For years, the basket has been used to collect flowers and greens. Though it doesn't hold water, it's light and easy to carry. If using a basket or trug, be sure to work quickly and avoid cutting during the hottest part of the day. As you pick, strip off unnecessary foliage right in the garden. Keeping a bucket or basket for compostables handy will keep the garden looking tidy. Stripping

Forsythia is among the easiest of all spring-flowering branches to force into bloom indoors. A large mass of forsythia can do much to chase away winter's gloom.

Gathering from the Wild

I often stop to collect a few blossoms from the highways and byways for inclusion in arrangements. There is something very special about some of nature's offerings to the cut flower marketplace. Queen Anne's lace, naturalized throughout the Northeast, goldenrod, the native asters and that horrible weed of wet places, purple loosestrife, all make welcome additions to the flower arranger's palette. Did I mention goldenrod? Poor goldenrod has been much maligned and is frequently confused with ragweed. Let's set the record straight: Goldenrod is not now nor has it ever been ragweed! Ragweed is an insignificant plant of roadsides and waste places where its green flowers produce abundant, wind-carried pollen. Goldenrod grows in the same locations, yet its pollen is heavy and not carried by the wind; rather, it requires bees to carry the pollen from blossom to blossom in order to become pollinated.

When cutting from the wild there are a few factors to take into consideration. Safety is of paramount importance, specifically when driving and parking your car. Be sure to get completely off the roadway, and as you look for a suitable place to stop and pick, don't create dangerous situations for other drivers. Waste places that support abundant wildflowers may support other forms of wildlife, so be on the look-out for snakes, wasps, poison ivy and poison sumac, which may lead you to regret your picking expedition.

Never pick from someone's property without his or her permission. That goldenrod may be part of a planting! State laws vary, and it's best to contact the Department of Environmental Conservation or its equivalent in your state to find out which plants are protected. Don't pick protected plants unless from your own property or with permission from the property owner. A good wildflower book is an important companion when you are collecting. Admire roadside "plantings" of wildflower mixes, but leave them for the enjoyment of others.

Harvest with moderation and consideration. Roadside flowers may be found in small pockets or colonies. When cutting from a stand of flowers it is always a good idea to leave a little behind to reseed that colony. If you remove every flower from a stand you will reduce that stand or possibly eradicate it. Good manners still dictate that we don't take the last cookie from the cookie plate.

excess foliage in the garden will lighten the load and reduce the amount of moisture loss through the foliage.

Always pick the most reliably sturdy flowers first. Don't begin with lilies and start stacking zinnias on top in your collecting basket. Flat foliage such as ferns will lie nicely in the bottom of the basket and be shaded by additions set on top. When gathering assorted treasures from the garden, such cuttings as faded blooms for potpourri and herbs for drying will be quite content if crushed under other flowers and foliage. Items such as statices and strawflowers can stand sun exposure longer if you are planning to dry them anyway. Always save the last few minutes of picking for those fragile flowers that will be ruined if crushed (lilies), or are difficult to revive if wilted (*Gaillardia* and roses).

Whenever cutting flowers, bring at least a basket, trug or container of water to carry your pickings. Even a few flowers will suffer if grasped firmly in the hand. It is amazing to me how quickly hand-held bouquets wilt, due in part to the heat emanating from the hand.

Have your conditioning containers ready for action as soon as you come in from cutting. Work quickly with the most fragile of your flowers, then with those that show signs of distress. Even if you have to get them into water before they are completely prepared, it is better to do so and go back later to finish preparing them.

Some plants produce sticky white sap, among them *Euphorbia* of all types and willow *Amsonia.* Caution must be exercised when harvesting from plants with milky sap. For some people the sap can produce a mild, itchy rash. The inside of the wrist and forearm seem to be especially sensitive areas. When cutting from a plant such as *Euphorbia,* be careful with the cut ends of the stem so that both you and the other cut flowers stay clean of the sap. In arrangements, the sap will foul the water and block uptake. When you are ready to place the *Euphorbia* in the conditioning water, take a moment to sear the cut end of the stems. This can be accomplished in one of two ways. The easiest and most sensible way is to place them in a shallow container of very hot (almost boiling) water for a few moments until the sap ceases to flow. Another method involves using the open flame of a match or candle to sear the stem ends. The flame is held to the cut stem until the sap congeals. I can't help feeling that this system is not as beneficial to the bloom, though I have used it successfully in the past. Once the flow of sap has been stopped, condition the stems in warm water as you do other flower and foliage stems.

Sometimes we simply can't get everything in water quickly enough. (That is not to say we didn't try.) When greens seem lackluster or wilted, try immersing them briefly in water completely, cut stems, leaves and all. This will immediately halt any further loss of moisture and often will be enough to revive them totally. After a few minutes, take them out of the water, gently shake off the excess moisture, recut the stems and place the ends in a very small amount of very hot (almost boiling) water. When the water has cooled, give them a very long, deep drink of warm water overnight. Not only will the foliage perk up nicely but it will last. For delicate greens such as ivy or ferns, seal them loosely in a plastic bag after soaking and store in the refrigerator overnight. Stacking the

Though improved varieties of goldenrod are lovely additions to the garden, this plant is abundant in many areas of the country and can be cut from roadsides and abandoned areas.

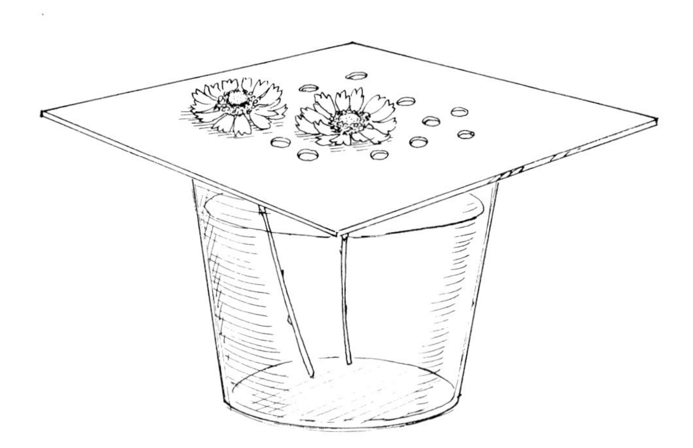

This simple device for conditioning difficult large-petaled flowers, such as daisies can be used to encourage strong, straight stems capable of supporting large flower heads.

fern flat between layers of damp paper toweling will keep them perfectly shaped. Those ferns or ivy will respond nicely.

Flowers frequently come into the workroom from the garden in less than satisfactory condition. For years I had trouble saving the larger perennial daisies. Shasta daisies, *Gaillardia* and *Rudbeckia* would wilt slightly, and the flower heads would never straighten up again. We learned a trick used by commercial florists to keep *Gerbera* daisy stems strong and straight. Take a sturdy piece of cardboard and punch out numerous holes about ½ inch in diameter, in rows about 3 inches apart. Set the cardboard over a deep, clean container of warm water. Prepare the flower stems and feed each stem through a hole in the cardboard. Be sure each stem extends into the water. The cardboard supports the flower, actually letting the stem hang down into the water; the flower petals are supported by the cardboard. When conditioned, the stems will be perfectly straight and the petals will be smooth and flat.

Professional florists use refrigeration to help preserve flowers in pristine condition. Most refrigerators in the home have two major problems, space and dehydration. Shorter flowers may be successfully stored in a refrigerator, yet unless carefully wrapped they will be dehydrated by the frost-free refrigerator standard on most refrigerators. Within a few hours, flowers left unwrapped in the fridge start to look like a slice of cheese left on the shelf without protection—definitely not suitable for use. As mentioned on page 31, however, make use of the refrigerator to condition greens such as ivy or fern fronds. Other flowers that can be treated the same way are flower heads harvested for garnishing or as food, among them nasturtium, *Calendula*, *Agastache* and violets. Place them on damp paper toweling in a shallow pan and cover tightly with plastic wrap. The individual blossoms will hold nicely for a day or two until you are ready to use them.

FORCING

Forcing branches of spring-flowering trees and shrubs into early bloom indoors is by far one of the easiest and most rewarding things you can do. I feel guilty accepting the accolades heaped on me at Mohonk for a few simple forsythia branches gracing a hall table in February. The forcing process is quite simple. Harvest the budding branches of spring-flowering trees and shrubs. Among the easiest to force are forsythia, flowering cherry, apple, peach, pear, quince and lilac. Winter forcing doesn't work with late-spring- and summer-blooming trees and shrubs such as mock orange and hydrangea.

Prepare the harvested branches for conditioning as you would any other woody branch. Place them in a deep, clean bucket or other container and keep that container filled with plenty of clean water. To hasten the forcing process, cover the branches with a clear plastic bag and place in a well-lit area away from direct sun. In a week or two you will see flower buds begin to emerge and blossoms will start to open. The amount of time it takes blossoms to form will depend on the species harvested, the time of year (the closer it gets to their natural bloom time, the quicker it is to force), and temperature of the room where the branches are stored while being forced. If you are forcing branches for a specific occasion or holiday, start two to three weeks ahead of time and cut branches for forcing at two- to three-day intervals. If the branches are proceeding at too slow a pace, you may be able to speed up the process by soaking the entire branch in warm water in a basin or bathtub for an hour or two before replacing in the bucket of warm water. Periodically adding warm water to the forcing bucket or misting with warm water will also speed things up, as will keeping the branches in a warm environment. Beware of too much heat, which may cause buds to blast, ruining any hopes of floral display.

If you want to slow things down and hold the flowers until the day of that special dinner party, employ just the opposite techniques. Move the forced branches to a cooler location. Temperatures just above freezing (34 to 40 degrees Fahrenheit) will hold blooms for quite some time. Adding ice to the water if a cool location is not available will also slow things down considerably.

A bright wreath of summer flowers welcomes special guests to your garden. These flowers were carefully conditioned and then arranged in a wreath form made of floral foam.

4

DESIGNING WITH CUT FLOWERS

Good floral design is in the eye of the beholder. It has been my experience that flowers can do no wrong. That's not to say that you can't look at your work with a critical eye and improve your skills. However, it seems that no matter how dissatisfied I might be with a bouquet (even masters pull arrangements apart and start all over again), someone will come along and drool over what I felt to be absolutely horrendous.

Good flower arranging is influenced by occasion, season, function, decor, container and, most important, the arranger's likes and dislikes. As we sometimes see in the fashion magazines, haute couture and high style may not be for everyone. Some basic design rules are good to fall back on, however, when you feel something is wrong but can't put your finger on it. I avoid step-by-step how-tos because I feel they stifle imagination when you're developing a design for your home, for your color scheme and to your taste!

The basic tools of design can be easy to assemble and need not be expensive or elaborate. Let's discuss containers first. With floral foam (Oasis), containers for arrangements may be anything that will support the floral foam, whether the container holds water or not. I prefer to work without foam, as flowers last longer in lots of plain, fresh water. Therefore, I prefer containers that will hold a generous supply of water. Bowls, tall cylindrical vases, cups, mugs, mason jars and crocks all are excellent for arrangements.

A handy type of container is actually an assortment of related vases or containers. They may be identical or merely similar in theme, shape or color. Three, five or seven small containers can be grouped together in the center of a table to make a centerpiece or set at individual dinner places as individual decorations. They may be antique medicine bottles, miniature pottery crocks, assorted small glass vases or a set of identical crystal vases. The advantage for the home-grown-flower designer is that these flower containers can be used in multiples or alone and will frequently be appropriate for small numbers of shorter flowers typically found in the garden at some times of the year.

Containers that don't hold water themselves but house water-holding vessels may be baskets, fruits and vegetables, even baked goods. If you can find a place to nestle a small container of water in an apple, you can use the apple to hold flowers. Houseplants such as philodendron and dracaena can provide a few blooms for special occasions. Such blossoms, if well conditioned, will last for a day or two when placed in well-watered potting soil. The soil will supply enough water to keep the flowers fresh; this is an old trick of commercial florists.

Remember that containers that are intricately molded are harder to clean. Some metal containers are made of materials that interact with

A dramatic mantle arrangement. Dark green candles and antique wooden fruit are an important part of this mantle arrangement which includes branches of Cornus kousa *(Japanese dogwood), green hydrangea blossoms and* Polygonum *foliage. A single brick of floral foam wrapped in plastic holds all the stems and is the "invisible" container.*

A favorite container such as this crock is equally at home with daffodils in spring and chrysanthemums in autumn. The nest of wooden robin's eggs completes the spring ensemble.

A container for an arrangement need not be a single vase. Here, six clear glass vials hold June flowers in an arrangement that can easily be re-arranged at a whim.

Late summer bounty is rich with the fragrance of herbs and the texture of fruits, gourds and strawberry corn. Dill and oregano flowers from the herb garden blend with other edibles.

water, perhaps ruining the container or resulting in a chemical reaction that may shorten flower life. Brass and stainless steel are stable, but many other metals react with water or water preservatives. If in doubt, protect your container; a liner will protect the metal as well as the quality of the water. A plastic insert, old drinking glass or recycled container that holds water will work well if hidden inside the decorative container.

The shape, size and style of the container will affect the shape, size and style of the finished arrangement. Open bowls make for open, spreading arrangements. It can be difficult to arrange in open bowls without some form of mechanical device to hold stems in place. Arrangements in bowls make wonderful centerpieces, and a bowl looks quite natural on the dining table. Tall, cylindrical vases are somewhat easier to arrange in than bowls. The form an arrangement in such a vase will take is usually more upright. Vertical arrangements can be very dramatic on tall accent tables and when placed where space is at a premium, such as the lavatory cabinet. Many vases are created with a narrow base and flaring top. These V-shaped vases are easy to design in; they hold many stems, but the water reservoir is deceptively small, and this can limit flower life and encourage rapid fouling of the water. Perhaps the most versatile of all vases are the classic rose bowl and urn styles. These containers have relatively narrow necks, which makes for easy placement of flowers and a generous reservoir to hold plenty of fresh, clean water.

Most people find certain containers that work well for them, and that container will show up again and again over the seasons and with different displays of flowers from tulips to goldenrod. No matter what your taste, develop a collection of vases and containers, and keep them handy and clean.

Many tools will help make your job easier when the time comes to put flowers in water. A variety of devices will help hold the stems of flowers and greens in place. The most commonly used devise today is floral foam. This product has become the mainstay of the commercial florist industry. Floral foam is designed to hold many times its own weight in water and will securely hold stems of flowers and greens in place in an arrangement.

Additional devices have been designed to work with the floral foam and hold accessories such as candles or hold flowers on cake tops; they may even attach to surfaces such as mirrors. There is no doubt that it is much easier to design with floral foam, as flowers are held exactly where you place them. Foam is great to use when creating an arrangement where flowers are placed on the horizontal or even angled downward. For maximum benefit when using foam, cut it while dry so it is tall enough to extend about ½ inch above the rim of the container, and leave plenty of space in the container around the foam to add water. Foam should be soaked thoroughly and held in place with florist's adhesive tape, sold in flower shops, craft stores and garden centers. There are a couple of drawbacks to using foam. The simple truth is that flowers last longer in lots of clean water. Floral foam is best used only once; with each additional use, the bacteria level in the foam increases and will hinder water uptake in flowers. When placing flowers in foam, be decisive; many changes in stem placement will cause the foam to break apart. When changing the angle or direction of a stem in foam, always take the stem completely out of the foam and reinsert it. Lifting a stem part way out of the foam will leave an air space at the bottom of the stem, and the flower will wilt and die.

If the floral foam that holds an arrangement is allowed to dry slightly, the flowers will suffer. Because floral foam is so adept at holding water, it will actually draw water away from the flowers and greens in an arrangement when it starts to dry out. Be sure to add plenty of good, clean water to your arrangement daily when using floral foam.

Pin holders are round or oval weighted bases that support vertical pins. The pins impale the stems of flowers and greens to hold them in place. This works extremely well with medium-size, soft stems, but pin holders are more difficult to use with woody stems or very fine, thin stems. Perhaps the most frustrating limitation when using pin holders is that it is very difficult to place stems in a horizontal plane. Although some recommend pin holders be held in place in the container using florist's clay, I find this isn't necessary as the weight of the holder is enough to secure most arrangements quite nicely. In general, I try to use a minimum of mechanics. It makes cleanup easier. Adhesive tape, florist's clay and other sticky devices can be difficult to clean off containers. A well-balanced arrangement won't need a lot of extra support. If an arrange-

A delicate crystal bowl inspires a mass arrangement of tulips and Amalanchier, *perfect on a lace cloth. The open bowl helps provide the "line" for the composition.*

The classic urn in miniature. The little glass vase is a perfect size for the average garden flower and can be used at any time of year.

Tulips combined in a free-flowing line. Lighter buds high in the arrangement add height without making the composition top-heavy. Foliage and flowers spilling over the edge of the container help to maintain a cohesive look.

This nosegay of tulips with the tiny flowers of Amalanchier *and cherry combine to create the feel of a gentler time.*

ment will be exposed to a breeze, is to be transported or moved frequently, it may then be desirable to use adhesive or clay.

Other devices have been developed to aid the flower arranger in holding flowers in a vase. There is a whole family of gadgets called "frogs," which may be wire cages, lead weights with holes in them and glass molded with holes to accept stems. All of these devices are helpful to some degree. (The holes of glass or metal frogs may be too large or small for some stems.) Their value depends on the effect you are trying to achieve. Additional materials that work well as design aids are balled-up chicken wire fencing, loosely crumpled aluminum foil, marbles or stones and twigs. Chicken wire is useful to keep on hand. You can wrap a block of floral foam with chicken wire for added support, or tape it flat over the top of a vase. Twigs cut in short lengths can be used to fill the vase somewhat and support the stems of flowers or foliage as you design. Using twigs in arrangements adds to the bulk of plant material and increases the risk of introducing bacteria and fouling the water, thereby reducing the vase life of your flowers.

The best approach with frogs and other holding devices is to use them just to get started. The first few stems of any arrangement are the most difficult to place and hold in position. Eventually, the stems will support each other and behave as you want them to. You can be successful with pinholders and frogs even in bowls, if you allow other stems in the arrangement to become part of the support mechanism of the arrangement. Even the lip of the container can support flowers and greens. The cardinal rule in flower arranging is that the cut end of the stem must be in water, the more water the better!

Let's look at some of the principles of design as they relate to flower arranging. As I've said, I don't follow them slavishly, but I refer to them when "troubleshooting" for an arrangement. When designing, I start with a container that pleases me and choose from the flowers at hand. Occasionally, I'm inspired as I pick and work an arrangement around a particular piece of vine, twig or special blossoms from a favorite plant. In the process of arranging, I simply start combining collected elements. As I approach completion, I may feel uncomfortable with the composition, and that is when I consider the elements of good design.

Proportion (scale) in flower arranging is important. The flowers and leaves should interact in a pleasing way not only together but with the container and their surroundings too. A bouquet of peonies might be a lovely composition but completely out of place when used in a small sitting area. A small demitasse cup of violets would be ridiculous as the centerpiece at a table for eight. Proportion can go awry when the flowers or foliage are out of synch with the container. A small crystal vase filled with

Visual weight is an important part of design. Dark colors carry more "weight" than their lighter-colored counterparts. The deep orange/red of the zinnia and gaillardia are placed low, while the bright yellow coreopsis is placed higher in the grouping.

delicate subjects is delightful, but the addition of a large, overbearing hosta leaf disturbs the scale. The rule of thumb is that the largest dimension of an arrangement should be about 1½ to 2 times the largest dimension of the container or vase that holds it. If this proportion is greatly exceeded or grossly underachieved, the container and arrangement will not look as though they belonged together.

To maintain proportion, the visual weight of the individual elements is important. Dark-colored elements appear heavier than light-colored elements of the same size. Light-colored flowers may appear slightly larger than dark blossoms of the same size. Place smaller, lighter flowers higher up in an arrangement and concentrate darker, larger blossoms closer to the base of the arrangement. This helps define the focal point, or visual center, of an arrangement. It appeals to our natural sense of proportion and helps develop a comfortable effect of balance, line and rhythm.

Balance is another easily understood, important element of design. I frequently use actual physical weight and balance as a guide to design. This works especially well when I use small mechanical devices to anchor my stems as the devices become the fulcrum of my balance. The tallest elements of the arrangement should counterbalance each other to keep the composition from toppling. Use visually—and physically—lighter elements such as buds and tiny flowers in the extremities of an arrangement. By concentrating the heavier flowers close to the base of an arrangement you create the impression of stability. This improves the overall composition and balance.

Line is a scary concept to some, yet it is an easy design principle to master. Line is simply the spatial relationship of individual elements to each other. The archenemy of line in design is even numbers. This is not to say that I haven't created many successful arrangements using four tulips. But, even numbers of like items in an arrangement will draw the eye toward them, and our carefully trained eyes will start to identify geometric shapes. Two red roses seem to have an imaginary line drawn between them, four will create a very nice box. In flower arrangements, these geometric shapes are overpowering and take away from the composition. Odd numbers of flowers, arranged in threes, fives, sevens and so on, usually behave nicely and create a natural, comfortable line.

Avoid placing any two identical elements in line in either a perfectly horizontal or vertical plane. Despite the use of odd numbers in total, the eye seeks out the horizontal or vertical line and focuses on it. Instead, place one bloom slightly lower and to the left or right to break up the lines. Avoiding an overpowering line is easy.

Rhythm is related to line and is most important in arrangements that rely on the placement of few blossoms for effect. In a line arrangement, a limited number of flowers are used to create a balanced design, so the flowers must be selected carefully. Flowers lead the eye from blossom to blossom toward the focal point. The simple effect of a good design is deceptive, because success with the line arrangement requires careful positioning of individual blossoms. Using the principles of proportion, balance and line help achieve the rhythm necessary for success in a line arrangement.

Color is fun, and we shouldn't have to worry about suitable color combinations in flower arranging. It is in regard to color that I too often hear the *can't* word. Some people feel that no one should use blue vases (why do they make blue vases then?). Others insist you can't combine pink with orange or red with purple. Let me take this opportunity to set

The placement of garden flowers in this monochromatic composition makes for a naturalistic grouping. Using flowers of different sizes and increasing the density of color at the base of the arrangement create balance and a focal point.

Related colors in shades of pink and voilet fill a simple glass vase. Aster, cosmos, verbena, foxglove, scabiosa and delphinium blend together in harmony.

the record straight. You can combine any colors successfully in floral design and can use any vase or container without disastrous results.

Horticulturally, there is no pure color. Crayon hues of pure orange, red, yellow and blue don't exist. Close examination of white flowers will show highlights of green, yellow, white or pink. Pinks are frequently blushed with coral or violet, even green. Yellows may have undertones of green or orange. And blue, well, blue is a very difficult color to find without some hint of violet. All this is a blessing in disguise. Color combinations are suggested within each blossom. Look toward the center, the base of the petals, the exterior of the petals or at the stamens and pistils, and you will see colors to which the flower is related. Introducing those colors to the arrangement will create wonderful harmony.

Green is the one constant in floral design. Even without adding the foliage of ferns or shrubbery, the various greens of stems and the natural leaves of each blossom introduce green to an arrangement. Green in the landscape or in the vase is an effective unifying element. The foliage of plants comes in an amazing assortment of colors, and greens can vary greatly. Green can be dark or light and have blue, yellow or red overtones. Foliage may be green, gray or variegated in any number of combinations from the vertical striping of ribbon grass to the almost-perfect golden edging of some hosta. The color of the variegation varies, too, yellow and green being the most common; green and white, green and silver, and tricolor variegations as in the tricolor sage are all suitable for inclusion in arrangements.

Color is a matter of personal taste and should be influenced by decor, vase and table linens (if any). Sometimes people feel the season or occasion dictates the colors used: white for weddings; pastels for Easter and baby showers; red and green for Christmas holiday festivities; and yellow, golds and russets in the autumn. Colors may be arranged together with like colors to create a monochromatic scheme, or with color opposites to develop a complementary color scheme. Blue and orange are complements, as are yellow and lavender, and red and green. Color "neighbors" work well together: russet with orange and yellow, blue with lavender and pink. Polychromatic color combinations are vivid blendings of a range of colors, bringing together the primary hues of red, yellow and blue with oranges, pinks, whites and violets for a riot of color. For pleasing color combinations, you should do as you like, not as some "expert" advises.

Try not to think of arranging as the art of vase decoration. I am very fond of and often choose to use a softly hued, medium green bowl. Glass containers are, of course, a non-color choice. White and black containers too frequently can become integral parts of the designs. Black can be very elegant and commanding of attention and calls for a dramatic sense of color in the arrangement. Colored vases by their very nature should become an

A small sampling of foliage from the garden. From top center, clockwise: Mountain laurel, viburnum, dusty miller, hay-scented fern, variegated weigelia, 'Purple Ruffles' basil, gardener's ribbon grass and Canadian hemlock.

A sampling of color in arrangements, from left to right: analogous shades of pink asters, carmine cosmos, and violet verbena and delphinium; complementary orange tithonia and blue salvia; complementary red Cardinal flower and red crab apples with assorted foliages; complementary yellow goldenrod and zinnia with lavender asters; anagolous yellow coreopsis with orange zinnias and gaillardia; and monochromatic white on white balloon flowers, snapdragons, asters, Queen Anne's lace and scabiosa.

Beauty and fragrance in the bedroom. Roses and lavender provide scent in the bouquet of mixed flowers of early summer. Lupine, columbine, mullein pink, allium and slender deutzia complete the arrangement.

A play for texture. Soft, feathery blooms combine with the rich texture of velvety rose petals in an old basket. The gardener's ribbon grass provides line and textural interest as well.

integral part of the color scheme of the design and demand the designer tie it together in some way.

Texture is the "color" of feel. In arrangements we experience texture visually and relate it to a tactile experience we recognize. We can visualize rough, smooth, velvety, glossy and spiny. Variation of texture enhances arrangements. By combining rough with smooth or velvety with glossy, another dimension comes into play. The use of texture is critical in a monochromatic scheme in which slight variations in color can be emphasized by contrasting textures.

Scent in Bouquets

I have frequently said that I garden as much with my nose as my hands. Gardening and flower arranging are joys to all the senses. The nose shouldn't be ignored. Incorporating scent in an arrangement is not a prerequisite of good design, but it should often be a consideration. Many flowers and foliages provide scent for bouquets. Here are a few of my favorites: Lilies of the valley, mignonettes, scented geraniums, basils and other herbs, garden pinks and carnations, lilacs, roses, sweet peas, lavenders (foliage and flowers), lilies, nicotianas, peonies, phloxes and sweet bay magnolias. Not all scents are for everyone. Boxwood foliage and marigolds offend some people, and strongly scented flowers may become overpowering in small, enclosed spaces.

Depth is a consideration in flower arranging as we are working with three-dimensional objects. Unfortunately, all too often we find that all the elements of an composition have been placed in one plane. This sort of design might have everything else going for it, but it misses depth. By layering flowers and foliage in the design, you can increase the interest level of the arrangement. Look at a garden. Are all of the flowers planted in a single row? Do all of the flowers face the same way? Of course not. A garden is three dimensional. The flowers are layered, and as you walk past, you see a slightly different composition from your changing perspective. The changing combinations of colors, textures and

Muted tones of cream, blue and yellow-green with the rich accents of foliage provide a delightful combination. The depth of flower placement helps to maintain the three-dimensional appearance even in a photograph.

Lilies should be a part of every cutting garden. The velvety colors are combined with dill, tansy and Klondike cosmos. When designing with lilies it is wise to remove the pollen-bearing anthers, as the pollen can stain.

lines are exciting. For an arrangement with depth, flowers are placed in the design at different levels, yet each is shown off to good advantage at different angles and when seen from various heights.

Mechanics is the term used by flower arrangers for the devices to secure the flowers. I don't often use them, though I sometimes use a frog or pin holder to anchor the first few stems to give me a head start with a design. The nasty thing about mechanics is that they must be camouflaged so they do not disrupt the beauty of the design. The most common means of hiding mechanics is to cover them with adequate foliage. In some instances, however, greens are not the answer. Other means of covering floral foam, pin holders or frogs is with Spanish or sphagnum moss (available at garden centers and craft shops), stones or marbles, shells, and even blossoms themselves. Whatever material is used should be clean so as not to foul the water (critical in the case of clear glass containers, where dirty water is immediately evident). Be leery of substances that become malodorous when in contact with water or produce a substance toxic to flowers and greens.

Our friends the flowers can be idiosyncratic. Not all behave as they should. Tulips, those delights of the spring garden and vase, are wonderful subjects when cut except for one minor problem, the tendency to grow. Tulips continue to grow in the vase and will, if allowed to do so, extend beyond the other flowers they were arranged with. There is no helping this phenomenon except to lift them out and cut back the ends of the stems. The flower petals will also open and close with the coming and going of daylight. I stop this bad habit by making a small vertical cut just below the flower head about ½ inch long and deep enough to reach about halfway into the stem.

Another flower that may disrupt the orderliness of your floral design is the snapdragon. Snapdragons are one of the best cut flowers, unparalleled in color and scent, but they have wayward tips. The last two or three inches of each snapdragon will reach upward. This is not an especially bothersome habit but it can turn a lovely centerpiece into something that more closely resembles Liberace's candelabrum.

Lilies don't move, grow or change once arranged, but lily pollen does seem to have a mind of its own. Most professional florists remove the pollen. It is a shame to have to do so because the nodding, pollen-heavy anthers add a certain charm. The sad truth is that lily pollen stains, sometimes permanently. Unless you are putting an arrangement in a safe place away from brushing sleeves and curious noses, I recommend removing the anthers. Use a tissue to grasp the pollen-bearing anther and pull gently—it's rather like blowing a child's nose. If you should inadvertently get pollen on a garment or tablecloth, resist the urge to brush it away immediately. Allow the pollen to dry for an hour or more, then lightly brush it away or use the vacuum cleaner.

Maintaining the flower arrangement is an integral part of success with home-grown cut flowers. Once the flowers have been arranged to your satisfaction, keep the arrangement looking good! Some locations in the home are ideal for placing cut flowers, some less so. It is never a good idea to mix flowers in water with electrical equipment such as televisions or entertainment systems. An accidental spill could cause an expensive repair or create a dangerous electrical shock. At Mohonk we never place arrangements on pianos or other musical instruments; experience has taught us that accidental spills of water can cause expensive repairs.

Avoid heat and direct sun with flower arrangements. Locations near fireplaces, radiators and strong, hot lighting all shorten the life of and enjoyment you'll receive from flowers. Flowers will do best in a cool room with adequate ventilation, but away from strong air currents and drafts.

Most florists finish a bouquet with a thorough misting with a spray bottle. Misting an arrangement not only keeps the flowers and foliages looking fresh but will help an arrangement last longer. The mist reduces moisture loss through the petals and leaves. In an overly warm house or apartment, misting will cool the flowers and, as the water evaporates, increase the humidity in the room.

The most common cause of failure with flower arrangements is lack of water. Ideally, all the stems of flowers and greens are well immersed in water. This isn't always the case, though, because to achieve the proper angle or use that special but short-stemmed rose, some stems are in only one or two inches of water. Adding water daily will maintain water level and help keep the water in the vase fresh. Use warm water to refresh most arrangements. However, to add hours to the enjoyment of bowls of cut spring-flowering bulbs such as tulips and daffodils, add a handful of ice cubes to help cool the arrangement and add water as they melt.

Some flowers last longer in the vase than others. As a flower begins to fade you may be able to eliminate it or replace it and continue to enjoy the rest of the bouquet for days afterward. Rather than try to pull out the spent bloom, cut it out as close to the vase as possible. Pulling a flower stem out of an arrangement may disrupt the entire composition.

A Word About Style

Several personalities have recently become big promoters of their "style." It's a great word and a wonderful concept. I have always felt it is more important to be comfortable than stylish, and our home reflects that philosophy. Preferences in styles and trends change dramatically over time (who would have thought the miniskirt would return?). What do not change are your personality and your love of fresh flowers. When arranging flowers in your kitchen or work room, do so because you enjoy doing so. If you want to mimic the great designers of the day, do it! Copying from fashion magazines or decorating books can be great fun.

Whatever style you choose, remember to be comfortable with your designs, enjoy the combination of gardening and bringing the garden indoors and wallow in the glory of a garden well tended, a bountiful harvest and the beauty you and nature helped create.

5

PLANT PORTRAITS

It has been difficult to limit the number of plants discussed in these plant portraits because an unlimited number of plants lend themselves to cutting and enjoying indoors. Anyone who has grown and harvested flowers for arranging will undoubtedly be perturbed with me for eliminating some special favorite. I have chosen plants that are valued for their size, shape, texture and lasting ability as well as those that may offer a specific challenge for the gardener or designer. The Plant Portraits represent all of the major horticultural groups: trees, shrubs, ornamental and edible plants and, of course, the annuals, biennials and perennials. As you use this book, you will find I have recommended species and varieties not described in the plant portraits; for many of these, specific information on their cultural requirements and landscape use can be found in other Burpee American Gardening Series books.

My father once said that you have to learn from the mistakes of others because you don't have enough time to make them all yourself. I encourage you to learn from my experience and mistakes, and hope this broadens your horizons enough so you learn from your future experiences.

The plants that follow are listed by their botanic names and cross-referenced by their common names. Common names, though easier to pronounce and frequently endearing (who can resist love-in-a-mist?) vary from area to area, but botanic names are understood from Boston to Bangkok. Botanic names are listed by the genus and include species and sometimes subspecies or cultivar names. Cultivar—cultivated variety—names usually appear in single quotation marks.

PLANT PORTRAIT KEY

Here is a guide to the symbols and terms used throughout this section.

Latin name of the plant is in boldface italic.

Phonetic pronunciation of the Latin name is in parentheses.

Common name of the plant is in boldface type.

The average hours of sun needed per day is indicated by symbols. The first symbol is what the plant prefers, but the plant is adaptable to all conditions listed.

○ *Sun*—Six hours or more of strong, direct sunlight per day.

◐ *Part shade*—Three to six hours of direct sunlight per day.

● *Shade*—Two hours or less of direct sunlight per day.

💧 *Drought resistant*

✸ *Heat lover*

✳ *Cool weather preference*

H *Condition in hot water (150 degrees Fahrenheit).*

W *Condition in warm water (100 to 120 degrees Fahrenheit).*

C *Condition in cool water (room temperature).*

S *Special conditioning requirements.*

Zones: Check the Plant Hardiness Map (pages 92-93), based on average annual temperature for each area—or zone—of the United States to see what zone you live in. Every plant portrait lists the zones best for that plant.

Whether it's exquisite foliage, charming buds or beautiful blossoms, every flower has something to offer the flower arranger. Penstemon has a delightful presence in the garden and makes a wonderful addition to any arrangement.

ANNUALS

Antirrhinum majus *are among the best cutting flowers, easy to grow and easy to harvest successfully. Pinch young plants to encourage basal branching.*

Ageratum houstonianum (aj-er-AY-tum hew-stōn-ee-AH-num) **blue flossflower,** ○ ◐ ✹ **W**

Characteristics: Ageratum is an old-fashioned, annual favorite known mostly for its value as a bedding plant. Fuzzy lavender-blue flowers are borne in clusters on top of medium-length stems. The typically compact, 8- to 10-inch plants are the result of much breeding, and today's *Ageratum* is not the *Ageratum* of our grandmothers. Avoid bedding varieties for cutting, and look for the *Ageratum* still available in heights of 20 to 30 inches.

Cultural Information: Ageratum does best in full sun in rich, well-drained garden soils, but it will produce good-quality cutting stems in light shade. *Ageratum* has few insect or disease problems. Seed in place after last frost or start indoors on a sunny windowsill about six weeks before last frost. The best *Ageratum* varieties for cutting are 'Bavaria' and 'Blue Horizon'.

Harvest and Use: In bouquets, *Ageratum* does very well with yellow roses (try 'Sunbright'), zinnias and snapdragons. It may be difficult to blend successfully with oranges and golden yellows.

Ageratum, *with its delightful, lavender-blue flowers, is available in heights of 24 to 30 inches, excellent for cutting. Try the variety 'Blue Horizon'.*

Amaranthus (am-a-RAN-thus) **amaranth,** ○ ✹ 💧 **H**

Characteristics: The amaranths comprise a group of frequently overlooked annuals that are wonderful additions to the annual border and the cutting garden. Several varieties available from seed are delightful garden performers, producing excellent cutting flowers and foliage. *A. caudatus*, also known as love-lies-bleeding and kiss-me-over-the-garden-gate, is characterized by long, weeping panicles of fuzzy burgundy flowers. The effect of these flowers is quite dramatic whether used fresh or dried. *A. caudatus* 'Scarlet Torch', producing shorter, upright spikes to 12 inches, is another heat- and sun-loving annual. It is effective used either fresh or dried.

Cultural Information: Amaranths are grown easily from seed sown in soils in spring after the danger of frost is past, or started indoors 6 weeks before planting outdoors. They thrive in well-drained soils of average fertility. Taller varieties may need staking.

Harvest and Use: It is best to remove all foliage before conditioning. Love-lies-bleeding is handsome when arranged to weep over the edge of a pedestal vase and puddle gently on the table below. Or arrange it on a mantle, letting it hang to its full length. The muted, deep red ropes blend well with many different colors and textures. Try it with orange lilies and deep green hosta foliage. The shorter, rust-colored spires of *A. c.* 'Scarlet Torch' combine well with the bright oranges of marigolds and cosmos, providing lovely textural and color counterpoint.

Amaranthus caudatus, *the quintessential romantic flower for bouquets.*

Annual aster; see ***Callistephus***

Annual baby's breath; see ***Gypsophila elegans***

Annual larkspur; see ***Consolida***

Antirrhinum majus (an-ti-RY-num MAH-yus) **snapdragon,** ○ ◐ ✳ **W**

Characteristics: The snapdragon is essential to the cutting garden. The offering of colors from pure white to deep burgundy and pale yellow to bronze and orange give the gardener a wonderful color range. The full-bodied spikes of delicate florets can be grown in two forms: the

closed-mouth "dragon style" and the bright, open-faced type such as 'Madame Butterfly'. For maximum height and color selection of the standard snapdragon form, the best choices are from the 'Rocket Series'.
Cultural Information: The seeds are easy to germinate in cool temperatures. Seedlings of Rocket "snaps" are available at many garden centers and nurseries in spring. When seedlings are about 4 inches tall and have several sets of leaves, pinch out the uppermost set of leaves and terminal bud to produce stockier, well-branched plants; they will perform better in the garden.
Harvest and Use: Harvesting spikes of snapdragons will encourage basal branching and more flower stems will be produced. Cut stems should be stripped of foliage before conditioning in warm water. An upright placement in an arrangement is more pleasing than a horizontal placement, as the tips of snaps continue to grow toward the light. All snapdragon colors are valuable, but one of my favorites is 'Rocket Series' bronze. Close inspection of this bronze flower reveals pink, yellow and orange overtones, making it ideal for blending with a wide range of flowers including blue *Salvia,* cosmos and lisianthus.

Aster, China; see ***Callistephus***

Baby's breath, annual; see ***Gypsophila elegans***

Bachelor's button; see ***Centaurea***

Bells of Ireland; see ***Moluccella***

Blue flossflower; see ***Ageratum***

Blue lace flower; see ***Trachymene***

Blue throatwort; see ***Trachelium***

Calendula officinalis

(ka-LEN-dew-la ōf-fish-in-AL-is) **pot marigold, ○ ◐ ✳ C**
Characteristics: Pot marigold is a wonderful, long-lasting cutting flower that is also one of the best of the edible flowers. This easy-to-grow annual blooms well throughout the season and produces numerous flowers for harvesting. Several improved varieties are available with colors ranging from cream to apricot. 'Pacific' at 24 inches provides stems suitable for cutting. As with other annuals, calendula responds well to cutting by producing more flowers.
Cultural Information: Calendula is extremely easy to grow and will thrive in almost any soil. Sow seed in early spring as soon as soil can be worked. Thin seedlings to six to eight inches apart to provide adequate room for proper development. Pot marigolds like plenty of moisture and benefit from a midseason fertilizer application.
Harvest and Use: Cut stems of *Calendula* should be placed in cool water until you are ready to design; they are easy to condition. The yellows of pot marigolds are among the purest of all yellow flowers, and combined with purple larkspur, it's dynamite.

Calendula *bright yellow or golden orange flowers are at home in fresh flower arrangements useful in potpourri, and excellent when tossed in a green salad.*

Callistephus chinensis *will fill late-summer and early-autumn bouquets with strong shades of blue, violet, red, rose, pink and white in single and double flowering forms.*

Callistephus chinensis

(ka-LEE-ste-fus chy-NEN-sis) **China (annual) aster, ○ W**
Characteristics: The China or annual aster is one of the most prized annual flowers for bouquets and arranging. Asters come in a range of lovely colors from crystal white to deep, pure blue; shades of palest pink to deep burgundy fill out the spectrum. Asters are available in single, daisylike and fully double forms. 'Totem Pole', 'Powder Puff Bouquet' and 'Single Rainbow' demonstrate the full range of colors and a diversity of bloom sizes from

the two-inch 'Powder Puff' to the four-inch 'Totem Pole'. When choosing varieties, look for a statement of wilt resistance, as aster wilt can devastate your crop. Asters bloom in late summer and are the backbone of the August and September cutting garden.

Cultural Information: Aster is easy to grow from seed and does well in most garden soils. Local greenhouses and garden centers usually offer an assortment of varieties each spring; avoid dwarf bedding asters that don't produce stems suitable for cutting. Thin asters 10 inches apart in well-prepared soil enriched with organic matter. Incorporate a balanced fertilizer into the soil before planting, and side-dress with additional fertilizer when flower buds begin to develop in July. Asters tolerate drought, but irrigation during dry periods will result in larger and superior blooms. Taller varieties should be staked in windy areas.

Harvest and Use: Asters combine well with many other cut flowers, and their straight, sturdy stems make them wonderfully easy for designing. Combine them with burgundy snapdragons, blue lisianthus and white phlox for a lovely late-summer bouquet.

Celosia *are bright, reliable additions to the annual cutting garden or integrated garden. They can be used fresh or dried for everlasting bouquets.*

Centaurea cyanus *is a favorite from Victorian times. The brilliant, clear blue combines well with many other flowers, but don't neglect the other colors: white, pale pink through rose, and maroon.*

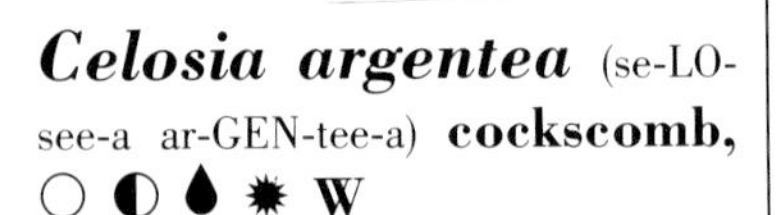

Celosia argentea (se-LO-see-a ar-GEN-tee-a) **cockscomb,** ○ ◐ ♦ ✹ W

Characteristics: Cockscombs are grown in two forms, each one worthwhile in small quantities in the cutting garden. Both forms are lovely garden specimens, providing long-lasting blossoms ideal for use fresh and dried. Cockscombs are available in many rich colors from red to yellow, including deep burgundy and orange. *Celosia argentea plumosa* or the plumed cockscomb has been the subject of much breeding work during the past several years, resulting in stockier, more dwarf plants. This does not always benefit the flower arranger. A highlight of the 1993 garden season is the new variety 'Flamingo Feather', growing to 24 inches and topped with a much smaller, more delicate version of the typical plumed cockscomb. 'Flamingo Feather' is a pleasant medium pink in color and an exciting textural contrast to some of its more staid garden colleagues such as lilies, roses, daisies and cosmoses. *Celosia argentea* 'New Look', 'Apricot Brandy' and 'Golden Triumph' are varieties worth including in the cutting garden. Dried blossoms will last for months and their velvety colors will enrich autumn bouquets and holiday arrangements.

Celosia argentea cristata, the crested cockscomb, is quite different from the plumed cockscomb. The crested cockscombs grow in undulating fans and form heads as they mature. Crested cockscomb is wonderful used fresh in late-summer and autumn bouquets and in dried arrangements year 'round. The texture is velvety, the colors deep and rich. The Burpee 'Floradale Series' in mixed colors is an excellent quality cockscomb.

Cultural Information: Cockscomb is an easy-to-grow annual that thrives in warm soils and full sun. A wide choice of varieties is usually available from the nursery or garden center each spring. Choose seedlings—from the greenhouse or garden center, or when growing your own from seed—that are actively growing, and make sure the young growth is not checked in the seedling flat. Look for young, vigorous plants that are not yet fully blooming. Foliage will not always be a deep green; plants with paler blooms frequently have pale or chartreuse foliage. Some of the reds have lovely burgundy foliage that sets off the bright flowers nicely in both garden and vase.

Harvest and Use: Condition cockscombs in warm water after removing all but the uppermost pair of leaves. Plumed cockscomb looks lovely combined with coreopsis and the strong-colored autumn mums. Crested cockscomb adds a great wealth of color and texture to any bouquet. For a festive holiday or harvest-time arrangement, arrange cockscomb in a hollowed-out pumpkin and surround with assorted gourds and Indian corn.

Centaurea cyanus (sent-OW-ree-a see-AH-nus) **bachelor's buttons, cornflowers,** ○ ✳ ♦ W

Characteristics: Centaurea cyanus is a standard of the cutting garden. Although most noted for the wonderful blue (cornflower blue!), shades of white, pink, violet and burgundy complete the color range, all of them desirable in the cutting garden and vase. 'Polka Dot' offers a full range of colors and produces nice, straight stems for cutting.

Centaurea is a large genus of several annuals and perennials, many of which are suitable for cutting. *C. moschata* is known as sweet sultan. The flowers are the same size as those of bachelor's buttons but appear as softer, rounded, powder-puff blooms. The colors range from white to lavender, all soft pastel shades.

Cultural Information: Seed bachelor's buttons where they are to grow in well-prepared garden soil. A full-sun location in well-drained soils will benefit *Centaurea,* which does not require extremely rich soils. Like some of the other garden favorites, bachelor's buttons will reseed themselves, and for the lazy gardener they will reappear year after year. In the garden, beware of powdery mildew, a death knell to these flowers not fond of heat and humidity. Regular harvesting of blossoms for fresh use and drying keeps the plants producing throughout the season. Staking may be necessary if they are grown in fertile ground. Avoid shade and crowded areas in the garden, which might further predispose bachelor's buttons to mildew problems.

Harvest and Use: It may be tedious to pull the leaves off the stems of bachelor's buttons, but this will reward you by keeping the water fresh and clean. Both bachelor's buttons and sweet sultan will serve you well in the vase for two weeks or longer if the water remains clean. I like the bright, pure blue of cornflowers with the pure yellow of coreopsis and bright orange Klondyke cosmos. *Centaurea* combines well with many spring-flowering and early-summer favorites.

China aster; see ***Callistephus***

Cockscomb; see ***Celosia***

Common garden cosmos; see ***Cosmos***

Consolida orientalis

(kon-SO-li-da o-ree-en-TAL-is) **annual larkspur,** ○ ◐ ✳ **W**

Characteristics: Larkspur provides one of the valuable blues of the cutting garden. The tall flower spikes are also available in white and pink shades and grow to four feet. 'Giant Imperial' is a mix of all the larkspur colors, and one packet of seeds will provide many cuts for fresh and dried use.

Cultural Information: Larkspur prefers cool temperatures, and by giving it a head start in spring you will have larger spikes and a longer season of bloom. To get the jump on spring, sow larkspur seed where they are to grow in the fall. Mark the location carefully so the garden spot is not tilled or inadvertently weeded out. Larkspur will need staking in exposed locations; use a medium-weight bamboo cane, and tie at about one foot and again 10 to 12 inches higher.

Harvest and Use: Larkspur dries nicely, holding its color into the winter, but it is the bright, elegant stems in fresh bouquets that makes it most valuable. 'Giant Imperial' is reliable, large and guaranteed to produce an abundance of cutting material. Be sure to remove all the ferny foliage when preparing for conditioning. Larkspur will last for 7 to 10 days in water. Try combining larkspur with roses for a traditional look or with masses of cosmos for a carefree arrangement. Care should be taken when handling the seeds and foliage of *Consolida* as they are poisonous.

Consolida orientalis *'Giant Imperial Mixed' is easily grown from seed and will provide ample cuts if seed is sown in autumn or very early spring. You'll want plenty for fresh and dry use.*

Cornflower; see ***Centaurea***

Cosmos

(KOS-mos) **common garden cosmos,** ○ ✸ 💧 **W**

Characteristics: Cosmos bipinnatus is an old-fashioned favorite that deserves space in any garden. The 'Sensation Series' is the most common form available, but 'Seashells' is an interesting variation, with its petals curved into shell or funnel shapes around the golden centers. *C. bipinnatus* comes in wonderful shades from pure white to carmine, with many gently striped and shaded forms available. Breeders are working on a pale yellow form that will be an interesting addition to our cutting garden at

Plant Cosmos bipinnatus *in the background where they will not shade smaller plants. If allowed to reseed themselves,* Cosmos *will form a larger clump with additional flowers for bouquets.*

Dianthus barbatus *is noted for its sweetly fragrant flower heads. Many ruffled and bicolor forms exist. Get the taller varieties, as dwarf forms may prove difficult to cut.*

Digitalis purpurea *is a true biennial, but 'Foxy' will bloom the first year from seed if sown early. The delicate spires of flowers add elegance to any arrangement.*

Mohonk. Cosmos are large-boned members of the garden, growing to five feet, with flowers up to 3½ inches across. The foliage is a soft ferny green.

C. sulphureus, the Klondyke cosmos, is a shorter, hotter-colored relative of *C. bipinnatus. C. sulphureus* has stiffer, almost marigoldlike foliage and grows to 24 to 30 inches, depending on variety. It produces a large number of flowers with 8- to 10-inch stems in colors from yellow to deep red.

Cultural Information: In the garden both cosmos forms described above require full sun, well-drained soil and moderate fertility. Too much fertilizer early in the season will delay bloom. If allowed to reseed, *C. bipinnatus* will return to the garden year after year, creating an ever-changing display of pink, white, magenta and carmine hues. It is always wise to stake cosmos early in the season with a heavy-duty bamboo cane or other suitable support.

Harvest and Use: Cosmos provides good, long cutting stems if you are not afraid to sacrifice some buds—buds look great in the flower arrangement. 'Sensation Series' cosmoses will last for 1 or more weeks in the vase if conditioned in warm water. The pink, deep rose and white blooms can be used with the blue of *Trachelium* and with larkspur to great advantage. The Klondykes are reliable and will last well if cut early. They shatter (petals fall rapidly off blossom) when past their prime. The colors are clean and clear. One of my all-time favorite combinations is orange cosmos with blue *Salvia.*

Dianthus barbatus (dee-ANTH-us bar-BA-tus) **sweet William, ○ ✳ C**

Characteristics: The sweetly fragrant flowers of sweet Williams are borne on flattened heads. The inflorescences are like individual, single pinks (perennial *Dianthus*) in shades from white to deep pink and purple. Many of the flowers are shaded, striped, blotched or edged in contrasting colors. Avoid wet soils and crowding for the greatest success with *Dianthus.* Count on sweet William to top out at about 18 inches with stems of 12 or more inches.

Cultural Information: D. barbatus is in fact a biennial, but it can be grown as an annual if started indoors in early spring. Sweet William can be sown in late summer to early fall where they are to bloom in the spring, or indoors to be moved into the border in the spring for early summer bloom.

Harvest and Use: D. barbatus is an excellent cut flower and will hold in water for two weeks or longer if conditioned properly. Combine sweet William with blue *Salvia* and mullein pink for delightful results.

Digitalis purpurea 'Foxy' (di-ji-TAL-is pur-pew-REE-a) **foxglove, ○ ◐ W**

Zones: 4 to 9

Characteristics: Digitalis 'Foxy' was a breakthrough in breeding when introduced several years ago. It is the first foxglove reliable as an annual. 'Foxy' is commonly found in garden centers and greenhouses in spring. Foxgloves make excellent specimens for cutting, with graceful spikes of flowers in shades from creamy white to rosy lavender. The throats of the blooms are intricately spotted with deep purples. *D. purpurea* Excelsior hybrids have individual florets produced around the stem for a much denser spike. The species *D. × mertonensis* is a true perennial form the color of strawberry yogurt. All species of *Digitalis* are poisonous and should be handled with care.

Cultural Information: Plant in well-drained garden soil enriched with organic matter. Foxgloves do well in partial shade and produce a large number of flowers suitable for cutting. *D. purpurea* is a true biennial, requiring 2 years to complete its life cycle. Allow the best of the plants to set seed and they will self-sow; in this way they will make a lovely, self-sustaining colony.

Harvest and Use: Harvest *Digitalis* when about one-third of the blossoms are open. *Digitalis* holds nicely in water for 2 weeks or longer if conditioned in warm water overnight. Combinations with hardy lilies, roses, cosmoses, shasta daisies or other rounded forms are especially handsome. Try the more purple shades with yarrow or tansy for a pretty, complementary arrangement.

Euphorbia marginata (EW-for-bee-a mar-ji-NAH-ta) **snow-on-the-mountain, ○ ◐ ✸ 💧 S, H**

Characteristics: Snow-on-the-mountain is a wonderfully bright member of the poinsettia family. It is tall, bold and makes an enchanting accent in the integrated border or cutting garden. *Euphorbia* produces a sticky white sap when cut and care must be taken in handling it (see page 31). Snow-on-the-mountain produces cleanly variegated foliage of gray-green striped with purest white. The tiny white flowers add some textural interest but are insignificant.

Cultural Information: Euphorbia is a strong grower that does best in full sun and warm locations. Sow seed directly outdoors in early spring where it is to grow, as the plants don't like to be moved. Snow-on-the-mountain will grow to 3 to 4 feet, and can fill a space in the back of the mixed border. Thin young plants to about 1 foot apart to allow them adequate space to mature. Staking may be required in exposed locations.

Harvest and Use: A searing dip in water that is boiling hot or exposing the cut stems to flame will congeal the sap and keep it from fouling water in the conditioning container and vase. After searing, give them a deep drink of hot water to condition overnight. The effect when mixed with flowers of any color is outstanding. For an elegant effect, use snow-on-the-mountain in an all-white bouquet with hydrangea, white snapdragon or gladiolus and white *lisianthus.*

Eustoma grandiflorum

(yew-STO-ma gran-di-FLO-rum)

lisianthus, prairie gentian, ○ ♦ H

Characteristics: Eustoma grandiflorum has had a somewhat uncertain beginning. A development of plant breeders, it was first named *Lisianthus Russellianus* and may still appear under this genus. Lisianthus, a child of the prairies, has become a cut flower of renown. It is available in pale shell pink, white, deep blue, rose, lilac and bicolored white with purple edges. Double varieties have been introduced in the past few years, adding to the versatility of this cut flower. The Yodel hybrid varieties have become the standards in the single types, whereas 'Lion' and 'Double Eagle' are excellent sources of the double forms of cut flowers in mixed colors. The buds are a great part of the plant's charm. Each petal swirls around the other, overlapping in a delicate pointed spiral, and the flower opens looking like a single poppy or tulip. The doubles don't have the grace of bud of the singles, nor do they possess the purity of form when open. They do provide a long-lasting, roselike flower that is very elegant in any flower arrangement.

Cultural Information: Eustoma is slow to germinate and sometimes fussy in the seed flat. Unless you have ideal growing conditions to start seedlings indoors early, you may be better off buying started seedlings from a greenhouse in spring. It takes about 140 days for flowers to be produced from seed, so direct seeding is not recommended in northern climates. Plant *Eustoma* seedlings in a full-sun location in well-drained garden soil. They will tolerate drought once established, but thrive in moist, well-drained soils. Staking is generally not necessary for these plants, which reach a maximum height of 2 feet.

Harvest and Use: The flowers are borne on sprays with sturdy, smooth stems. The gray-green foliage stays neat and is not demanding when cut. Lisianthus is a reliable cut flower that will last for 3 weeks in a vase of water. Harvest an entire spray to get stems that are suitably long for design work or cut just the individual blooms on 4- to 6-inch stems for smaller vases. Conditioning cut stems is easy in hot water; lisianthus is almost always successful as a cut flower. Unlike some other annuals, it is slow to produce new stems, producing only three to four sprays of flowers over the course of the growing season. The primary flower will open first and be followed by a number of secondary buds. Though the buds

Euphorbia marginata *will thrive in hot, sunny locations. When harvesting, scald the stem ends in very hot water to arrest the flow of milky sap.*

Eustoma grandiflorum *may be difficult to grow from seed, but the end result is breathtaking. Cut and placed in water, the flowers may last for three weeks in an arrangement.*

last well in water, smaller buds will not mature when cut. Combine lisianthus with any number of other cuts for a variety of looks. The satiny petals harmonize nicely with snapdragons, stocks, sweet peas and lilies. Or provide a contrast in texture with *Astilbe*, yarrows or gayfeathers.

Flossflower; see ***Ageratum***

Flowering tobacco; see ***Nicotiana***

Foxglove; see ***Digitalis***

Garden sage; see ***Salvia***

The cloverlike blossoms of Gomphrena globosa *will delight the gardener and flower arranger alike. Grow plenty of these drought-tolerant flowers for fresh and dry use.*

Baby's breath is easily cultivated in well-drained soil that is slightly alkaline, hence the generic name Gypsophila. *The annual 'Covent Garden White' will provide pure white flowers on graceful stems.*

Globe amaranth; see ***Gomphrena***

Gloriosa daisy; see ***Rudbekia***

Gomphrena globosa (gom-FREE-nah glo-BO-sa) **globe amaranth,** ○ ✸ 💧 **W**

Characteristics: Globe amaranths are easy-to-grow, sun-loving annuals that are a must for every cutting garden. The rounded, cloverlike blossoms come in shades of white, pink, lavender, magenta, orange and strawberry red. Upon close inspection, the flowers appear to have reflective, shiny surfaces, but the overall effect in the garden and bouquet is that of rather coarse, bristly flowers. *G. g.* 'Buddy' was bred as a bedding plant and grows to 8 to 10 inches. Look for tall mixed strains, 'Strawberry Fayre' (or 'Strawberry Fields'), 'Lavender Queen' and *G. haageana,* which is a bright orange.

Cultural Information: There are several varieties available for growing from seed. Seedlings are purchased at the garden center or greenhouse in spring. Plant them out after danger of frost in full sun. *Gomphrena* does well in heat and tolerates drought, though it will thrive if it receives adequate moisture.

Harvest and Use Most frequently used as an everlasting, *Gomphrena* lasts indefinitely in water and is among the few flowers that last well in both water and floral foam. All of the colors combine well with many different flowers. The magenta form is stunning when used with creamy white zinnias.

You will find it necessary to harvest smaller flower buds with mature flowers; these will continue to enlarge somewhat in the arrangement, adding texture and interest. Condition the prepared stems in warm water because hot water will damage them. To use dried, hang upside down in a warm, dry, dark location. The color of the dried flower is almost as bright as that of fresh *Gomphrena.*

Gypsophila elegans (jip-SOF-i-la ay-le-GANZ) **annual baby's breath,** ○ **H**

Characteristics: Baby's breath is strongly associated with commercial florists, but it is worth including a small number of plants to provide filler for your bouquets. Annual baby's breath is a pleasant change from the *G. paniculata* 'Bristol Fairy' type typically found in flower shops. The flowers are flat, white or pale rose, and feature a single layer of five petals. Baby's breath is found in loosely branched panicles.

Cultural Information: For success over the long season, repeat sowings of seed at 2- to 3-week intervals. *Gypsophila* requires full sun and perfectly drained soils. Additions of ground agricultural limestone to the soil will aid its growth. Staking may be necessary during wet weather as "gyp" can become leggy.

Harvest and Use: Baby's breath is an excellent accent flower and gives a light airiness to bouquets. I enjoy masses of baby's breath in a vase with accents of small, colored flowers such as rose buds, bachelor's buttons and sweet Williams.

Helianthus annuus *is a vigorous addition to the sunny garden. Those not cut for inclusion in bouquets can be ripened to feed the birds.*

Helianthus annuus (hee-lee-ANTH-us AN-ew-us) **sunflower,** ○ ◐ ✸ 💧 **H**

Sunflowers are a basic ingredient of many vegetable gardens where they are grown to provide food for the chickadees. Varieties such as 'Mammoth' are large flowers of the sort Van Gogh painted. They work very nicely in autumn arrangements indoors and out. However, sunflower selection need not stop at the 'Mammoth' types. A wide variety of cultivars is available in heights ranging from 2 to 12 feet. 'Color Fashion' and 'Sunburst' offer smaller versions of the favorite at a more manageable height (5 feet) and in a wider range of colors, from creamy white to yellow, gold, mahogany and brown. Many of the 3- to 5-inch flowers are made distinctive by concentric bands of contrasting color or petals accented by darker hues of the same color.

Cultural Information: Sunflowers are easy to grow in average garden soil in full sun. Sow the seed where it is to grow, thinning to a final spacing of 1 foot. Though sunflowers tolerate drought, the quantity and quality of blooms produced will be better when they receive adequate moisture. Staking of the taller varieties should be done early as there may be a tendency for stems to be knocked over by heavy winds and late-summer rains.

Harvest and Use: Sunflowers condition nicely in hot water. Remove most of the large, coarse foliage as it taxes the stem's ability to supply water to the flower. Try combining the large forms of sunflower with other late-summer favorites. Cornstalks and other garden produce make an attractive display for the rustic porch. Smaller varieties combine well with apricot dahlias and goldenrods and look right at home in an old bronze vase.

Immortelle; see ***Xeranthemum***

Kiss-me-over-the-garden-gate; see ***Amaranthus***

Lace flower; see ***Trachymene***

Larkspur, annual; see ***Consolida***

Lathyrus odoratus (LATH-ear-us owe-DOR-ah-tus) **sweet pea,** ○ ◐ ✳ **C**

Characteristics: Sweet peas are among the truly romantic flowers of the cutting garden. They speak of a gentler time when the delicately colored blooms might be included in a nosegay or tussy-mussy. Sweet peas range from white to soft pinks, pastel lavenders and stronger shades of purple and red.

*Charm, innocence, fragrance and beauty—*Lathyrus odoratus *offers it all.*

There are varieties that offer mottled flowers, bicolors and stripes. The flowers, which resemble miniature sun bonnets, are borne on short, stiff stems that branch off tendril-covered vines to 5 feet long.

Cultural Information: Sweet peas like a well-drained soil, sweetened with lime. Like other peas, the sweet pea should be planted in early spring as soon as the soil can be worked. To speed germination, soak the seed overnight to soften the seed coat. Sweet peas are a legume and do best when inoculated with a beneficial bacterium that works with the plant roots to make nitrogen available for growth. Legume Aid and Burpee Booster are two products available for this purpose. Be sure to provide a climbing support for the growing vine, be it a string trellis, teepee of poles or fencing, as unsupported sweet peas can become an unmanageable tangle.

Harvest and Use: All parts of this plant are desirable for floral design when conditioned in cool water. The gray-green foliage and twisted tendrils add charm to floral designs. Consider combining sweet peas with delicate shades of roses, forget-me-nots and blue veronicas, or keep them all to themselves for a delightfully old-fashioned bouquet.

Lisianthus; see ***Eustoma***

Love-in-a-mist; see ***Nigella***

Love-lies-bleeding; see ***Amaranthus***

Marigold; see ***Tagetes***

Marigold, pot; see ***Calendula***

Mignonette; see ***Reseda***

Moluccella laevis (mo-lu-KEL-la lee-VIS) **bells of Ireland,** ○ ◐ W

Characteristics: Green flowers are so unusual that they always receive attention. Bells of Ireland is just such an annual. The flowers are insignificant white blossoms surrounded by attractive, bright, apple green bracts (modified leaves). The bract remains showy after the flower fades. The spires of bell-shaped bracts are harvested to be used fresh or dry in bouquets.

Cultural Information: Bells of Ireland is easy to grow in a well-drained location in full sun. It is not fussy about soil but is difficult to start from seed. Refrigerate the seed for at least 5 days before soaking overnight in warm water. Press the prepared seed into the soil without covering it; the seeds need light to germinate. The bells will slowly mature through the season and in ideal circumstances reach 2 or more feet.

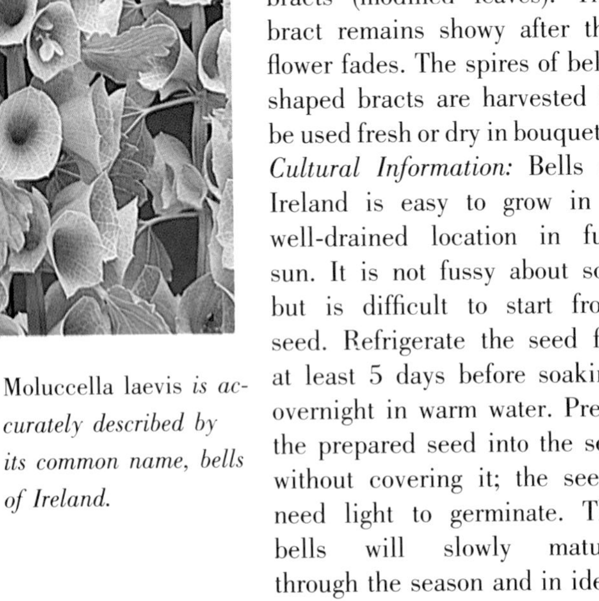

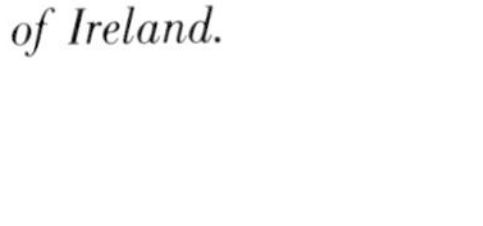

Moluccella laevis *is accurately described by its common name, bells of Ireland.*

Harvest and Use: Take a few moments to remove the extra leaves that appear between the bracts—I feel they detract from the form of *Moluccella.* The flowers condition well in warm water and last for 7 to 10 days as fresh cuts. To dry, hang bells of Ireland upside down in a dark, warm, dry place. Although the green will fade slightly, the spires will continue to provide interesting color and texture in dried arrangements into the winter months.

Bells of Ireland combines well with any of the "everlastings" in dried bouquets but works well with fresh flowers, too. I especially like them with some of the late-summer–blooming annuals and perennials such as *Tithonia, Aconitum,* asters and goldenrods, and there is something very pleasing about *Moluccella* with zinnias. For a change of pace, try an all-green arrangement with foliages and the flowers of the 'Envy' zinnia and 'Lime Green' nicotiana, seed heads of garlic chives, the foliage of hosta and, of course, bells of Ireland.

Mourning bride; see ***Scabiosa***

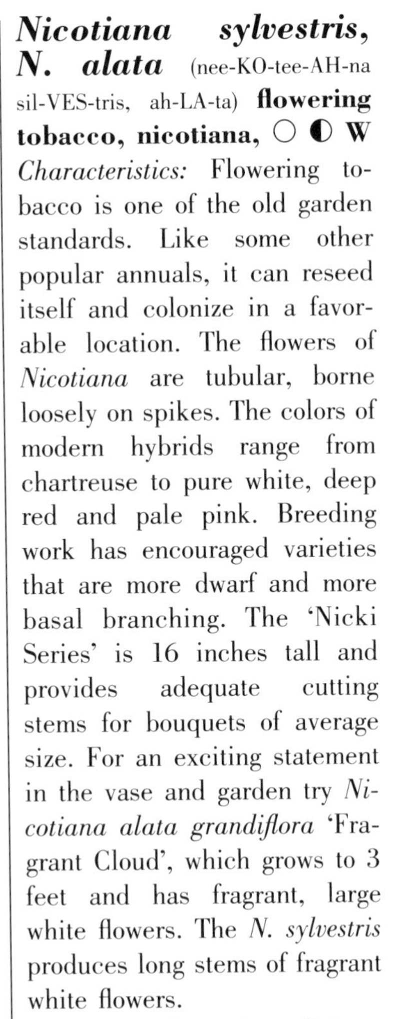

Nicotiana sylvestris, N. alata (nee-KO-tee-AH-na sil-VES-tris, ah-LA-ta) **flowering tobacco, nicotiana,** ○ ◐ W

Characteristics: Flowering tobacco is one of the old garden standards. Like some other popular annuals, it can reseed itself and colonize in a favorable location. The flowers of *Nicotiana* are tubular, borne loosely on spikes. The colors of modern hybrids range from chartreuse to pure white, deep red and pale pink. Breeding work has encouraged varieties that are more dwarf and more basal branching. The 'Nicki Series' is 16 inches tall and provides adequate cutting stems for bouquets of average size. For an exciting statement in the vase and garden try *Nicotiana alata grandiflora* 'Fragrant Cloud', which grows to 3 feet and has fragrant, large white flowers. The *N. sylvestris* produces long stems of fragrant white flowers.

Cultural Information: Culture in the garden is easy. Seed can be sown where the plants are to grow in a well-drained, rich soil. Press seeds into the soil but do not cover, as they require light to germinate. Taller varieties may need staking. Ni-

Nicotiana alata *'Nicki Hybrid Mixed' will grow in partial shade and provide many lovely blooms for cutting.*

cotiana does well in full sun but it thrives in partial shade. In the integrated cutting garden, plant it near a terrace or bedroom window where the intoxicating fragrance can be enjoyed in the evening, when it is strongest. It may be attacked by slugs and occasionally infested with spider mites, so watch for signs of these pests.
Harvest and Use: Nicotiana can be difficult to harvest as the flowers, stems and leaves are sticky and can become so entwined they damage themselves when one tries to separate them. Harvest them individually and separate individual stems as much as possible. Give them a deep, wide bucket of warm water and spread the stems around the perimeter to avoid their tangling. Nicotiana is an exotic-looking flower for arrangements and goes well with hardy lilies, phloxes, purple coneflowers and the largest of the cosmos blossoms. In the home, place it where the fragrance can be enjoyed in the evening.

Nigella damascena (ny-JELL-a dam-a-SKAY-na) **love-in-a-mist, ○ W**

Characteristics: How the Victorians loved their romantic names and romantic flowers. The common name above offers a vivid picture of this excellent cut flower. *Nigella* is a small, starlike flower surrounded by a delicate spray of ferny foliage just below the flower head. Flowers range in color from pale blue-green to white, pink, blue and purple. The variety 'Persian Jewels' gives the full color range on 18-inch plants.
Cultural Information: Love-in-a-mist is a true annual, growing from seed, to flower, to fruit in short order. Once the attractive seedpods have developed, the flowers will no longer be produced. Blooming will be prolonged somewhat on plants whose flowers are harvested regularly. *Nigella* is easy to grow from seed and is likely to reseed itself if you allow a few seed heads to remain on the plant. Sow the seed every 2 to 3 months for continuous bloom from June until frost.
Harvest and Use: Harvesting love-in-a-mist is easy, and conditioning in warm water will harden cut stems nicely for use in arrangements. The seedpods can be collected and dried for use on wreaths or in dried arrangements for display throughout the autumn and winter months. The delicate colors and soft texture of *Nigella* make it easy to combine with other flowers from the garden. Choose similarly delicate flowers such as the light, snapdragon-like blooms of *Linaria*. It combines well with the smaller blooms of *Dianthus* too.

Nigella damascena *is a delightful, old-fashioned flower that produces fascinating seedpods for everlasting bouquets.*

Painted tongue; see ***Salpiglossis***

Pincushion flower; see ***Scabiosa***

Pot marigold; see ***Calendula***

Prairie gentian; see ***Eustoma***

Purple umbrella; see ***Trachelium***

Reseda odorata (ree-SEE-da oh-do-RAH-ta) **mignonette, ○ C**

Characteristics: Mignonette is not an extravagant beauty that catches the eye of every passerby, but a delicate charmer with greenish blossoms that delight the sense of smell. The sweet scent of mignonette was a favorite 100 years ago, but today the plant has all but disappeared from American gardens. It grows to about 1 foot in height. The medium green leaves are topped by short spikes of dense greenish flowers often tinged with red or cream.
Cultural Information: Reseda should be sown where it is to grow in early spring. Plant in full sun and well-drained garden soil. Supplemental fertilizing will help maintain production throughout the summer, as will maintaining adequate soil moisture. A small amount included in the cutting garden is enough to provide fragrance for several bouquets all summer.

Reseda odorata *is not a glamorous beauty, but will delight everyone's sense of smell with its clean, sweet aroma.*

Rudbeckia hirta is a lovely addition to any flower arrangement or late-summer garden. The flowers may be difficult to condition, but the end result is well worth the extra effort.

Harvest and Use: Condition *Reseda* in cool water before including in bouquets. The colors are not significant enough to alter even the most delicate of color schemes very much. Use it as a filler to cover the mechanics of an arrangement while it perfumes the air.

Rudbeckia hirta (rood-BEK-ee-a her-TA) **gloriosa daisy,** ○ 💧 ✹ **W**

Zones: 3 to 9

Characteristics: Gloriosa daisies are among the most dependable summer bloomers, offering up their sunny, daisy flowers all summer long. Sometimes listed as an annual, biennial and even as a perennial, the truth of the matter is it's a free-seeding annual and will turn up in the cutting garden or integrated border season after season if allowed to go to seed. The coarse leaves and spiny stems suit this earth goddess of the garden. Muted tones of gold, brown, yellow, burgundy and orange are typical of the varieties of this easy-to-care-for annual. Some of the more delightful specimens offer deep markings on the petals surrounding a prominent, dark brown, center cone. The variety 'Irish Eyes' has a distinctive green center that makes it a delightful accompaniment to variegated foliage.

Cultural Information: Choose a sunny place in the garden for this common roadside plant. It doesn't require an overly rich soil. *Rudbeckia* is widely available in the spring, and container-grown plants will transplant nicely. For ease in culture and cost savings, seed directly in the garden where the plants are to grow. Allow several of your favorite plants to self-sow and you will find a colony of bright, sunny blossoms each year.

Harvest and Use: Rudbeckia can be tricky to harvest and condition successfully. Cutting the stems and placing them directly into water in the garden improves chances of success, but at Mohonk we have found the florist's trick described on page 32 gives the straightest stems and the most perfect petals. Give gloriosa daisies plenty of room in the conditioning container; the blooms are up to 5 inches across, and the petals are easily damaged. Once turgid after conditioning, the flowers are long lasting and will grace a vase of fresh water for more than a week.

Arranging with gloriosa daisies is fun, as their bright colors and sturdy, no-nonsense look are always uplifting. Combine them with other rugged members of the cutting garden such as yarrow and blanketflower, add some down-home roadside selections such as grass heads and sedges, and you'll have the quintessential all-American bouquet! What better way to accent a picnic table for a summer barbecue?

Few flowers offer the richness of color and velvety texture of Salpiglossis sinuata.

Sage, garden; see ***Salvia***

Salpiglossis (sal-pi-GLOSS-iss sin-yew-AH-ta) **velvet flower, painted tongue,** ○ ◐ ✳ **S,W**

Characteristics: This petunia relative is a delightful addition to the cutting garden where summers are cool. The intensely colored flowers in shades of gold, blue, purple, maroon and yellow are rich additions to almost any flower arrangement. The variety 'Casino' is an 18- to 24-inch annual that features the full mix of colors, many with brightly streaked and veined throats.

Cultural Information: Salpiglossis can be sown directly in the garden, successfully started indoors or purchased from the nursery. Plant in a rich, light, well-drained soil in full sun to partial shade. Those planted in shade tend to be a little taller, but where summer heat is a problem, light shade will make for better success.

Harvest and Use: Cut *Salpiglossis* carefully, for like their cousin nicotiana, *Salpiglossis* clings to itself. Always cut them last, and carefully arrange them on top of other flowers in the cutting basket; try to keep them away from each other.

Painted tongue's velvety texture and rich colors give it a commanding presence in the vase. Combine it with other strong colors such as cherry red snapdragon or blue *Salvia,* or choose a more subtle cast of players with the delicate shadings of *Digitalis* and the gray foliage of *Artemisia.*

Salvia (sal-VEE-a) **garden sage, ○ W**
Zones: 4 to 9
Characteristics: The garden sages, a marvelous group, may be perennial or annual. The most common form, *Salvia splendens,* scarlet sage, is an old-fashioned favorite in the garden but perhaps should no longer be referred to as the scarlet sage. *S. splendens* comes in a variety of sizes and colors, including purple, rose, coral and white. The flowers of this member of the mint family are tubular and relatively short lived. The calyx, a long-lasting, brightly colored tube, remains showy long after the actual flower has faded. This is a warm-weather garden grower.

Salvia farinacea, mealycup sage, offers one of the best blues for the cutting garden and integrated border. This delightful native American provides an excellent source of true blue spikes for arrangements. The variety 'Argent' (or 'White Porcelain') is a silvery white companion. The 6- to 8-inch flower spikes top 8- to 10-inch stems. Consider 'Blue Bedder', which grows to about 30 inches, or for a shorter plant (18 inches), 'Victoria'. *S. farinacea* and *S. splendens* are perennials in warmer climates. In the Northeast it is best to treat them both as annuals.

Salvia horminum, Joseph's coat, is a delightful, small, textured sage and a true annual, completing its life cycle in 1 year. It may also be called the clary sage, which is a misnomer (clary sage is *S. sclarea*). The colorful bracts in pale pink, white or blue will provide a copious supply of color for fresh-cut or dried bouquets. Sow the seed where it is to grow. Joseph's coat will frequently reseed itself and return to the garden for many seasons.

Salvia patens, the gentian sage, is a lesser-known cousin of the other annual and tender perennial sages. This salvia is perhaps one of the boldest of blue flowers. Although the flowers are not as prolific as the other sages, the clear azure blue of gentian sage will bring a bright, bold accent to the garden.
Cultural Information: Give the sage a hot, sunny spot in the garden, and you will be happy with the profusion of blooms suitable for fresh and dry use. *Salvia* varieties are available at local greenhouses each spring; look for varieties that will be tall enough to provide good length in cutting stems. Although *Salvia* tolerates poor soils and drought, give it a rich soil with plenty of organic matter and adequate moisture to see it thrive. *S. horminum* will reseed and colonize in the garden, providing years of cutting materials from one sowing.
Harvest and Use: Floral combinations are unlimited with the blues of *S. horminum, S. farinacea* and *S. patens.* Combinations with summer-blooming annuals such as marigolds and zinnias work well, as do such elegant flowers as lilies and roses. The upright flower spikes are the ideal counterpoint to the rounded flower forms like those of zinnias. The brilliant scarlet sage will become a delightful accent for marigolds in late summer or early autumn.

Scabiosa atropurpurea
(skāb-ee-O-sa ah-tro-pur-PEWR-ee-a)
pincushion flower, mourning bride, ○ W
Characteristics: The reaction to *Scabiosa* is always the same: "Why does such a pretty flower have such an unpleasant name?" *Scabiosa* is an arrestingly beautiful flower. Its simplicity is deceiving. The fully double, rounded heads are composed of intricate series of individual blooms in deep red, blue, white and every pastel shade in between. Light-colored stamens extend above the petals of the flowers like pins from a pincushion, hence one of its common names. Plants may reach 3 feet in height, and individual flower stems average 1 or more feet, making them long-lasting favorites of the home flower arranger.
Cultural Information: Scabiosa is easy to grow in a well-drained, rich garden soil. Start plants indoors or sow seed directly in May for good cut-flower production from August through a killing frost. Few pests bother the pincushion flower. Look for the 'Giant Imperial' variety for cutting. Offering a superior mix of colors, it behaves nicely in the garden and rarely needs staking.

*The garden sages (*Salvia spp.*) will provide many flowers for cutting and drying. Blue salvia (*S. farinacea*) is among the best of all the blue flowers for cutting.*

Scabiosa atropurpurea *has wonderful, mounded flowers in a rich range of colors. The wiry stems support the flowers well in arrangements.*

*The Signet Marigolds (*Tagetes signata *'Pumila') will delight you. These tiny blossoms are borne in sprays with fernlike foliage.*

Harvest and Use: Cutting *Scabiosa* is easy as the foliage is mostly basal. Properly conditioned in warm water, it isn't unusual for pincushion flowers to last as long as 2 weeks. The range of colors represented in *Scabiosa* makes the blossoms easy to use with many other garden flowers. August and September are rich months in the cutting garden, with abundant selections and combinations from which to choose. Try the deep red, almost black *Scabiosa* with garden phlox and globe amaranth for an intriguing contrast of forms and textures. The pastel shades are well offset by the deep blue-violet hues of *Aconitum,* and any of them will work well with lisianthuses which run in a similar color range and will harmonize well in an analogous color scheme.

Snapdragon; see ***Antirrhinum***

Snow-on-the-mountain; see ***Euphorbia***

Sunflower; see ***Helianthus***

Marigolds, Tagetes erecta, *are some of the most rewarding flowers for the cutting garden: they are easy to grow and inexpensive and their garden performance is matched by their beauty in the vase.*

Sweet pea; see ***Lathyrus***

Sweet William; see ***Dianthus***

Tagetes (ta-GAY-teez) **marigold, ○ ● ✸ W**

Characteristics: The common marigold, an excellent cut flower, is probably not used as much as it should be. Perhaps this is because it is often one of the first plants many of us grow, and we associate it with our unsophisticated beginnings. It's true some people are repelled by the pungent foliage. I'm one of those people who takes comfort in that familiar smell. But for those who are hesitant, many of today's marigolds have a less pungent foliage than their ancestors, and some varieties have odorless foliage.

Cultural Information: Marigolds are Mexican natives and thrive in a hot, dry garden environment in well-drained soil. Purchase plants from the nursery in spring or seed them where they are to grow in the sunny garden. Like many annuals, marigolds will tolerate drought but produce more cuttable stems when grown in well-prepared, fertile soil with adequate moisture. Their ease in culture, bold color and long-lasting vase life make them ideal subjects for the cutting garden.

Harvest and Use: *Tagetes* is easily harvested and conditioned. Cleaned stems can be placed in warm water to harden, for use in fresh water or floral foam. They last equally well in water and floral foam. During the cooler autumn months, harvest marigolds in the warmer part of the day; they are better able to absorb water when warm.

Three species of *Tagetes* are typically available as seedlings: *T. erecta* (the African marigold), *T. patula* (the French marigold) and *T. signata pumila* (the signet marigold). The names are ironic, as all marigolds are native Americans. The African marigold is also called the American marigold or hedge marigold. These are the tallest of the marigolds, growing to 3 or more feet with flowers to 4 inches across. I like using the big, bold, brassy African marigold with the bright red *Salvia* 'Early Bonfire' for a neon announcement that summer is over!

The French marigolds are dwarfs, with heights of 6 to 12 inches. Free flowering, French marigold blooms are 1 inch across and may be single, fully double, anenome-flowered or crested in form. These are delightful garden subjects but frequently don't provide adequate stem length to make them worthwhile in the cutting garden.

The African and French marigolds have been crossed and are called triploid, mule or Afro-French marigolds. Many of these are only 12 to 14 inches high, bearing large flowers similar to those of the African types. Their short stems are difficult to use in flower designs.

To me the most delightful and useful of the marigolds is the signet marigold. These 12- to 14-inch plants produce the smallest of the marigold blooms at ½ inch across. The single blossoms are borne in profusion atop ferny foliage that has a distinctly lemony fragrance. This marigold produces 8- to 10-inch stems of flower sprays that add delightful texture when used as filler in arrangements. The variety 'Lemon Gem' is clean medium yellow. Combine it with *Lisianthus* 'Yodel Blue' or with *Gomphrena globosa* 'Strawberry Fields'. The individual blossoms of 'Lemon Gem' can be added (if they have not been sprayed) to a tossed salad for extra color and a unique, pungent flavor.

Tobacco, flowering; see ***Nicotiana***

Trachelium caeruleum

(tray-KEEL-ee-um see-RU-lee-um)

blue throatwort, purple umbrella, ○ W

Characteristics: Trachelium, a tender perennial, will overwinter in the South. It forms dense heads of smoky, deep purple flowers borne on tough, wiry stems. The stems in and of themselves are of interest and appear almost black. The panicles of flowers are useful in bouquets where their distinctive form, texture and faint fragrance complement almost any other flower types.

Cultural Information: Trachelium seeds are tiny and should be started indoors on a sunny windowsill 6 to 8 weeks before the last spring frost. They tolerate cool temperatures and will bloom from midsummer until frost when planted in a sunny location.

Harvest and Use: Trachelium is so stiff you can almost use it without conditioning. The flowers will last for 1 month or longer in arrangements and show no preference to either water or floral foam. Combine *Trachelium* 'Purple Umbrella' with *Tithonia,* the Mexican sunflower, or the orange zinnia for a bright contrast in colors. Or, use them with *Delphinium,* dahlias or lilies for a more elegant effect. The white form ('White Umbrella') is available but doesn't appeal to me, as the white blossoms appear almost dirty against the dark stems.

Trachymene coerulea

(tra-kee-MAY-nee ko-ROO-lee-ah)

blue lace flower, ○ ✳ W

Characteristics: The Victorians loved these umbels of pale blue, fragrant flowers. This little-known, easy-to-grow annual is best grown in the cutting garden as plants may become scrappy looking as the season progresses. These plants produce dozens of blooms and resemble pale blue Queen Anne's lace. Flower production may slow down during the hot summer months if night temperatures exceed 70 degrees Fahrenheit.

Cultural Information: Sow the seeds where they are to grow about the time of the last spring frost. The plants will grow to a height of 18 inches and will spread to 1 or more feet. Space seedlings 8 to 10 inches apart for best flower production. *Trachymene* doesn't like to dry out, so water well during drought. Regular harvesting will help promote flower production.

Harvest and Use: Cut, stripped of its light green, deeply lobed foliage, and conditioned in warm water, *Trachymene* is one of the longest-lasting cut flowers. Try combining it with other flowers of delicate hue such as sweet peas, pale pink lisianthuses and pink *Salvia horminum,* or try the pale yellow of *Calendula,* deep green foliage of *Arborvitae,* and a stronger blue as of larkspurs. This blossom becomes "something blue" in wedding bouquets, especially lovely when mixed with creamy white roses and baby's breath.

Umbrella, purple; see ***Trachelium***

Trachelium caeruleum *has wiry stems supporting deep purple-blue flowers borne in flat-top clusters. The flowers, though small, create a wonderfully hazy look in arrangements.*

Try old-fashioned Trachymene *in combination with other pastel flowers for a delicate, feminine bouquet.*

Verbena bonariensis often reseeds and colonizes in the garden. It is best to plant this vigorous, 4-foot-tall grower in the background.

Grow Xeranthemum annuum for fresh or dry use in the sunny garden.

Zinnias are never out of style.

Velvet flower; see ***Salpiglossis***

Verbena bonariensis

(ver-BEE-na bon-AR-ee-EN-sis) **verbena,** ○ ● ✸ **W**

Characteristics: There are many verbenas available from seed catalogs for growing in sunny spots of the garden, but none will provide the stem length and garden show of *Verbena bonariensis. V. bonariensis* reaches 4 to 5 feet, and its strong, stiff, upright stems support the dense clusters of rosy purple flowers without staking.

Cultural Information: Seed directly into the garden in full sun and thin to 12 inches apart. The young plants will appear leggy and spare when young, but a cluster of six to eight plants will quickly put on a display of note. Allow a few blossoms to ripen at the end of the season as the plant will reseed and a natural-looking colony will develop. In the garden combine *V. bonariensis* with cosmos, cleome and *Artemisia ludoviciana* 'Silver King' for a free-flowing, long-flowering display of self-sufficient plants.

Harvest and Use: Verbena is easy to condition and will last for 7 to 10 days in water. Use warm water to condition the stems, which require little or no stripping of foliage. In the vase, combine it with some of its garden friends, cosmos and the silvery foliage of *Artemisia.* The color will glow among pink and lavender flowers of any type.

Xeranthemum annuum

(ze-RAN-the-mum an-NEW-um) **immortelle,** ○ ✸ ● **W**

Characteristics: Frequently listed among everlastings, immortelle is an easily grown, trouble-free flower for use in fresh and dried bouquets. These composite flowers are on 3-foot plants characterized by white, softly furred leaves and stems. The plants will bear blossoms of pale pink, white, rose and lilac in single and double forms. Individual blossoms are small (1¼ inches in diameter), but the plants produce generous amounts suitable for fresh and dried use as well as plenty left over for garden display.

Cultural Information: Like so many of the everlastings, *Xeranthemum* requires full sun in average, well-drained garden soil. It can be started indoors in a sunny, warm location in March for transplanting into the garden after all danger of frost. Seed it directly out of doors after danger of frost for late-summer bloom.

Harvest and Use: Immortelle combines well with other everlastings such as *Gomphrena* and *Helichrysum* in either fresh or dried form. However, the soft, grayish white stems and shiny flowers mix best with flowers of more satiny texture. Try combining it with *Salpiglossis* or *Ageratum.* I like the colors and textures mixed with the deep red foliage of *Ocimum basilicum* 'Purple Ruffles' (purple basil) or *Perilla,* too.

Zinnia elegans

(zin-EE-ah EL-e-ganz) **zinnia,** ○ **W**

Characteristics: Zinnias are like old friends: They are comfortable to be around, and though undemanding, they do much to enrich our lives. Zinnias are true summer annuals, basking in bright sun and hot days. Zinnia colors are strong, and flowers make a bold statement in form and colors. The petals have an unusual satiny quality and seem to shine as if coated with reflective dust. This gives the zinnia blossom an inner light. Two of the best varieties for cutting are 'Cut and Come Again', with 1½-inch blooms, and 'State Fair', with blossoms up to 3 inches across. These two varieties complement each other well, with flowers that range from creamy white to soft pink, hot pink, magenta and deep rose to bright red. Interspersed are plants producing flowers from the palest yellow to deep gold and clear orange to bronze. Both grow on sturdy plants to 36 inches. *Zinnia* 'Envy' is a green variety that may have some people looking askance, but when combined with the whites of snapdragons, nicotianas, bells of Ireland and the foliage of snow-on-the-mountain, the effect is remarkably cool and elegant.

Cultural Information: Zinnias can be seeded directly in the garden or purchased as seedlings in spring. Wait until the soil has warmed and all danger of frost is past before planting. Zinnias are prone to powdery mildew in late summer and will benefit from a full-sun location with plenty of room around them for good air movement. If possible, avoid watering with overhead sprinklers, as this promotes conditions favorable to the disease. 'State Fair' may need staking, but the smaller-flowered 'Cut and Come Again' will do very nicely on its own.
Harvest and Use: Zinnias are delightfully easy to cut for use in flower arrangements. Like many annuals, zinnias produce more and better blooms as the season progresses; don't be afraid to cut heavily. The leaves are attached tightly to the stem and care must be used in removing them as the stems are easily bent. Zinnia blooms should be cut in the warmer part of the day during the cool autumn months as they will not condition well when stems are cold. Condition zinnias in warm, not hot, water; even though the plants thrive in summer heat, the flower stems can be damaged by excessive heat.

Zinnias are among the most versatile of all the cutting flowers. They will last for 1 or more weeks in water, and are in bloom for such a long period in the garden that you will be able to create different combinations from June through October. Try deep rose zinnias with creamy white *Astilbe* in June, hot pink and magenta zinnias with *Liatris* in July, yellow zinnias with yellow lilies and ferns in August, and greet autumn with orange and bronze zinnias with *Gaillardia* and gloriosa daisies in September.

PERENNIALS

Achillea (ah-KEEL-ee-a) **yarrow, ○ ♦ H**
Zones: 3 to 8
Characteristics: The yarrows are easy additions to the cutting garden, where they perform well in hot, sunny, dry conditions and even in poorer soils. Yarrows are native Americans and bring with them an inbred hardiness and disease resistance. Several species are worth including in the cutting garden, many producing blooms suitable for both fresh and dry use.

Achillea × 'Coronation Gold' is a standard in the perennial border and should be planted in the cutting garden for its profuse display of quality flowers. The stems of the brilliant golden yellow flower heads reach 3 feet, giving them the height needed for even the largest floral designs. Individual heads may be as much as 3 inches across, easy to use in almost any bouquet. Like that of many *Achillea* varieties the foliage of *A.* × 'Coronation Gold' is mostly basal, finely serrated and soft gray-green.

A. filipendulina is the fernleaf yarrow. It is the tallest of the yarrows, topping out at close to 5 feet. The flower heads are a strong golden yellow and reach 4 to 5 inches across. The gray-green foliage can reach 10 inches long and makes a suitable cut green when harvested and conditioned in warm water.

A. millefolium, common yarrow, offers several suitable cutting varieties. Try 'Cerise Queen', 'Rubra' or 'Rosea' for their flower heads in pinks and reds borne atop 2- to 2½-foot stems. 'Summer Pastels' is a new introduction, named an All-America Selection winner. The softly muted pinks, cream, buff and pale yellow flowers offer a soft, muted palette.

Cultural Information: Yarrow is one of the easiest plants to cultivate. Purchase named varieties from a reliable nursery or mail-order catalog in spring. Plant them in a well-dug garden site in full sun; take care to avoid creating an overrich soil because lush growth will be weak and floppy, requiring

Achillea *'Summer Pastels' from the Mohonk Gardens. The delicate shading of rose, yellow, blush and creamy white blend well in the garden and the vase.*

Aconitum *is a great cutting garden perennial. The blue cowls borne on spikes up to 4 feet tall give it the common name monkshood.*

Aquilegia *spp. will delight the gardener in partial shade. Try combining columbine with tulips or bleeding heart and bring spring indoors in a vase.*

staking. *A. millefolium* varieties become weedy in the garden; don't hesitate to divide them regularly to avoid overcrowding and reduce production. Yarrow is easily grown from seed and will flower the first year. Though yarrows tolerate drought when established, maintain adequate soil moisture during dry periods to promote high-quality flowers and healthy plants.

Harvest and Use: The yarrows offer coarse texture for the garden and vase, yet there is something very rich looking about the brilliant yellow heads, especially of *A. filipendulina* 'Gold Plate'. Cut and condition overnight in hot water for longest-lasting blooms in either fresh water or floral foam.

I like combining the yellow yarrows with strong foliages such as hosta which contrast nicely in texture. In a vase with deep purple *Delphinium* and *Astilbe*, yarrow is a standout. When dried, the heads can be cut from their stems and used in wreaths, where they'll hold their color long into the season.

Aconitum (ah-KO-ny-tum)

monkshood, ○ ◐ ✳ H

Zones: 5 to 8

Characteristics: Monkshood is a reliable alternative to *Delphinium* for the late-summer and early-fall border and cutting garden. The individual flowers in deep, rich blues and purples look like the cowled hoods worn by the brothers in the monastery, hence the name "monkshood."

There are actually several colors available in the genus *Aconitum*: Choose *A.* × *bicolor* for distinctive white flowers edged in blue; *A. napellus* 'Albus' for white; and for yellow or creamy white flowers, grow *A. vulparia.* In my estimation, the finest of form and color is the azure monkshood (*A. carmichaelii*), which grows to 4 feet. The flowers of azure monkshood, a deep purple-blue, are borne on long, tapering spikes.

Cultural Information: Aconitum prefers cool climates and rich garden soils that receive regular applications of organic matter and fertilizer. Purchase plants from a local nursery or buy the bare-root plants sold through many reputable mail-order houses. Soak the roots of bareroot plants overnight in warm water before planting for the best results.

Planted in light shade, *Aconitum* thrives for many years without being divided. A light, organic mulch will help conserve moisture and keep roots cool through the hot summer months.

Harvest and Use: Cut stems should be conditioned in hot water. In an arrangement, monkshood is happiest in plenty of water. Combine monkshood with yarrows, China asters, phloxes and hardy asters.

Aquilegia (ak-will-EE-jee-a)

columbine, ◐ ○ ● ✳ C

Zones: 4 to 8

Characteristics: Columbines are old-fashioned favorites that surely graced grandmother's garden as they grace our own in May and June. The multicolored, nodding blossoms are held above light green foliage reminiscent of maidenhair ferns. The intricate blossoms appear to be fragile, which belies the lasting quality they possess. Brightly colored sepals that may form elongated spurs add an exotic flair to the flowers in blues, pinks, yellows, red and white. The foliage can be cut for inclusion in flower arrangements, as can the seed heads, which are four-parted, upright cylindrical chambers. Columbines grow to 3 feet, depending on site and variety.

Try growing *A. caerulea* for its lovely blue and white flowers. The various varieties of *A.* × *hybrida* offer the largest assortment of colors and flower types. 'Nora Barlow' is a double flower with pink, red, green and white tones. The McKana Giant hybrids are among the largest flowered of all the varieties, with a full artist's palette of colors. 'Snow Queen' is pure white and very elegant.

Cultural Information: Columbines will grow in full sun, but do even better in partial shade as it provides a cooler environment. They require a perfectly drained soil to avoid root rot, which makes columbines relatively short-lived perennials.

The plants are easily grown from seed and may resist transplanting because of their tap root. Be prepared for them to reseed and form colonies. Hybrid columbines will generally not come true from seed collected in the garden, and an interesting selection may be found in subsequent generations, but don't be surprised if the color assortment and exotic spurs both start to disappear. Consider reseeding columbine

every other year or so to keep a fresh supply of a wide range of colors and form. Columbine will occasionally suffer from leaf miners, which feed between the upper and lower leaf surfaces, leaving irregular trails to mar the foliage.
Harvest and Use: Harvest back to the crown of the plant to get the longest stems possible. Columbines should be conditioned in cool water, which firms them nicely without hastening their demise. Fresh columbines last in the vase for 5 to 7 days. Combine columbines with other spring-flowering favorites. Try forget-me-nots, bleeding hearts, daffodils and tulips for a lighthearted, romantic garden bouquet.

Artemisia (ar-tay-MIS-ee-a) wormwood, mugwort, ○ ♦ ✹ H

Zones: 5 to 8
Characteristics: Artemisia is a native American and always a valued addition to the landscape and the vase. Typically, the wormwoods are grown for their finely cut, silvery foliage. Wormwood is a long-lived addition to the garden and easy to care for, with few pests or diseases.

Artemisia ludoviciana albula is the full Latin name for two of the best varieties for cutting and drying. 'Silver King' is a 3-foot plant, and 'Silver Queen' is a shorter relative; they produce large amounts of silvery white foliage.
Cultural Information: Plant the nursery-grown or bareroot plants in the garden in a well-drained soil in full sun. The soil should not be too rich, as this encourages legginess and weak stems that may require staking.
Harvest and Use: Harvest in late morning after the dew has dried, and condition the stems in hot water. If the foliage is wetted, it will appear to be green until it dries to a silvery white again. The yellow blossoms that form in June do not become a significant element of any display. I like to combine the silvery foliage of *Artemisia* with strong colors of the richest hues. *Celosia* and *Salvia* combine well with *Artemisia,* as do bold, red dahlias. Wormwood combines well with other foliage, and it is wonderful to see what happens when burgundy foliage is combined with silver. Pure white flowers of any species combine elegantly with *Artemisia.*

Aster (A-ster) Michaelmas daisy, ○ ◐ H

Zones: 3–8
Characteristics: Asters are among the best of the late-summer perennials for the cutting garden. They are long lasting in water and offer a color range to please even the most jaded. Several varieties provide suitable cuts. *Aster* × *frikartii* is one of the best, with an unparalleled season of bloom; these plants produce a large number of pale lavender-blue flowers singly at the ends of stems. *A. novae-angliae,* the New England aster, produces beautiful pink to lilac, daisylike flowers on plants that may grow 4 to 5 feet tall. *A. novi-belgi,* the New York aster, is not nearly as tall as its New England cousin but produces flowers that range from white to navy blue on plants to 3 feet. Both the New York and the New England aster are commonly found along roadsides and in waste places and meadows throughout the Northeast. The colors range from grayish white to deep blue, and although the flowers are usually quite small in the wild, you may find some that are showy and worthy of cutting.
Cultural Information: The taller asters may require staking, as they are prone to damage from the wind and heavy rains that may plague the late-summer garden. Give asters plenty of space in the border or cutting garden as they may mildew during the dog days of summer when humidity abounds and air sits stagnant. Dividing clumps of asters regularly is beneficial, not only to keep plants rejuvenated but to refresh the soil and space the plants out for better growth and development. Asters may be grown from seed, but the best results usually are obtained from container-grown or bareroot specimens purchased for spring planting.

Choose a rich garden site in full sun or light shade. Asters will frequently tolerate poor soils, but the plant height and flower size may suffer. Once established, hardy garden asters are likely to overrun the garden, and despite their loveliness they should be rogued out like any other weed. I always enjoy garden flowers that have a little spunk and offer "extras" to any gardening neighbor willing to take some off my hands.
Harvest and Use: Asters are easy to harvest and condition. The foliage, borne along the

The silvery-grey foliage of Artemisia ludoviciana *'Silver King' performs well in the sunny garden even in poor soils. Use it in arrangements either fresh or dried. Wormwood's grey foliage will combine well with a large variety of strong-colored flowers and foliages.*

Asters can often be found growing along the roadsides or in waste places. The improved varieties of Aster × frikartii *come in shades of blue, violet, rose, pink and white.*

length of the flower stem, easily strips off for additions to the compost pile. The flowers firm up very nicely in warm to hot water. Asters last well in floral foam but, like other flowers, really do best in clean water. Asters, with their yellow centers and petals in shades of blue and violet, combine well with many garden flowers. Try large masses of goldenrod with equally large masses of *A. novi-belgi* 'Sailor Boy' for a delightfully wild-looking summer bouquet. Or combine white nicotianas with a mixture of asters in blue, pink and violet for a visual and fragrant sensation.

Astilbe (a-STIL-bee) **false spirea, ◐ ○ ✳ H**
Zones: 4 to 8
Characteristics: With frosty spires of delicate white or pink blooms, or in bold red or maroon, *Astilbe* is a graceful garden perennial that excels in fresh flower arrangements and dried bouquets. *Astilbe* ranges in height from 1 to 4 feet and will happily occupy a moist location in the shady garden. The ferny, dark green foliage is excellent in the garden and can be harvested for use in a vase of fresh-cut flowers. By carefully selecting varieties, you can have *Astilbe* in bloom from June into September.

Astilbe *is a charming perennial for partial shade and woodsy soils rich in organic matter. The delicate spires of frothy blooms can be cut.* Astilbe *foliage is a natural addition to any* astilbe *bouquet.*

Cultural Information: Astilbe is best purchased from the nursery or through a reputable mail-order house; bareroot plants should be planted in spring. As with any bareroot perennial, soak the plants overnight in warm water before planting. *Astilbe* requires soil deeply prepared with plenty of organic matter such as compost, leaf mold or well-rotted manure. A protected, partially shady site is ideal for these garden favorites that don't like extreme heat. Divide *Astilbe* every three years or so, to allow you to enrich the soil. They will reward you with larger blooms and more of them.
Harvest and Use: Harvest while the plants are quite young. If you wait until all of the flowers have opened on these graceful spires, they will shatter and not last in water. White blooms may turn brown as they fade. *Astilbe* has little foliage on the strong, wiry stems. Condition cut spires overnight in hot water before arranging them in a deep vase with a large water reservoir. I love to design with astilbes in all of their colors and will combine them with lilies, delphiniums, roses, snapdragons, *Allium* and almost any other flower. Their natural beauty and texture complement so many other flowers. Remember to save some for drying. In the integrated garden you will be hard-pressed to leave some behind for garden display.

Baby's breath, hardy; see ***Gypsophila***

Bee balm; see ***Monarda***

The genus Campanula *is a large one with many cultivars. The peach-leafed bellflower offers a tall spire of bell like flowers in pristine white or deep blue.*

Bellflower; see ***Campanula***

Bergamot; see ***Monarda***

Blanketflower; see ***Gaillardia***

Campanula (kam-PAN-new-la) **bellflower, ○ ◐ ● H**
Zones: 3 to 7
Characteristics: The bellflowers are a large group of herbaceous biennials and perennials, many of which are suitable for cutting. Perhaps one of the best for cutting is *Campanula persicifolia,* the peach-leafed bellflower, which has long been a popular cut flower in Europe and for several years a Dutch import to the United States for the florist trade. The peach-leafed bellflower is available in shades of blue and pure white.
Cultural Information: C. persicifolia is an easy-to-grow peren-

nial that will adapt to conditions from full sun to shade. Plant seed in late spring in the nursery row, and transplant in August where they are to bloom the following spring. Nursery-grown plants are also available. Most varieties grow to about 3 feet and should be spaced at about 12 inches in rich garden loam. Irrigate regularly during the blooming period from late June through July. Plants can be divided easily once established to propagate new plants and improve soil fertility.

Harvest and Use: These wonderfully stately spires are superb companions for peonies, and complement lilies in both color and form. Combine them with many of the spring-blooming shrubs such as rhododendron and beautybush. The foliage is mostly basal and conditioning in hot water is recommended. Once conditioned, bellflowers will last for 10 to 14 days in water.

Chrysanthemum (kris-ANTH-em-um) **shasta daisy, painted daisy, hardy garden chrysanthemum, ○ ◐ ✳ S,W**

Zones: 5 to 9

Characteristics: Chrysanthemum is a large genus of composite flowers, many of which are suitable for cutting. *C.* × *superbum* is one of the best, the shasta daisy. These are the large white "daisy" daisies, with yellow centers and white petals that are the essence of early summer and purity. Several varieties are available for cutting. Shasta 'Alaska' is a 2-inch daisy on 2-foot stems; it is manageable in bouquets and easily conditioned. Shasta 'Majestic' is one of the largest, with flowers almost 6 inches across on 2-foot plants. These may be "majestic," but they are not easily conditioned or used in flower bouquets, because the large flowers are awkwardly out of proportion to their stem length.

The painted daisy, *C. coccineum,* is a yellow-centered flower in shades of pink and crimson. The plants are typically straight stemmed with soft, ferny foliage. 'Robinson's Pink' and 'Robinson's Carmine' are two named varieties suitable for cutting.

Hardy garden chrysanthemums, or "mums," are the delight of the autumn garden. *C.* × *morifolium* is a diverse group of plants that includes single, daisylike varieties and fully double forms, in colors ranging from white to maroon and some that are truly bronze. These garden favorites, sold by the roadsides each autumn, are delightful late-summer additions of color to porches and planting beds. The large assortment of flower types, colors and season of bloom make this an ideal addition to the cutting garden. Choose several varieties for a full range of characteristics.

Cultural Information: Shasta daisies are easily grown from root divisions, seed or plants bought from the nursery or mail-order house. They are gregarious in the garden and multiply, sometimes becoming a nuisance. Seed mixes of painted daisy are available, but selected plants should be chosen from the mix as some

Daisies are the very essence of innocence and summer fun. Chrysanthemum maximum *are easy to grow and harvest for use in flower bouquets.*

flowers will be imperfect in form and unsuitable for use in design. Once you have selected the flowers and colors suited to your needs, discard the rest and propagate your selections by division.

For best results with hardy mums in the cutting garden, purchase young rooted cuttings or bareroot plants in spring. Division of existing garden plants each spring will give you an endless supply of vigorous plant stock for the cutting garden. The culture will vary with their use. In the ornamental garden you may want to pinch new growth back every few weeks until the Fourth of July; flower buds will follow. Pinching produces the well-rounded, bushy plants we have come to recognize as the hardy garden mum. For cutting, however, we don't want to pinch out new growth and encourage densely branched plants. We want to encourage good stem length. Toward the end of the season, the mum will naturally branch out and you will have a spray of blossoms suitable for cutting and use in bouquets.

Chrysanthemums are not fussy about soil but should be grown in full sun or, at most, very light shade. A well-prepared, rich soil will give you longer stems for cutting. Fall-flowering mums should be divided each spring and will give you a large number of young, vigorous shoots to plant; discard the woody stems. Divide shastas and painted daisies after they bloom each year in midsummer. Take that opportunity to improve the soil with plenty of compost or well-rotted manure. Staking may be necessary in very fertile soils or in shade to keep the stems off of the ground.

Harvest and Use: Chrysanthemums are easy to condition and use. For shastas the florist's cardboard trick described on page 32 will keep the stems straight and allow the flower petals to become turgid in a flat plane. Combine shastas with astilbes, larkspurs or *Campanula.* The pinks and reds of the painted daisies combine nicely with mock orange and white *Salvia horminum.* Autumn mums are fine all by themselves, but when combined with other late-summer and fall bloomers such as asters, sunflowers and the heads of ornamental grasses or roadside weeds, they become the official welcoming committee for the glories of autumn.

Convallaria majalis *will form a dense groundcover in moist, shady areas and provide generous numbers of stems with which to fill delicate vases. Their fragrance and simple beauty need no accompaniment.*

Columbine; see ***Aquilegia***

Coneflower, purple; see ***Echinacea***

Convallaria majalis (kon-val-AIR-ee-a may-JALL-iss) **lily of the valley, ◐ ● C**

Zones: 3 to 9

Characteristics: Lily of the valley makes a wonderful groundcover for the shadiest places in the integrated cutting garden. In the right location it forms a dense groundcover with fragrant white blossoms that sweeten the garden each June. The flowers are small, white bells on delicately arching stems and may reach only 6 inches in height. There are several varieties available, including a pink form and a double form, but quite frankly, only the species is worth growing.

Cultural Information: Lily of the valley requires a rich, well-drained soil with plenty of moisture. Annual topdressings of peat moss or well-rotted manure will benefit this garden beauty. Basically trouble free, foliage of *Convallaria* will become pale and shabby looking if it dries out or is overcrowded. Additional plants are propagated through division of established clumps in early spring. Both the roots and the orange-red globular fruits are poisonous if ingested.

Harvest and Use: The best way to harvest lily of the valley is to grasp the stem close to where it emerges from the foliage and gently tug it straight up. This will maximize the stem length and leave the plants looking tidy. Recut the stems with sharp snips or shears before conditioning in cool water. When picking, cut a few leaves to complement the flowers, as the long, parallel-veined leaves look better with lily of the valley than any other foliage. *Convallaria* is best used alone or with other small-scale, spring-flowering plants such as grape hyacinths, violets and forget-me-nots.

Coralbells; see ***Heuchera***

Coreopsis (ko-ree-OP-sis gran-di-FLO-ra) **lance coreopsis, tickseed, ○ ◐ 💧 ✸ W**

Zones: 3 to 9

Characteristics: Coreopsis is a native American plant that produces a profusion of golden yellow blossoms from June through the fall months. The basal foliage is composed of dark green, lance-shaped foliage; the flower heads are produced on strong, straight, leafless stems. The variety 'Early Sunrise' will bloom the first year from seed and is ideal for cutting.

Coreopsis lanceolata *with black-eyed Susan and gray lamb's ear fill this perennial border with more than enough flowers. A few won't be missed when cut and brought indoors for enjoyment at the dining table.*

Coreopsis grandiflora *'Early Sunrise' is a perennial that is easily grown from seed and will bloom the first year.*

Cultural Information: Coreopsis is an easy-to-grow perennial that will thrive in deep, well-drained soils enriched with organic matter in hot, sunny locations. Sow the seed where they are to grow and thin to 8 inches apart. Coreopsis needs no staking and welcomes supplemental watering during periods of dry weather.
Harvest and Use: Harvesting flowers is the key to a continuous display in the garden, and the flowers will last for 1 or more weeks in an arrangement. When coreopsis is conditioned and turgid, combine it with blue larkspurs, lavenders or blue *Salvia* for the natural complement of yellow and blue, or combine it with bronze snapdragons, *Gaillardia* and mahogany sunflowers or gloriosa daisies for a celebration of earth tones.

Daisy, painted; see ***Chrysanthemum***

Daisy, shasta; see ***Chrysanthemum***

***Delphinium elatum* hybrids** (dell-FIN-ee-um ee-LAY-tum)

delphinium, ○ ◐ ✳H
Zones: 3 to 8
Characteristics: No garden should be without delphiniums, and no one who seriously wants to produce an exciting spring bouquet can pass them up. Delphiniums are tall, stately garden specimens, demanding of the site and gardener alike. The elegant spikes in shades ranging from the deepest purple to the palest blue and pure white are frequently accented with white or black centers, known as "bees."

Many strains of excellent garden delphiniums are available. The 'Blackmore and Langdon Strain' is exceptional and ranges from 4 to 6 feet tall. The 'Pacific Coast Strains' are even taller and will produce blooming stems almost 6 feet in height. For less ambitious sites, *Delphinium* 'Magic Fountains' is a little more demure at 3 feet.
Cultural Information: Delphiniums are heavy feeders and demand a deep, rich, well-drained soil to which copious amounts of organic matter have been added. If you do not have the wherewithal to double dig your entire garden site, double dig for your delphiniums. Delphiniums appreciate an application of ground agricultural lime, bone meal or wood ash to sweeten the soil as they don't care for acid soils.

Plants are typically started from seed. Seed where they are to grow in spring, or seed them in fall, transplanting in spring. Many nurseries and greenhouses offer them as well.

Delphinium *will provide a grand display of flowers for the garden and vase. A few spikes harvested and conditioned will combine with peonies for a breathtaking arrangement.*

Dianthus *'Spring Beauty' will provide years of enjoyment in the garden. They do best in a well-drained, slightly alkaline soil.*

Dianthus *'Helen' will seem much more fragrant indoors where its beauty can be appreciated more closely.*

Echinacea purpurea *appears in the cutting garden, herb garden and perennial borders at Mohonk Mountain House.*

Fertilize delphiniums heavily throughout the growing season, when new shoots emerge, flower buds form, after flowers are harvested, and as a second flush of growth emerges in late summer. Keep the roots moist, but never allow soggy soils to persist, as this encourages root rot. Organic mulches help discourage weeds and maintain even moisture levels in the soil, but may increase the incidence of slugs, which can be devastating. Delphiniums need a sunny place in the garden and prefer cool summer nights and moderate winters. Where ideal conditions exist, delphinium clumps will continue to grow and produce more and more flowers each year. For many of us, however, we must start each year with new seedlings and do all that we can to make them happy.

The taller strains of *Delphinium* require staking to protect the heavy flower stems from breaking away at the base in heavy winds and rains. Some gardeners stake each stem, fastening it to the stake at 1-foot intervals. For cutting purposes, however, it may be desirable to create a "corral" of stakes around each plant.

Harvest and Use: Harvest delphinium spikes by cutting the stem down to the basal foliage. At the time of harvest, fertilize with well-rotted manure or 5-10-5 slow-release fertilizer to encourage a second flush of growth that will bloom in August and September. Flower stems should be placed in hot water for conditioning overnight. Don't use shortcuts when conditioning delphiniums. The height of the spikes taxes the stems' ability to provide enough water to support them to the top. Delphiniums can be designed in floral foam for a special occasion, but for the best results use a vase with a deep reservoir that will hold a large amount of water, and keep the container full at all times; delphiniums are as demanding in the vase as in the garden. Combine the stately spikes of delphiniums with peonies. Together they are unbeatable and complement each other in every way.

Dianthus (di-ANTH-us) **garden pinks, ○ C**

Zones: 3 to 8

Characteristics: Garden pinks are unparalleled for scent in the garden. The evergreen tufts of gray-green foliage make them ideal edging plants for the integrated border and rockery. Perennial pinks do best in full sun and will not grow in less-than-perfect drainage. They do not require overly rich soils, thriving in sandy soils or spilling over rock walls. *D. plumarius,* the cottage pink, is a vigorous grower to 1½ feet. There are several named varieties of the cottage pink, all suitable for cutting and including in small bouquets. The single, semidouble and double forms are available in colors ranging from white to pale pink, salmon, rose and crimson.

D. deltoides, the maiden pink, grows to 1½ feet with bright green basal foliage that forms loose mats. Colors of *D. deltoides* varieties range from white through pinks and purples. Many are accented with contrasting rings of color on the single row of petals. The fragrance is distinctly clovelike and a delightful addition to any bouquet.

Cultural Information: Pinks should be grown only in full sun and perfectly drained soil. Imperfect drainage will cause crown rot and death. Pinks can be grown from seed or cuttings, and starter plants are often available at nurseries. Established clumps should be divided in spring every 3 or 4 years; discard the older centers. Soil should be slightly sweet, and pinks respond well to ground agricultural limestone. A mulch of marble chips placed around the base of each plant will improve air circulation and drainage around the plant crowns.

Harvest and Use: Condition *Dianthus* blossoms in cool water after removing lower leaves. Flowers last equally well in water and floral foam, for as long as 2 weeks. Combine pinks with bachelor's buttons in a small crystal vase for an endearingly old-fashioned arrangement. Add pinks to bouquets of lily of the valley and violets, and the heady arrangement will perfume an entire room.

Echinacea purpurea (ek-in-AY-see-a pur-PEWR-ee-a) **purple coneflower, ○ ◐ 💧 ✷ H**

Zones: 3–9

Characteristics: Purple coneflower turns up everywhere in the gardens at Mohonk. In the perennial border, its rosy purple, daisylike flowers bloom from June until frost. In herb gardens, *Echinacea* is an example of the medicinal herbs used in tinctures to strengthen the immune system. In cutting gardens, *Echinacea* is a prolific source of cut flowers for an extended season and into the fall, when the cone-shaped centers can be collected for use in dried bouquets. The single row of flower petals tip back gently, giving this plant a look distinctive from that of other daisies. The variety 'Bright Star' will grow to 3 feet and has rosy plum petals surrounding a lovely orange cone. 'White Swan' has pure white rays, a delightful honey scent and grows to 18 inches in the garden.

Cultural Information: Easy to grow, *Echinacea* doesn't require rich soil and will, in fact, thrive in any full sun location in well-drained average soil. Planted in spring, purple coneflower will bloom the first year; or, buy seedlings from the greenhouse or garden center. Allowing some flowers to set seed each year will increase the colony and provide for an endless supply of cuts all season long.

Harvest and Use: Cut flowers close to the basal foliage; in this way, you can get stem lengths of 18 or more inches. Condition in hot water before designing. Try purple coneflower with *Liatris* for a rough-textured, boldly colored arrangement.

Eulalia grass; see ***Misanthus***

False spirea; see ***Astilbe***

Funkia; see ***Hosta***

Gaillardia* × *grandiflora (gay-LARD-ee-a ex gran-di-FLO-ra) **gaillardia, blanketflower, ○ ● ✸ S, H**

Zones: 3 to 9

Characteristics: For summer bouquets and summer gardens, nothing is more rewarding than *Gaillardia.* The single flower heads are composed of brightly colored, single petals surrounding a fuzzy, rounded dark center. The petals come in a range of sunset colors and are frequently banded in multihued combinations of yellow, gold, burgundy and red. There are double and semidouble forms available.

Cultural Information: Gaillardia, easily grown from seed, is undemanding of soils and does best in rather poor soils that are perfectly drained. Sow the seed in spring after all danger of frost, or up to 2 months before frost in fall. *Gaillardia* detest cold, wet, heavy soils and thrive in hot, sunny locations. Although they will tolerate drought, they prefer an adequate supply of moisture. Where conditions are less than ideal, treat them like annuals and start with new seeds each year. For those of us with ideal sites, periodic division will be necessary to keep the individual plants vigorous and maintain flower production.

Harvest and Use: Harvest toward the end of your picking sessions, as the petals don't have much substance and will not recover if crushed or badly wilted. Condition in hot water, suspending the stems as described in the florist's trick on page 32. In the cool autumn months, it is wise to harvest during the warmer part of the day when stems are pulling water up from the roots. Harvest regularly to keep plants producing from July through frost. Save the centers from spent blossoms for use in dried bouquets or other crafts.

Garden pinks; see ***Dianthus***

Garden phlox; see ***Phlox***

Gayfeather; see ***Liatris***

Goldenrod; see ***Solidago***

Gooseneck loosestrife; see ***Lysimachia***

Gypsophila paniculata (jip-SOFF-ill-a pan-i-KEW-la-ta) **hardy baby's breath, ○ S, H**

Zones: 3 to 10

Characteristics: Gypsophila has as its root *gypsos,* Greek for "chalk." And like the word rooted in chalk, so the plant likes to be rooted—in "chalk." Baby's breath is a perennial that requires very well drained

Gaillardia grandiflora *is as useful when it's past its prime as when it's perfect. The globular seed heads can be used effectively in many arrangements.*

Gypsophila *can provide an abundance of tiny double flowers for fresh or dry use. Be sure the soil is very well drained and enriched with lime.*

soils enriched with copious amounts of ground limestone. Baby's breath, or "gyp," can reach 4 feet in height and a similar spread. It is valued for the profusion of tiny white blossoms found on wiry stems.
Cultural Information: Grow named varieties from root divisions purchased from mail-order catalogs or purchase container-grown plants from your favorite nursery or garden center. For the border, plant them 4 feet apart toward the back, in full sun. Gyp is frequently grown near old-fashioned bleeding heart and Oriental poppies to cover the void left by the latter after their brief display of spring foliage. *Gypsophila* needs staking, and most gardeners agree the best method of supporting the profusion of tangled stems is to corset the plants in a bamboo cage held together with strong twine. The great mass of flowers will spill over the twine and do much to cover the mechanics.
Harvest and Use: Harvest masses of blossoms in full bloom for drying in a warm, dark, dry place. For fresh flowers, cut in the evening and place in buckets with generous amounts of hot water to which 2 or 3 drops of liquid detergent and 2 or 3 drops of liquid chlorine bleach have been added. The liquid detergent will assist in the absorption of water and the bleach will not only keep the water fresh and bacteria free but seems actually to whiten the flowers!

Baby's breath works well with everything. Its only drawback is that the commercial florists have used it *ad nauseum* and so we sometimes consider its use as trite. For a change of pace, try generous amounts of gyp with a few blooms of garden pinks, bachelor's buttons, *Coreopsis, Gomphrena* or other quarter-size blooms. The effect is delightfully feminine and will be pleasing at a wedding reception, bridal shower or as a gift to a new mother. One plant of baby's breath, if harvested completely, may yield as much as three full displays of blooms over the course of the growing season.

Heuchera *'Palace Purple' has wonderful burgundy foliage that can be harvested for use with many flowers. Consider using it with coreopsis for a bold scheme.*

Hardy baby's breath; see ***Gypsophila paniculata***

Hardy garden chrysanthemum; see ***Chrysanthemum***

Hardy garden phlox; see ***Phlox***

Heuchera × *brizoides*

(hew-KER-a ex bri-ZOY-deez) **coralbells, ◐ ○ C**
Zones: 4 to 8
Characteristics: I think we all have sentimental favorites. *Heuchera* will always remind me of my first gardening job at the house down the street, where in partial shade the coralbells grew lushly. I learned at 10 years of age that flowers don't have to be huge neon signs boldly crying out their glories to be of value. Coralbells are North American natives grown for their handsome, evergreen foliage and delicate racemes of tiny coral, pink, red or white blossoms. The leaves are rounded or kidney shaped, frequently mottled, veined or banded in white or maroon. *H. micratha diversifolia* 'Palace Purple' is a new cultivar to the garden scene and has already won acclaim for its deep purple-bronze foliage, which is deeply lobed, shiny above and bright red below. The flowers and foliage are excellent cuts, suitable together, of course, or in mixed flower bouquets.
Cultural Information: Most *Heuchera* can be grown successfully from seed. Named varieties may be purchased from nurseries and mail-order catalogs. The Bressingham hybrids will grow to 18 inches and provide plenty of flowers for cutting in the full color range. 'Palace Purple' is reliable from seed; plant the seed in partial shade in well-drained garden soil ammended with lots of organic matter. Do not cover the seed because it needs to be exposed to light to germinate. Coralbells will bloom the second year, starting in June, with sporadic repeat bloom throughout the summer. Bareroot plants are available, as are container-grown plants of many varieties each spring. Divide

coralbells every 4 to 5 years to avoid overcrowding. Be careful not to bury the crown with applications of organic matter or dense protective winter mulches, as crown rot will follow. A light protective mulching of pine straw or evergreen boughs should be applied after the ground has frozen to avoid frost heaving and protect evergreen foliage. When removing the mulch in spring, take the time to clean away dead leaves of *Heuchera* or other organic debris.

Harvest and Use: Harvest by cutting back to the base any flower stems as they start to open; condition in cool water. Coralbells combine nicely with shasta daisies, and seem a natural pairing with columbines. Try mixing the leaves of 'Palace Purple' with the flowers of coreopsis for a strong statement of color.

Hosta (HOS-ta) **plantain lily, funkia, hosta, ● ◐ W**

Zones: 3 to 9

Characteristics: Hosta is a large genus with many exciting variations suitable for growing in the deepest shade. Unfortunately, few people remember the lowly hosta when it comes time to create flower arrangements. Try *H. plantaginea* 'Royal Standard' for its smooth green leaves and deliciously fragrant blossoms; the white flowers are held 18 inches above basal foliage mounding to 16 inches. *Hosta* 'So Sweet' is a variegated form with glossy green leaves with white margins; the white flower spikes are 24 inches tall, with individual florets that are sweetly fragrant. The variety of hostas never fails to amaze. Leaves will be small or large, narrow or broad, smooth, puckered or quilted. Leaf colors range from chartreuse to deep green, golden to blue, and many are variegated in gold, cream or startling white. Flowers borne on leafless stems may be white or, more commonly, mauve or violet. Many are fragrant.

Cultural Information: They are extremely easy to grow as long as they receive shade from the hottest sun and adequate moisture. Hostas rarely need division, and over time will form competitive root systems that discourage weeds, making them admirable groundcovers. Purchase container-grown plants from the nursery in spring, or bareroot plants, which may be ordered through the mail.

Harvest and Use: Flowers should be harvested for arranging as the first flower opens; the other buds on the stems will continue to open. Conditioning in warm water before use will encourage their ability to last. Leaves should also be conditioned before use. Place the leaf stems in warm water overnight, or submerge the entire leaves in a pan of warm water for 30 minutes before standing up in water. This also washes off dust and pollen that frequently dull the shiny, broad leaves.

The tubular- to trumpet-shaped flowers look well with the rounded forms of dahlias. Try variegated hosta foliage with an all-white flower arrangement—very cool, sophisticated and summery.

Hosta *(here, 'Honey Bells') can provide not only foliage but fragrance and beauty from their flowers.*

Hosta fortunei *'Aureo-marginata' has green leaves boldly accented with gold. Consider playing upon this theme and building an arrangement of golds and greens with accents of deep blue.*

Lance coreopsis; see ***Coreopsis***

Lavandula officinalis (lav-AN-dew-la of-fiss-IN-al-is) **lavender, ○ 💧 W**

Zones: 5 to 9

Characteristics: Lavender is considered an herb, and rightly so; for centuries, lavender has been grown to scent linens, create perfumes and repel insects, and it has been eaten fresh in salads and dried in culinary herb mixtures. The delicate lavender blue spikes are ideal for the home cutting garden. Lavender adds not only beauty but distinctive fragrance to bouquets.

Lavender brings to mind clean, crisp images and was a favorite of our grandmothers. The flowers and silvery foliage of Lavandula officinalis *both offer strong scent.*

Liatris spicata is a native American prairie flower. Give it a location in full sun and you will raise flowers excellent for cutting.

Strong stems and grey-green foliage are what makes Lychnis coronaria an excellent choice for garden and vase.

Lavender will bloom periodically from June until frost. The variety 'Munstead', one of the most prolific bloomers, is a slightly darker blue than the common English lavender. 'Jean Davis' is considered a pink lavender (why grow pink lavender?), but it is a dull, pale, pinkish gray; I can't recommend including it in your garden unless you are collecting lavenders. Both the flowers and foliage are fragrant and suitable for use in fresh and dried bouquets.

Cultural Information: Lavender is actually a small, evergreen shrub and grows to 18 inches tall. It can be grown from seed, but usually it is easier to purchase plants. Prepare the soil in a well-drained, sunny location by adding lime, bone meal or wood ash to increase the alkalinity. Space the plants 10 to 12 inches apart for the best display and to provide plenty of room for plant growth. In the North, plants may need some light protective winter mulch to prevent die back, caused by severe temperatures or strong winter winds. If damage has occurred, cut back affected parts in spring to newly emerging buds. Lavender will bloom on new growth. Periodically side dress established plants with lime or bone meal to maintain a neutral soil pH.

Harvest and Use: Strip off only the foliage that would be submerged in water. (Save the strippings for inclusion in potpourri, or simply set them out in a basket to enjoy the fragrance.) Use warm to hot water to condition the flower stems, anywhere from 6 to 10 inches in length. Consider mixing lavender with other delicately fragrant flowers such as roses, garden pinks or lily of the valley in a small vase to brighten the room of a bed-ridden friend; the fragrance will do as much to lift the spirits and promote healing as the beauty will.

Lavender; see ***Lavandula***

Liatris spicata (lee-AT-riss spik-AH-ta) **gayfeather, ○ ✸ W**

Zones: 3 to 9

Characteristics: Liatris is a native American from the prairie states. It is bold and rather coarse—in other words, perfect for making a bright statement in your flower design. From heavy, mostly basal foliage emerge dense spikes of fuzzy, magenta-purple flowers. The spikes of some varieties will grow to 6 feet. They are distinctive in that they open from the top down, the opposite of how snapdragons and gladioluses open.

Cultural Information: Plant *Liatris* corms or young, nursery-grown plants in a sunny location. Good drainage is important; although they will thrive in copious amounts of moisture during the height of the growing season, they will disappear from the garden if soils are soggy during the winter months. An annual side dressing of 5-10-5 slow-release fertilizer will keep them happy and healthy.

'Kolbold' has 2-foot spikes of slightly deeper purple than the species. 'White Spires' (*L. scariosa*) is a 3-foot white form that can be useful in the garden. The Kansas gayfeather is the tallest of the genus (*L. pycnostacha*), growing to 6 feet with a somewhat more open flowering spike. In wetter soils or windy locations it may be necessary to provide support for the tallest gayfeathers, but most will be fine without staking.

When harvesting, leave as much foliage as possible on the plants to feed the roots. *Liatris* does not need regular dividing, but note that diminished flower size or production may indicate overcrowding. Divide the cormous roots with a sharp knife and discard the oldest, woody portion of each plant.

Harvest and Use: After conditioning in warm water, *Liatris* can be combined with all manner of flowers from the garden. Purple *Liatris* and bright yellow 'Connecticut King' lilies is a bold-as-brass combination suitable for a large centerpiece. *Liatris* with cosmoses and purple coneflowers is a more subtle approach, though equally enjoyable.

Lily of the valley; see ***Convallaria***

Loosestrife, gooseneck; see ***Lysimachia***

Lychnis coronaria (lik-NISS ko-ro-NAY-ree-a) **mullein pink, rose campion, ○ ✸ 💧 H**

Zones: 4 to 8

Characteristics: This delightfully old-fashioned perennial favorite is easy to grow and will provide bold, hot pink to magenta blossoms throughout summer into fall. The mostly basal, pubescent gray foliage shows off these bright flowers.

Cultural Information: A seed packet planted in full sun in spring will provide a lifetime supply of plants and flowers. The plants themselves are short lived but reseed readily, creating colonies of plants. Unwanted seedlings can be rogued out, transplanted elsewhere or given away. *Lychnis c.* 'Alba' is a white-flowered form; 'Angel Blush' is a seed mix with a color range from white to cerise, most of the plants white with pinkish centers.

Harvest and Use: Hot water should be used to condition flower stems, which will last up to 1 week. The stems are multibudded and 18 to 24 inches tall. Combine the hot pink forms with white or silver foliage. Try *Lychnis* massed with *Artemisia ludoviciana* 'Silver King'.

Lysimachia clethroides

(li-si-MAK-ee-a kleth-ROY-deez) **gooseneck loosestrife,** ○ ◐ **W**

Zones: 4 to 9

Characteristics: Plant this one and step back! Gooseneck is more than gregarious, more than aggressive—it is invasive. The 3-foot-high plants are topped with white spikes of little flowers. Each spike bends in the middle and the tip faces up, giving the overall impression of a goose neck.

Cultural Information: Whether planted in full sun or partial shade, the vigorous rhizomatic root system of gooseneck will spread like wildfire. Choose a location for this where its groundcoverlike habit will not cause trouble. Gooseneck will do best in sites with plenty of moisture. Prepare any good garden soil with generous amounts of organic matter.

Harvest and Use: Don't be afraid to harvest gooseneck stems right back to the ground; this plant has enough energy to support the loss of foliage. Strip the foliage by grasping loosely and pulling it down toward the base of the stem. Condition cut and cleaned gooseneck in warm water overnight. The joy is in its wonderful line, and the slightly arching flower spikes provide charm and interest to any arrangement. Combine it with blossoms from any mixture of summer-flowering annuals: snapdragons, cosmos, zinnias and lisianthus (*Eustoma*) will all benefit from the association.

Michaelmas daisy; see ***Aster***

Miscanthus sinensis

(mis-KAN-thus syn-EN-sis) **eulalia grass,** ○ ◐ **W**

Zones: 4 to 9

Characteristics: *Miscanthus* is an excellent ornamental grass for gardeners who don't want an invasive grass filling their flower borders. It has some endearing qualities for the floral designer as well—gently recurved tips create little pig tails. The grass plumes have a shimmering pink quality when fresh, and when mature and dry, *Miscanthus* has wonderfully fluffy white plumes suitable for use in bouquets fresh or dried.

M. sinensis 'Gracillimus' has green and yellow stripes (variegation) that follow the vertical parallel veins of the grass blades. *M. sinensis* 'Zebrinus', the zebra grass, is variegated with gold banding across the leaf blade.

Cultural Information: *Miscanthus* is easy to grow and will adapt well to almost any garden situation. For best results plant in full sun in rich, moist soils. But, consider *Miscanthus* for use in trouble spots, wet locations, dry locations and full sun, too. It never needs dividing and will produce more blooms each year.

Harvest and Use: The flower plumes can be harvested when fresh or dry and need not be conditioned. The leaf blades of *Miscanthus* should be condi-

Lysimachia clethroides *is typified by a gracefully arched spire of pure white flowers. Gooseneck may be invasive in the garden and should be planted where it can colonize.*

Many ornamental grasses are valuable in the border and should not be overlooked for inclusion in the cutting garden. Miscanthus sinensis *(background) has silvery white panicles in autumn on 4-foot plants.* Pennisetum alopecuroides *(foreground) will also provide plenty of flower heads for fresh and dry use.*

tioned in warm water before use. Try the dried plumes with freshly cut hardy mums or asters. The unripened flower heads are shown off to perfection against the deep colors of dark-hued *Salvia*, the bronzed foliage of autumn peonies, and mahogany sunflowers.

Nothing compares with Paeonia *for beauty of fragrance and form. Plant extras for bountiful June bloom and superb cut foliage throughout the growing season.*

Monarda didyma *is a member of the mint family, and its flower clusters will attract hummingbirds and bees. Divide* Monarda *every year to keep plants young and vigorous.*

Monarda didyma (mo-NAR-da di-DEE-ma) **bee balm, bergamot, Oswego tea, ○ ◐ H**

Zones: 4 to 9

Characteristics: This fine garden perennial was used by Native Americans for making tea, hence one of the common names, Oswego tea. Bee balm is a wildflower of meadows and roadsides, where its unusual flowers are usually pale lilac.

Bee balm is a member of the mint family and its active rootstocks will form dense clumps and may become invasive. This plant will do well in full sun or light shade, in moist or dry soils. The flowers are borne in terminal clusters and are frequently surrounded by brightly colored rings of bracts. The color range extends from white through pink and red to violet. To enjoy this summer-blooming perennial fully, plant it where you can watch the hummingbirds that will come to feed on the sweet nectar.

Cultural Information: Bee balm is nearly always grown from root division, a means of reproduction that produces specimens identical to the mother plant. Mildew is a problem with *Monarda,* and care should be taken to plant in an area with good air circulation. For greatest success, plant in rich garden soil with abundant moisture and divide every 2 to 3 years, eliminating the oldest, woody portions of the root stocks. This is best done in spring, and presents an opportunity to enrich the soil with well-rotted manure or compost.

Harvest and Use: Harvest bee balm from your cutting garden regularly to stretch the blooming period to 2 months or longer. Flowers should be stripped of their foliage and conditioned in hot water. Clean, disease-free (unsprayed) leaves can be steeped in boiling water to make an aromatic and refreshing beverage. Try *Monarda* 'Blue Stocking' in arrangements with white garden phlox and yellow coreopsis. The reds and pinks ('Cambridge Scarlet' or 'Croftway Pink') work well in combination with blue larkspurs and lisianthus.

Monkshood; see ***Aconitum***

Mugwort; see ***Artemisia***

Mullein pink; see ***Lychnis***

Oswego tea; see ***Monarda***

Paeonia lactifolia (pie-ON-ee-a lac-ti-FOL-ee-a) **peony, ○ ◐ ✻ W**

Zones: 3–8

Characteristics: This herbaceous plant is truly the queen of the garden. It is long lived, relatively pest free, and creates some of the most stunning, exquisitely fragrant flower arrangements. Peonies may be single, fully double or anenome flowered, and the flowers pure white, deep red, or any shade of pink from coral to raspberry.

Cultural Information: Peonies are exacting in their site requirements, but once established they are long lived, undemanding perennials. Choose a sunny location where the soil is deep, well drained and free from tree roots. Peonies dislike disturbance and competition. Do not crowd them with plants that will compete for air, light and nutrients, nor should you place them near annuals where the soil will be dug every year.

Peonies are best divided in late summer, and the largest selection is available at that time of year. (Too often we think to plant flowers when we see them in bloom in other peoples' gardens.) Plants that are container grown will be available in spring, but typically the variety selection is poorer than catalog selections. Prepare the soil well, adding steamed bone meal to hasten early root formation. Plant the tuberous roots about 1½ inches deep and water in well. Provide a mulch once the ground has frozen the first winter to prevent frost heaving. Young peonies benefit from an application of balanced slow-release fertilizer in the spring.

Harvest and Use: Peony blossoms can be harvested from the time the buds begin to show color, when they are about the size of golf balls. They will open in the vase, so cutting them young will extend your enjoyment. Cut the stems only as long as you need them to minimize unnecessary foliage loss, though taking the occasional stem back to the ground on a mature peony will not damage the plant. Don't overlook the single peony; not only is it a lovely cut, with its bright yellow stamens, but the singles frequently have fewer disease problems in the garden. The doubles may collect water in the petals during spring rains, causing the plants to break over and botrytis (gray mold) to proliferate.

Condition cut stems in warm water overnight. Don't discard leaves from the peony; they are long-lasting in arrangements. Peony foliage can be cut from mature peonies any time during the season for use in bouquets; it is attractive and holds up nicely. I especially like peony foliage in the autumn when it becomes bronzed. Try bronze peony foliage with orange and yellow American marigolds.

Peonies are ideal design subjects in any number of combinations. Three peonies of any color with an armload of lilacs is all you need to create fragrant magic. Try white, single peonies with delphiniums of deep blue, or mass peonies and mountain laurel cuttings for an elegant centerpiece.

Painted daisy; see ***Chrysanthemum***

Peony; see ***Paeonia***

Phlox paniculata (FLOX pan-i-KEW-la-ta) **hardy garden phlox, ○ ◐ H**

Zones: 3 to 9

Characteristics: Phlox reminds me of sunny August days spent vacationing in Maine; masses of pink, white and magenta blooms spilling through white picket fences by seaside cottages is still a vivid image for me. Phlox is an easy-to-grow perennial and can be the mainstay of the late-summer flower border.

Cultural Information: Plants are propagated by root cuttings in spring and should be planted out in the garden in full sun to light shade. Where still, humid days are common, watch out for mildew, which can disfigure foliage and weaken plants. Look for resistant varieties at your favorite nursery. Plant cuttings or young plants into freshly prepared soil to which organic matter has been added. Plant 15 to 18 inches apart with the eyes (buds) just below the soil surface. A light organic mulch will help conserve moisture and reduce weeds.

Phlox (here, Phlox paniculata *'Starfire') is a wonderful flower for the late-summer border and vase. Divide the plants regularly and choose varieties that resist mildew.*

As plants mature, they weaken and so benefit from dividing. Choose only the most vigorous of the new shoots each spring and space them out in newly enriched soil. It may be necessary to control mildew during some seasons; if mildew is caught early, a fungicidal application will help curb the disease. In the garden, be very conscientious with fall cleanup. Remove any diseased foliage from the base of plants and destroy or discard it—do not compost it. Harvesting flowers for arrangements and bouquets prolongs bloom, but it is a good idea to deadhead phlox to prevent reseeding and varieties that may revert to the common, muddy magenta.

Harvest and Use: After stripping off the lower foliage from cut phlox, condition it in a deep container of hot water. Bouquets of phlox with *Aconitum,* hot pink phlox with *Hydrangea paniculata* or just armloads of phloxes all by themselves will prove to be beautiful additions to any decor.

A weed is a plant out of place, but Solidago *'Crown of Rays' deserves a place in every garden.*

Pinks, garden; see ***Dianthus***

Plantain lily; see ***Hosta***

Purple coneflower; see ***Echinacea***

Rose campion; see ***Lychnis***

Shasta daisy; see ***Chrysanthemum***

Solidago (so-lid-AH-go) **goldenrod,** ○ ◐ 💧 **H**

Zones: 2 to 9

Characteristics: The goldenrods are often maligned—and unfairly—as the source of hayfever and have been shunned for years. The tall, stately spires of this bright golden native American should be included in every summer border where their sunny color and hardy disposition will cheer even the dourest heart. Goldenrod is a hardy perennial that forms vigorous clumps of mostly basal foliage and gently curved flower spikes up to 6 feet.

Cultural Information: Choose a sunny location for this gregarious member of the composite (daisy) family. It is easily propagated from root division. Be sure to deadhead to avoid unwanted seedlings. Much breeding work has been done in Europe where *Solidago* is grown for use in borders and is frequently seen in the flower shops. 'Cloth of Gold' has deep yellow flower heads on 2-foot stems. *S.* × 'Peter Pan' is a late-blooming variety and slightly taller, at 2½ to 3 feet.

Harvest and Use: Don't neglect the roadsides where goldenrod abounds. Cut it as it begins to open and it will dry beautifully and maintain its glorious golden color. Harvest whole stems and strip off the foliage. The stems will condition and become turgid if placed in hot water overnight. After conditioning, use them in masses all by themselves or with cattails or dried grasses. For a bolder look, arrange goldenrod with the smaller-flowered sunflowers in old crocks.

Speedwell; see ***Veronica***

Spirea, false; see ***Astilbe***

Tanacetum vulgare (tan-ah-SEE-tum vul-GAR-ee) **tansy,** ○ ◐ **H**

Zones: 4 to 10

Characteristics: Tansy is a versatile composite with lovely, fernlike foliage and broad heads of buttonlike, bright yellow flowers.

Cultural Information: Grow tansy in full sun in average garden soil. At Mohonk, we grow tansy in our herb garden because it acts as a natural insect repellant. Try *T. vulgare* 'Crispum' for its tight, crisp foliage, as well as the species. Both of these grow to 3 feet in height and produce abundant flowers. Sow seed in autumn, or plant root divisions or nursery-grown specimens in spring. Do not try to create a rich soil for tansy as it will become invasive, overly lush, and require staking.

Harvest and Use: Harvest tansy with long stems. As you strip off the foliage, save some for use in arrangements and add

Tanacetum vulgare *is a delightful specimen for the herb garden, where it is grown for its insect repellant properties. The yellow buttons borne atop 2½-foot stems are ideal for use in fresh and everlasting arrangements.*

the rest to a natural moth-repellant potpourri with lavender, thyme and rosemary. Tansy should be placed in containers of hot water for conditioning. Combine it with other late-summer perennials or annuals such as *Aconitum*, asters and *Celosia*. Be sure to harvest some to dry, hung upside down in a dark, dry, warm location.

Tansy; see ***Tanacetum***

Tickseed; see ***Coreopsis***

Veronica spicata (vu-RON-i-cah spi-CAH-ta) **speedwell,** ○ ◐ ✸ 💧 **W**

Zone: 3–10

Characteristics: Veronica is an easy, free-blooming perennial for the foreground of the sunny, integrated border or cutting garden. The delicate spikes of blue, violet, rose, pink or white are ideal subjects for smaller arrangements and small-scale gardens. *Veronica* grows to 15 to 24 inches tall and produces spikes as much as 1 foot long.

Cultural Information: Plant *Veronica* in rich, well-drained soil 1 to 2 feet apart. The plants are exceptionally heat and drought tolerant. Most varieties need no staking. By regularly harvesting flowers, you can extend the season of bloom for several weeks.

Harvest and Use: Try 'Minuet', which has rich pink blooms in July, or 'Sunny Border Blue', with intense blue flower spikes. Condition the flower stems in warm water. Try *Veronica* with *Dianthus* or *Nigella*. The rosy pink forms can be prettily used with *Lychnis* 'Angel Blush'. Try 'Sunnyborder Blue' with pale yellow *Calendula* and chive blossoms.

Wormwood; see ***Artemisia***

Yarrow; see ***Achillea***

Veronica spicata *(here, 'Minuet') comes in a variety of colors, from blue to pink to white.*

BULBS, CORMS, TUBERS AND RHIZOMES

Acidanthera bicolor (ah-sid-ANTH-e-ra by-COL-or) **peacock orchid, dark-eye gladixia,** ○ ✸ **W**

Zone: 10

Characteristics: Bright white butterflies blotched with chocolate brown and black, the flowers of *Acidanthera* are borne above the swordlike foliage from July until frost in the sunny garden.

Cultural Information: Acidanthera is related to the gladiola and requires similar culture, but it offers an unusually exotic cut flower for late-summer bouquets. The fragrant flowers will continue to be formed on the loosely branching stems throughout autumn. *Acidanthera* is easy to grow in average soil in full sun. It is native to Ethiopia, and enjoys summer heat. In warmer climates it will overwinter without being dug and stored. In the Northeast it is necessary to dig, clean and store the corms over winter. After the foliage has been killed back by frost, carefully dig up the corms. Cut back the stem to within 2 inches of the corm and remove any fibrous roots. Allow the coarse, papery cover to remain. Store in peat moss or sawdust in a cool, slightly damp location until spring. Plant outdoors where they are to grow after danger of frost is past. As you lift the mature corms, watch for cormels (baby corms); these may be grown on in a nursery row for two seasons until they reach blooming size.

Harvest and Use: Harvest by removing individual flowers, entire stems or entire plants, depending on the length of stem desired. Pulling the plant from the ground and cutting the corm off at the base of the stem will give you the greatest stem length for designing, but will sacrifice the corm, which must be discarded. Cut stems should be placed in warm water in a container deep enough to support the flower spikes. After conditioning, combine with dahlias for a lovely display. I like the exotic look of individual buds, leaves and full blossoms of *Acidanthera* arranged in hollowed-out eggplants. Clustered together on a pewter platter or in a handsome flat basket, the eggplants and peacock orchids complement each other in form and color, making an elegant centerpiece for a summer Sunday brunch.

Acidanthera bicolor murielae *is best treated like its relative, the gladiolus. The fragrant white flowers with chocolate-purple throats are topped by gently nodding buds waiting to open.*

Allium caeruleum is an important color accent in this arrangement of green, chartreuse and creamy white. Alliums are easy to grow in most garden soils.

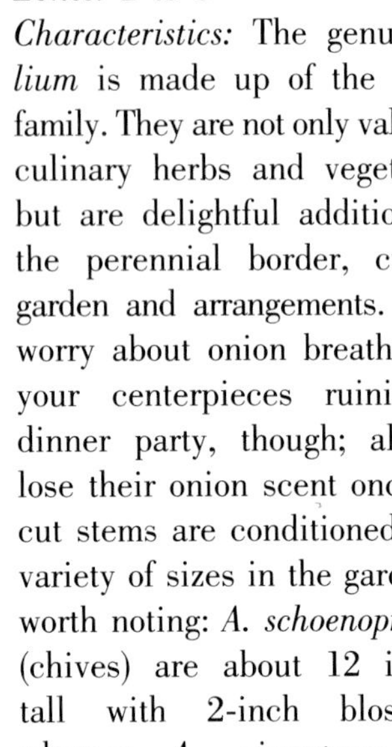

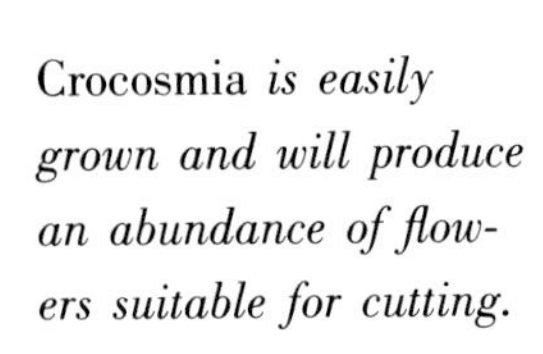

Crocosmia is easily grown and will produce an abundance of flowers suitable for cutting.

Allium (AL-ee-um) **flowering onion, giant allium, chives,** ○ ✳ **C**

Zones: 2 to 8

Characteristics: The genus *Allium* is made up of the onion family. They are not only valuable culinary herbs and vegetables but are delightful additions to the perennial border, cutting garden and arrangements. Don't worry about onion breath from your centerpieces ruining a dinner party, though; alliums lose their onion scent once the cut stems are conditioned. The variety of sizes in the garden is worth noting: *A. schoenoprasum* (chives) are about 12 inches tall with 2-inch blossoms, whereas *A. giganteum* (the giant allium) will top out at 4 to 5 feet tall with flower heads 6 or more inches across. *A. giganteum* is only marginally hardy in northern gardens, so it is critical that it be planted in a perfectly drained soil; a winter mulch of evergreen boughs, pine straw or straw will help protect it from severe cold. *A. sphaerocephalum* (drumstick allium) has 2-inch heads of tightly clustered blossoms that are deep violet when open and bright green in the bud. This is an excellent, long-lasting cut with 2-foot stems, and one of the least expensive of the alliums. Plant plenty of these in the garden for fresh and dry use. *A. caeruleum* (blue garlic) is one of the finest of the alliums, easy to grow and hardy. Blue garlic will produce 1-inch balls of bright cornflower blue on 2-foot stems in June.

Cultural Information: Alliums need a sunny garden site with well-drained soil. They will accept poor garden soils and live for season after season, but poor drainage will cause them to fail. The foliage of alliums is basal. Some, like the giant allium, are flat and hug the ground; chives are tubular and upright. Most of the foliage has a lovely blue-green cast and is a delightful garden accent. Plant enough alliums for fresh and dried use. Chives are usually sold as plants in spring; all other alliums should be purchased in autumn and planted in September or early October. Plant bulbs in well-prepared soil enriched with organic matter and bone meal, which will encourage early root formation. Some alliums will produce growth in autumn, but this won't hurt flower formation or display.

Harvest and Use: Harvest blossoms when they are about halfway open, as they will continue to mature in the vase. Condition alliums in cool water to help reduce any oniony fragrance. Giant alliums are handsome with white delphiniums or yellow lilies. The chives are ideal in bouquets of herbs and other edible flowers such as rose buds, nasturtiums and *Calendula*. There is no limit to the floral combinations for this delightfully easy perennial bulb.

Chive; see ***Allium***

Crocosmia (kro-KOS-mee-a) **crocosmia, montbretia,** ○ ◐ ✹ **W**

Zones: 7 to 10

Characteristics: Crocosmia is a tender bulb sold in spring. In northern gardens it is treated like a tender annual. In gardens south of Zone 6 it can be left in the ground where it will colonize and behave as a perennial. This African native is available in shades of yellow, orange and bright, bold red. The flowers are borne on strong stems 15 to 20 inches tall in August and September. Typically, the flower stems branch and curve slightly, the ends of the spikes bearing a couple rows of buds, very much like freesia.

Cultural Information: Plant *Crocosmia* in spring in a sunny or partially shady location when soils are warm. Plant at least 10 bulbs for a suitable display in the integrated garden, with an additional 10 for cutting. Mulch the planting during the first winter for extra insulation or, if you garden in the North, lift and store as you would gladiolas.

Harvest and Use: Harvest only as much stem length as you need for your vase arrangement. By leaving some buds on the branched, leafless stems, you can continue to produce more blooms. Condition in warm water for use with variegated grasses, zinnias and *Monarda.* Try combinations of goosenecks with crocosmias as their shapes are so similar.

Daffodil; see ***Narcissus***

Dahlia (DAH-lee-a) dahlia, ○ S,W

Zones: 9 to 10

Characteristics: The native American dahlia is a popular, old-fashioned garden favorite. Dahlias offer a range of colors from pure white to yellow, orange, red, pink, lilac and burgundy. Many bicolors are available with contrasting striped or banded petals. Although all dahlias cut well and last in water, not all are suitable for use in bouquets. The decorative dahlias may produce blooms the size of dinner plates, but how do you use them in bouquets? For flower arrangements, choose the water-lily types, with flowers 3 to 4 inches across on plants 3½ to 4 feet tall. These upward-facing dahlias are wonderfully shaped with gently curved, clearly defined petals, on strong stems. The pompon types will produce lovely, rounded blossoms 2 to 3 inches across on plants 3 feet tall.

Cultural Information: Dahlias like plenty of moisture in deep, fertile, well-drained soil. They may need staking to stand upright in the middle or background of the sunny border or cutting garden. Dahlias may be started indoors in flats of potting soil mixed with peat moss 2 to 3 weeks before the last spring frost, then planted out when growth starts. In fall, allow the frost to kill back the plants and then dig the tubers. Cut the stems back to within 2 inches of the tubers, which should then be washed free of soil, allowed to dry and stored in peat moss or sawdust in a cool, damp area.

Harvest and Use: Cut stems of dahlias should be briefly conditioned in very hot (almost boiling water) for 5 minutes before conditioning in warm water. I like combining the water-lily dahlias in delicate pastel shades with summer annuals—bronze snapdragons with yellow or pink dahlias are delightful. The startling white dahlias are a beautiful addition to bouquets of red *Celosia* and *Hydrangea paniculata.*

Dark-eye gladixia; see ***Acidanthera***

Flowering onion; see ***Allium***

Gladiolus (glad-E-o-lis) gladiola, ○ W

Zones: 9 to 10

Characteristics: The poor *Gladiolus* has been given a bad rap. For years it has been persistently used for funeral flowers and so has become associated with bereavement. It is unfortunate that a flower that has so much to offer the flower enthusiast, with a broad color range, stately presence and long-lasting flower spikes, should be shunned. "Glads" can be pure white to deep blue, with yellows, pinks, corals and oranges filling out the spectrum. The yellows range from the palest cream to deep gold and even greenish. Plant breeders have developed some varieties with spots and blotched throats and

I find the smaller-scaled dahlia flower heads, such as the Pompon Dahlia *'Potgieter' here, easier to use in arrangements.*

Even dwarf forms such as Dahlia *'Bonnie Esperance' can provide the terrace gardener a few flowers for a vase.*

Gladiolus *come in every color of the rainbow, and some the rainbow has yet to see. Easy to grow and rewarding, a few "glads" make a strong color statement in an arrangement.*

Iris are long-lived perennials that form dense clumps. Cut iris blooms when they begin to unfurl and they will last well in water. (Iris germanica *'Gay Parade'*).

others with heavily ruffled petals more magnificent than any orchid. Plants range in height from 3 to 4 feet for standard "glads," and 2 to 3 feet for the miniature gladiola. The sword-like foliage is a bold accent to the integrated cutting garden, where "glads" should be massed for greatest affect.

Cultural Information: Gladiolus is easy to grow in any soil in full sun. Choose corms that are large and firm but not dry and rock hard to the touch. For best results, prepare the soil deeply, incorporating leaf mold or compost to increase water-holding capacity. Gladiolas should be planted in groups over a period of weeks, starting when the ground can be worked in spring and completing the last planting about the Fourth of July. Staggering the planting dates will stagger the blooming period and give you a supply of flowers from July until frost.

Just before planting soak corms in a Lysol solution (1 tablespoon Lysol to 1 gallon warm water) to control thrips and disease. Beware of thrips, minute insects that cause tan, vertical stripes along the length of gladiola leaves, mottle flowers and destroy plantings. To avoid thrips, rotate planting sites annually, and discard any suspect corms. In areas exposed to wind be prepared to support plantings with individual stakes or 4 × 4-inch support wire fixed horizontally about 1½ feet off the ground.

Harvest and Use: When harvesting gladiolas, cut the thick stems just above the foliage. Consider sacrificing the occasional corm by pulling the entire plant out of the ground and cutting the stem at the corm. (This is how commercial growers harvest gladiolus with extra-long stems.) Flowers and foliage are easily conditioned in warm water. Before use, remove the last few flower buds to encourage all the florets to open. Where flower stems are too long, cut the spike into sections and use two florets here, three there and the budded tip somewhere else. I think masses of gladiolas with their natural foliage look best. Try white and pink gladiolas with hydrangeas in autumn, or lilies with gladiolas for summer bouquets. For smaller-scale gardens, and smaller, easier-to-use flower spikes, 'Tiny Tots' will give you miniature gladiolas with 18- to 20-inch flower spikes.

Iris (EYE-ris) **iris, ○ ◐ W**

Zones: 3–10

Characteristics: The irises are a diverse group of plants from all over the world. There are two groups that seem particularly to shine for use in the vase. The bearded or German iris is widely hybridized and offers the enthusiast an incredible assortment of flower colors and combinations with bicolors and heavily ruffled petals abounding. I'm still drawn to the smaller-flowered, old-fashioned varieties that used to grace grandmother's garden. The Japanese iris is an outstanding cut flower and will thrive in wet places (even along the edge of a shallow pond); it ranges in color from white to purple, and may have variegation, veining or blotches in a contrasting shade, often yellow.

Cultural Information: All irises are relatively easy to grow and, once planted, will be part of the garden for many years. Bearded irises have shallow-rooted rhizomes requiring a perfectly drained location for success. Plant in full sun, and take the time to encorporate organic matter into the soil. Bearded irises are available in September and should be planted as soon as they are received. The rhizome can be left slightly exposed, but it may be helpful to use a flat rock to weight the rhizome the first winter to avoid frost heaving. Bearded irises are prone to iris borer, an insect that can be devastating. It is wise to lift and divide rhizomes every 3 to 4 years to provide them with fresh soil. Cut out any signs of borers with a sharp knife. If borers are present, transplant the irises into fresh soil in a new location in the garden.

Japanese irises are at home in wet locations in the garden; don't attempt these in dry soils as failure is ensured. The soil should be rich in organic matter and free from lime. Plant the stout rhizomes in fall and be prepared to divide every 3 to 4 years.

Harvest and Use: Irises are easy to cut and use. Choose young blooms that are just starting to open, and harvest the entire stem, taking with it three or more buds. Although not especially long lasting as a cut flower, the bearded iris will continue its display in the vase as buds open along the prepared stem. Bearded iris can remain showy in an arrangement for up to 1 week. The Japanese iris will also last for 1 week in water if harvested as the flowers start to emerge from the bud. Both are easily conditioned in warm water before being combined with other garden flowers in arrangements. I like the flowers of bearded iris alone in a vase. Be prepared to do a little house-keeping, as the faded flowers should be picked off of the stem. Try combining the purple bearded irises with peonies or Japanese irises with shasta daisies.

Jonquil; see ***Narcissus***

Lilium (LIL-ee-um) **lily, ○ ◐ W**
Zones: 5 to 9
Characteristics: The lilies are the grand ladies of the garden, tall, stately and elegant. There are many species within this genus of hardy perennial bulbs. The Asiatic hybrids make some of the finest cut flowers. Bred for their upward-facing blooms, the Asiatic, or Hardy, hybrids range in height from 2 to 5 feet. The color range of Asiatic lilies, which bloom in June and July, seems to expand each year. Look for white, pink, yellow, red and mauve. Many of the blossoms, from 4 to 6 inches across, will be freckled with brown or purple, adding interest to their bright, clear colors. 'Enchantment' remains one of the best oranges. Try 'Connecticut Lemonglow' for an unsurpassed yellow and 'Bianca' for its ethereal white flowers.

The Oriental lilies are a little more difficult to grow, but offer fragrance, form and color not seen in other lilies. They are later to bloom in the garden, not making an appearance until August and September. Typically shorter than their Asiatic cousins, the white, pink and cerise blossoms are wonderfully bright with their knobby petals frequently spotted. Try the pure white 'Casa Blanca' or the beautiful pink 'Stargazer'.
Cultural Information: Lilies are generally easy to grow and are long lived in the proper garden site. Choose a position in full sun or light shade and prepare the soil deeply in fall. Use plenty of organic matter and incorporate some bone meal to encourage early root development. Soil for lilies must be perfectly drained for long-term survival and colonization. Lily bulbs are delicate, unprotected bulbs. Look them over before planting them; they should be large, and their multiple layers of scales should be clean, light colored, and free from scars and rot. Plant the bulbs 5 to 6 inches deep. Lilies are best planted in fall but may not be available until early spring. Plant lily bulbs as soon as you purchase them in fall or spring for best garden performance.
Harvest and Use: Like other bulbs, lilies should be cut with a minimum of foliage. Remove no more than one-third of the lily foliage if you don't want to reduce flower displays in future years. Lily stems should be cut when the first blossom or two has opened. The remaining buds will open in the vase. Take the time after harvesting to remove the pollen-heavy anthers, as they can stain. Remove the lower leaves and place stems in warm water to condition. Lilies can be used as individual blossoms taken from the stem or as entire stems. Try combining lilies with delphiniums or larkspurs; they are compatable with other spike flowers, too, such as snapdragons and gladiolas.

Lilium *'Enchantment', one of many Asiatic hybrids available for gardeners today, is one of the finest cut flowers.*

Narcissus, daffodils and jonquils all belong to the genus Narcissus. *Varieties such as 'Accent' are lovely additions to the landscape and will form clumps, providing ever more flowers with each passing year.*

Lily; see ***Lilium***

Montbretia; see ***Crocosmia***

Narcissus (nar-SIS-sus) **daffodil, narcissus, jonquil, ○ ◐ ✳ S,C**
Zones: 4 to 8
Characteristics: Daffodils and narcissus are the promise of spring after a long and bleak winter. Narcissus are available in many forms, from the dwarfs suitable for the rockery, to bold and brassy trumpet daffodils. Colors range from white to green, yellow, orange and pink,

and many offer contrasting trumpet and petal colors. The selection of varieties is seemingly endless, with large trumpets, small trumpets, single and double forms, and single and multiple blooms per head. Daffodils will bloom early, midseason and late, with a bloom time from late March through May. They are easy to force for winter bloom indoors.

Cultural Information: Daffodils are among the hardiest of all the spring-flowering bulbs and are notoriously long-lived perennials, returning each spring for many years. Planted in a deep, rich, well-drained soil, daffodils and narcissus can be naturalized among groundcovers, hardy ferns and even perennials such as hostas. Beds of daffodils may pose a problem for the neat freak, as "daff" foliage will last well into July before it begins to die back for summer dormancy. This can look messy in the garden. An old gardener once taught me to braid daffodil foliage when it starts to look unattractive, and tie the tip of the braid to the base of the foliage for a nice, neat topknot of foliage. When the foliage can be pulled from the bulb with a light tug, remove the foliage and compost it. In naturalized settings, it isn't necessary to go through all the bother, as the foliage will be covered by the groundcover, fern fronds, leaves of hostas, daylilies or other growth where it will ripen naturally.

Plant firm, large bulbs in September and October for bloom the following spring. Triple-nosed bulbs will give you four or five flowers the first year. A handful of bone meal at the base of each planting hole will help promote early root formation. Commercial bulb fertilizers are well worth the investment; side dress bulb plantings with a handful each spring as new growth emerges. Daffodils will grow and bloom for many years without dividing; when the flower display begins to diminish, lift and divide bulbs before replanting in fall.

Harvest and Use: Narcissus can be a little messy to harvest but are almost always successfully conditioned in cool water. Daffodil stems will drool a clear, viscous liquid that can inhibit the lasting ability of other cut flowers. Always take the time to condition daffodils alone in their own container for at least 1 hour (overnight is better) before mixing them with other flowers. Care should be taken in harvesting "daffs" as their stems are hollow and the flower heads will not be supported by stems that are bent. Use a sharp knife or garden snips to cut stems. When designing with daffodils and narcissus, a thin, smooth stem from another plant can be inserted into the narcissus' hollow stem to allow for easier placement into pin holders or floral foam. Some florists use chenille stems (similar to large, fuzzy pipe cleaners and available from craft suppliers) to insert up the stems for added support and water absorption ability.

Combine daffodil and narcissus blooms with any of the spring-flowering bulbs such as tulips and *Scilla,* delicate stems of forget-me-nots and the emerging buds of trees and shrubs, or the brilliant flowers of forsythia. Don't forget to include a few daffodil leaves for a natural accent of foliage.

Peacock orchid; see ***Acidanthera***

Tulipa (TOO-lip-a) **tulips,** ○ ◐ ✳ C

Zones: 4 to 8

Characteristics: Tulips are elegant perennial bulbs, much revered for their formal, upright habit in flower beds. The tulips are a diverse group of species and varieties in a range of heights and colors to please any palate. Look for flower colors ranging from white to deep red, yellow to brilliant orange, and violet to almost black! Variegation abounds in this genus with stripes, spots, picotee edges, and leaping, flamelike markings. Some of the species tulips may grow to only 3 to 6 inches in height, and others are much more stately, with the single late tulips topping the chart at 30 inches.

Several groups of tulips are worth including in the cutting garden. Single early or hybrid Darwin tulips reach to 24 inches tall in colors ranging from brilliant gold to deep red, with many orange and yellow-red bicolors. There are several pink varieties in the single early group that tend toward shell pink, pale orange and salmon. Single early tulips bloom in late March to early April. Triumph tulips are midseason, blooming in mid- to late April. They boast a full range of colors and will top out at about 20 inches tall. Look for 'Garden Party', white petals with a vivid rose edging, and 'Apricot Beauty', with fragrant, pale apricot blossoms.

Single late tulips are the tallest of all. These tulips, in bloom in mid-May, are available in the full range of colors. Try combining one of the "black" tulips with pale pink or creamy yellow. Blooming at the same time are the fringed tulips with strong, pure-colored petals edged in delicate fringe, or lily-flowered tulips with their delicately pointed, vase-shaped blooms on stems that seem always to be bending in a light breeze. Parrot tulips are another addition to the late-spring cutting garden, their contorted blooms a wild blend of paisley colors with pale pinks, white and green or orange, yellow, red and green. Perhaps some of the finest of the cutting tulips, the peony-flowered or double late tulips are elegant additions to any bouquet in bold pinks, reds or white.

Cultural Information: Tulips are easy to grow in any well-drained soil. Look for bulbs that are large, free from bruises and cuts, and firm but not dried out. Prepare the planting bed with well-rotted manure, compost or peat moss, and enrich it with the addition of Bulb Booster or bone meal to enhance root development. Tulips should be planted slightly deeper than recommended (up to 8 inches deep); deeper planting prolongs their useful life. Annual additions of Bulb Booster will also help maintain vigor and flower production. Be sure to water bulbs in after planting to encourage good root development.

Harvest and Use: Harvest tulips when they are still in a fairly tight bud but fully colored. Tulips that have been allowed to open and close in the garden day after day will be worn out before they get into the vase. Cut the flower stem above the foliage or cut one or more leaves. Cutting leaves will reduce flowering in future years but the effect of the foliage in arrangements is worth it. Where maximum stem length is necessary, pull up the entire plant by the roots and cut the bulb off. This bulb will not grow next year and should be discarded. Use a bucket filled with cool water to condition flowers before use.

Tulips can be challenging to the floral designer. Their tendancy to continue to grow in the vase will disconcert and may upset a carefully composed arrangement. Tulip petals open during the day and close at night; this causes them to age faster than tulips that are kept closed. By keeping tulips cool, you can keep the petals from opening. Try adding ice to finished arrangements to chill the tulips and replenish the water supply. Another trick is to make a small vertical cut with a sharp knife just below the blossom. The incision should be ¼ to ½ inch long and should prevent the flower from opening.

Tulips can be combined with any number of flowers and foliages in bouquets. I like tulips all by themselves by the bowlful on a dining table. With forget-me-nots, forsythias or lilacs, tulips add an elegance unsurpassed by other flowers.

Tulips are reliably easy spring bulbs suitable for most cutting gardens. A variety of flower types are available, including 'Angelique', a double late-flowering pink.

Rembrandt tulips such as 'Burpee's Masterpiece Mixture' come in multicolored blends that work well in combination with many other flowers.

TREES AND SHRUBS

Any number of trees and shrubs can be grown for use in arrangements and to enhance the landscape. Your garden probably offers some woody selections suitable for the vase now. I prefer cuttings from small rather than large trees, as larger trees offer logistical problems when it comes time to harvest. Trees and shrubs not only offer suitable flowers but in many cases can be a source of dramatic, long-lasting foliages. I will identify a few favorites you may consider including in your garden. It is critical that you choose woody plants hardy in your USDA zone.

Evergreens are plants that maintain their foliage year 'round. Some turn bronze during the winter months. Evergreen foliage may be needled or broad-leaved, coarse or fine, solid or variegated. Evergreens offer the designer a wide range of foliage patterns, and colors from deep burgundy to yellow-green and blue-gray, suitable for mixing with flowers or other foliages. Most of the evergreens will hold for a month or longer in water without special treatment.

Sappy stems of conifers should be conditioned in cool water, as hot water encourages the sap to bleed; do not split the stems of coniferous plants. Other plant types benefit from having their stems split vertically with a cross cut and conditioning in hot water. Properly handled, evergreen foliage can be used again and again with different flowers. Be sure to recut the stems and use plenty of fresh, clean water to avoid a buildup of bacteria.

Consider some of the following for foliage accents in bouquets:

Aucuba japonica (golddust plant or Japanese aucuba)
Buxus (boxwood)
Euonymus (wintercreeper)
Ilex (holly)
Kalmia (mountain laurel)
Pachysandra (Japanese spurge)
Pinus (pines)
Rhododendron (rhododendron, azalea)
Thuja (arborvitae)
Tsuga (hemlock)

Almost all of the flowering shrubs offer something to the floral designer. Many of the spring bloomers can be forced for bloom indoors in the late winter; forsythia (*Forsythia* × *intermedia*) and flowering quince (*Chaenomeles japonica*) are two of the best. The summer bloomers will not force indoors in the summer because they bloom on new growth produced from the spring buds; butterfly bush (*Buddleia*) and hydrangea are two that fall into the summer category.

Harvest shrub flowers when they are fully developed and beginning to open up. Almost all types of woody plants will do best if all of the foliage is removed before conditioning. Condition stems in hot water after splitting the cut end of the stem with a cross cut. If you are having trouble conditioning a specific type of woody plant flower, consider placing the prepared stem in 2 inches of very hot—almost boiling—water for a few minutes before plunging them into a deep drink of warm water. If a specific stem still causes trouble, try shortening it. Extremely long stems are more difficult to condition than shorter stems. Allow woody plants to condition overnight before using them.

The following shrubs are good choices for harvesting for use in flower arrangements:

Abeliophyllum (white forsythia)
Amelanchier (shadblow)
Buddleia (butterfly bush)
Chaenomeles (flowering quince)
Deutzia (slender deutzia)
Forsythia (showy border forsythia)
Hydrangea (panicle, 'Peegee Hydrangea')
Kolkwitzia (beauty bush)
Philadelphus (mock orange)
Rhododendron (rhododendron, azalea)
Spiraea (spirea)
Syringa (lilac)
Viburnum (viburnum)
Weigela (weigela)

THE ROSE—QUEEN OF THE CUT FLOWERS

Rosa (ROE-sah) **rose**

Characteristics: The rose is revered in song and poem. Long the symbol of love, it has eased the way for many a heartsick young man. *Rosa* is a large genus of shrubs and has representatives from all over the world.

There are many types of roses suitable for the garden, but not all are good cutting roses. Some of the old-fashioned roses that perfume the air with their single blossoms will not last in water. Some of the very largest roses may be awkward and clumsy looking in a bouquet. Many of the newest rose introductions offer the gardener fragrance, beauty and improved hardiness and disease resistance.

For cutting, most of us are looking for roses that will produce cuttable stems and provide long-lasting blossoms. Hybrid Tea roses have long dominated the rose garden, prized for their beauty of form; range of color from white to deep red, yellow, orange and violet; and prolific flower production. Best picks from the Hybrid Tea group are 'Garden Party', a creamy white blushed with pale rose, 'Touch of Class', a delightful pink touched with coral, the rich, deeply red 'Chrysler Imperial', and the incomparably yellow 'Sunbright' and 'Lowell Thomas'. There are many Hybrid Tea roses, and any may make a worthy addition to the cutting garden.

Floribunda and Grandiflora roses combine Hybrid Tea purity of form with increased

Roses are ideal candidates for cutting from the garden. Varieties such as 'Gold Medal', a Grandiflora rose, are suitable for use singly in a bud vase or as sprays of roses in a larger arrangement of flowers.

'Red Meidiland' is one of a new generation of rose, combining the best of the modern roses with the scent, hardiness and vigor of old roses. These "shrub" roses are best cut and used in sprays.

The hybrid tea rose is the classic modern rose. Many new varieties such as 'Touch of Class' bring increased disease resistance to the garden.

Fresh roses from the garden. Cut roses should be plunged immediately into hot water in a clean container, to condition them before they are used in arrangements.

vigor and disease resistance. Consider 'Ivory Fashion' for bouquets; its creamy white blooms borne in clusters are very elegant. 'Queen Elizabeth' is a strong, medium pink Grandiflora. The Grandifloras have slightly smaller, single blooms on good cutting stems. The coral pink of 'Sonja' is considered one of the finest of the cutting roses offered in the commercial market and can be grown in the home cutting garden. 'Gold Medal' is a bright golden yellow Grandiflora.

For the floral designer, miniature roses may offer the largest group of roses superior in the vase as single blooms or sprays of multiple blooms. They range from tiny beauties that grow to 6 inches to varieties that produce smaller blossoms on stems to 3 to 4 feet in height. The flowers are an ideal size for use in bouquets of smaller flowers such as bachelor's buttons and *Nigella.* Miniature roses and sweetheart roses are usually grown on their own root stocks—they are not grafted—and offer superior hardiness to the Hybrid Teas, Floribundas and Grandifloras. 'Jean Kenneally' is a delightful apricot; 'Adam's Smile' is a blend of pink, yellow and coral, and 'Figurine' is a soft white rose with pink undertones. In the garden these roses will produce cuttable stems of a foot or more in length.

Shrub Roses are the roses of the future: tough, resilient, resistant to disease and hardy. Breeders are working to develop the traditional tough characteristics of the Shrub Roses with the everblooming qualities of the Hybrid Teas. The Meilland group of shrub roses are superior in all aspects: hardiness, fragrance, quality of bloom and reblooming ability.

Cultural Information: Roses should be planted in an area where they will receive a minimum 6 to 8 hours of sun per day. A southeastern exposure is ideal, providing adequate sunlight in the morning, yet protecting the shrubs from the hot sun of late afternoon. Roses tolerate a wide range of soil types. Paramount is soil drainage, which must be perfect. Prepare the soil deeply, incorporating peat moss or other organic matter that will improve the soil structure and nutrient-holding capacity of the soil.

Roses can be purchased as container-grown plants or bareroot nursery stock wrapped in fiber or moss. Soak bareroot plants in warm water overnight before planting. (Container-grown plants can be planted without soaking the roots.) Prune dormant plants back to 12 inches at the time of planting, cutting back to an outward-facing bud. Follow planting with a thorough watering and apply a 2- to 3-inch layer of organic mulch such as pine straw, cocoa shells, buckwheat hulls or ground corncobs. When roses begin to show growth, fertilize with a well-balanced, slow-release fertilizer such as 5-10-5. Repeat fertilizer applications when flowers start to open in June and again about 6 weeks later. Roses will flourish with adequate water during dry weather. Soaking the soil at the base of the roses is preferred to overhead irrigation, which can encourage disease.

Overwintering roses varies from region to region. In the Northeast, we usually apply a protective mulch around the base of the plants to cover the lower canes and, in grafted roses, the graft. Choose a mulching material that drains well so it doesn't hold moisture around the roots. After the plants are completely dormant in fall and the ground has started to freeze, apply the mulch in a cone-shaped mound over the crown of each plant. We frequently supplement this winter mulch with evergreen boughs that help hold the mulch in place and add extra insulation from winter winds, cold and the damage caused by alternate freezing and thawing. When the forsythia begins to bloom in spring, carefully remove the mulch from around the roses and spread it out over the surrounding soil to help conserve moisture and prevent weeds. For more information on overwintering, consult *Roses,* another book in the Burpee American Gardening Series.

Insects and disease can be a problem with roses, especially Hybrid Teas. By carefully choosing and preparing the site, maintaining good plant vigor, and selecting disease-resistant plants, we can do much to discourage disease. Cleanliness is critical with roses. Remove diseased leaves from the site and destroy them; do not add them to the compost heap. Organic, botanical and biological controls are available to combat many rose insects and diseases.

Harvest and Use: Harvesting roses is, in fact, a pruning job. Roses should always be cut back to a bud just above a leaf with five or seven leaflets. Never prune back to a leaf with three leaflets as the growth resulting from that bud will, in all likelihood, be blind (will not produce a flower bud). Wherever possible, choose a bud that is facing out, away from the center of the plant. This pruning technique will encourage an open, uncluttered interior for the shrub. The rose shrub that is free from the clutter of many crossing branches and with an open habit will have better sun exposure and air circulation, and be less prone to disease.

Harvested roses should be stripped of any foliage that would sit under water and any thorns. The stems should be immediately placed in hot water for conditioning overnight. Roses treated in this way will last for 1 week or longer in fresh water. Roses can be enjoyed singly in bud vases, clustered with other flowers in a nosegay, or combined with lilies and delphiniums for an elegant centerpiece. Whatever the use, count on roses to provide unparalleled elegance of fragrance and form.

PLANTING LISTS FOR THE CUTTING GARDEN

FLOWERING TREES FOR THE CUTTING GARDEN

Many trees suitable for the small garden will produce flowers that will last well in water. In addition to fragrance and beauty of bloom, these trees may offer foliage, autumn color, ornamental fruits and twig formation. Consider incorporating one of the following trees in your landscape for cuttings.

Amelanchier laevis (shadblow)
Cercis canadensis (redbud)
Cornus spp. (dogwood)
Hamamelis virginiana (witch hazel)
Ilex spp. (holly)
Magnolia spp. (magnolia)
Malus spp. (apple, crabapple)
Oxydendrum arboretum (sorrel tree, sourwood)
Prunus spp. (cherry, plum, peach; ornamental and edible varieties)
Pyrus spp. (pear, ornamental pear)
Salix spp. (willow, pussy willow)
Tamarix (tamarisk, salt cedar)

FLOWERS FOR THE SHADY CUTTING GARDEN

ANNUALS

Ageratum houstonianum (blue flossflower)
Browallia speciosa (blush violet)
Coleus × *hybridus* (coleus)
Nicotiana spp. and hybrids (flowering tobacco)
Torenia fournieri (wishbone flower)
Tropaeolum majus (nasturtium)
Viola spp. (pansy, violet, Johnny-jump-up)

PERENNIALS

Aquilegia spp. and hybrids (columbine)
Astilbe spp. (false spirea)
Cimicifuga racemosa (black snakeroot)
Convallaria majus (lily of the valley)
Epimedium spp. (barrenwort)
Ferns (many genera)
Heuchera spp. (coralbells)
Hosta spp. and hybrids (plantain lily)

SHRUBS/GROUNDCOVERS

Enkianthus campanulatus (red-vein enkianthus)
Hedera helix (English ivy)
Kalmia latifolia (mountain laurel)
Pachysandra terminalis (pachysandra, Japanese spurge)
Rhododendron spp. (rhododendron, azalea)
Vinca minor (periwinkle)

WHITE FLOWERS FOR THE CUTTING GARDEN

ANNUALS

Antirrhinum majus (snapdragon)*
Callistephus chinensis (China aster)*
Cosmos bipinnatus 'Sensation' (cosmos)*
Eustoma grandiflorum (lisianthus, prairie gentian)*
Gomphrena globosa (globe amaranth)*
Gypsophila elegans (baby's breath)
Nicotiana spp. (flowering tobacco)*
Salvia farinacea 'Argent' (salvia)
Zinnia elegans (zinnia)*

PERENNIALS

Aquilegia spp. and hybrids (columbine)*
Astilbe spp. and hybrids (false spirea)*
Campanula spp. (bellflower)*
Chrysanthemum maximum (shasta daisy)
Convallaria majus (lily of the valley)
Echinacea purpurea 'White Star' (echinacea)
Gypsophila paniculata (baby's breath)
Hosta × 'Royal Standard' (hosta)
Paeonia lactifolia (peony)*
Phlox paniculata (garden phlox)*
Physostegia virginiana (obedience plant)*

BULBS, CORMS, RHIZOMES AND TUBERS

Acidanthera bicolor (dark-eye gladixia)
Dahlia hybrids (garden dahlia)*
Gladiolus hybrids (gladiola)*
Narcissus spp. (narcissus, daffodil)*
Tulipa spp. (tulip)*

TREES AND SHRUBS

Deutzia gracilis (slender deutzia)*
Hydrangea paniculata (peegee hydrangea)
Kalmia latifolia (mountain laurel)*
Magnolia virginiana (sweetbay magnolia)*
Malus spp. (ornamental crabapple)*
Oxydendron arboretum (sorrel tree)
Rhododendron spp. (rhododendron, azalea)*
Syringa vulgaris (lilac)*

*White flowers available as part of a seed mix of colors or by purchasing individually named varieties.

BLUE/LAVENDER FLOWERS FOR THE CUTTING GARDEN

ANNUALS

Ageratum houstonianum (blue flossflower)
Browallia speciosa (bush violet)
Callistephus chinensis (China aster)*
Centaurea cyanus (bachelor's button)*
Consolida orientalis (larkspur)*
Eustoma grandiflorum (lisianthus, prairie gentian)*
Lathyrus odoratus (sweet pea)*
Matthiola incana (stock)*
Nigella damascena (love-in-a-mist)*
Salvia farinacea (mealycup sage, gentian sage)*
Scabiosa atropurpurea (pincushion flower)*
Trachelium caeruleum (purple umbrella)
Trachymene coerulea (blue lace flower)
Verbena bonariensis (verbena)

PERENNIALS

Aconitum napellus (monkshood)
Aquilegia × *hybrida* (columbine)*
Baptisia australis (false indigo)

*Blue or purple flowers available as part of a seed mix of colors or by purchasing individually named varieties.

Delphinium elatum (delphinium)
Hosta spp. (plantain lily)
Hyssopus officinalis (hyssop)
Iris spp. (iris)*
Lavandula angustifolia (lavender)

Nepeta spp. (catmint)
Phlox paniculata (garden phlox)*
Platycodon grandiflorus (balloonflower)*
Veronica spicata (speedwell)*
Viola spp. (garden violet)

BULBS, CORMS, RHIZOMES AND TUBERS

Allium spp. (allium, chive, onion)
Endymion hispanicus (wood hyacinth, Spanish squill)*
Gladiolus hybrids (gladiola)*
Tulipa hybrids (tulip)

*Blue or purple flowers available as part of a seed mix of colors or by purchasing individually named varieties.

YELLOW FLOWERS FOR THE CUTTING GARDEN

ANNUALS

Antirrhinum majus (snapdragon)*
Callendula officinalis (pot marigold)*
Celosia cristata (cockscomb)*
Cosmos sulphureus (Klondyke cosmos)*
Gaillardia pulchella (blanketflower)*
Helianthus annuus (sunflower)*
Hunnemannia fumariifolia (Mexican tulip poppy)
Tagetes spp. (marigold)*
Zinnia elegans (zinnia)*

PERENNIALS

Achillea spp. and hybrids (yarrow)*
Aquilegia × *hybrida* (columbine)*
Chrysanthemum × *morifolium* (hardy garden chrysanthemum)*
Coreopsis grandiflora (lance coreopsis)
Rudbeckia hirta (black-eyed Susan)
Solidago spp. (goldenrod)
Tanacetum vulgare (tansy)

BULBS, CORMS, RHIZOMES AND TUBERS

Dahlia hybrids (dahlia)*
Gladiolus hybrids (gladiola)*
Narcissus spp. (daffodil, narcissus)*
Tulipa spp. (tulip)*

TREES AND SHRUBS

Berberis vulgaris (common barberry)
Cytisus praecox (broom)
Forsythia × intermedia (showy border forsythia)
Hamamelis virginiana (common witch hazel)
Kerria japonica (Japanese kerria)*
Syringa vulgaris and hybrids (lilac)*

*Yellow flowers available as part of a seed mix of colors or by purchasing individually named varieties.

PINK AND RED FLOWERS FOR THE CUTTING GARDEN

ANNUALS

Amaranthus caudatus (love-lies-bleeding)
Antirrhinum majus (snapdragon)*
Callistephus chinensis (China aster)*
Celosia cristata and *C. plumosa* (cockscomb)*
Centaurea cyanus (bachelor's button)*

*Pink and red flowers available as part of a seed mix of colors or by purchasing individually named varieties.

Cosmos bipinnatus 'Sensation' (cosmos)*
Dianthus barbatus (sweet William)*
Eustoma grandiflorum (lisianthus, prairie gentian)*
Gomphrena globosa (globe amaranth)*
Lathyrus odoratus (sweet pea)*
Salvia splendens (garden sage)*
Scabiosa atropurpurea (pincushion flower)*
Xeranthemum annuum (immortelle)*
Zinnia elegans (zinnia)*

PERENNIALS

Aster spp. (Michaelmas daisy, aster)*
Astilbe spp. (false spirea)*
Chrysanthemum × morifolium (hardy garden chrysanthemum)*
Chrysanthemum coccineum (painted daisy)
Dianthus spp. (pinks)
Digitalis purpurea (foxglove)
Heuchera × hybrida (coralbells)
Liatris spicata (gayfeather)
Lilium spp. and hybrids (hardy lilies)*
Lychnis coronaria (rose campion, mullein pink)
Monarda didyma (bee balm)
Paeonia lactifolia (peony)*
Phlox paniculata (garden phlox)*

BULBS, CORMS, RHIZOMES AND TUBERS

Crocosmia spp. (montbretia)*
Dahlia hybrids (dahlia)*
Gladiolus hybrids (gladiola)*
Tulipa spp. and hybrids (tulip)*

TREES AND SHRUBS

Chaenomeles lagenaria (flowering quince)
Hydrangea paniculata grandiflora (peegee hydrangea)
Kalmia latifolia (mountain laurel)
Malus spp. (flowering crabapple)
Prunus spp. (ornamental cherry)
Rhododendron spp. (rhododendron, azalea)*
Syringa spp. (lilac)*

*Pink and red flowers available as part of a seed mix of colors or by purchasing individually named varieties.

ORANGE, RUSSET AND BROWN FLOWERS FOR THE CUTTING GARDEN

ANNUALS

Amaranthus caudatus (love-lies-bleeding)
Antirrhinum majus (snapdragon)*
Calendula officinalis (pot marigold)*
Celosia cristata and *C. plumosa* (cockscomb)*
Cosmos sulphureus (Klondyke cosmos)*
Gomphrena globosa (globe amaranth)*
Helianthus annuus (sunflower)
Reseda odorata (mignonette)
Zinnia elegans (zinnia)*

PERENNIALS

Chrysanthemum × morifolium (hardy garden chrysanthemum)
Gaillardia × grandiflora (blanketflower)
Rudbeckia hirta (gloriosa daisy)

BULBS, CORMS, RHIZOMES AND TUBERS

Crocosmia spp. (montbretia)*
Dahlia hybrids (dahlia)*
Lilium spp. and hybrids (hardy lilies)*
Gladiolus hybrids (gladiola)*
Tulipa spp. and hybrids (tulip)*

*Orange, russet or brown flowers available as part of a seed mix of colors or by purchasing individually named varieties.

ORNAMENTAL TREES

Charles O. Cresson

INTRODUCTION

One of the great satisfactions of life is to watch a young tree grow to majestic proportions as it reaches maturity. Results may not be long in coming, for many trees grow rapidly. This can be a lifelong fascination. Enlist the help of children when planting a tree and they will have an early start in this pursuit.

Trees are beautiful. Throughout the year, they give interest to the landscape. Tall, stately evergreen conifers provide fresh green color, even in the depths of winter, among the silhouettes of their deciduous counterparts. Spring foliage of some trees emerges in shades of red, purple, and even gold, and for a few trees, these colors will persist through the summer. People often think of a tree's beauty only in terms of foliage, but imagine the spring or summer spectacle of a large tree bedecked with flowers. Fall is the season of brilliant foliage, which can equal the brilliance of the brightest flowers. Colorful fruit and berries often last well into winter or even the following spring, catching the sun, contrasting with the snow, cheering dull days, and feeding wildlife. Some trees even transform the color of their twigs to reds, yellows and bright greens in winter as if seizing the opportunity to attract your attention and invite you outdoors for companionship.

Trees are the dominant element, the backbone, of most landscapes. They create the setting in which other plants grow. Established trees impart a sense of age and establishment even to young gardens in which other plants, such as shrubs and perennials, may still be quite small. Because it takes so many years to grow large trees, they should be preserved and cared for if you already have them.

Aside from their beauty and landscape value, trees have an additional, even greater importance: They help to preserve the environmental balance of our piece of the earth. They provide a habitat where wildlife can thrive. Trees clean the air, removing pollution and toxins while transforming carbon dioxide into oxygen. Their roots hold the soil, preventing erosion. Tree leaves make nutritious compost and mulch, which builds soil fertility and creates a home for organisms that become food for wildlife. Their flowers attract hummingbirds, and their fruit and seeds sustain numerous other birds through the winter. Their branches, especially evergreen branches, shelter birds in adverse weather. Even dead trees have a role in nature, because many animals and birds require their cavities for shelter and nesting.

Trees also contribute to our own comfort by preserving valuable resources. Deciduous trees provide shade and absorb heat in the summer, cooling your patio and house, and indeed the whole neighborhood. After leaf drop in winter, they allow the sun's rays to warm the earth. Evergreens on the windward side of your house will break the force of cold winter winds, reducing your heating bill. On a property containing several mature trees, routine care and trimming can provide wood for occasional use in the fireplace. Trees not only will save you money but, when well selected and placed in the landscape, can add to your property value.

Both shrubs and trees are long-lived, woody plants and may be so similar that the distinction is sometimes blurred. Generally, trees have single trunks and shrubs have many trunks, or woody stems. Trees are usually taller, although some small trees may be smaller than the largest shrubs. To confuse the matter even further, some large-growing shrubs can be trained as single-trunked small trees. Trees can also be multi-trunked. To keep it as simple as possible, the trees in this book are able to grow to more than 15 feet, and usually have just one trunk. Dwarf trees, including dwarf conifers, are not included.

Though not requiring a wet site, weeping willows grow and look best next to water. This golden weeping willow, Salix alba *'Tristis', is a special treat mirrored in the lake in autumn.*

TYPES OF TREES

Trees vary tremendously. The most apparent difference is between deciduous and evergreen trees. Deciduous trees lose their leaves in winter. Evergreens hold their leaves all year 'round. In the North, most evergreens are needled conifers that bear their seeds in cones (pines and spruces, for example). Deciduous trees usually have broad leaves, and many, such as the maple, assume brilliant colors in autumn. Others, such as crabapples and fringe trees, delight us with a breathtaking display of flowers and perhaps colorful fruits. It must be pointed out, however, that not all evergreens are conifers and not all deciduous trees are broad leaved. In the South, there are many fine broad-leaved evergreen trees such as the southern magnolia (or bullbay) and the live oak. Larches, on the other hand, are deciduous conifers. In other words, although generalizations are helpful, there are exceptions.

NATURAL TREE SHAPES

Tree Forms and Shapes

Trees grow in a variety of shapes according to their kind. For example, conifers tend to be pyramidal and oaks are generally rounded. On the other hand, mutations of many trees have been discovered through the centuries that have shapes different from the norm. These mutations have been propagated specially for use in gardens. The columnar Lombardy poplar was a mutation found in Lombardy, Italy, nearly 300 years ago; it is now common worldwide. The weeping flowering cherry, also a mutation, was introduced from Japan.

Some tree shapes, such as espalier, are not natural. They are created by training and pruning, and without regular shaping will resume growing in their natural forms.

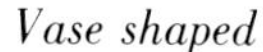

Vase shaped

Globe shaped

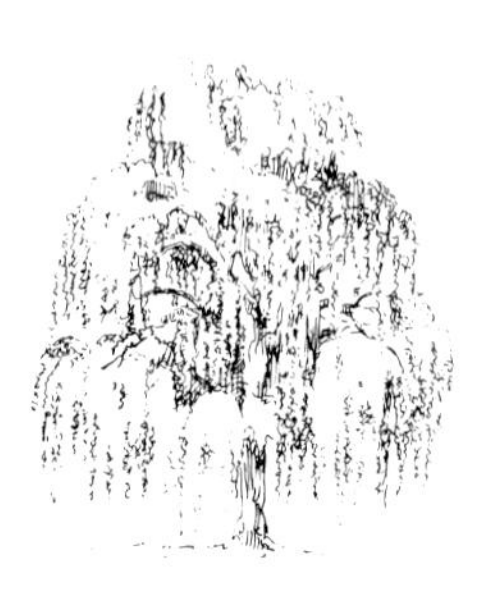

Weeping

Spreading

Pyramidal or conical

Fastigiate

ARTIFICIAL (MAN-MADE) SHAPES, CREATED BY TRAINING AND PRUNING

Pollarded

Pleached

Bonsai

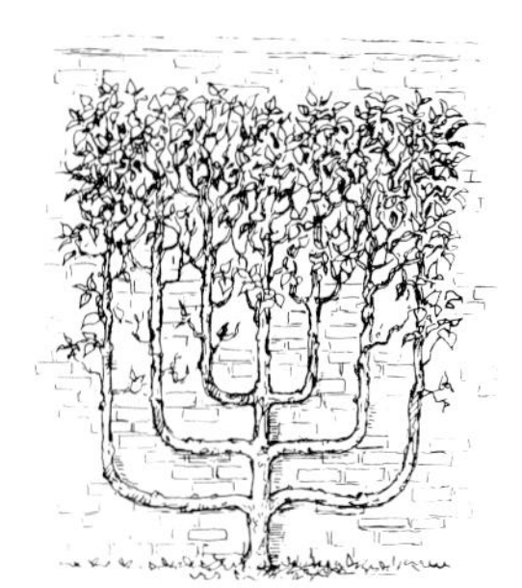

Espaliered

Hedge (hemlocks and hollies)

LEARNING ABOUT TREES

One of the best ways to learn about the trees that will grow well in your garden is to take a walk around your neighborhood and see what is growing nearby. Your neighbors probably have the same kind of soil and climate you do. Look at the kinds of locations and conditions where the healthiest trees are growing. Ask your friends about their trees; people usually enjoy sharing information about their gardens. Take a trip to a local public garden or arboretum where the names are often attached to the trees, so that you can find out what they are and learn more about them. Garden or arboretum staff members are often available to answer your questions. The cooperative or agricultural extension service in your state probably publishes free bulletins about trees. Reputable nurseries and garden centers also have knowledgeable staff that can answer your questions and recommend trees for local conditions. No book such as this can account for all climates and growing conditions, and the best advice will often come from those with experience in your area.

In the following pages you will learn the basics about trees: how to select them, how to grow them and how to solve their problems. The "plant portraits" will tell you about some of the best kinds for temperate climates.

1

THE GARDEN PLANNER

Before placing anything as permanent and important as a tree on your property, you should develop a scheme for how you will use and design the space. You probably already have ideas. Begin by looking at the different ways in which areas are used now. Look at how physical barriers such as hedges, fences and even your house and garage divide the property into sections. For instance, the front yard is probably separate from the back, but the side might be a separate area, too.

Next, consider what uses and activities are appropriate to various areas. The front area is likely to be viewed by the public. You want it to look attractive and inviting, but you may not spend much time there. The back is more likely to be private, and reserved for family activities and recreation. It may include a patio or deck for outdoor living. Consider the layout of your house, as well as your yard. Walk around inside your house and look out the windows. Think about the views from important rooms, such as your living room and den. You will need a utility area where trash cans, firewood and compost can be kept out of sight. You might want a flower garden, located in either sun or shade, and a vegetable garden, which will need to be in sun. All of these considerations will help you make your whole garden more attractive and functional. Placement of trees will be one of your first decisions in shaping these areas. (Chapter 2 explains what kinds of trees to plant for various purposes in your garden.)

YOUR GARDEN'S ENVIRONMENT

Now consider the characteristics of your piece of land. Look at the USDA Plant Hardiness Map of the United States (pages 92–93) to determine your approximate climatic zone. This map is based on normal winter cold, the most important factor in determining winter hardiness of plants. Local conditions also influence your climate. If you live at a high elevation, your climate will be colder than an elevation several hundred or thousand feet lower. A south-facing slope will be hotter and drier than a north-facing one because its angle catches more of the sun's rays. This means that if you have a south slope or a lower elevation you may be able to grow a plant that is not hardy for other properties nearby, even if they're in the same USDA hardiness zone.

The weeping Alaska cedar, Chamaecyparis nootkatensis *'Pendula', is a particularly graceful conifer.*

Rainfall

Find out the average annual rainfall for your area, and during which seasons it falls. This is not as critical as the characteristic temperature extremes, because you can water to supplement shortages of rain. Most trees need about 40 inches of rain per year to grow well, so in climates with little summer rain, you will need to water many trees. Some kinds will get along with less water, so if you live in a dry region it is especially important to get advice on what these trees are to avoid the need for extra watering.

Soil

Soil is an important feature of your garden's environment. Water availability is related to soil conditions. Sandy soils dry out quickly because the water drains right through. Clay soils hold water but are heavy and difficult to work; they are often compacted, with poor aeration and poor drainage. Roots need oxygen to grow, so they need good aeration in the soil. If puddles take more than half a day to seep in after a rain, you can tell your soil has poor drainage.

Drainage is also affected by topography. On a slope, the uppermost soil is likely to be dry, whereas the lower part will stay moist longer. Fortunately, many desirable trees thrive in adverse soil conditions, whether the soil be poorly drained or very dry. And don't despair; soils are usually mixtures of sand, clay and other particles that combine the advantages of each and are suitable for most of the trees you would wish to plant.

One condition few plants can tolerate is severe root competition. Densely matted, shallow roots take all the nutrients and water before less-established plants have a chance at them. Norway maples are notorious for their tenacious roots. If you have one, you'll note few things will ever grow beneath it. Some people have tried adding a layer of soil over the roots, but that is eventually a harmful measure: Generally it leads to the slow death by suffocation of venerable specimens. The roots are still there and will grow up into the new soil, if the tree survives. Filling over tree roots with additional soil changes the delicate balance of aeration to the roots.

Soil pH is one of the most important indicators of the suitability of your soil for specific plants; pH is a measure of the acidity or alkalinity of the soil, a scale that runs from 0 to 14. Below 7 is acid, and above 7 is basic (or alkaline). Rhododendron and their relatives, such as sorrel trees, are well known for requiring acidic soils. Soil pH affects the availability of many nutrients, and an extreme pH can actually cause a nutrient deficiency even though there is plenty of the nutrient in the soil. The best balance of available nutrients for most plants occurs near neutral, specifically pH 6.8. Most trees prefer slightly acidic soils, but many will grow satisfactorily in slightly alkaline soils, too.

The best way to learn about your soil is to have a soil test done. You can often buy a special envelope from the cooperative extension service of your state or from a local garden center, fill it according to directions, and send it through the mail to be tested by professionals. The results will tell you the pH, nutrient availability, and how to correct your soil in order to grow what you would like. The cost is generally modest, and a real bargain considering the invaluable information it furnishes about your soil.

Sargent's cherry, Prunus Sargentii, *is one of the finest flowering trees for early spring, but the early flowers are often spoiled by frost. In this situation, the pond may save the flowers by radiating enough heat to prevent light frosts.*

Air Circulation

Winds can hamper good tree growth. Surrounding trees, buildings and hills provide shelter from the wind. Hilltops and coastal locations are especially windy. Very sheltered sites, on the other hand, may have such poor air circulation that they encourage disease for susceptible trees, particularly in humid climates.

Sunlight

The amount of sunlight you receive determines the kinds of trees you can grow, too. Large surrounding buildings or trees on the south side cast a lot of shade, but the same trees on the north side will cast little shade. Overhead trees can cause heavy or light shade, depending on their size, type and how they are trimmed. Such densely foliaged trees as Norway maples cast a heavy shade, whereas oaks allow dappled sun to shine through. High shade is brighter and can be created by removing lower limbs along the trunk. Many trees and other plants can be grown well in high or dappled shade.

Existing Trees

If you already have trees on your property, your first priority should be to incorporate them into the landscape plan. Before removing any tree, be sure it really must go. A tree hastily removed and later regretted will take decades to replace. Of course, there are situations in which a tree cannot stay. It may be simply dead or damaged or sick beyond recovery. Perhaps it is just in the wrong place and you can't plan around it.

If you are considering removing a tree, first try to work with it. Ugly or misshapen trees can become fascinating specimens with great character. Through imaginative pruning you can reveal interesting trunk character, branch shapes and bark texture. You will create effects that can't be purchased at any price and that take years to develop. A low-branched tree that seems to be in the way can be limbed up, leaving an overhead canopy. If trees are too crowded, thin out the stand by selecting the best specimens in the best locations and removing the rest. Don't be overzealous—you can always take out more later. These decisions can affect the success of your property's design, and mistakes can take years to fix. If you feel unsure, seek the help of an experienced horticulturist or arborist with some design background.

2

DESIGNING WITH TREES

THE CHARACTER OF TREES

Because of their size, trees are dominant elements in any landscape. By virtue of their grandeur, they set scale. Alone or combined with shrubs, they shape your landscape and garden by enclosing it or dividing it into sections for different uses. They can create vistas and channel the eye toward desired points or block out and hide unsightly objects or areas. Overhead, they break the force of the sun to make a restful patch of shade. In addition, the trees you choose will shape the character of your garden.

Manipulate the sense of scale to your advantage. A very large tree next to a small house will dwarf it, whereas a large tree next to a large house will make it seem less imposing. Large foliage, like that of some magnolias, tends to make a small space such as a courtyard seem even smaller. In the landscape, large or coarse foliage will appear to be closer. The fine foliage of needled evergreens, such as spruce, recedes in the landscape, giving a greater sense of distance, losing detail and focusing attention on the overall tree shape.

Tree forms and shapes are as important as scale. Upright trees draw the eye up. Weeping trees draw the eye down. Pyramidal shapes attract attention to that part of the landscape and can add to the formality or symmetry of a design. They attract attention most dramatically when used singly or in pairs. High-branched trees allow us to see past the trunk, to focus on a distant object; they have space and air under them. Low-branched trees present a visual barrier in the landscape and stop the eye. They seem anchored to the ground and act as dividers. See pages 8–9 for illustrations of tree shapes.

The type of foliage plays a role in the character of design. Dark evergreen foliage can be somber, even overpowering; but used in moderation, or mixed with other foliage, it can create an attractive contrast or background to lighter elements that change with the seasons. For instance, bright yellow witch hazel flowers will show up more effectively in midwinter against a dark background of evergreens. Colorful crabapple fruits are particularly visible after their leaves have fallen, and even more so when they are backed by an evergreen. Foliage of deciduous trees and shrubs is usually of lighter shades of green. Deciduous trees are welcome additions to the winter garden, because after their foliage has fallen, more light reaches into dark corners on dull days. Illustrations of leaf shapes are found on the following page.

A classic combination of flowering dogwood, (Cornus florida) *and azaleas.*

LEAF SHAPES

Foliage type and shape varies widely from one tree species to another. Understanding basic foliage shapes is critical to identifying and choosing the right tree for landscape use. "Plant Portraits" describe basic leaf types as shown below.

BROAD-LEAVED SHAPES:

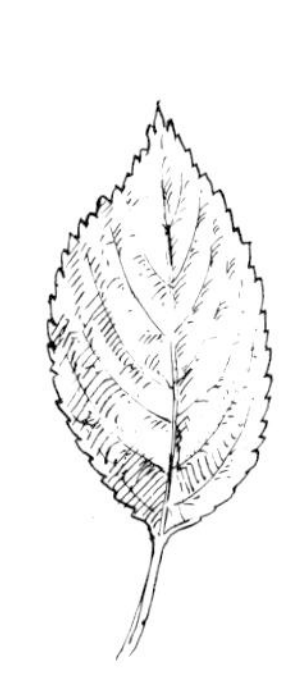

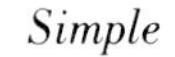

Simple

Palmately lobed

Pinnately lobed

Trifoliate

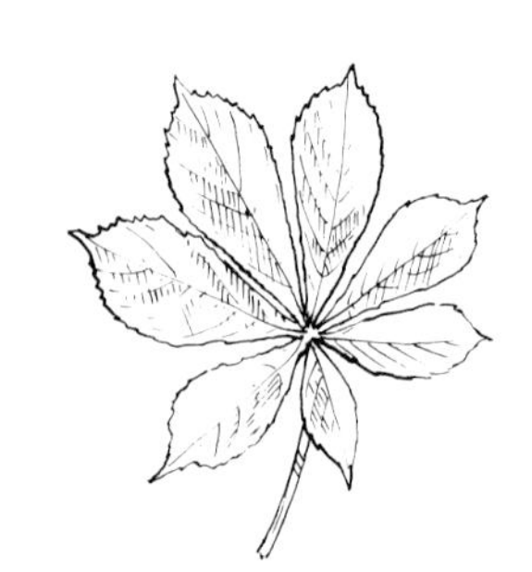

Palmately compound

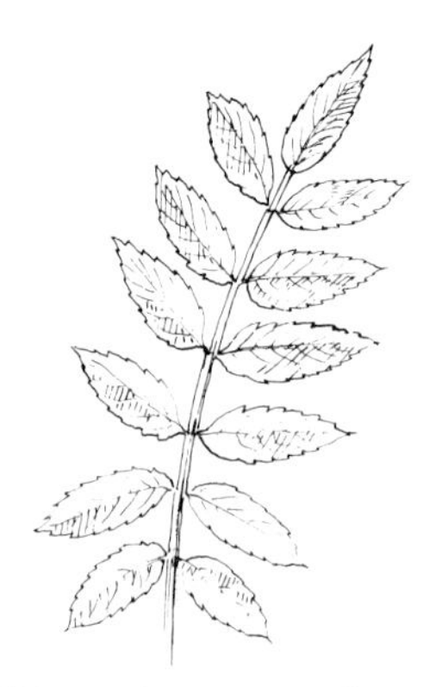

Pinnately compound

Bipinnately compound

NEEDLED SHAPES:

Scalelike needled (i.e., arborvitae)

Short needled (i.e., spruce)

Long needled (in clusters, i.e., pine)

The magnificent autumn color of this deciduous conifer from China, Pseudolarix Kaempferi, *inspired the common name of golden larch.*

The native red maple, Acer rubrum, *is so named for its brilliant autumn color. It grows best in sunny locations. Here it grows with poplar, a pioneer species, that has not yet assumed its autumn color.*

Dwarf Trees

There are many kinds of dwarf trees. Some, such as Japanese bonsai, are kept small by pruning the shoots and roots regularly so that they are not allowed to grow large. But most dwarf trees in gardens are either genetically small or are dwarfed by being grafted onto dwarfing rootstocks. Genetic dwarfs naturally grow more slowly. In time they may become quite large, but it will take many years and they will never reach the size of their normal counterparts. Examples of genetic dwarfs are many varieties of conifers, smaller-growing forms of Japanese maples and some kinds of fruit trees, such as the small peach trees bred for patio containers.

Other trees, primarily apples and pears, are grafted onto roots developed by breeders to stunt the tree's growth. The relationship between the top of the tree and the different root is complex, but it is known that certain rootstocks will grow a tree of a very specific height and vigor. Dwarf fruit trees are most useful to growers or home gardeners who wish to pick fruit without the need of a ladder. Dwarfing rootstocks are less frequently used for ornamental trees.

SEXUALITY AND TREES

Although the great majority of trees are hermaphroditic (possessing both sexes on the same tree), there are a few, such as hollies, that are dioecious (having male and female flowers on separate trees). Male trees do not bear fruit, and neither will females unless there is a male tree nearby to provide pollen. Because hollies are grown for their attractive red berries, it is essential to have both sexes in your garden or neighborhood, along with a population of bees.

Luckily, bees frequent most gardens and can effectively pollinate about eight female trees from a single male tree. Bees are such efficient pollinators that the trees don't even have to be planted next to each other. Bees find all the trees, and travel freely between them. Many gardeners plant a male tree in a less promiment location and put the females where their berries will be most visible. Most nurseries stock both male and female cultivars of dioecious species, so you will be able to buy both sexes in order to have berries.

YOUR GARDEN

Trees help define and enhance garden areas. They are such dominant elements that they should be the first plants you place, if possible. Shrubs, perennials, annuals and bulbs should follow, in that order. The remainder of this chapter will explain how to fit trees into the landscape and what to look for in trees you are selecting for different uses.

Few flowers can match the winter beauty of hollies with evergreen foliage and red berries. The variegated leaves of this English holly, Ilex Aquifolium *'Golden King', are an extra feature.*

Design Principles

Several design principles will assist you in evaluating the success of your garden and the feasibility of your ideas. Repetition of plants, objects, colors and forms help to unify a landscape. For example, you might place a tree in the foreground, and then place another one or more of the same kind in the distance. The eye will be drawn through the landscape as it moves from one tree to the next. In a small garden it may not be possible to repeat such large elements as trees, particularly when you want several different kinds to provide interest at different seasons. Instead, consider repeating smaller elements such as shrubs and choose kinds that will complement trees by blooming at the same time. (You can figure this out by observing your neighborhood or visiting public gardens.) You could also repeat a shape with smaller-growing trees of a different kind, but with a similar appearance.

Balance, or equalizing weights visually in the landscape, also imparts unity to a design. For instance, in a formal design, symmetry will provide balance, perhaps in the form of two identical trees on opposite sides of an object or space. It is slightly more complicated to achieve a sense of balance in an informal, asymmetrical scheme. But again, the concept of balancing visual weights applies. Create balance by using a large object on one side and several smaller ones on the opposite side. You can also use a large object closer to the pivotal point on one side to balance a smaller object placed farther away on the opposite side.

A focal point helps to unify a design by encouraging the eye to focus on a particular object or element, whether the setting be formal or informal. This simply means that a single element or area should stand out, and the design should be balanced on either side of it. The focal point may be a tree, shrub or flowers, but a nonplant feature, such as a bench or statue, is likely to be most effective because, being different, it will stand out better.

The principle of sequence uses time to create a progression of such seasonal features as bloom of different plants, foliage colors and winter interest. The greater the variety of plants in your garden, the greater the potential for a continuous sequence of events and display. But the need for variety must not undercut repetition and balance, which are so necessary to good design. The principle of sequence itself should be used according to the principles of repetition and balance. All the seasonal interest should not be confined to one spot, but be repeated and balanced throughout the garden.

Think in terms of plant combinations. Combine trees and other plants to bloom together with complementary colors. Flowering dogwood with azaleas is a classic spring combination in many regions. Harmonious foliage color and shape provide a long season of interest. A single golden-foliaged Hinoki false cypress is a striking exclamation point among Colorado blue spruces and deep-green Norway spruces. Plant larger-leaved deciduous trees with needled conifers, for a contrast of textures. Locate an early pink-flowering saucer magnolia in front of a background of dark evergreens.

Needless to say, planting a small tree that will become a large specimen someday requires long-term vision. Full size may come in about 30 years for a flowering cherry, 50 to 60 years for a pin oak, or several hundred to a thousand years for a giant redwood. How should a gardener deal with the continuously increasing size of a tree when designing a planting? Landscape architects decide on a target time at which they want a landscape to "mature." This might be 5, 10 or more years.

Middleton Place, near Charleston, S.C., is famous for its old, magnificent, spreading live oaks, Quercus virginiana.

Oriental spruce, Picea orientalis, *is one of the best garden spruces because of its refined shape.*

This is the time at which the trees reach the size for which they were spaced. Of course, you can't stop them from growing, so after that the landscape may become crowded and need some major revisions.

In a commercial landscape, the plan may be to remove half the trees in 10 years when they become crowded. For the homeowner this is usually not a happy prospect. We become attached to our trees. Besides, they are a major investment in time and, perhaps, money. In home gardens, it is usually best to place trees to allow for their mature size, especially large-growing, long-lived kinds such as oaks, tulip trees and pines. Mature spread must be considered, as well as mature height. Use smaller, shorter-lived cherries, dogwood and mountain ashes to fill in the spaces. They will have finished their life cycles by the time the larger trees finally mature. Face down and fill in the planting with shrubs and perennials.

CHOOSING TREES FOR SPECIAL PLACES

About Shade Trees

All too often shaded areas have a barren appearance because there is not enough light for most flowering and foliage plants to grow well. A more hidden problem is competition in the soil from shallow tree roots. This need not be. The best shade trees are those that have deep roots and branch from high on the trunk. Deeply rooted trees are compatible with shade plants and will allow you to create an attractive garden in the shade. Such shallow-rooted trees as lindens and Norway maples cause severe competition with underplantings for water and nutrients.

High shade is preferable to low shade because it allows more diffused light from the side for plantings beneath, yet it still breaks the force and heat of the overhead sun. High shade also allows more air circulation, which contributes to plant health, as well as human comfort on hot days. Another issue to consider when assessing the quality of shade is the density of foliage. It's easier to grow plants in the light shade of a honey locust than the heavy shade of a densely foliaged linden.

Broad-leaved trees make the best shade trees because of their spreading habits. Most are deciduous, but in the South, such evergreens as live oak are widely used. Conifers are less suitable as shade trees because they tend to be narrower. But if you have a grove of mature conifers, don't cut them down! They can be adapted to provide the right kind of shade by such techniques as limbing up (removing lower branches) and by thinning them out—removing the more crowded, weaker individuals.

Evergreen and deciduous trees cast different kinds of shade and have different uses on your property. Although evergreens impart a refreshing green to the winter landscape, too many of them will cast a somber darkness on those short, dull days. Evergreen trees provide more shelter to plants growing under them, especially evergreen shrubs, because they block the

Some Shade Plants for Under Trees

SHRUBS:

Camellia species
Enkianthus campanulatus
Hamamelis species (witch hazel)
Hydrangea species
Pieris japonica (Japanese andromeda)
Prunus Laurocerasus (cherry laurel)
Rhododendron species (includes azaleas)
Viburnum species

PERENNIALS:

Anemone × hybrida (Japanese anemone)
Astilbe species (goatsbeard)
Cimicifuga species (bugbane)
Dicentra species (bleeding heart)
Epimedium species (barrenwort)
Hosta species (plantain lily)
Pulmonaria species (lungwort)

GROUNDCOVERS:

Euonymus Fortunei (wintercreeper, euonymus)
Ferns, various
Hedera Helix (English ivy)
Liriope species (lilyturf)
Pachysandra terminalis (Japanese spurge)

BULBS:

Caladium species
Colchicum species
Crocus species
Narcissus species (daffodil)
Scilla sibirica (Siberian squill)

ANNUALS:

Begonia species
Browallia americana (bush violet)
Coleus species (flame nettle)
Impatiens species (busy lizzy)
Torenia Fournieri (wishbone flower)

Weeping willowleaf pear, Pyrus salicifolia *'Pendula', is prized for its silvery foliage and pendulous mounded habit.*

winter sun and wind, which can cause winter burn. On the windward side of a building they break chilly winds, saving on heating bills. But don't use them on the sunny side; they will block the sun's warmth. Use deciduous trees on the sunny side where they will shade the house from the hot summer sun but allow the sun to provide some heat in winter. A deciduous tree on the south side of a patio will make it a sunny, warm and more inviting place in early spring, as well as a cool shaded spot through the summer. In the garden, spring flowers prefer to be planted under deciduous trees. Daffodils, crocuses, winter aconites and many other early bulbs begin growth in late winter when the bare trees allow plenty of sun to shine through. By the time trees leaf out, the bulbs will have nearly finished growing.

SCREENING TREES AND WINDBREAKS

Some trees can fulfill these three functions: visually hiding an unwanted view or object, absorbing or reducing noise, and breaking the force of strong winds. They should be well branched to the ground, and evergreen to function fully through the winter. Deciduous trees are usually not as effective in winter, but when wider plantings, such as a strip of woods, can be made on larger properties, they can function equally well. On small properties, evergreens with a narrow habit are preferable to save space. In very tight spaces, hedges are the only option. Large hedges are a lot of work to trim but can be successfully made from hemlock (*Tsuga canadensis*), white pine (*Pinus Strobus*), arborvitae (*Thuja occidentalis*) and holly (*Ilex* species). Small hedges should be made of shrubs.

Good planning is essential to the long-term success of a screen planting. The results of impulsive planting can be unfortunate and far-reaching. Planting a single row of large-growing conifers in too much shade or too little space can mean that in a few years the trees will have lost their low branches, with the screening effect lost and the trees casting too much shade to permit another effective screen to be planted beneath them. If space is at a premium, consider such small shade-tolerant evergreen trees as hollies or arborvitaes (*Thuja occidentalis*) or use shrubs.

Eastern arborvitae, Thuja occidentalis, *is an evergreen well suited to tall hedges and tolerates some shade.*

European hornbeam, Carpinus Betulus *'Fastigiata', makes a fine deciduous hedge, as seen here at Longwood Gardens, Kennet Square, Pa.*

Recommended Trees for Hedges

- *Carpinus Betulus* 'Fastigiata' (European hornbeam)
- *Chamaecyparis pisifera* (Sawara false cypress)
- ×*Cupressocyparis Leylandii* (Leyland cypress)
- *Fagus sylvatica* (European beech)
- *Ilex* species (holly)
- *Juniperus* species (juniper)
- *Pinus Strobus* (eastern white pine)
- *Prunus lusitanica* (Portugese cherry laurel)
- *Quercus ilex* (holm or holly oak)
- *Thuja occidentalis* (eastern arborvitae)
- *Tsuga canadensis* (hemlock)

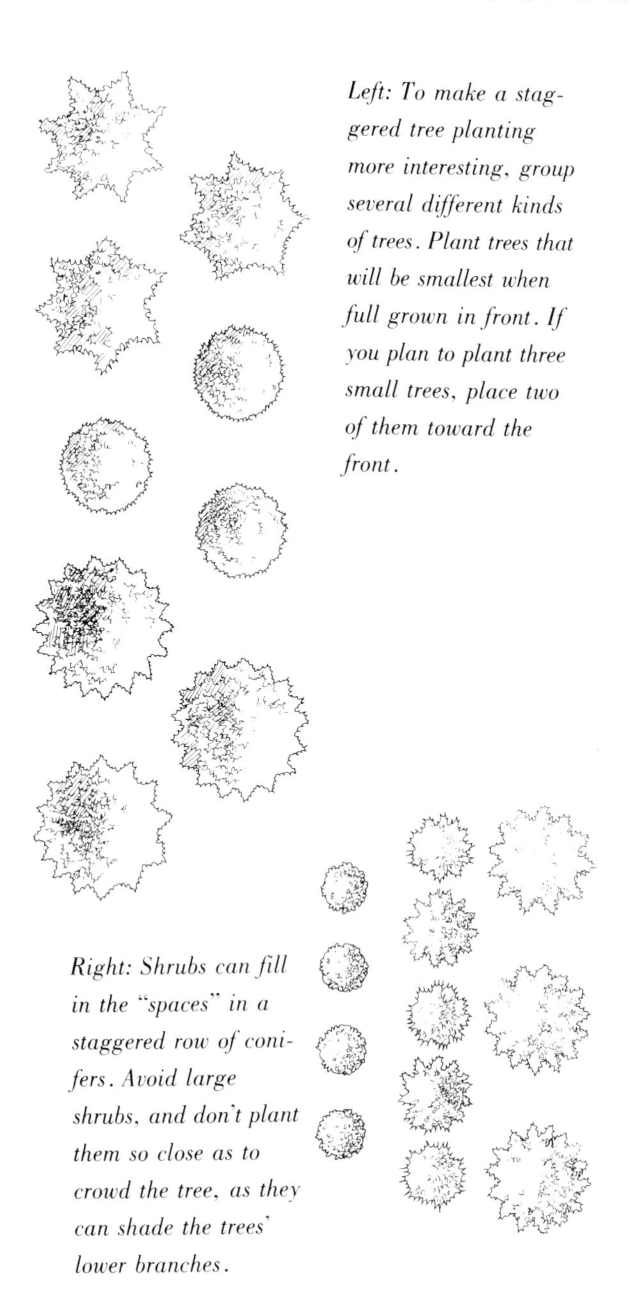

Left: To make a staggered tree planting more interesting, group several different kinds of trees. Plant trees that will be smallest when full grown in front. If you plan to plant three small trees, place two of them toward the front.

Right: Shrubs can fill in the "spaces" in a staggered row of conifers. Avoid large shrubs, and don't plant them so close as to crowd the tree, as they can shade the trees' lower branches.

Proper spacing is important to allow for the long-term growth of trees. If planted too closely and not trimmed, the stronger trees will gradually crowd out the weaker ones in an irregular pattern. Alternatively, when young trees are given enough space to grow, it will be many years before they fill in the gaps. The best solution is to space the trees widely in two staggered rows. When viewed straight on, the trees in one row will appear to fill the spaces between the trees in the other row. To fill the spaces even faster, interplant with shrubs. A less monotonous scheme is to use several groups of different kinds of trees.

Vegetation windbreaks are superior to the solid barriers produced by fences, walls and buildings, for several reasons. Because they allow air to pass through, they break the force of the wind without channeling it around the edges. (Wind can whip around solid objects, increasing in velocity and the potential to cause damage. Anyone living in a city in the midst of tall buildings knows this phenomenon well.) A windbreak of moderate density can reduce wind speeds for a distance of up to eight times its height. In addition, the permeability of vegetation windbreaks increases the area of the quiet zone behind the windbreak.

The effectiveness of sound reduction is enhanced by the density of foliage closest to the ground and by distance. The density of low foliage is most important because sound, such as road noise, travels along the ground. A sound barrier is most effective when planted close to the source of the noise, with as much distance as possible between the barrier and the listener. The initial volume of the sound is broken by the barrier, and then the remaining volume decreases while traveling the distance to the listener.

Screen plantings are valuable long-term investments. Protect them from crowding by any weed trees, shrubs and vines that might grow up with time; these create shade that will cause the foliage to thin out, and branches, especially low ones, to die out. If you give screen plantings enough space and keep them free from competing vegetation, they require little maintenance.

ABOUT SPECIMEN TREES

A tree considered a specimen or focal point is in a prominent location and has striking features, flowers or unique foliage color, for example. For the best effect, it must not be crowded. A specimen tree should be chosen with care, so that its mature size will be in proportion to the property. A small tree is often the best choice for a home garden of moderate size. It stands to reason that a prominently placed tree should possess as many striking features as possible, whether they be flowers, fruit, foliage or overall form. Crabapples (*Malus* species) and mountain ashes (*Sorbus* species) have both flowers and decorative fruit, but one must take care to select disease-resistant varieties that will not defoliate at the height of summer. Goldenrain tree (*Koelreuteria paniculata*) has yellow flowers in summer, strikingly coarse, deep green foliage and papery pods that hang into the winter. Weeping English beech (*Fagus sylvatica* 'Pendula') lacks showy flowers or fruit, but its magnificent pendant form is sufficiently striking when provided with enough space in a large landscape.

TREES FOR WILDLIFE

Consider wildlife when selecting trees for your garden. Birds and other animals add beauty and interest to the landscape during all seasons. To encourage these creatures to stay in your garden, you will want to plant a variety of trees, to provide them with fruits and seeds over a long period of time. Some fruits become palatable earlier than others. Less tasty types will be left alone until later, when the more favored kinds are no longer available. Robins and cardinals like the fruit of dogwood (*Cornus* species), crabapples (*Malus* species), mountain ashes (*Sorbus* species), hawthorns (*Crataegus* species), hollies (*Ilex* species) and junipers (*Juniperus* species). Seeds of birches (*Betula* species), sweet gums (*Liquidambar* species), spruces (*Picea* species) and pines (*Pinus* species) are eaten by goldfinches. In autumn, squirrels bury acorns and other nuts to provide food all winter long. Hummingbirds are attracted to the flowers of many trees, including horse chestnuts (*Aesculus* species) and black locusts (*Robinia* species). Many birds feed on the insects that live on trees among the foliage, branches and bark crevices.

Trees provide safe places for nesting and shelter from inclement weather. Evergreeens are especially valuable for shelter in winter. Cavities in dead trees and branches are required by many species of birds and animals for nesting, but because few dead trees are left standing in residential areas, birdhouses hung on living trees are good substitutes. Each species has its own preference as to the type of house and tree. The greater the variety of trees and other plants, the better wildlife habitat you will have.

Junipers have soft, berry-like cones. Many ripen to a bluish color, as in the case of western red cedar, Juniperus scopulorum, *and are eaten by birds.*

Some Trees Adapted to City Conditions

MODERATE SIZE	*NORMAL LANDSCAPE SIZE*
Acer campestre (hedge maple)	25 to 35 feet
Crataegus species (hawthorn)	15 to 30 feet
Koelreuteria paniculata (goldenrain tree)	30 to 40 feet
Malus species (crabapple)	12 to 20 feet
Pyrus Calleryana (callery pear)	20 to 40 feet
LARGE SIZE	
Betula nigra 'Heritage' (river birch)	40 to 70 feet
Cercidiphyllum japonicum (katsura tree)	40 to 50 feet
Fraxinus species (ash)	50 to 80 feet
Ginkgo biloba (maidenhair tree)	60 to 80 feet
Sophora japonica (Japanese pagoda tree)	50 to 70 feet
Zelkova serrata (Japanese zelkova)	60 to 80 feet

ABOUT STREET AND CITY TREES

Conditions in the city present special challenges to trees. City soils are often compacted by machinery and foot traffic and surrounded by pavement. These conditions result in poor soil aeration. City trees are also constantly assaulted by air pollution. When the wrong trees are chosen for street planting, they can grow too large for the space available. Their tops threaten utility lines and may be cut off, resulting in the kind of open wounds where the exposed stubs are most susceptible to decay-causing fungi. Their roots heave pavement, sidewalks and curbs out of line. Nevertheless, street trees need to be large enough to form a trunk with the lowest branch about 8 feet high for

Callery pears, Pyrus Calleryana, *make fine street trees.*

pedestrian and small vehicle clearance. On the street side, low branches should be 14 feet high to allow for big trucks. Fortunately, most of these problems can be averted by selecting trees of moderate size. For locations away from the street, where more space is available, it is still important to select trees tolerant of pollution and soil compaction.

SEASONAL FEATURES OF TREES

Trees are year-'round companions in our gardens. They change their appearance; but unlike herbaceous plants, which die down, they remain standing, even after their leaves have fallen. We often think of trees as large foliage plants, but many have a season of prolific bloom or showy fruit.

The greatest number of trees flower in spring. Who could deny the breathtaking beauty of a saucer magnolia in full bloom, covered with pink petals in advance of its summer foliage, or the graceful Japanese flowering cherries in our nation's capital? Even in the coldest regions, crabapples can be relied on for sumptuous displays of pink, white and red. The impact of these early-flowering trees is compounded because they flower while the emerging leaves are still insignificant.

Later in spring and through the summer, blossoms are enhanced by lush foliage. Yellow flower clusters hang below fresh young leaves on golden chain trees (*Laburnum* × *Watereri*). Stewartias follow, with white camellialike flowers nestled among light green foliage. In midsummer, Japanese pagoda (*Sophora japonica*) take center stage with creamy white pealike flowers against deep green leaves. The large white flowers of bullbays, or southern magnolias (*Magnolia grandiflora*), are deliciously lemon scented and sit singly among the large evergreen foliage like white doves. Mimosas (*Albizia Julibrissin*) are curiously tropical in appearance with their pink brushlike flowers among the lacy light green leaves, providing a long display during the warmest months. The sourwoods (*Oxydendron arboreum*) also have a long display. Their small white flowers, along pendant stems, appear in early summer, but give way to creamy seedpods that effectively continue the display through summer. Latest to bloom, from August to October, are Franklin trees (*Franklinia Alatamaha*), also with white camellialike flowers. Their final flowers open as the leaves change to crimson. The flowers of lindens (*Tilia* species) are

In cool climates, where golden chain trees, Laburnum × Watereri, *grow well, they can be trained over an arch, through which their pendant flower clusters hang. This is the laburnum arch at Barnsley House, England.*

The summer-flowering hardy silk tree, Albizia Julibrissin, *has a tropical appearance.*

not particularly showy, but their summer fragrance is a not-to-be-forgotten experience. Although summer-blooming trees are not as common as spring bloomers, they need not be in short supply in the landscape.

In the North, autumn- and winter-flowering trees are few. But they are scarcely needed, because the winter landscape is rich with colorful fruit, waxy, colored twigs and textured bark. As spring is the season of flowers, so autumn is the season of fruit. More berries and fruit ripen at this season than any other. Depending on the variety of tree, some will ripen early among green foliage and remain as the foliage assumes the tints of autumn. Others color later, along with the foliage, which makes some remarkable contrasts. Many trees retain their fruit in such profusion after the leaves have fallen that they create a major visual impact in the winter garden. Fruits can be red, orange, yellow, blue or nearly black. Bright colors are preferred by humans because they show up better in the autumn or winter landscape, but wildlife seek out black and blue berries as winter food. Crabapples (*Malus* species) are among the most valuable trees bearing decorative fruit; they have a range of colors, some varieties hold their fruit until spring, and they can be grown in most regions of North America. Mountain ashes (*Sorbus Aucuparia*) have some of the showiest fruit of all trees, but do best in the North where summers are cool. Farther south, idesias (*Idesia polycarpa*) are good substitutes for mountain ashes, with similar clusters of fruit. Evergreen hollies (*Ilex* species) are small trees with red berries. Autumn arrangements of cut branches of foliage and fruit can be as striking as flowers and more in keeping with the season.

Cones of pines (*Pinus* species), spruces (*Picea* species) and other conifers often remain attractive for the whole year, because many kinds continue to hang on the tree for indefinite periods. Cones come in all sizes from less than an inch to a foot long. Immature cones may take on attractive colors during the growing season, such as those of Korean firs (*Abies koreana*), which become a striking purple. Through the summer, slender, pendant green cones hang from the branches of eastern white pines (*Pinus Strobus*). And in the winter, use mature cones, in all their variety, for holiday decorations indoors.

Through the winter, dried capsules and papery fruit catch the snow and rustle in the wind. The swollen papery capsules of goldenrain trees (*Koelreuteria paniculata*) hang in great clusters, while the smaller capsules of sourwoods continue to cling to their pendant stems until spring.

Color and contrast in the winter landscape are not confined to berries and cones. White trunks of birches (*Betula* species) stand out so prominently that they catch the eye and make it stop—they punctuate views. Up close, the papery, cinnamon-colored bark of paperbark maples (*Acer griseum*) joins with ordinary evergreens for an extraordinary composition. Lacebark pines (*Pinus Bungeana*) provide their own evergreen foliage as an interesting counterpoint to bark mottled with gray-brown, olive and tan. Twigs of some trees assume bright colors especially for the winter season. Those of golden weeping willows (*Salix alba tristis*) glow against a blue sky. Some upright willows are grown for their twigs that become red or orange with the onset of winter. Only the youngest twigs have the striking color, so these trees are often pollarded, or cut short, each spring to encourage vigorous growth. No one could forget the spectacle of coral bark maple (*Acer palmatum* 'Senkaki') in the snow. Contorted willows (*Salix Matsudana* 'Tortuosa') and Japanese cut-leaf maples (*Acer palmatum dissectum* varieties) show off their fascinating twisted branches best after the leaves have fallen. Planted in front of a wall, their shadows cast a silhouette that changes throughout the day as the sun moves across the sky.

Nevertheless, foliage is still the single most important characteristic of trees. In the garden,

The lacy beauty of European larch, Larix decidua, *a deciduous conifer, is highlighted by ice and snow.*

Eastern white pine, Pinus Strobus, *bears attractive cones.*

In addition to the pastel yellow and sometimes orange, autumn tints of katsura tree, Cercidiphyllum japonicum, *the freshly fallen leaves also have a delicious burnt-sugar fragrance.*

foliage has the longest-lasting impact on the landscape. Foliage is also the part of the tree with which we are most familiar. Show someone a maple leaf, and chances are, he or she can identify it. Show someone a piece of bark, a twig or even a single flower, and chances are he or she will be lost.

From the first emerging leaves of spring, foliage is a changing feature through the year. The fresh green of the first tiny willow leaves and the reddish tints of red maple leaves along the roadside are welcome sights. These early colors lose their intensity or fade to green in summer, but some trees retain interesting foliage color all summer long. For regions with cool summers, golden black locusts (*Robinia Pseudoacacia* 'Frisia') are unsurpassed for their yellow foliage. Trees with reddish foliage are more common, and include bloodgood Japanese maples (*Acer palmatum* 'Bloodgood'), purple-leaf plums (*Prunus cerasifera* 'Thundercloud'), crimson king maples (*Acer platanoides* 'Crimson King') and European purple beeches (*Fagus sylvatica* 'Atropunicea').

Variegated foliage in trees is often regarded as gaudy, but can be attractive if it is clean looking and if the tree is sited well in the landscape. In hot climates, variegated plants are more subject to foliage burn than their all-green counterparts. Some are tough enough, though, to be used in most regions where they are hardy. One form of Norway maple (*Acer platanoides* 'Drummondii') has a clean white edge around each leaf. There is a variety of tulip tree (*Liriodendron Tulipifera* 'Aureo-marginatum') with a yellow edge to each leaf. Several different kinds of flowering dogwood are now available with variegated foliage. Any branches reverting to normal green foliage must be pruned out of variegated trees, because these are often more vigorous and tend to take over.

The transition to winter is a time for great change in foliage. Many trees exhibit brilliant or clear pastel colors before shedding their leaves. The renowned October oranges and yellows of sugar maples throughout New England is testament to this phenomenon. Just as trees are planted in gardens for their flowers, they are also planted for their autumn tints, particularly in regions where fall colors are normally dull. Black gums (*Nyssa sylvatica*), Katsura trees (*Cercidiphyllum japonicum*), red maples (*Acer rubrum*), Japanese maples (*Acer palmatum*), sourwoods (*Oxydendron arboreum*), scarlet oaks (*Quercus coccinea*), sweet gums (*Liquidambar Styraciflua*) and golden larches (*Pseudolarix amabilis*) are just a few of the trees planted especially for this purpose. Even the foliage of some so-called evergreens take on reddish or golden tints in winter. One form of Japanese cedar (*Cryptomeria japonica* 'Elegans') assumes a reddish coloration as the weather cools.

TREES IN NATURE

Observing trees in nature will help you understand their place in your garden. In nature most trees grow in forests or with other trees. In a mature forest, young trees grow up among the older trees to replace those that die. A mature forest is called a "climax" forest and the young trees that grow there are able to grow in the shade of other trees. Oaks, tulip trees and hemlocks typically grow in such forests, where individuals of all ages can be seen together. Mature forests have smaller "understory" trees, ones that never become large. These small trees spend their entire lives in the shade, and many, including the dogwood, flower spectacularly. Other trees, such as birches, will not grow in the shade. These "pioneer" trees are found growing in open fields that are reverting to forest. Once the forest is established, they die out.

Trees that grow on slopes or in well-drained soils will probably suffer in wet, poorly drained locations. Others, such as willows, bald cypresses and red maples, grow best where they have wet feet. Those found thriving at the top of a hill are probably fairly tolerant of drought and dry conditions. Many kinds of pines grow in such dry locations.

How well you match a tree to the conditions of the planting site will determine your chances of success. You can plant most shade-tolerant climax trees in the sun, but you won't succeed with a pioneer species planted in the shade. If you have a sunny property, there is a wide choice of trees from which to choose. If you have a wooded property and want to add more trees, a birch won't grow but a young oak will. To add more color, plant such understory flowering trees as dogwood, Japanese snowbells and stewartias, rather than crabapples, which prefer more sun. Surprising as it may seem, you can even have trees in a low wet spot—if you make the right choice.

Cypress knees develop from the roots of bald cypress, Taxodium distichum, *when it grows in wet, swampy soils.*

What to Look For:

DESIRABLE QUALITIES

Small leaves or leaflets, don't need raking (honey locust)

Leathery leaves, make good mulch without packing down (oak)

Small, attractive fruit that does not become messy (callery pear, crabapple)

Disease and pest resistant (katsura tree)

Deep roots compatible with other plantings (oak)

Neat habits—doesn't constantly drop leaves, bark, branches (katsura tree)

UNDESIRABLE QUALITIES

Shallow roots (Norway maple, plane tree, linden)

Roots apt to grow into and clog sewer lines (willow, poplar)

Large soft leaves that smother small plants and bulbs (London plane tree)

SHED DEBRIS ALL SUMMER

Leaves (many trees)

Bark (London plane tree, white oak)

Branches and twigs (tulip tree, white oak)

SHED NUISANCE FRUIT

Spiney (Chinese chestnut, horse chestnut)

Smelly (female ginkgo)

Large pods (honey locust, catalpa)

Toxic to other plants (black walnut)

DISEASE AND PEST SUSCEPTIBLE

Aphids (tulip tree, linden)

Borers (mountain ash, many birches)

Leaf miner (American holly, birch)

Dutch elm disease (American elm)

3

THE PLANTING AND GROWING GUIDE

HOW TREES GROW

The most commonly asked questions about tree care refer to the proper times for fertilizing, pruning and planting, and the answers call for a basic knowledge of how trees grow. Despite the wide variety of tree types, all grow in pretty much the same way. Extension growth occurs at the ends of both shoots and roots, where the tips have zones of actively dividing cells called meristems. Trunks do not stretch, and a branch will not become higher above the ground with age. Trunks thicken from the cambium, a layer of actively dividing cells under the bark. The cambium lays down new rings of wood, which thicken the trunk, and new layers of bark. The wood inside the cambium conducts water and nutrients up to the leaves where they are transformed into sugars, the tree's food, by photosynthesis. These sugars are taken down to the roots by the phloem, located under the bark outside the cambium layer.

The growth cycle of trees is regulated by the length of the days at different seasons. Shortening days of late summer and autumn signal preparation for winter dormancy and the formation of leaf buds for the following year. Once dormant, trees have a cold requirement that must be satisfied before the tree can grow again. This cold requirement, different for different trees, simply is the number of consecutive days when the temperature is below a critical level, usually around 40°F. A tree will not have normal spring growth unless it has had enough cold days the preceding winter. This is a safeguard for the tree against leafing out in an early warm spell and then being damaged by the return of cold weather. Northern trees have longer cold requirements than southern variants, one reason many northern trees don't grow well in the Deep South. With the coming of spring, longer days and warmer temperatures stimulate growth until the shorter days of mid- and late summer signal growth to slow down again. Different kinds of trees have different bloom seasons because they produce flowers in response to different day lengths.

A tree's metabolism changes with the seasons. Although trees might be able to withstand bitterly cold temperatures in midwinter, even a light frost in summer can cause severe damage. In spring, soft tissues and low starch reserves render trees most susceptible to pest and disease attacks. The cool seasons of fall, winter and spring are the periods of most active root growth. These seasons are the best times to plant and transplant trees because lost roots are quickly and easily replaced when the starch reserves needed to grow roots are at their highest. It's also a good time because dormant trees have lower moisture requirements. The best times to fertilize trees are late fall and early spring, when the developing roots absorb nutrients in

The great majority of trees flower in spring, as does this May-blooming red buckeye, Aesculus Pavia, *a small native tree.*

In spite of the covering of snow on this Canadian hemlock, Tsuga canadensis, *its roots may still be active below ground.*

preparation for spring growth.

Perhaps the least understood aspect of a tree is the root system. It is not the same shape as the top, and does not go as deep as the tree is high, as some people may believe. In fact, most feeder roots are in the top few inches of soil, where most nutrients are, and they spread farther than the branches. Well-drained and aerated soil will encourage roots to grow more deeply, adding to the strength and drought tolerance of the tree.

OBTAINING TREES

Once you've decided what types of trees to plant, the next step is to obtain them. Most any tree you want is available from a nursery somewhere. You'll find the most popular kinds for your area at local nurseries and garden centers. If you shop around a bit you can get the best values in a range of sizes to suit your budget. Both rare and very new varieties are usually available only from specialty nurseries, and most of these are mail order. Local nurseries offer trees in any of three ways. The smaller sizes are available in pots or containers. The largest containers can hold sizable landscape specimens, but large trees are usually balled-and-burlapped, often termed "B&B." (These trees have been field grown and dug with a ball of the field soil around the roots. This ball is wrapped in burlap and tied with rope to hold it together.) A really large landscape specimen must be dug and transplanted with a mechanical tree spade. Very large trees are always expensive, and purchasing them is not necessarily the quickest way to get a big tree, because they take longer to resume normal growth rate and become fully established. A smaller tree will become established faster, and may actually outgrow the large transplant.

Mail-order nurseries supply smaller trees due to the limitations and expense of shipping. But it is often worth the several years' wait for that extra-special variety to grow. Because you can't see the mail-order merchandise before you buy, check the guarantees of quality and customer satisfaction and buy from reputable mail-order firms. The smallest trees are sent in containers, but larger deciduous broad-leaved trees are often sent bareroot. This saves on postage and enables you to get a larger plant. Planting bareroot trees is not risky if it is done at the correct time. Many nursery owners believe that planting bareroot trees is preferable to planting balled-and-burlapped trees. The exposed roots can be spread more easily, thereby coming into direct contact with the soil in which they are to live. Experts feel that root growth is inhibited by a change from one kind of soil to another, particularly when the new soil is poorer; this is the case when roots must grow forth from a rich potting soil into field soil.

WHEN TO PLANT

Container-grown trees can be planted at just about any time that you can buy them—year 'round where winters are mild. It's best to avoid planting in very warm weather, however. Bareroot trees must be planted when dormant, before the leaves appear. Many can be planted in fall; some should be planted only in spring. Your nursery will supply them at the correct time for planting. The advantage of planting in the fall or as early in spring as possible is that the new tree has plenty of time to spread its roots into new soil before summer, a time of potential drought and a time when trees can rapidly dehydrate. Summer is the season when most newly planted trees die. Trees planted in late spring and summer need more attentive watering.

Once you have purchased or received your trees they must be held in good condition until they can be planted. Mail-order plants (particularly evergreens or anything in leaf) should be opened immediately on arrival to check on their condition and allow air to get to the tops. Without air circulation and light, the foliage is susceptible to disease and mold. The soil or packing material around the roots of bareroot trees should be moistened if dry and then rewrapped. All trees are best kept out of strong light and in a cold place until planted, but they should be protected from freezing temperatures. Under these conditions, bareroot trees can easily be kept for a week or so if checked regularly. Container-grown trees are more easily cared for because their roots are established in the pots. They can be kept outdoors until planting, provided they are kept moist and protected from freezing temperatures and hungry animals.

SOIL PREPARATION

Good soil preparation is the first step to planting. The most important task is to reduce compaction by breaking up the soil as thoroughly as possible. Break up the soil when it is moderately moist or dry, so that it crumbles, never when it is wet and sticky because it will become more compacted. Usually, it is best not to loosen the soil deeper than the depth of the root ball or pot, or else the tree may sink too deeply when the soil settles later. If you do loosen the soil in the bottom of the hole more deeply, use your foot to press it down again. Your body weight is about the right pressure to settle the soil properly without unwanted compaction.

Experts used to recommend adding such soil amendments as leaf mold, peat moss and sand to improve the soil around the roots of a new tree. This is no longer advocated. It is impractical to improve all the soil into which a tree's roots will eventually extend, of course, and just a pocket of amended soil discourages roots from growing into the surrounding, unimproved soil. It would be like planting the tree in a big pot. It reduces drought resistance and, therefore, the tree's chances of survival. Merely loosening the soil thoroughly is enough to encourage strong root growth.

The danger of root strangulation cannot be overemphasized. The effects may not become evident for several years, when the tree becomes sick and dies. Grown commercially, young trees often become pot bound or their roots are crammed into the ground in such a way that they get twisted around the trunk or each other. This can cause some roots to encircle other roots or the trunk. As the tree grows, these encircling roots kill the tree by cutting off sap flow. Straightening or removing encircling roots at planting is the best corrective treatment, and will not threaten the life of the tree. If you provide good aftercare, the tree can easily recover from the loss of even a quarter of its roots.

Planting a Container-grown or Bareroot Tree

1. Be sure tree is not dehydrated. Water containers the day before planting or soak roots of bareroot tree in water overnight. Keep all roots moist at all times.

2. Dig hole at least twice as wide as the pot or root ball, but not deeper.

3. Mound soil in bottom of hole high enough for tree to sit so soil level from nursery or pot is about 2 inches above the surrounding soil level. As the tree settles, this prevents a depression from forming that can collect water and cause root or crown rot in compacted or poorly drained soils.

4. Remove tree from pot or wrapping and set in hole.

5. Orient tree for best side to face forward.

6. Loosen soil around sides and bottom of root ball.

7. Trim all damaged or dead roots back to healthy tissue with clean cuts to stimulate new root growth.

8. Spread roots over mound, including encircling and matted roots, to promote growth into new soil and prevent root strangulation. Remove encircling roots that can't be spread.

9. Install stakes outside diameter of root ball as required to support tree.

10. Backfill hole, spreading roots in layers.

11. Firm soil in hole with foot.

12. Form soil basin, at least as wide as hole, to contain irrigation water, so when you water the tree, the water will soak in before it runs off.

13. Apply mulch 2 to 3 inches deep to prevent moisture loss, cracking of dried soil surface and competition from grass and weeds.

14. Secure tree to stakes with appropriate ties.

15. Water thoroughly.

Planting a Balled-and-burlapped Tree

1. Be sure tree is not dehydrated. Water thoroughly the day before planting.

2. Dig hole at least twice as wide as root ball, but not deeper.

3. Set tree in hole so soil level from nursery is about 2 inches above the surrounding soil level. As the tree settles, this prevents a depression from forming that can collect water and cause root or crown rot in compacted or poorly drained soils.

4. Orient tree for best side to face forward.

5. Remove rope or twine around trunk and top of ball.

6. Natural fiber burlap may be left around the roots of the tree, but it must be folded down into hole or cut away. None must be exposed above the soil because it acts like a wick to dry the soil and roots. All synthetic or plastic twine and burlap must be removed to prevent strangulation.

7. Check for encircling and strangulation roots. This may require temporarily removing soil on surface of ball to examine major roots at the base of the trunk.

8. Trim all damaged or dead roots back to healthy tissue with clean cuts to stimulate new root growth.

9. Spread encircling and matted roots to promote growth into new soil and prevent strangulation. Remove encircling roots that can't be spread.

10. Install stakes outside diameter of root ball as required to support tree.

11. Backfill hole, spreading roots in layers.

12. Firm soil in hole with foot.

13. Form soil basin, at least as wide as hole, to contain irrigation water, so when you water the tree, the water will soak in before it runs off.

14. Apply mulch 2 to 3 inches deep to prevent moisture loss, cracking of dried soil surface and competition from grass and weeds.

15. Secure tree to stakes with appropriate ties.

16. Water thoroughly.

STAKING

Young trees are staked for two reasons. Staking supports the tree and prevents it from leaning or being uprooted until it is strong enough to stand on its own. It protects a tree from damage by lawn mowers, other machinery or vehicles and people. Generally, it is best to provide support only when necessary, for as short a period as possible. Some trees, including smaller bareroot trees and conifers branched low to the ground, do not need staking at all. High trees with a long trunk and wide top, or those in locations subject to strong winds, nearly always need to be staked.

Stakes should be installed at the time of planting, before you fill the hole, to avoid damage to the tree roots. Use two or three stakes, and place them outside the diameter of the root ball. Almost any material can be used for stakes, including old metal pipes, "T" fence stakes, rebar (concrete reinforcement rods) and wooden poles up to 2 inches in diameter (for large trees).

Ties must not damage the bark and should allow the trunk to move. Bark injury can result in the death of the top of the tree, and trunks tied too tightly are subject to breakage at the point of attachment. Wire covered with pieces of old hose are the most common materials used for large trees, but not the best. Experts recommend the use of soft materials such as rubber or canvas straps, which are less damaging to the bark. Make broad loops between each of the stakes and the trunk or use a figure eight, rather than a smaller loop around the trunk. Keep in mind that trunks thicken and strengthen faster when they can move freely. The stakes and ties can usually be removed after a year.

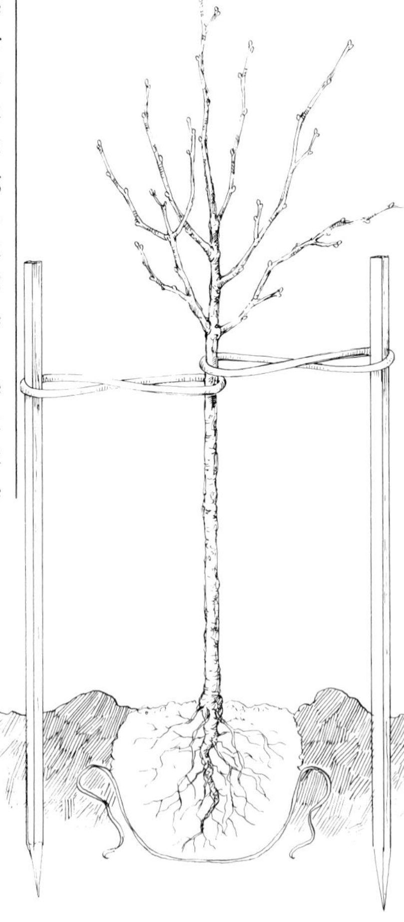

A newly planted tree that needs staking should be secured at the lowest height that will still hold it in place. Wide straps, tied loosely in a figure-eight, will adequately support the trunk yet avoid damaging it.

TREE CARE

Watering is the most important concern for a newly planted tree in its first year, especially in the summer. Most regions are subject to at least one period of drought each year, and this can kill or seriously damage a new tree. A neighbor of mine once asked about his conifers, planted about a year before, that had lost their tops. This was almost certainly due to lack of water during a summer dry spell. Drought-damaged trees may or may not recover. Check your trees weekly, and if need be, dig down into the original root ball to make sure the soil is moist. If it's not, water deeply immediately. Don't be fooled by a light rain—it will only make a fool out of you. At least 1 inch of rain, maybe more depending on your soil, is required to wet the whole root area deeply enough to satisfy your tree.

Even for established trees, the general rule is that they need 1 inch of rain per week. Most established trees can easily survive intermittent dry spells, but keep an eye on them for signs that they want some help. Watch for drooping leaves or wilting that does not recover once the sun is off the foliage.

If you live in an arid region, you can either plant trees adapted to your climate or commit yourself to regular watering for the life of the tree. With water becoming scarcer in many regions, it is much wiser to plant drought-tolerant trees. Even if you are willing to water, you may not be permitted to because of shortages. If you live in an arid region, you may be fortunate enough to have a native tree or two already on your property. Be aware that these trees are not adapted to having additonal irrigation. If you water a lawn around these trees, the extra water is likely to cause a root rot and the trees may die as in the case of many California live oaks. It is an all-too-common scenario in which fine old specimens needing little care are killed by ignorance and replaced by trees needing more water and care.

MULCHING

There are few situations where mulch is not beneficial. Mulch is put on top of the ground, not dug in. In time, organic mulches break down into fine, dark humus. Most trees are adapted to growing with something covering the soil; indeed, the litter on a forest floor is a natural mulch. Mulch maintains moisture in the soil, adds organic matter and nutrients, and helps keep the soil cooler in summer and warmer in winter. Mulch also allows more water to penetrate the soil by preserving the porosity of the surface and holding water in place so it can soak in. By slowing runoff, it reduces soil erosion. If you are looking to save work, remember that a good mulch will suppress weeds very effectively without the toxicity of herbicides.

The best kinds of mulch for trees are wood chips and bark. These will last for a year or two. Grass clippings can also be used in moderation and are a good source of nitrogen. Pine needles (straw) and stiff leathery leaves of such trees as oaks make a good mulch, because they will not pack down. Maple leaves are less suitable because they are too soft and a thick layer may mat down on the soil, restricting aeration.

Use mulch properly. You will often see trees with 6 or more inches of mulch around them. This is a labor-saving technique that can have fatal results. Overmulching can keep the soil too wet, reduce aeration, encourage some diseases and even prevent water from reaching the soil. It also provides a home for hungry mice that can damage bark. The proper depth for a bark or wood-chip mulch is about 3 inches. A loose leafy mulch can be deeper because it will settle. Remember that the need to replace mulch is a good sign. It is being broken down into nutrients that your tree can use.

GROUNDCOVERS

A groundcover planting is a natural way to complete your landscape because it acts as a living mulch, and helps to hold a mulch of leaves in place. Grass is less suitable, especially around young trees, because it competes vigorously with tree roots for water and nutrients. A groundcover under the drip line of your tree will promote the tree's health and vigor. Good groundcover subjects are *Pachysandra* and *Vinca*. English ivy will survive among the toughest roots of such trees as Norway maples and lindens, but it is too competitive for best growth of other trees.

PRUNING AND TRAINING

Pruning is one of the most useful techniques for shaping a tree and controlling growth. It can also prevent future problems. It is an art that warrants extensive study, but its principles are quite simple. "Apical dominance" is a term that describes the influence of the tip of a shoot over the buds and side branches below it. The terminal bud suppresses, or limits, the growth of side buds below it. The strength of apical dominance is partly determined by the plant species. Trees with strong apical dominance have a single leader and horizontal side branches below it, as do most conifers. Trees with weaker apical dominance lack a single strong leader and have many upright branches, as with many broad-leaved trees. Terminal buds on side branches perform a similar function, suppressing the growth of buds immediately behind them. When a terminal bud is damaged or pruned off, dominance is broken and several side buds come into growth. One or more of these will begin to behave as terminals. It is for this reason that frequent pruning makes a plant more bushy. If it is indiscriminately done, however, the natural shape of the plant will be lost. When pruning is properly done, a plant's shape can be corrected and its health improved.

Young trees should be lightly pruned to shape them for the future. For spreading broad-leaved trees, select and keep strong, evenly spaced scaffold branches. These branches will determine the basic shape of the tree. Remove rubbing and crossing branches that will cause wounds subject to infection. Suckers and branches that point in toward the center of the tree should also be pruned out. Avoid narrow crotches as they are structurally weak and apt to break away when the tree gets bigger, leaving a wound that is difficult to heal. Narrow crotches

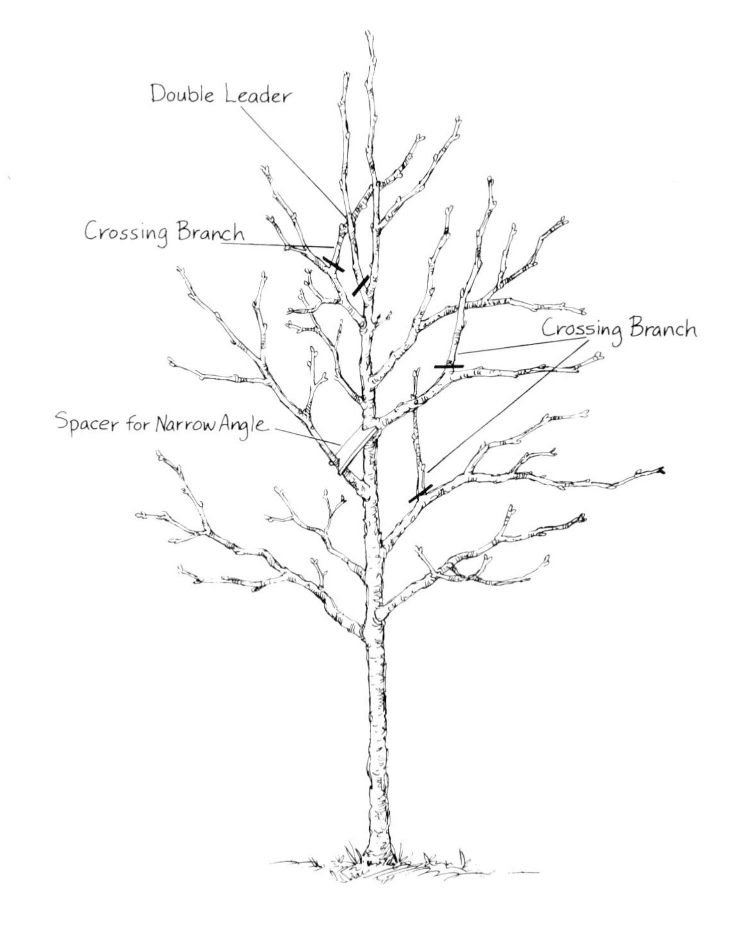

Young trees usually need some pruning to encourage them to develop a strong branch structure. First, prune out any dead or damaged branches. Next, remove the smaller or less shapely leaders when there is more than one. Finally, cut out any rubbing branches to prevent worn bark, an invitation to insects and disease. The upper branches and ultimate leader indicate the shape of the mature tree.

in young trees can be widened with a spreader to increase the angle between the branch and the trunk. A spreader is nothing more than a dowel or stick, with a notch in each end, that is wedged in the crotch. The branch will take the shape in which it is held after a year or so (depending on the size of the branch). Remove competing leaders. For a strong tree, even broad-leaved trees that will ultimately develop several leaders should be held to a single leader when young. Conifers need virtually no scaffold pruning, but they should always be kept to a single leader.

Shaping a tree doesn't have to be accomplished in one year, nor must all nonscaffold branches be removed from the start. The more branches you leave on the tree, the more leaves it will have for photosynthesis, the stronger it will be and the faster it will grow. Leaving small branches along the trunk will help to thicken and strengthen it. These can be removed without harm in future years.

When to Prune

If you have just planted a tree, you will probably want to trim a few branches to shape it. But you should leave major pruning until winter or early spring, when the tree is dormant. During dormancy a tree has its highest food reserves stored for the spring flush of growth. Pruning during the dormant season simply rechannels the energy, causing different buds to grow. When you remove leaves during the summer, you take away some of the tree's ability to make and store food. It can be useful, however, if you are pruning to control size.

Peculiarities of different tree types influence the ideal time to prune. Cherries, elms, birches and maples tend to bleed from fresh cuts made in the spring, so they should be pruned in fall. Bleeding is not usually harmful to the tree, but it is alarming to the gardener and can hinder healing or encourage certain infections if it is prolonged. Evergreens are best pruned shortly before growth begins, because they can use their foliage to photosynthesize at a reduced level during the winter, adding strength to the plant. There is also the danger of winter damage to bark suddenly exposed to winter sun when the evergreen branches shading it are removed. Otherwise, prune most trees anytime during the winter, when there is little else to keep you busy in the garden.

How to Prune

Removal of a branch of any size opens a wound that increases risk of infection by fungi, bacteria and insects. The size and kind of wound are factors that influence the tree's ability to resist infection. Small cuts heal quickly and pose little risk. The larger the cut, the higher the risk of infection before the wound heals over. Soft-wooded trees are more prone to rot. You can help the tree by making the cut properly.

Dr. Alex Shigo spent 25 years with the United States Forest Service, wounding and dissecting trees to discover how they become infected and heal. He recommends that all branches be cut where the branch meets the collar, a swollen area at its base. The collar has an increased resistance to infection, and it has the ability to isolate infection to keep it from spreading. If you cut close to the trunk and remove or damage the collar, you leave the tree defenseless. Experts used to recommend "flush cuts," but these are now considered harmful by Dr. Shigo and others. Nor should stubs be left beyond the collar, as the tree cannot heal them over, and they provide an ideal entry point for infections.

Removal of large branches with a saw involves the risk of tearing the bark down the trunk. To prevent this, make three cuts. The first cut should be several inches out from the collar from the underside of the branch for about a third of its diameter. Then make a second cut from above, just beyond the undercut, until the branch breaks off. This will leave you with a short stub that can be safely cut at the proper point without the risk of its weight tearing the bark. Dr. Shigo says that you can tell a good cut by the way that it heals. The healing wood should form evenly around the whole cut like a donut, not thicker in some areas. When removing dead branches, cut back to the living bark, but do not cut into or damage it.

Wound dressings on tree cuts are a controversial subject, but are no longer recommended by Dr. Shigo. He says that the environment of the wood sealed under the dressing is ideal for infectious organisms.

The London plane tree, Platanus × acerifolia, *is commonly used in* allée *plantings in Europe, where it is pruned regularly to maintain a uniform size. This is the famous* allée *at the Jardin des Plantes, Paris.*

To cut a large branch: First, make a partial cut from the underside, about 4 or 5 inches from the branch collar; this will prevent the branch from tearing the bark down the trunk. Next, make a cut from above, beyond the first cut. Now, make the final cut next to the branch collar.

The practice of topping mature trees (indiscriminately cutting off the tops of trees) is a despicable one. It has been likened to a haircut, but it is more accurately compared with cutting off an arm somewhere between the wrist and elbow. The problem with this kind of pruning is that when the top of a trunk is cut off, there is no branch collar to fight infection and it moves directly down into the heart of the tree. Topping also forces many weakly attached shoots to form around the decayed stumps. Many of these will grow into large branches that can snap off at their bases. As decay progresses down through the tree, it seldom shows external symptoms, but the structure of the tree is continuously weakened, leading to unexpected breakage in the future.

There are several alternatives to topping trees. The most sensible is to choose trees that will not outgrow their spaces. However, many problem trees are already in place. Rather than shortening the tree to below utility lines, it can be pruned to grow around them, with the wires passing through the center. In the long run, this is cheaper, because it requires less frequent maintenance. If you are concerned about a tree hanging over your house, shorten branches back to forks and crotches that can heal quickly or remove only particularly large branches that hang directly over the house. Such steps reduce the risk of damage from the tree, while simultaneously preserving its shade and aesthetic value. Seek the services and advice of a reputable tree surgeon for such work. Tree climbing is dangerous and should only be attempted by trained professionals.

Trimming small branches and shaping with hand pruners is a simple procedure. When removing a whole branch, don't leave stubs but rather cut back to the swelling at the base of the branch. When shortening a shoot or twig, make the cut about a quarter inch above a bud. Cut back to a bud that points in the direction that you want the branch to grow. Buds at the ends of side branches should point out or down, whereas those on a leader should point up.

When the terminal or leader of a tree is damaged or destroyed, a new one may be slow to form, especially in conifers. To reestablish a new leader, tie a side branch into a vertical position until it becomes fixed there, and begins to behave like a leader. It may take a year or two for the adjustment. If several leaders form, remove all but the one that is strongest and in the best position.

FERTILIZING TREES

Fertilization of trees is another controversial topic. Advice differs on how, when and what nutrients are most important. One point of agreement is that fertilization is not a universal cure-all for poor or compacted soil, bad drainage, excessive shade or a tree that is ill-suited to its environment. Many trees grow and thrive for years without any fertilizing. Under ideal conditions, where trees have a natural mulch and groundcover, or grow in woodland conditions, fertilizer is rarely necessary. A great way to simulate these conditions is to spread compost under your trees. Many trees, however, are grown in situations where naturally occuring nutrients, in the form of leaves, are swept away and their roots must compete with voracious grass roots. These trees may benefit from fertilization. In other cases, a specific symptom, such as off-color foliage, indicates the need to correct a nutrient deficiency.

The three nutrients that plants need in greatest quantity are nitrogen (N), phosphorus (P) and potassium (K). The analysis of a fertilizer is given on the package as percentages of these nutrients in a series of three numbers. For example, 10-6-4 means 10 percent N, 6 percent

P and 4 percent K. (The remaining percentage is mostly inert ingredients.) Such other nutrients as iron, boron and magnesium are required in much smaller quantities and are termed micronutrients, or trace elements. They are less often included in standard fertilizers and applied only when specifically called for due to local soil conditions or to correct symptoms, for which an expert should be consulted. Too high a concentration of trace elements can be toxic to some plants.

Fertilizing is often termed "feeding," but this is an inaccurate description. Fertilizer only supplies nutrients. The nutrients are transformed by photosynthesis into sugars and starches, the tree's real food. The easiest method of application is to broadcast dry, granular fertilizer on the surface of the soil or lawn. (Be sure to do it when grass and foliage are dry, or it may burn the plants because it will stick to wet foliage.) As most feeder roots are shallow, they will pick up the nutrients. Fertilizing is best done in late fall to early spring, for two reasons. First, grass and other plants are dormant at these times and less likely to absorb the fertilizer before the trees get it. Second, the tree roots are actively absorbing and storing nutrients in preparation for the spring flush of growth, when they are most needed. Don't fertilize when the soil is frozen; it is likely to get washed off rather than absorbed, and tree roots are not active when the soil temperature is below about 40°F.

You may wonder why many arborists fertilize trees by drilling holes in the soil and why it is not recommended here. The theory behind fertilizing in holes is that it puts the nutrients below the depth of other plant roots where only the tree can get them. We feel that placing fertilizer in holes is unnecessary, because feeder roots are shallow. It is also more difficult for the homeowner to do.

Blanket recommendations about how much fertilizer and what specific nutrients to apply are impossible to give. It depends on your soil and the conditions under which the tree is grown. First consider the health of your trees. Are they growing well? Is the foliage a healthy color? Are there any pest problems? It may be that no fertilizer is necessary. Next, get a soil test. Soil tests are often provided through your state cooperative extension service. Inquire at local nurseries, garden centers and public gardens about how to get a soil test in your area. The results will recommend a treatment for your soil conditions. General rates on a fertilizer bag will tell you how much of that formulation can be safely applied without harming your tree, but this will not reflect your tree's actual need. There is also debate as to whether trees should be fertilized in their first year. Certainly it is not advisable to push newly planted trees too fast, before their root systems are established enough to support such growth. Most experts agree that when you fertilize, a slow-release fertilizer is better because it releases nutrients gradually so the tree can use them more efficiently. There is no doubt that it is far more important to keep the trees watered when newly planted. Fertilizing your trees is just one of several things you can do to increase their health and vigor, which in turn helps them to resist pests and diseases and perhaps grow faster for a quicker landscape effect.

The grand southern live oak, Quercus virginiana, *live to great ages and develop strong, wide-spreading branches.*

4

PLANT PORTRAITS

PLANT PORTRAIT KEY

Scientific names of trees are in boldface italics. They are essential for precision when discussing specific trees. Common names vary so much from region to region that readers and nursery owners alike cannot be sure what tree to plant. Scientific names can tell you something about the plants by showing their relationships to each other.

They are usually based on Latin or Greek, languages that don't change and so will always be understood internationally. Each name is a subdivision of the former. The first name is the genus (plural, genera), which is always capitalized. The second name is the species, which need not be capitalized, although some botanists will capitalize it if it is derived from a proper noun, such as a person's name (i.e., *Chamaecyparis Lawsoniana*, the Lawson cypress). These names are in italics. All plants have at least two botanical names.

Additional names may be added to designate a variety, subspecies or a cultivar. A variety usually occurs naturally, in the wild. It is written in the same way as the species name. *Cultivar* means *culti*vated *var*iety and is a variant created or found only in gardens. The name is usually a modern-language name, is not italicized, is always capitalized and is placed in single quotes (i.e., the Japanese maple cultivar 'Bloodgood').

Many garden trees are hybrids. This may be indicated in the name by an "×" (but it is not required). The position of the × tells you what has been hybridized. When placed before the species name, × tells you that it is a hybrid between two other species. Saucer magnolia (*Magnolia ×Soulangiana*) is a hybrid of Yulan magnolia (*M. denudata*) and lily magnolia (*M. liliiflora*). It might be explained this way: *Magnolia ×Soulangiana* (*M. denudata* × *M. liliiflora*). It is also possible, but less common, to have hybrids between two genera, which is indicated by placing the × before the name of the genus. Leyland cypress is the only example in this book: *×Cupressocyparis Leylandii* (*Cupressus macrocarpa* × *Chamaecyparis nootkatensis*). There are many hybrid cultivars.

Unfortunately, there is sometimes more than one scientific name for the same tree. One name is considered to be more correct than the others. When other names are in common use, the synonyms are given in parentheses immediately following the preferred name.

Phonetic pronunciation of the scientific name is in parentheses.

Common name of tree is in boldface type.

Primary ornamental features: the most important features of a tree. These are found directly after the common name in lightface type.

Seasons of bloom: SP = Spring, SU = Summer, F = Fall, E = Early, M = Middle, L = Late, i.e., ESP = Early Spring

The average hours of sun needed per day is indicated by symbols. The first symbol is what the tree prefers, but the tree is adaptable to all conditions listed.

The deodar cedar, Cedrus Deodara, *from the Himalayas, makes a graceful specimen.*

○ Sun: 6 hours or more of strong direct sunlight per day.

◐ Part Shade: 3 to 6 hours of direct sunlight, light dappled shade all day or high shade all day. (High shade means that the shade is cast by high branches, allowing plenty of diffuse, indirect light to come from the sides.)

● Shade: 2 hours or less of direct sunlight, relatively dark locations. Few trees work as specimens in full shade.

Life Span (approximate):

Short: less than 60 years

Moderate: 60 to 120 years

Long: More than 120 years

Very long: approximately 1,000 years or more

Zones: Hardiness zones are derived from The USDA Plant Hardiness Map (pages 92–93). This map is based on average minimum winter temperatures, the most important factor determining hardiness. Other factors affect plant survival and health, too. High summer temperatures in the Southeast may kill or limit a plant's growth, whereas the same plant will grow successfully in the cooler summers of an equivalent zone of winter cold along the Pacific coast. Other trees will not grow well in the cooler summers because they require hot summers to complete their growth cycle. Factors that can also affect hardiness include exposure to wind (which can dehydrate), winter sun (which can burn foliage and thin bark), and late frosts (which can kill early shoots or flowers).

Foliage Description: These descriptions are meant to provide an overall sense of appearance. Evergreen trees hold their foliage all year long, summer and winter. Deciduous trees lose their leaves in winter. Basic leaf shapes are illustrated on page 16.

Height: Two measurements are separated by a semicolon. The first is "landscape" size: the height most often reached in gardens, parks and yards. The second is "maximum size known": the largest size that this kind of tree has been known to reach either under ideal conditions or with great age. Both of the sizes listed apply only to the species discussed in this book.

Shape and width: See pages 8–9 for an explanation and illustrations of tree shapes.

Characteristics: Describes appearance and features of the trees. Includes information about where the tree is native. "N:" means "native to."

Cultural Information: Explains optimal soil, placement and care.

Abies concolor

Abies koreana *(detail of cones)*

Abies (A-beez) **fir,** Evergreen foliage ○ ◐

Zones: Variable

Height: 15 to 70 feet; 100 to 130 feet

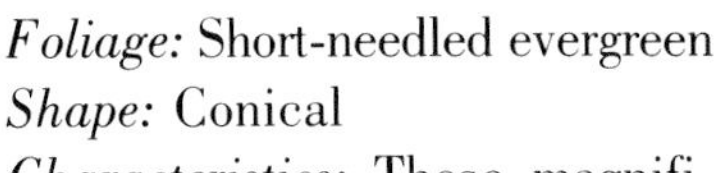

Foliage: Short-needled evergreen

Shape: Conical

Characteristics: These magnificent conifers with straight trunks and nearly horizontal branches make impressive specimens in the landscape. Fat, oblong cones are held upright on the branches. The white fir (*Abies concolor*; Zones 3 to 7; N: Rocky Mountains) has attractive blue-green foliage and is one of the most adaptable firs, tolerating more summer heat than most and even doing well in some city conditions. Usually grows to about 50 feet, width is about 25 feet. Nikko fir (*A. homolepsis*; Zones 4 to 6; N: Japan) is a midsize tree that grows to about 50 feet in gardens, often flat topped, with bright green foliage. Korean fir (*A. koreana*; Zones 5 and 6; N: Korea) is a smaller tree with deep green foliage, normally reaching only 30 feet in cultivation, but up to 60 feet in the wild. The immature cones are an attractive purple and may appear even on young trees.

Cultural Information: Firs generally prefer moist, humid conditions and grow best in northern or mountain climates in a well-drained, acid soil. Under these conditions they have few pest and disease troubles. Pruning often destroys their shape. Branches are not regenerated once lost, so avoid crowding by other trees. The foliage of the balsam fir (*A. balsamea*; Zones 3 to 5; N: North America) has a delicate fragrance, but it is the least heat tolerant of firs, dying mysteriously after a few years, except in cool mountainous climates.

Acer (A-ser) **maple,** Fall color, bark, some with colorful twigs in winter ○ ◐ ▙ ▙

Zones: Variable
Height: 15 to 75 feet; 30 to 120 feet
Foliage: Palmately lobed (rarely compound), broad-leaved deciduous
Shape: Globe, some as wide as tall
Characteristics: Maples are one of the most important groups of ornamental trees. Large or small, maples have many desirable attributes, including brilliant fall colors and striking winter bark textures and color. Hedge maple (*Acer campestre*; Zones 4 to 8; N: Europe) resembles Norway maple in appearance with deep green leathery leaves, but normally reaches only about 35 feet. Paperbark maple (*A. griseum*; Zones 4 to 8; N: China) has decorative, peeling cinnamon-colored bark and grows to 30 feet. Its unusual leaves are composed of three leaflets and assume a reddish fall color. The Japanese maple (*A. palmatum*; Zones 5 to 8; N: Asia) is one of the most variable species of trees. Generally, they are medium to small trees, growing to 15 to 25 feet, with brilliant fall color. Some have colored twigs in winter. *A. palmatum* 'Atropurpureum' has deep reddish purple foliage in summer. *A. palmatum* 'Bloodgood' has the deepest red folige and maintains good color all summer. Coral bark maple (*A. palmatum* 'Senkaki' or 'Sangokaku') has twigs that become a striking salmon pink in fall and winter and has golden fall foliage. Members of the *A. palmatum dissectum* group are characterized by deeply cut, lacy foliage and a picturesque contorted branching and trunk pattern. They are slow growing with a low, mounded habit when young and include *A. palmatum* 'Crimson Queen' with lacy, burgundy red foliage all summer, and *A. palmatum* 'Ornatum' which is an old cultivar with reddish spring foliage that becomes bronzy light green in summer and fiery orange and yellow in fall. Old specimens may become picturesque specimens more than 12 feet tall.

Amur maple (*A. Ginnala*; Zones 2 to 8; N: China) and Tatarian maple (*A. tataricum*; Zones 3 to 8; N: southeast Europe and western Asia) are small trees with stiff habits, mainly grown for fall color in the North where the Japanese maple is not hardy.

Another group of midsize trees is the striped-bark maple group, which is characterized by interesting green-and-white striped branches and trunks. The moosewood maple (*A. pensylvanicum*; Zones 3 to 6; N: eastern North America) grows well in mountainous and northern regions with cool summers; it prefers part shade. The red-vein maple (*A. rufinerve*; Zones 5 to 8; N: Japan) is better suited to warmer areas. They both grow about 30 feet high.

Some of the larger-growing maples make excellent shade trees, but they require adequate space, because they can grow to 60 feet or more and nearly as wide. Red maple (*A. rubrum*; Zones 3 to 9) colors to brilliant red and yellow tints in autumn and is native to eastern North America. Perhaps the finest autumn foliage display of the larger species is that of sugar maple (*A. saccharum*; Zones 3 to 8). In its native New England, entire mountainsides are lit up with glorious shades of pastel orange and yellow. It grows about half as wide as tall. Norway maple (*A. platanoides*; Zones 3 to 7; N: Europe) is one of the most commonly planted shade trees, with dense, deep green foliage and yellow fall color. It is spreading, often growing as wide as it does tall. *A. platanoides* 'Crimson King' is a popular cultivar with reddish purple foliage all summer. The leaves of *A. platanoides* 'Drummondii' are edged with white. Unfortunately, large maples, particularly Norway maples, tend to have shallow roots that can heave sidewalks and starve lawns and shrubs. Young Norway maples will grow in dense (full) shade and are invading woodlands in some regions, crowding out the native trees.

Cultural Information: Maples generally do best in rich, well-drained soils. A notable exception are the red maples, which will grow in wet soils with poor drainage. Most will grow in partial shade, and the smaller species are often understory species in nature. Striped-bark maples usually do not grow well in sun. All are generally free of serious pest or disease problems.

Acer griseum

Acer saccharum

Acer palmatum *'Atropurpureum'*

Aesculus Hippocastanum

Aesculus Hippocastanum (ES-kew-lus hip-o-kas-TA-num) **horse chestnut,** Flowers, MSP ○ ◐
Zone: 3 to 8
Height: 60 feet; 100 feet
Foliage: Palmately compound, broad-leaved deciduous
Shape: Globe, nearly as wide as tall
Characteristics: The common horse chestnut, native to Europe, is grown for its spectacular clusters of small white flowers with golden centers. Few large trees can exceed its beauty when in full bloom. It does, however, have drawbacks, the most serious of which is scorched foliage in mid- to late summer due to leaf diseases. Control measures are unnecessary, because the tree is not harmed, but it is unsightly. Horse chestnut is a poor choice for such high-use areas as patios: In spring, the expanding buds drop their sticky resinous coverings all over the ground and the petals fall, and in autumn it sheds large seeds with spiny coverings. *A. H.* 'Baumannii' is a double-flowered, seedless cultivar.
Cultural Information: Easy to grow and adaptable to most soils, if reasonably moist. Forms a tap root, so best transplanted balled-and-burlapped or from containers when young.

Alaska cedar; see ***Chamaecyparis***

Albizia Julibrissin (al-BIZ-ee-a ju-lee-BRI-sin) **hardy silk tree, mimosa,** Flowers, LSP–SU ○
Zones: 6 to 9
Height: 20 to 30 feet; 35 feet

Albizia Julibrissin

Foliage: Lacy, bipinnately compound, broad-leaved deciduous
Shape: Vase, often wider than high
Characteristics: This small tree (native from Iran to China) is popular for its tropical, brushlike pink flowers, feathery foliage and long bloom season, but is limited in hardiness. *A. J.* 'Rosea' and 'E. H. Wilson' are smaller-growing cultivars that can be grown farther north in milder parts of Zone 5. Seeds prolifically, which can cause a big weed problem.
Cultural Information: Adaptable to many soil types and locations. Recently, a serious wilt disease has killed trees in many areas. *A.* 'Charlotte' and *A.* 'Tryon' are reputedly wilt-resistant.

Aleppo pine; see ***Pinus***

Amelanchier arborea (am-el-ANG-kee-er ar-BOR-ee-a) **shadbush, serviceberry, service tree, sarvis tree,** Flowers, fruit, fall color, MSP ○ ◐
Zones: 4 to 9
Height: 20 to 30 feet; 40 feet
Foliage: Simple broad-leaved deciduous
Shape: Upright, rounded, taller than wide
Characteristics: The common name, shadbush, refers to the bloom season, which corresponds to the season in which shad run in the rivers. White flowers are followed by small, edible red fruit in early summer, which attract wildlife. Showy fall colors range from yellow to orange and red. Botanists disagree about the correct names for the different members of *Amelanchier. A. canadensis* and *A. laevis* are similar

Amelanchier arborea

to *A. arborea.* Native to eastern North America.
Cultural Information: Adaptable to many soil types, but grows best in moist soils. Neat in habit and needs little pruning.

American beech; see ***Fagus***

American elm; see ***Ulmus***

American holly; see ***Ilex***

Amur chokecherry; see ***Prunus***

Amur maple; see ***Acer***

Araucaria araucana (ar-row-KAR-ee-a ar-row-KAN-a) **monkey puzzle tree,** Evergreen foliage ○ ◧
Zones: 7 to 9
Height: 40 to 60 feet; 90 feet
Foliage: Stiff, flat, spiny, needled evergreen
Shape: Rounded pyramidal
Characteristics: The monkey puzzle tree, native to Chile, is the hardiest species of *Araucaria.* All other species are tropical or subtropical. The foliage of this conifer is deep green and stiff with a sharp spine on the end of each wide leaflike needle. A unique and coarse form in the landscape.
Cultural Information: Grows best where summers are cool and moist, as in the Pacific Northwest. Has also grown as far north as Wilmington, Delaware, in the East.

Araucaria araucana

Arborvitaes; see ***Thuja***

Arizona cypress; see ***Cupressus***

Ash; see ***Fraxinus***

Ash, European mountain; see ***Sorbus***

Ash, green; see ***Fraxinus***

Ash, Korean mountain; see ***Sorbus***

Ash, mountain; see ***Sorbus***

Ash, white; see ***Fraxinus***

Austrian pine; see ***Pinus***

Bald cypress; see ***Taxodium***

Balsam fir; see ***Abies***

Beeches; see ***Fagus***

Bell, Carolina silver; see ***Halesia***

Bell, mountain silver; see ***Halesia***

Bell, silver; see ***Halesia***

Betula (BET-you-la) **birch,** Fall color, bark ○ ◧
Zones: Variable
Height: 40 to 70 feet; 80 to 90 feet
Foliage: Simple broad-leaved deciduous
Shape: rounded pyramidal, about ⅔ as wide as tall
Characteristics: Birches are best known for the white peeling bark of the native paper birch. This tree is a poor choice in warm climates, where it is susceptible to borers. The best choice for white trunks in most regions is the Japanese *B. platyphylla japonica* 'White Spire' (Zones 4 to 7). Another fine landscape plant is the native river birch (*Betula nigra* 'Heritage'; Zones 5 to 7). It has beautiful peeling bark of salmon and tan. The yellow fall color is of short duration. Both of these should be planted as single-trunked trees to avoid future snow and ice damage. Gray birch (*B. populifolia*; Zones 3 to 6; N: northeastern North America) is a smaller tree, growing to about 30 feet, with a grayish white bark. It normally forms several weak trunks, is likely to be damaged by snow and ice when older and is subject to serious leafminer damage. Resistant to borers, but not a recommended landscape plant.
Cultural Information: Prefers a moist, acid soil, but will grow on drier sites. River birch tolerates poor drainage. Borer is the most serious threat to birches. River birch is one of the most resistant, and *B. platyphylla japonica* 'White Spire' seems to be the most resistant of the white-trunked birches.

Betula platyphylla japonica

Birches; see ***Betula***

Bishop pine; see ***Pinus***

Black locust, golden; see ***Robinia***

Black pine, Japanese; see ***Pinus***

Black tupelo; see ***Nyssa***

Bloodgood maple; see ***Acer***

Blue Atlas cedar; see ***Cedrus***

Blue spruce; see ***Picea***

Bullbay; see ***Magnolia***

California incense cedar; see ***Calocedrus***

California live oak; see ***Quercus***

Callery pear; see ***Pyrus***

Calocedrus decurrens (kal-oh-SED-rus dee-KER-enz) **California incense cedar,** Evergreen foliage ○ ■

Zones: 5 to 8

Height: 40 to 50 feet; 150 feet

Foliage: Scalelike, needled evergreen

Shape: Fastigiate-conical

Characteristics: This stately conifer, native to the mountains of Oregon and California, is similar in appearance to arborvitae. It tends to be more narrow in shape in the East than in the West.

Cultural Information: Grows best in moist, well-drained soil but is also drought tolerant when well established. Grows well in the southeastern states as well as many other regions.

Calocedrus decurrens

Canadian hemlock; see ***Tsuga***

Canary Island pine; see ***Pinus***

Canyon live oak; see ***Quercus***

Carolina silver bell; see ***Halesia***

Carpinus Betulus **'Fastigiata'** (kar-PI-nus BET-you-lus) **European hornbeam,** Refined shape, foliage ○ ◐ ■

Zones: 4 to 7

Height: 40 to 50 feet; 75 feet

Foliage: Simple broad-leaved deciduous

Shape: Fastigiate, about ⅔ as wide as high

Characteristics: Carpinus Betulus 'Fastigiata' (native to Europe and Asia Minor) is the most noteworthy form of this species. Its rounded upright habit and neat green foliage make a shapely specimen tree. Fall color is yellowish green.

Cultural Information: Adaptable to a wide range of soils and requires infrequent pruning.

Catalpa (ka-TAL-pa) **catalpa,** Flowers, ESU ○ ◐ ■

Zones: Variable

Height: 30 to 60 feet; 100 feet

Foliage: Large, simple, heart-shaped, broad-leaved deciduous

Shape: Globe, spread varies

Characteristics: Spectacular summer-flowering trees with large clusters of small bell-shaped white flowers with yellow and purple spots, followed by long

Carpinus Betulus *'Fastigiata'*

Catalpa bignonioides

beanlike pods. The large, heart-shaped leaves turn yellowish green in fall. Northern catalpa (*Catalpa speciosa*; Zones 4 to 8) grows 40 to 60 feet tall and about half as wide as high. Common or southern catalpa (*C. bignonioides*; Zones 5 to 9) is small growing, reaching only 30 to 40 feet but forming a tree as wide as tall. Both are native to the southeastern United States.
Cultural Information: An adaptable species that tolerates hot, dry conditions, but grows best in moist, rich soils.

Cedar; see ***Cedrus***

Cedar, Alaska; see ***Chamaecyparis***

Cedar, blue Atlas; see ***Cedrus***

Cedar, California incense; see ***Calocedrus***

Cedar, deodar; see ***Cedrus***

Cedar, eastern red; see ***Juniperus***

Cedar, Japanese; see ***Cryptomeria***

Cedar, Port Orford; see ***Chamaecyparis***

Cedar, western red; see ***Juniperus***

Cedar, white; see ***Thuja***

Cedar of Lebanon; see ***Cedrus***

Cedrus (SEE-drus) **cedar,** Evergreen foliage ○ ■
Zones: Variable
Height: 40 to 70 feet; over 100 feet
Foliage: Short-needled evergreen
Shape: Broadly pyramidal, about ⅔ as wide as high
Characteristics: Cedars mature to grand, massive trees with a broader shape than most conifers, so they must be allowed plenty of space in which to grow. Blue Atlas cedar (*Cedrus atlantica* 'Glauca'), popular for its bluish needles, has the most striking foliage color of the true cedars. Native to the Atlas Mountains of northern Africa, hardy in Zones 6 to 9. Deodar cedar (*C. Deodara*; Zones 7 to 9; N: Himalaya) has longer green needles than the other cedars and a soft, graceful appearance in the landscape. *C.* 'Shalimar' is a hardier cultivar, growing in Boston in Zone 6. The famed cedar of Lebanon (*C. libanii*; Zones 5 to 7; N: Asia Minor) is the widest-growing species and has dark green foliage.
Cultural Information: Adaptable to various well-drained soils. Seldom bothered by pests and diseases.

Cercidiphyllum japonicum (ser-si-di-FIL-um ja-PON-i-kum) **katsura tree,** Summer foliage, fall color ○ ◐ ■
Zones: 4 to 8
Height: 50 feet; 100 feet
Foliage: Heart-shaped, broad-leaved deciduous
Shape: Globe, about as wide as tall
Characteristics: One of the most beautiful of the nonflowering trees. Its clean, deep green, heart-shaped foliage emerges reddish purple in spring and changes to pastel yellow and apricot-orange in autumn. The freshly fallen leaves have a delightful, spicy fragrance. Native to Japan and China.

Left: Cedrus Deodara
Middle: Cedrus atlantica *'Glauca'*
Bottom: Cercidiphyllum japonicum

Cultural Information: Katsura trees are easy to grow and tolerant of city conditions. They are generally pest and disease free.

Cercis canadensis (SER-sis kan-a-DEN-sis) **eastern redbud,** Flowers, SP ○ ◐

Zones: 4 to 9
Height: 20 to 30 feet; 30 feet
Foliage: Heart-shaped, broad-leaved deciduous
Shape: Globe-vase, as wide, or wider, than high
Characteristics: Small lavender to purplish pink flowers bloom along branches before leaves in early to midspring. Blooms just before dogwood and evergreen azaleas. Foliage may color to yellow in autumn. *Cercis canadensis* 'Forest Pansy' has purplish foliage all summer. Native to eastern North America.
Cultural Information: Adaptable to a wide range of soil types if they are well drained. Grows well as an understory tree in light shade. Appearance is improved when dead wood is pruned out periodically.

Cercis canadensis *'Forest Pansy'*

Chamaecyparis pisifera *'Filifera'*

Chain, golden; see ***Laburnum***

Chamaecyparis (kam-ee-SIP-ar-is) **false cypress,** Evergreen foliage, bark ○ ◐

Zones: Variable
Height: 50 to 75 feet; more than 150 feet
Foliage: Scalelike needled evergreen
Shape: Pyramidal-conical, ¼ to ⅓ as wide as high
Characteristics: False cypresses are reliable garden conifers that are slightly smaller than firs, true cedars and larger pines. Many have warm reddish brown bark. There are numerous varieties, including many dwarf or slow-growing selections (not discussed in this book). *Chamaecypacis pisifera,* The Sawara false cypress or retinospora (Zones 3 to 8; N: Japan) is probably the most commonly grown species with many different foliage forms and colors. *C. p.* 'Boulevard' has soft plumy blue foliage. It is somewhat untidy as a large tree because dead foliage is held among the branches. Thread-leaf cypress (*C. p.* 'Filifera') has long, stringy branchlets that create a unique foliage texture. It is slow growing and remains a small tree. Golden thread-leaf cypress (*C. p.* 'Filifera Aurea') has stringy golden foliage that colors best in winter. *C. p.* 'Plumosa' has dark green, feathery foliage. Moss cypress (*C. p.* 'Squarrosa') has soft, plumy, light blue-green foliage.

Hinoki false cypress (*C. obtusa*; Zones 4 to 8; N: Japan) is most often seen in its dwarf forms, but the normal form makes a fine tree to 75 feet with lustrous dark green foliage and rich reddish brown bark. *C. o. 'Crippsii'* is an excellent golden-foliaged conifer with somewhat slower growth. There are also many different varieties of Lawson false cypress or Port Orford cedar (*C. Lawsoniana*; Zones 5 to 7; N: Pacific Northwest) but they do not thrive in heat, and are not commonly grown in most of the United States. *C. L.* 'Columnaris' is especially useful for its steely blue foliage and refined, narrow, conical habit. Weeping nootka false cypress or Alaska cedar (*C. nootkatensis* 'Pendula'; Zones 5 to 9; N: Alaska to Oregon) makes a smaller, broadly pyramidal tree with drooping branchlets and deep green foliage. It reaches only about 40 feet in gardens, but more than 100 feet in the wild.
Cultural Information: Most are easy to grow and adapted to a variety of soils if well drained, but prefer soil to be rich and moist. Sawara and Hinoki false cypresses are better suited to warmer, drier climates than the others.

Cherry; see ***Prunus***

Cherry, Cornelian; see ***Cornus***

Cherry, double sweet; see ***Prunus***

Cherry, Higan; see ***Prunus***

Cherry, Japanese flowering; see ***Prunus***

Cherry, Yoshina; see ***Prunus***

Cherry laurel, Portugese; see ***Prunus***

Chestnut, horse; see ***Aesculus***

China fir; see ***Cunninghamia***

Chinese elm; see ***Ulmus***

Chinese fringe tree; see ***Chionanthus***

Chinese juniper; see ***Juniperus***

Chinese quince; see ***Pseudocydonia***

Chionanthus (ky-oh-NAN-thus) **fringe tree,** flowers, LSP. ○

Zones: Variable
Height: 20 feet; 30 feet
Foliage: Simple broad-leaved deciduous
Shape: Spreading, globe, about as wide as high
Characteristics: Small, fragrant flowers in fluffy clusters cover the tree when in full bloom. Leathery foliage is a lustrous dark green, yellow-green in fall. The blue berries ripen in early fall and, although not particularly showy, are attractive to birds. If not trained to have a single trunk, trees may become attractive, large multistemmed shrubs. Usually dioecious, so you'll need both sexes in the same vicinity to produce fruit. *Chionanthus virginicus* is native to the southeastern United States, and hardy in Zones 3 to 9. The Chinese fringe tree (*C. retusus*; Zones 5 to 8; N: Asia) has smaller, lighter green leaves. Both are fine ornamentals.
Cultural Information: Prefers rich, acid, moist soil. Requires little pruning and is seldom attacked by pests and diseases.

Chokecherry, Amur; see ***Prunus***

Cladrastis lutea (kla-DRAS-tis lew-TEE-a) **yellowwood,** Flowers, bark, LSP ○

Zones: 3 to 8
Height: 40 feet; 50 feet
Foliage: Pinnately compound, broad-leaved deciduous
Shape: Spreading globe, as wide as high
Characteristics: Pendulous clusters of white pea-like flowers hang from the ends of the branches. Leaves are light green; bark is smooth and gray, much like that of beech. Native to southeastern United States.
Cultural Information: Requires well-drained soil, which may be either acid or alkaline. Prune only in summer to avoid bleeding in winter and spring. Tends to form weak, narrow crotches, which should be spread or corrected by pruning when young.

Coast redwood; see ***Sequoia***

Colorado spruce; see ***Picea***

Common catalpa; see ***Catalpa***

Contorted willow; see ***Salix***

Coral bark maple; see ***Acer***

Cork oak; see ***Quercus***

Cornelian cherry; see ***Cornus***

Chionanthus retusus

Cladrastis lutea

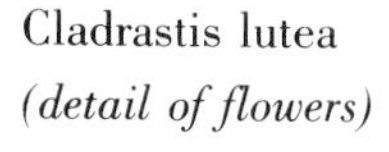

Cladrastis lutea
(detail of flowers)

Cornus florida

Cornus Kousa

Cornus (KOR-nus) **dogwood,** Flowers, fruit, fall color, bark, SP-ESU ○ ◐

Zones: Variable
Height: 20 to 30 feet; 40 feet
Foliage: Simple broad-leaved deciduous
Shape: Spreading vase, as wide, or wider, than high
Characteristics: Best known is the showy flowering dogwood (*Cornus florida*; Zones 5 to 9) native to the eastern United States. Its showy "petals" are actually colored leaf bracts that may be white, pink or a deep pink approaching red, depending on the tree. In many of the eastern states, this tree is part of a classic combination, blooming with azaleas in midspring. Many cultivars are available with improved bract color and size. In fall, the foliage colors to reddish purple with clusters of red berries. Kousa dogwood (*C. Kousa*; Zones 5 to 8) is a similar species from Japan and China, but it flowers about a month later, in late spring to early summer. Bracts are usually white; however, rare pink cultivars are now becoming available. Red fall color and edible round red fruits appear in fall. Bark mottled with tan and gray-brown is attractive all year. Cornelian cherry (*C. mas*; Zones 4 to 8; N: Europe) is very different. It does not have bracts, but it does produce many clusters of small yellow flowers in early spring, long before other trees. Combines well with the early small bulbs. Edible red "cherries" may be used for preserves in fall. *C. officinalis* (Zones 5 to 8; N: Japan and Korea) is similar, but flowers a week or so earlier and has more attractive mottled bark.
Cultural Information: Grows best in well-drained, moist, acid soil, under semiwoodland conditions. In recent years, *C. florida* has been afflicted by a debilitating anthracnose disease in many areas. Trees located where there is good air circulation and suitable soil seem to do best. Provide good care, including water in drought periods, to maintain vigor. Trees are seldom killed outright and may remain fine ornamentals if infection is moderate. Dogwood are damaged especially easily by such things as lawn mowers bumping into the trunks. These wounds give entry to borers and diseases that lead to the tree's decline.

Corylus Colurna (KOR-i-lus ko-LUR-na) **Turkish filbert, Turkish hazel,** Flowers, fall color, ESP ○

Zones: 4 to 7
Height: 50 feet; 75 feet
Foliage: Simple broad-leaved deciduous
Shape: Pyramidal, about ½ as wide as tall
Characteristics: An attractive, moderate-size tree, native to southeastern Europe and Asia Minor. Grown for its clean, dark green foliage and stately, low-branching formal shape. Both male and female flowers occur on the same tree, but it is the male flowers that are showy. They are produced in the very early spring in long, hanging greenish catkins. Fall foliage is not striking, but may develop shades of yellow and purple.

Corylus Colurna

Corylus Colurna *(detail of catkins)*

Crataegus viridis *'Winter King'*

Cultural Information: Plant Turkish filberts in well-drained soil. They will withstand more drought than many shade trees, and so are useful for drier sites. Also tolerant of heat and city conditions. Seldom bothered by pests and diseases.

Crabapple; see ***Malus***

Crataegus (kra-TEE-gus) **hawthorn,** Flowers, fruit, fall color, MSP ○ ■
Zones: Variable
Height: 15 to 30 feet; 35 feet
Foliage: Palmately lobed, broadleaved deciduous
Shape: Globe, as wide as high
Characteristics: Named for the long thorns, characteristic of many species. Most have clusters of white flowers followed by small red fruits in fall. Fall color ranges from yellow and orange to purple tints. The English hawthorn (*Crataegus oxycantha*) is popular for its pink or red flowers, particularly the double red cultivar *C. o.* 'Paul's Scarlet'. But the English hawthorn is very susceptible to leafspot disease and lacks fall color and fruit. It grows to 15 feet. Winter king hawthorn (*C. viridis* 'Winter King'; Zones 5 to 7; N: eastern North America) is one of the best for general landscape use. It has shorter and sparser thorns, a more vaselike tree shape to 30 feet, white flowers and profuse, bright red fruit that lasts through much of the winter.
Cultural Information: Despite various insect and disease problems, hawthorns are easy to grow in a variety of conditions. They will tolerate either acid or alkaline soils as well as drought. Training and regular pruning is necessary to produce a well-shaped tree, because they tend to sucker and develop crossing branches. Pests and diseases may include lace bugs, aphids, borers, scales, mites, scab and fire blight.

Cryptomeria japonica (krip-to-MEE-ri-a ja-PON-i-ka) **Japanese cedar,** Evergreen foliage, bark ○ ◐ ■
Zones: 6 to 9
Height: 60 feet; 100 feet
Foliage: Prickly scalelike needled evergreen
Shape: Fastigiate-conical, ⅓ to ½ as wide as high
Characteristics: Japanese cedars, native to Japan and China, make handsome specimen conifers throughout the year, with deep green foliage in spring and summer that becomes bronzy in winter. They tend to retain their lower branches. The shredding bark is reddish brown. *Cryptomeria japonica* 'Elegans' has softer, bushier foliage that turns reddish in winter, and it reaches only 10 to 15 feet. *C. j.* 'Lobbii' is a full-size tree, but somewhat sparsely branched, which makes for an open, picturesque effect. *C. j.* 'Sekkan' is slower growing with golden new growth. *C. j.* 'Yoshino' is perhaps the finest cultivar, with a dense branching habit and an evenly shaped tree.
Cultural Information: Grows best in a rich woodland soil that is well drained, light and moist. Few pests and diseases bother Japanese cedars.

Cryptomeria japonica *'Yoshino'*

Cunninghamia lanceolata

Cunninghamia lanceolata (kun-ing-HAM-i-a lan-see-oh-LAY-ta) **China fir,** Evergreen foliage ○ ◐ ■

Zones: 7 to 9
Height: 60 to 75 feet; 150 feet
Foliage: needled evergreen
Shape: Pyramidal, about ⅓ as wide as high
Characteristics: These native Chinese conifers have a unique, almost tropical appearance because of their long, flat needles. Branches tend to be held horizontally, and trees that have been broken may develop more than one trunk. *Cunninghamia lanceolata* 'Glauca' has blue-green foliage.
Cultural Information: Of limited hardiness, this conifer will often grow in the warmer parts of Zone 6. Unfortunately it is susceptible to breakage from strong winds, ice and heavy snow, and most specimens seem to lose their tops at least once. New tops readily form, a trait unusual among conifers, but these should be thinned to a single new leader. Also unusual is the ability to sprout from the base of the trunk. Plant in an acidic, well-drained soil. Usually pest and disease free.

×Cupressocyparis Leylandii (kew-press-oh-SIP-ar-is lay-LAN-dee-i) **Leyland cypress,** evergreen foliage. ○ ■

Zones: 6 to 10
Height: 70 feet; more than 100 feet
Foliage: Scalelike needled evergreen
Shape: Fastigiate to pyramidal, less than ¼ as wide as high
Characteristics: This hybrid conifer (*Cupressus macrocarpa* ×*Chamaecyparis nootkatensis*) is rapidly becoming one of the most popular landscape plants where hardy. It is one of the fastest-growing evergreen trees, easily making 3 feet of growth a year under good conditions. There are many cultivars. ×*Cupressocyparis Leylandii* 'Haggerston Grey' has grayish green foliage with a narrow tree shape. *C. L.* 'Leighton Green' has bright green foliage. *C. L.* 'Robinson's Gold' and *C. L.* 'Castlewellan' have yellow foliage in cool climates, but not where summers are hot. The foliage of *C. L.* 'Silver Dust' is attractively flecked with white, making it one of the best large variegated conifers.
Cultural Information: Adapted to a wide range of conditions and well-drained soils. Trees tend to be unstable and topple over in wind, due to small root systems. Plant as young as possible from containers and be sure to spread roots. An excellent screening plant that makes a good hedge if pruned yearly to maintain size. Also good for seashore plantings. No serious pests or diseases.

Cupressus (kew-PRES-sis) **cypress,** Evergreen foliage ○ ■

Zones: Variable
Height: 30 to 40 feet; 75 feet
Foliage: Scalelike needled evergreen
Shape: Fastigiate to pyramidal, ½ as wide as high
Characteristics: These true cypresses are conifers for the South, rather than for cold climates. Perhaps the most famous to Americans is the Monterey cypress (*Cupressus macrocarpa*; Zones 8 to 10) of coastal California. It forms a widely fastigiate to pyramidal tree that broadens out with age to reveal a picturesque form. Arizona cypress (*C. arizonica*; Zones 6 to 9) is a hardier but smaller tree growing to 35 feet with bluish gray

Cunninghamia lanceolata *(detail of cones)*

×Cupressocyparis Leylandii

Cupressus macrocarpa

Cupressus arizonica and C. macrocarpa

foliage. Italian cypress *(C. sempervirens*; Zones 7 to 10) is the narrow, spiky tree seen in classical landscapes of Italy. In the United States, it grows best in the similar climate of coastal California.

Cultural Information: Cypresses are easy to grow because established trees are quite drought resistant, need little pruning unless used as a hedge, and are pest and disease resistant. Arizona and Monterey cypresses are subject to canker diseases. Plant in a well-drained soil.

Cypress; see ***Cupressus***

Cypress, Arizona; see ***Cupressus***

Cypress, bald; see ***Taxodium***

Cypress, false; see ***Chamaecyparis***

Cypress, golden thread-leaf; see ***Chamaecyparis***

Cypress, Hinoki false; see ***Chamaecyparis***

Cypress, Italian; see ***Cupressus***

Cypress, Lawson false; see ***Chamaecyparis***

Cypress, Leyland; see ×***Cupressocyparis***

Cypress, Monterey; see ***Cupressus***

Cypress, moss; see ***Chamaecyparis***

Cypress, Sawara false; see ***Chamaecyparis***

Cypress, thread-leaf; see ***Chamaecyparis***

Cypress, weeping nootka false; see ***Chamaecyparis***

Davidia involucrata (day-VID-i-a in-vol-u-KRAY-ta) **dove tree, handkerchief tree,** Flowers, bark, MSP ○ ◑ ■

Zones: 6 to 8

Height: 20 to 40 feet; 65 feet

Foliage: Simple broad-leaved deciduous

Shape: Spreading pyramidal, usually narrower than tall

Characteristics: The common names of this Chinese native are suggested by the large white bracts (petallike leaves) that hang below the branches when the tree is in bloom. The shiny, dark green leaves are attractive all summer, but do not color in autumn. The scaly bark is showy all year with warm shades of brown and orange-brown. Young trees are slow to reach flowering age.

Cultural Information: This Chinese woodlander prefers light shade, but will tolerate full sun if not drought stressed. Soil should be rich, moist and well drained.

Davidia involucrata

Dawn redwood; see ***Metasequoia***

Deodar cedar; see ***Cedrus***

Dogwoods; see ***Cornus***

Double sweet cherry; see ***Prunus***

Douglas fir; see ***Pseudotsuga***

Dove tree; see ***Davidia***

Dragon's claw willow; see ***Salix***

Eastern arborvitae; see ***Thuja***

Eastern redbud; see ***Cercis***

Eastern red cedar; see ***Juniperus***

Eastern white pine; see ***Pinus***

Elms; see ***Ulmus***

English hawthorn; see ***Crataegus***

English holly; see ***Ilex***

English oak, Fastigiate; see ***Quercus***

European beech; see ***Fagus***

European hornbeam; see ***Carpinus***

European larch; see ***Larix***

European mountain ash; see ***Sorbus***

Fagus (FAY-gus) **beech,** Bark, foliage ○ ◐ ■

Zones: Variable

Height: 50 to 70 feet, more than 100 feet

Foliage: Simple broad-leaved deciduous

Shape: Globe or pyramidal, about ⅔ as wide as high

Characteristics: Beeches are well known for their smooth, light gray trunks. The American beech (*Fagus grandifolia*; Zones 3 to 9) forms a fine rounded shade tree with green foliage that becomes golden yellow in autumn, then turns to light tan. The foliage clings on many branches through the winter. European beech (*F. sylvatica*; Zones 4 to 7) has a more pyramidal shape; but the many variations of this species provide a remarkable array of tree shapes and foliage types. Fern-leaved beech (*F. s.* 'Asplenifolia') has deeply cut green leaves. Purple beech (*F. s.* 'Atropunicea') has deep purple foliage all summer. Weeping beech (*F. s.* 'Pendula') is distinctive for its weeping branches, which eventually form

Fagus sylvatica *'Asplenifolia'*

Fagus sylvatica *'Pendula'*

a large mound shape. All beeches need plenty of space in order to grow into grand specimens.
Cultural Information: Plant in a well-drained, preferably acid soil. Transplant in spring. Tolerant of shade, but grows best in full sun. Not good under city conditions. The shallow roots compete with underplantings.

False cypresses; see ***Chamaecyparis***

Fastigiate English oak; see ***Quercus***

Fern-leaved beech; see ***Fagus***

Filbert, Turkish; see ***Corylus***

Fir; see ***Abies***

Fir, balsam; see ***Abies***

Fir, China; see ***Cunninghamia***

Fir, Douglas; see ***Pseudotsuga***

Fir, Korean; see ***Abies***

Fir, Nikko; see ***Abies***

Fir, white; see ***Abies***

Flowering cherry, Japanese; see ***Prunus***

Flowering dogwood; see ***Cornus***

Foster holly; see ***Ilex***

Fragrant snowbell; see ***Styrax***

Franklin tree; see ***Franklinia***

Franklinia Alatamaha (frank-LIN-i-a a-la-ta-MA-ha) **Franklin tree,** Flowers, fall color, LSU-EF ○ ◐
Zones: 5 to 9
Height: 15 to 20 feet; 30 feet
Foliage: Simple broad-leaved deciduous
Shape: Spreading globe, often nearly as wide as high
Characteristics: This beautiful, small tree has not been seen in the wild since discovered and collected in Georgia by Philadelphia botanist John Bartram, in the late 1700s. He named it after his friend Benjamin Franklin. It is one of the finest small flowering trees or large shrubs, often forming several trunks. White camellialike flowers with yellow stamens are borne for more than a month extending into autumn, when they combine with reddish foliage. The growth habit is rounded and spreading, but open so that larger specimens combine well with underplantings.
Cultural Information: Grows best in a rich, acid, well-drained, moist soil, such as along a stream bank, but performs well in many garden situations. Flowers most prolifically in full sun. Easiest to transplant when small.

Fraxinus (FRAK-si-nus) **ash,** Foliage, fall color ○
Zones: 3 to 9
Height: 50 to 80 feet; more than 100 feet
Foliage: Pinnately compound broad-leaved deciduous
Shape: Globe
Characteristics: Ashes are useful shade trees because of their rapid growth and their adaptability to a variety of sites and soils where other trees may not perform well. Leaves are composed of several leaflets and are coarse in texture. Some ashes produce abundant seeds that may lead to a weed problem, so male cultivars, which are seedless, are recommended. Green ash (*Fraxinus pennsylvanica*) is the most adaptable and transplants readily, but often lacks fall color. *F. p.* 'Marshall's Seedless' and *F. p.* 'Patmore' are seedless. White ash (*F. americana*), although less adaptable,

Franklinia Alatamaha

Fraxinus pennsylvanica *'Summit'*

is entirely suitable for most home garden conditions and has superior ornamental value. Fall color ranges from yellow to purple. *F. a.* 'Autumn Purple' is seedless. Both species are native to eastern North America.
Cultural Information: Adaptable to both acid and alkaline soils, and green ash tolerates drier sites and salt. Easily transplanted. May be attacked by numerous pests and diseases, but these are usually not severe, because trees tend to maintain their health under adverse conditions. Prune in fall.

Ginkgo biloba

Gleditsia triacanthos *'Sunburst'*

Fringe trees; see ***Chionanthus***

Giant redwood; see ***Sequoiadendron***

Ginkgo biloba (GINK-go by-LOW-ba) **maidenhair tree,** Foliage, fall color ○
Zones: 3 to 9
Height: 80 feet; more than 100 feet
Foliage: Fan-shaped broad-leaved deciduous
Shape: Fastigiate to spreading globe, usually narrower than wide.
Characteristics: Ginkgos have been cultivated in China for centuries and have even been found in fossils. The leaves, shaped like little fans, are bright green in summer and golden yellow in fall. The seeds ripen in fall and have a fleshy covering, which ferments to a strong putrid odor. Because ginkos are dioecious, you can prevent the formation of fruit by planting only male trees. *Ginkgo biloba* 'Sentry' is a fastigiate male cultivar.
Cultural Information: Adapted to wide range of soil conditions, tolerant of air pollution and city conditions, and mostly pest and disease free.

Gleditsia triacanthos (gle-DIT-see-a try-a-KAN-thos) **honey locust,** Foliage, fall color ○
Zones: 3 to 9
Height: 70 feet; more than 100 feet
Foliage: Lacy pinnately or bipinnately compound, broad-leaved, deciduous
Shape: Spreading vase, often about as wide as high
Characteristics: The leaves are composed of many small leaflets that cast a light shade. In autumn, these leaflets fall individually, and are small enough virtually to eliminate the need for raking. Fall color of these trees, native to eastern North America, is yellow. Typical honey locusts have long, sharp thorns along the trunk and branches, so only selections of the thornless variety (*Gleditsia triacanthos inermis*) are planted in gardens. The young foliage of *G. t.* 'Sunburst' is golden yellow, eventually fading to green. *G. t.* 'Ruby Lace' has reddish foliage, but is inferior in habit and pest resistance to other types. Many thornless cultivars with green foliage, including *G. t.* 'Moraine', are available in nurseries.
Cultural Information: Adaptable to a wide range of soils, but seems to prefer those that are moist, rich, and alkaline. Also tolerant of salt and drought. A very popular tree in recent years, but is subject to a number of pests and diseases, including webworm, that may become serious. Seems to do especially well in cities where leaf litter (in which webworm overwinters) is usually cleaned up.

Golden black locust; see ***Robinia***

Golden chain; see ***Laburnum***

Golden larch; see ***Pseudolarix Kaempferi***

Goldenrain tree; see ***Koelreuteria***

Golden thread-leaf cypress; see ***Chamaecyparis***

Golden weeping willow; see ***Salix***

Gray birch; see ***Betula***

Green ash; see ***Fraxinus***

Gum, sour; see ***Nyssa***

Gum, sweet; see ***Liquidambar***

Halesia (ha-LEE-zi-a) **silver bell,** Flowers, fall color, MSP ◐ ○ ■

Zones: Variable
Height: 40 to 60 feet; 60 to 80 feet
Foliage: Simple broad-leaved deciduous
Shape: Pyramidal globe, about ⅔ as wide as high
Characteristics: Silver bells are among the best native ornamental trees; they are native to southeastern North America. The small white flowers hang below the branches. Fall color is yellow or greenish yellow. The Carolina silver bell (*Halesia carolina*; Zones 4 to 8) reaches about 40 feet in normal situations. The mountain silver bell (*H. monticola*; Zones 5 to 8) grows to about 60 feet and has larger flowers. There are pink-flowered forms of both species.
Cultural Information: Grows best in rich, moist, acid soil as an understory tree in light shade, but will take full sun. Few pest or disease problems.

Handkerchief tree; see ***Davidia***

Hardy silk tree; see ***Albizia***

Hawthorns; see ***Crataegus***

Hazel, Turkish; see ***Corylus***

Hedge maple; see ***Acer***

Hemlocks; see ***Tsuga***

Higan cherry; see ***Prunus***

Himalayan pine; see ***Pinus***

Hinoki false cypress; see ***Chamaecyparis***

Hollies; see ***Ilex***

Holly oak; see ***Quercus***

Hollywood juniper; see ***Juniperus***

Holm oak; see ***Quercus***

Honey locust; see ***Gleditsia***

Hornbeam, European; see ***Carpinus***

Horse chestnut; see ***Aesculus***

Idesia polycarpa (eye-DEE-zee-a poly-KAR-pa) **idesia,** Flowers, fruit, LSP-ESU ○ ◐ ■

Zones: 6 to 8
Height: 40 to 60 feet; 60 feet
Foliage: Simple broad-leaved deciduous
Shape: Pyramidal globe, as wide as tall
Characteristics: This rarely seen, but attractive, tree is native to Japan and China. It has large, deep green, heart-shaped leaves and clusters of reddish orange fruit in autumn. The clusters of greenish flowers are not especially showy.
Cultural Information: Plant in a moist, well-drained soil. Idesias are dioecious, so both sexes must be present in order for fruit to be produced.

Ilex (EYE-lex) **holly,** Fruit, evergreen foliage, SP ○ ◐ ■

Zones: Variable
Height: 30 feet; 50 feet or more
Foliage: Simple broad-leaved evergreen
Shape: Pyramidal, about ⅓ as wide as tall
Characteristics: Red berries among spiny evergreen foliage on shapely trees make holly one of the showiest ornamentals of late fall and winter. Most kinds also have yellow-berried varieties, especially pleasant when combined with the red-berried types. American holly (*Ilex opaca*; Zones 5 to 9) is the best species for eastern North America, where it is native. It is the hardiest broad-leaved evergreen tree in the North. The foliage is an olive green. *I. o.* 'Stewarts Silver Crown', a female, is the first American holly to have foliage variegated with cream. Foster holly (*I.* ×*attenuata* 'Foster #2'; Zones 7 to 9) bears abundant crops of berries and has smaller leaves that are easier to use in cut arrangements. English holly (*I. Aquifolium*; Zones 6 to 9) is the finest-looking ornamental holly with deep green glossy foliage and bright red berries. It resents excessive heat

Halesia carolina

Idesia polycarpa

Ilex Aquifolium
'Golden King'

and grows best in the Pacific Northwest, although it does reasonably well in the Mid-Atlantic region. There are also forms with leaves variegated with white or cream. Native to Europe, North Africa and western Asia. *I.* 'Nellie Stevens' (Zones 6 to 9) is a popular hybrid of English holly that does well in the Southeast. Long-stalk holly (*I. pedunculosa*; Zones 5 to 8) is native to Japan and China. It has friendly, spineless, dark green, glossy leaves and bright red berries on long peduncles (fruit stems). It often grows with multiple trunks, but can be trained to a fine single-trunked tree. Normally about 15 feet tall, but may reach 30 feet. Some hollies are deciduous, but those are usually shrubs, and not discussed in this book.

Cultural Information: Hollies grow best in a moist, well-drained, acid soil and will be more densely branched in full sun. American holly is often afflicted with leaf miner, but trees in partial shade and woodland conditions seem less bothered by this. Because they are dioecious, both sexes must be planted for fruit production. Similar species can pollinate each other if they bloom at the same time.

Juniperus scopulorum *'Tolleson's Weeping' (detail)*

Juniperus chinensis *'Hetzii Columnaris'*

Incense cedar, California; see ***Calocedrus***

Italian cypress; see ***Cupressus***

Italian stone pine; see ***Pinus***

Japanese birch; see ***Betula***

Japanese black pine; see ***Pinus***

Japanese cedar; see ***Cryptomeria***

Japanese flowering cherry; see ***Prunus***

Japanese larch; see ***Larix***

Japanese maple; see ***Acer***

Japanese pagoda tree; see ***Sophora***

Japanese snowbell; see ***Styrax***

Japanese stewartia; see ***Stewartia***

Japanese umbrella pine; see ***Sciadopitys***

Japanese zelkova; see ***Zelkova***

Junipers; see ***Juniperus***

Juniperus (jew-NIP-er-us) **juniper,** Evergreen foliage ○ ◼

Zones: 3 to 9

Height: 20 to 50 feet; 30 to 90 feet

Foliage: Scalelike needled evergreen

Shape: Fastigiate to pyramidal, less than ⅓ as wide as high

Characteristics: Junipers are workhorses of modern landscapes because they are tolerant of so many adverse conditions. They are extremely variable, with the same species encompassing both shrubby and upright tree forms. Foliage is fine textured and may be prickly, especially on young trees. Foliage color varies from deep green to a grayish blue, depending on the variety. Most common of the tree types is the Chinese juniper (*Juniperus chinensis*), native to Asia. One of the most popular cultivars of this species is *J. c.* 'Kiazuka', also known as 'Torulosa' and Hollywood juniper. It has an irregular branching habit with bright green foliage; it grows to about 25 feet. *J. c.* 'Mountbatten' has a narrow columnar shape and gray-green foliage, and seldom exceeds 12 feet. Western red cedar (*J. scopulorum*; N: western North America) usually grows to about 35 feet and is best known for *J. s.* 'Skyrocket', a strongly narrow, upright cultivar. *J. s.* 'Tolleson's Weeping' has bluish pendulous foliage hanging from weeping branches. Eastern red cedar (*J. virginiana*; N: eastern and central North America) is similar to the western red cedar, but somewhat taller, often reaching 40 to 50 feet. Cultivars include *J. v.* 'Cupressifolia' with dark

green foliage and *J. v.* 'Manhattan Blue', both with a pyramidal habit.
Cultural Information: Generally a tough group of plants. Adaptable to a wide range of soils, including poor, dry, gravelly, acid and alkaline. They prefer an open, sunny location with good air circulation.

Katsura tree; see ***Cercidiphyllum***

Koelreuteria paniculata (kol-roo-TE-ri-a pan-ik-you-LAY-ta) **goldenrain tree,** Flowers, fruit, ESU-MSU ○ ▆L
Zones: 5 to 9
Height: 30 to 40 feet; 60 feet
Foliage: Pinnate or bipinnately compound, broad-leaved deciduous
Shape: Globe, as wide or wider than high
Characteristics: Small yellow flowers in large clusters among large leaves composed of many smaller leaflets. Large clusters of papery seedpods remain through the winter and are useful in dried arrangements. Native to Asia.
Cultural Information: Adaptable to a wide range of acid and alkaline soils. Tolerates heat, drought and city conditions. Usually not bothered by pests and diseases. Prune to remove crowded or crossing branches in winter.

Korean fir; see ***Abies***

Korean mountain ash; see ***Sorbus***

Korean pine; see ***Pinus***

Korean stewartia; see ***Stewartia***

Kousa dogwood; see ***Cornus***

Laburnum* × *Watereri (la-BER-num wa-TER-er-i) **golden chain,** Flowers, MSP ◐ ▆L
Zones: 5 to 7
Height: 15 feet; 30 feet
Foliage: Trifoliate broad-leaved deciduous
Shape: Vase, nearly as wide as tall
Characteristics: A small tree, popular for its hanging clusters of yellow flowers. Beanlike pods in fall are not particularly decorative.
Cultural Information: Grows best in cool regions such as the Pacific Northwest; not suitable for the southeastern United States. Young trees perform well in the East, but decline when they reach middle age. Adapted to well-drained acid or alkaline soils. Locate where they will receive shade during midday.

Lacebark elm; see ***Ulmus***

Lacebark pine; see ***Pinus***

Larch; see ***Larix***

Larch, European; see ***Larix***

Larch, golden; see ***Pseudolarix***

Larch, Japanese; see ***Larix***

Larix (LAR-iks) **larch,** Foliage, fall color ○ ▆L
Zones: Variable
Height: 70 to 90 feet, more than 100 feet
Foliage: Short-needled deciduous
Shape: Pyramidal, about ⅓ as wide as high
Characteristics: The needles of this deciduous conifer are bright green and turn yellow in fall. Larches are northern trees. They are not suitable for the southeastern United States because they dislike summer heat. They have a fast rate of growth. Japanese larch (*Larix Kaempferi* or *L. leptolepis*; Zones 4 to 7; N: Japan) is considered a better ornamental, is more disease resistant and is faster growing than the European larch. European larch (*L. decidua*; Zones 2 to 6; N: Europe) is similar in appearance and hardier.
Cultural Information: Plant in acid soil, avoid droughty locations. Transplant when dormant. Prune in summer.

Koelreuteria paniculata

Laburnum × Watereri

Larix decidua

Laurel; Portuguese cherry; see ***Prunus***

Lawson false cypress; see ***Chamaecyparis***

Lebanon, cedar of; see ***Cedrus***

Leyland cypress; see ***×Cupressocyparis***

Linden, small-leaved; see ***Tilia***

Top left: Liquidambar Styraciflua *Top right:* Liriodendron Tulipifera *'Aureo-marginatum' Bottom:* Liriodendron Tulipifera *(detail of flower)*

Liquidambar Styraciflua

(lik-wid-AM-bar sty-ra-se-FLOO-a) **sweet gum,** Fall color, summer foliage ○ ■
Zones: 5 to 9
Height: 60 to 75 feet; more than 100 feet
Foliage: Palmately lobed broad-leaved deciduous
Shape: Pyramidal, about ⅔ as wide as tall
Characteristics: One of the best trees for brilliant autumn colors of yellow to purplish red. The deep green foliage is somewhat star-shaped, with five pointed lobes. The spherical fruit can be a nuisance in fall and winter, especialy on walkways. *Liquidambar Styraciflua* 'Moraine' is considered the hardiest cultivar. *L. S.* 'Obtusiloba' has rounded leaf lobes and does not produce fruit. Native to eastern North America and Mexico.
Cultural Information: Requires a deep, moist, acid soil to grow best. Not tolerant of city conditions, pollution or drought, but is adapted to both the eastern and western regions of the United States. Transplant only in spring. Prune during winter.

Liriodendron Tulipifera

(lir-ee-oh-DEN-dron tew-li-PIF-er-a) **tulip tree, tulip poplar,** Flowers, fall color, LSP ○ ◐ ■
Zones: 5 to 9
Height: 70 to 90 feet, more than 150 feet
Foliage: Palmately lobed broad-leaved deciduous
Shape: Pyramidal, rounded with age, ½ as wide as tall
Characteristics: Native to eastern United States, tulip trees are tall and stately with long trunks and an open, branching habit. The bright green foliage turns yellow in autumn and has a distinctly flat-ended shape. The orange and green flowers, similar in shape to tulips, are interesting, but not particularly showy because they are often high in the tree and blend with the foliage. *Liriodendron Tulipifera* 'Aureo-marginatum' has very attractive yellow-edged leaves. They do not seem to burn as easily as leaves on some variegated trees. *L. T.* 'Fastigiatum' is tall and narrow in habit.
Cultural Information: Requires a rich, acid, well-drained soil. Not tolerant of soil compaction or city conditions. Difficult to transplant except when small because roots are thick, fleshy and widely spaced. Often subject to aphid attack in spring with resulting honeydew deposited on surfaces below. Healthy trees are not harmed and spraying is unnecessary.

Live oaks; see ***Quercus***

Loblolly pine; see ***Pinus***

Locust, golden black; see ***Robinia***

Locust, honey; see ***Gleditsia***

Loebner magnolia; see ***Magnolia***

Lombardy poplar; see ***Populus***

London plane tree; see ***Platanus***

Long-stalk holly; see ***Ilex***

Magnolia (mag-NOH-lee-a)
magnolia, Flowers, fruit, evergreen foliage (sometimes), SP, SU ○ ◐ ■
Zones: Variable
Height: 20 to 60 feet; 90 feet
Foliage: Simple broad-leaved deciduous or evergreen
Shape: Spreading globe or pyramidal, often as wide as high
Characteristics: Magnolias are an important and varied group of flowering trees. Most are spring blooming and deciduous, and many have a light, delicate fragrance. Swamp magnolia has a strong, sweet fragrance and southern magnolia has a deliciously lemony fragrance. Fruits are conelike pods that split open to reveal fleshy pink or red seeds. These seeds may drop out and hang briefly from threads. "Cones" may ripen to pink or red, depending on the variety, and can be quite striking.

The following deciduous magnolias all bloom in early spring. 'Betty' (Zones 3 to 8) is a hybrid that grows to 10 feet and has reddish purple blooms. 'Galaxy' (Zones 6 to 8), also a hybrid, reaches 20 feet and has deep pink blooms. Loebner magnolia (*M.* ×*Loebneri*; Zones 3 to 8) has white or pink blooms and grows to 30 feet. Saucer magnolia (*M.* ×*Soulangiana*; Zones 4 to 9) also grows to 30 feet, with pink or white blooms. And star magnolia (*M. stellata;* Zones 3 to 8) reaches 20 feet and has white or pink blooms. The semievergreen swamp magnolia (*M. virginiana*; Zones 5 to 9) blooms in white in late spring.

Southern magnolia or bullbay (*M. grandiflora*; Zones 6 to 9) is one of the finest ornamental trees native to North America and it is now grown throughout the world, wherever it is most hardy. Few trees can match its beauty at every season. It has lustrous evergreen foliage, often with the added richness of felty brown hairs, called indumentum, on the underside. Large creamy white, lemon-scented flowers are normally borne for about 6 weeks during late spring or early summer, but some varieties will flower continuously into fall. The best trees develop large showy cones that ripen to bright red in autumn. Unfortunately, the large leaves predispose southern magnolias to damage from heavy snow and ice in winter. It is one of the largest of flowering trees, with some individuals in the wild reaching 90 feet. There is so much variation among the different cultivars that they should be carefully chosen to fit your specific needs. *M. g.* 'Bracken's Brown Beauty' (Zones 7 to 9) is an especially fine foliage plant for its heavy, rusty brown indumentum. Compact habit and smaller leaves add to its beauty. Flowers are in scale at 5 to 6 inches in diameter. Grows to about 30 feet. *M. g.* 'Edith Bogue' (Zones 6 to 9) was awarded the Pennsylvania Horticultural Society's Gold Medal Award for its superior cold hardiness. Narrow, deep green leaves with light indumentum. Flowers are 9 to 12 inches wide with strong fragrance from late spring to early summer. The cones are a reddish color and of moderate size. Upright shape resists snow and ice damage. Maximum size in the North is about 35 feet. *M. g.* 'Glen St. Mary' or 'St. Mary'

Magnolia stellata

Magnolia ×Soulangiana *'Alexandrina' (detail of flower)*

Magnolia grandiflora *(detail of flower)*

(Zones 7 to 9) is one of the most widely sold cultivars. It has fine foliage backed by good indumentum and a smaller, more compact habit than the most vigorous kinds. Noteworthy for flowering at a younger age. Grows to about 20 feet tall. *M. g.* 'Hasse' (Zones 7 to 9) is of upright, compact, narrow habit with dark green foliage and good indumentum. Moderate vigor and size. *M. g.* 'Little Gem' (Zones 7 to 9) is a popular cultivar due to its small size (10 to 20 feet tall). Leaves and flowers are less than half that of other cultivars. Blooms spring and fall, and begins blooming at a very young age. *M. g.* 'Samuel Sommer' (Zones 7 to 9) is an upright, wide-spreading tree with some of the largest of all flowers, up to 14 inches across. Good indumentum. Grows 40 feet tall and almost as wide. *M. g.* 'Timeless Beauty' (Zones 6 to 9) is a new variety with upright habit, flowering continuously through the summer. It is a hybrid with *M. virginiana*. *M.* 'Victoria' (Zones 7 to 9) is considered the hardiest cultivar in the Pacific Northwest. Rusty brown indumentum. Grows to 20 feet tall, about ⅔ as wide.

Cultural Information: Magnolias require rich, acid, well-drained, but not droughty soil. The swamp magnolia will grow in wet, poorly drained soils as well as drier locations. Because magnolias have thick, fleshy roots, they should be transplanted when young from containers or balled-and-burlapped, not bareroot. Magnolias are woodlanders and like the shelter of nearby trees, as long as they are not crowded. They are seldom seriously troubled by pests and diseases, although scale can be a problem. The flowers of early blooming varieties may be damaged by frosts, especially when planted in southern exposures that encourage the flowers to open even earlier. Southern magnolia is subject to winter foliage damage in the North and should be sited in locations sheltered from wind and extreme cold. *M. grandiflora* 'Edith Bogue' is probably the most cold-tolerant cultivar of southern magnolia currently available.

Malus floribunda

Malus *'Donald Wyman' (detail of fruit)*

Magnolia, southern; see ***Magnolia***

Maidenhair tree; see ***Ginkgo***

Malus (MAY-lus) **crabapple,** Flowers, fruit, fall color, MSP ○

Zones: Variable
Height: 12 to 20 feet; 40 feet
Foliage: Simple broad-leaved deciduous
Shape: Weeping, spreading, or globe, often wider than high
Characteristics: Crabapples are one of the most important groups of flowering trees for northern climates because of their extreme hardiness. Depending on the species, they are native to North America, Japan and China. There are so many kinds that they offer a range of characteristics unequaled by most other trees. In spring, before the leaves have expanded fully, the branches are covered with pink,

red and white flowers. These are often followed by a crop of small red, yellow or amber fruit that may hang on the tree into winter or spring, providing food for wildlife. Fruit of some varieties makes excellent jelly. Young foliage may be tinted red in spring and color again in fall. Some varieties maintain reddish foliage through the summer. Most types have a broad, rounded shape, but some are more upright and spreading, while a few have a weeping habit. Choose the combination of characteristics that suits your needs.

Dr. Thomas L. Green, research plant pathologist at the Morton Arboretum in Lisle, Illinois, has been evaluating crabapples for many years and considers the following varieties to be among the best for general landscape use. All are hybrids and grow to about 20 feet, unless noted. *Malus* 'Adams' (Zones 4 to 8) becomes a rounded tree with red flowers. The red fruit remains attractive on the tree from fall to spring. Reddish young foliage enhances the flowers before turning green for the summer. *M.* 'Bob White' (Zones 5 to 8) has a broad, spreading tree habit with small, light green leaves and white flowers. Attractive yellow fruit ripens in fall and often stays on the tree until spring. *M.* 'Donald Wyman' (Zones 4 to 8) grows into a rounded tree. The white flowers are followed by red fruit in fall that lasts well through winter. *M. floribunda* (Zones 4 to 8; N: Japan) is considered one of the finest species of crabapple with pink buds that open to white flowers. It is a graceful tree with a spreading habit. The amber fruit is showy throughout autumn. *M.* 'Indian Magic' (Zones 4 to 8) has pink flowers and dark green foliage. Orange-red fruit lasts from fall to spring. The tree has an upright, spreading habit. *M.* 'Jewelberry' (Zones 5 to 8) is perhaps the best dwarf (almost shrubby) cultivar. It may grow to about 12 feet tall and 15 feet wide but is usually seen half as large. White flowers are followed by red fruit that persist until December. *M.* 'Orminston Roy' (Zones 4 to 8) is another fine upright, spreading tree. It bears white flowers and amber fruit that lasts until spring. *M.* 'Prairifire' (Zones 4 to 8) has red flowers complemented by purplish foliage that becomes dark green during the summer. The red fruit holds well until spring. This tree has an upright, spreading habit. *M.* 'Professor Sprenger' (Zones 4 to 8) has white flowers, persistent orange-red fruit and an upright, spreading tree shape. *M.* 'Profusion' (Zones 4 to 8) has purple-bronze foliage through summer and red flowers in spring. The maroon fruit holds well through winter. This rounded tree reaches 25 feet. *M.* 'Sugar Tyme' (Zones 5 to 8) is an upright, spreading tree growing to only about 18 feet. White flowers and red fruit are enhanced by dark green foliage. The fruit persists until spring. *M.* 'White Cascade' (Zones 4 to 8) is a weeping crabapple, growing to 15 feet tall, with fine textured green foliage and white flowers. The amber fruit does not persist well through winter.

Cultural Information: Plant in a well-drained, acid to slightly alkaline soil. Moderately drought resistant. Bareroot trees are easy to transplant when dormant, or plant container-grown and balled-and-burlapped stock when in growth. Crabapples need pruning from the start to train them to a desirable shape. Always prune as lightly as possible to avoid stimulating water sprouts and suckers. During winter, prune out undesirable suckers and branches. Most crabapples are grafted, and any suckers from below the graft and from the roots should be removed. Crabapples are attacked by many diseases, including scab, fire blight, cedar-apple rust and powdery mildew. Extremely susceptible varieties can be eyesores for much of the summer. Their desirability as ornamentals depends on their ability to resist infection. Spraying with fungicides is unnecessary if resistant varieties are planted. Few are highly resistant to every disease, but those varieties with mild susceptibility still make acceptable landscape trees.

Maples; see ***Acer***

Metasequoia glyptostroboides (met-a-se-KWOY-a glip-tow-strow-BOY-deez) **dawn redwood,** Foliage, fall color, bark ○■L

Zones: 4 to 8

Height: 70 feet; more than 100 feet

Foliage: Short-needled deciduous

Shape: Sharply conical, about ⅓ as wide as high

Characteristics: One of the few deciduous conifers. Similar to bald cypress, but grows into a broader, more pointed tree. Foliage is soft and feathery, with the short needles arranged along

Metasequoia glyptostroboides

short deciduous twigs. Summer foliage color is light green, becoming rusty orange-brown in fall. Dawn redwood is one of the fastest-growing conifers, often exceeding 3 feet in one year. Found in fossils from fifty million years ago, it was discovered growing in western China in 1941.
Cultural Information: A very adaptable tree that grows well in both the North and South. Does best in a rich, deep, moist, acid, well-drained soil. Easy to transplant and needs almost no pruning. Pest and disease free.

Mimosa; see ***Albizia***

Monkey puzzle tree; see ***Araucaria***

Monterey cypress; see ***Cupressus***

Moosewood maple; see ***Acer***

Moss cypress; see ***Chamaecyparis***

Mountain ashes; see ***Sorbus***

Mountain silver bell; see ***Halesia***

Nikko fir; see ***Abies***

Nootka false cypress, weeping; see ***Chamaecyparis***

Northern catalpa; see ***Catalpa***

Norway maple; see ***Acer***

Norway spruce; see ***Picea***

Nyssa sylvatica (NIS-a sil-VAT-i-ka) **sour gum, black tupelo,** Fall color, foliage ○ ◐ ■

Zones: 3 to 9
Height: 40 to 50 feet; over 100 feet
Foliage: Simple broad-leaved deciduous
Shape: Pyramidal to rounded with age
Characteristics: One of the most spectacular native trees (eastern United States) for fall colors of bright orange, red and yellow. It is one of the first trees to show fall color, often on a few branches in late summer. Foliage is deep green in summer.
Cultural Information: Prefers a deep, moist soil but is adaptable to a wide range of soils including poorly drained and dry, if they are acid. Not tolerant of city conditions. Difficult to transplant due to long, spreading roots. Plant young container-grown specimens. Pests and diseases are not serious.

Oaks; see ***Quercus***

Nyssa sylvatica

Oxydendrum arboreum

Oxydendrum arboreum *(detail of seed capsules)*

Oriental spruce; see ***Picea***

Oxydendrum arboreum

(ok-si-DEN-drum ar-BO-ree-um) **sourwood, sorrel tree,** Flowers, fruit, fall color, LSP-ESU ○ ◐ ▙

Zones: 5 to 9
Height: 30 feet; 75 feet
Foliage: Simple broad-leaved deciduous
Shape: Pyramidal globe, ½ to ⅔ as wide as tall
Characteristics: The sorrel tree, native to the southeastern United States, has one of the longest seasons of interest of any flowering tree. Small white flowers, borne on pendulous stalks, are followed by cream-colored seed capsules that remain showy through summer (making the tree look as if it is still in bloom). In autumn, the seed capsules ripen to brown and remain on the tree for the winter. The foliage is a deep, lustrous green through the summer, turning to yellow and deep red in fall.
Cultural Information: Plant in rich, well-drained, acid soil. Relatively drought tolerant. Minimal pruning is required to remove dead branches.

Pagoda tree, Japanese; see ***Sophora***

Paperbark maple; see ***Acer***

Parrotia persica

(par-ROW-tee-a PER-si-ka) **parrotia,** Flowers, fall color, bark, ESP ○ ◐ ▙

Zones: 4 to 8
Height: 20 to 40 feet; 50 feet
Foliage: Simple broad-leaved deciduous
Shape: Spreading globe, sometimes wider than tall
Characteristics: This small tree, native to Iran, often grows with several trunks, but can be trained to a single trunk. It is grown for its bark and brilliant fall color. The bark is of year-'round interest, mottled with gray, green and brown. The lustrous, deep green foliage colors to bright orange and yellow in autumn. In early spring, the small flowers with reddish stamens are attractive. Related to witch hazels, winter flowering shrubs.
Cultural Information: Prefers well-drained, acid soil, but will tolerate slightly alkaline soils. Pest and disease free.

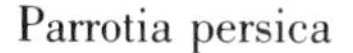

Parrotia persica

Parrotia persica *(detail of bark)*

Pears, see ***Pyrus***

Picea glauca *'Conica'*

Picea pungens*'Glauca'*

Picea (PY-see-a) **spruce,** Evergreen, foliage ○ ◐ ■

Zones: Variable

Height: 40 to 60 feet; more than 100 feet

Foliage: Short-needled evergreen

Shape: Pyramidal, ⅓ to ½ as wide as tall

Characteristics: Spruces are among the most common landscape conifers. The most often seen and fastest-growing species is the Norway spruce (*Picea Abies*; Zones 2 to 7, possibly 8; N: Europe). It has dark green needles and a characteristic weeping habit at maturity. While the main branches are held almost horizontally, the smaller branches along them are strongly pendulous, giving the tree an open, airy appearance. This is the most heat-tolerant species and grows to 60 feet or more. White spruce (*P. glauca*) has gray-green foliage and is the most tolerant spruce of wet sites. It is native to northern North America, hardy in Zones 2 to 6 and grows 40 to 50 feet tall. Serbian spruce (*P. Omorika*; Zones 4 to 7; N: southeastern Europe) is one of the finest species and is rapidly becoming popular. It has a very narrow pyramidal shape, requiring less space than any of the others, but may still reach 50 or 60 feet. The needles are deep green with white undersides, which give flashes of white as the branches move in the wind. Grows in both acid and alkaline soils. Another excellent ornamental species is Oriental spruce (*P. orientalis*; Zones 4 to 7; N: Caucasus and Asia Minor). It has shorter needles, a denser habit and is considerably more shade tolerant than the other spruces mentioned here. It also has a slower growth rate, but will eventually achieve 60 feet. *P. o.* 'Aurea' has attractive golden new growth. Colorado spruce (*P. pungens*; Zones 2 to 7; N: Rocky Mountains) is best known in gardens for the grayish blue foliage form of the blue spruce (*P. pungens* 'Glauca'). It has the longest needles and is almost as commonly planted as Norway spruce. It grows to 60 feet.

Cultural Information: Spruces are northern trees and grow best in cool climates. However, they are more successfully grown than firs (*Abies* species) in warm regions (including the Mid-Atlantic states). They prefer a well-drained, moist, acid soil, but are somewhat drought tolerant. *P. orientalis* is susceptible to winter foliage burn in dry, exposed locations. A dense root system makes spruces easy to transplant. Pests and diseases are more serious in southern areas where the trees are stressed by heat. Watch for mites and bagworms in particular.

Pin oak; see ***Quercus***

Pine; see ***Pinus***

Pine, Aleppo; see ***Pinus***

Pine, Austrian; see ***Pinus***

Pine, bishop; see ***Pinus***

Pine, Canary Island; see ***Pinus***

Pine, eastern white; see ***Pinus***

Pine, Himalayan; see ***Pinus***

Pine, Italian stone; see ***Pinus***

Pine, Japanese black; see ***Pinus***

Pine, Japanese umbrella; see ***Sciadopitys***

Pine, Korean; see ***Pinus***

Pine, lacebark; see ***Pinus***

Pine, loblolly; see ***Pinus***

Pine, Scotch; see ***Pinus***

Pine, Swiss stone; see ***Pinus***

Pine, umbrella; see ***Pinus***

Pinus (PY-nus) **pine,** Evergreen foliage, bark, cones ○ ■

Zones: Variable

Height: 30 to 60 feet, more than 100 feet

Foliage: Long-needled evergreen

Shape: Pyramidal, about ½ as wide as high

Characteristics: Pines differ from other conifers in their needles, which are held in clusters of twos, threes, or fives. There is remarkable variety in size and adaptation, and many have interesting shapes or variegated foliage. Some become huge trees, whereas others are of slower growth and ideal for small gardens.

The five-needled, or white pines, are especially beautiful due to their bluish or gray-green foliage. In contrast to other pines, they are more northern trees, and do poorly in the South. Eastern white pine (*Pinus Strobus*; Zones 3 to 8; N: eastern North America) is the best known and is frequently used in landscape plantings because of its commercial availability and fast growth. It can become a large tree, exceeding 80 feet (150 feet in the wild), and often outgrows the space provided for it. With age, wet snows snap the brittle branches and leave a picturesque or deformed specimen, depending on your point of view. Long narrow cones hang prominently at the ends of the branches. *P. S.* 'Fastigiata' has upright branches and narrower shape when young, becoming rounded with age. Said to be more resistant to snow and ice damage. Himalayan pine (*P. Wallichiana* or *P. Griffithii*; Zones 5 to 7; N: Himalayan Mountains) is fuller and bushier in appearance owing to its longer needles. A fine ornamental for large properties. The needles of *P. W.* 'Zebrina' are banded with gold. Korean pine (*P. koraiensis*; Zones 3 to 7; N: Korea) has shorter needles and a slower, tighter habit of growth. A refined white pine for smaller properties, it reaches about 40 feet and keeps its low branches. The most refined and shapely white pine is the Swiss stone pine (*P. Cembra*; Zones 4 to 7). It is one of the best pines for small gardens because it is densely branched with a narrow shape, and reaches 40 feet only after many years. Native to mountains of central Europe and southern Asia.

The three-needled pines are more tolerant of heat and have stiffer, sharper needles. Lacebark pine (*P. Bungeana*; Zones 4 to 8), from China, deserves a special situation to show off its beautiful bark, which is mottled with gray, brown and olive green. It is often multitrunked and grows slowly to a height of 30 to 50 feet (75 feet in the wild). Loblolly pine (*P. Taeda*; Zones 6 to 9; N: southeastern United States) is one of the most common pines in the Southeast. It often grows in dense forests, but in open situations it is shorter. It has an open habit and casts a light shade, but requires full sun, even as a young tree. The needles are light green. Canary Island pine (*P. canariensis;* Zones 9 to 10; N: Canary Islands) is an important landscape tree in southern California, with notable long needles. Young trees are conical and pointed in shape, rounding on top as they mature. They usually grow to about 60 feet.

The two-needled pines are a tough and serviceable group. Japanese black pine (*P. Thunbergiana*; Zones 5 to 7; N: Japan and Korea) tolerates coastal salt spray, sandy soils and drought. It is irregular in shape, with a leaning or crooked trunk and seldom grows much above 30 feet. The needles of *P. T.* 'Oculus-draconis' are banded with yellow, giving the tree a beautiful golden cast. Austrian pine (*P. nigra*) is a taller tree, growing 50 to 60 feet (more than 100 feet in the wild). It is characterized by dark green needles, thick branches and a prominent trunk with rough bark mottled gray and brown. It tolerates city conditions, seashore conditions, drought and a range of soils, including those that are high in clay and alkaline. Native to southern Europe, it is hardy in Zones 4 to 7, and possibly 8. Scotch pine (*P. sylvestris*; Zones 2 to 8; N: Europe, northern Asia) has shorter blue-green or yellowish green needles, and orange- or reddish brown bark. It is tolerant of various soils, including poor, dry sites. It normally grows 30 to 60 feet. Aleppo pine (*P. halapensis;* Zones 8 to 10; N: Mediterranean) is useful in California where tolerance of heat, wind, salt and drought are needed. It grows to about 60 feet tall. Bishop pine (*P. muricata*; Zones 7 to 10; N: California) is a finer ornamental than *P. halapensis* and grows to only about 45 feet. Italian stone pine or umbrella pine (*P. pinea*; Zones 9 to 10; N: Mediterranean) is a broad, flat-topped tree that reaches about 80 feet at maturity. The large seeds are the edible pine nuts of Europe. *Cultural Information:* On the whole, pines are better suited to dry, poor soils, hot climates and city conditions than other

Pinus Bungeana *(detail of bark)*

Pinus Wallichiana

conifers. They require good soil drainage. Austrian and Japanese pines are tolerant of salt spray. Austrian pine is susceptible to diplodia tip blight.

Plane tree, London; see ***Platanus***

Platanus ×acerifolia

Platanus ×acerifolia

(PLAT-a-nus a-sir-e-FO-lee-a) **London plane tree**, Bark, foliage
○ ◐ ■

Zones: 4 to 8
Height: 70 feet; more than 100 feet
Foliage: Palmately lobed broad-leaved deciduous
Shape: Globe, nearly as wide as tall
Characteristics: The London plane tree originated as a hybrid of the American and Oriental plane trees and proved to be very tolerant of conditions in London and other cities around the world. Unfortunately, it grows too large for cramped spaces along streets and next to buildings, and is losing favor in preference to other smaller city trees now available. As a tree for home landscapes, there are other trees with better habits and more ornamental value. Plane trees drop leaves and twigs all summer, and in autumn shed spherical fruits. The striking bark is mottled with brown, olive and cream, but is shed in large sheets in early summer. There is no significant fall color.
Cultural Information: Grows almost anywhere, including in cities and compacted alkaline soils, which accounts for its popularity for urban planting. Less susceptible to anthracnose than the native sycamore, *Platanus occidentalis*.

Plums; see ***Prunus***

Poplar; see ***Populus***

Poplar, Lombardy; see ***Populus***

Poplar, tulip; see ***Liriodendron***

Populus

(POP-ew-lus) **poplar,** Foliage ○ ■

Zones: Variable
Height: 70 feet; 90 feet
Foliage: Simple broad-leaved deciduous
Shape: Fastigiate, globe or pyramidal
Characteristics: Poplars are valued for their fast growth and ability to grow under difficult conditions, including cities and the Midwest. But they are short-lived, weak wooded and subject to a variety of diseases that can seriously disfigure them. Their roots are notorious for growing into and clogging sewer lines and heaving sidewalks and pavement. Many cities prohibit planting them. Poplars must be used with caution in the landscape, and homeowners should resist the temptation of sensational catalog claims. Use them for short-term purposes where trees are needed quickly, but also plant longer-lived, higher-quality trees for the future. Lombardy poplar (*Populus nigra* 'Italica'; Zones 3 to 9) has long been a popular landscape plant for its narrow columnar form, up to 90 feet tall. Unfortunately, it is often seen with dead tops and branches from pest and disease attacks. Originated in the 1600s in the Lombardy section of Italy.
Cultural Information: Grows best in deep, rich, moist soil, either acid or alkaline. Prune in summer and fall, because wounds in winter and spring bleed. Subject to many pests and diseases including many cankers, rusts, mildews, leaf spots, caterpillars, aphids and scales, which can cause serious damage.

Populus nigra *'Italica'*

Port Orford cedar; see ***Chamaecyparis***

Portuguese cherry laurel; see ***Prunus***

Prunus (PROO-nus) **cherry** and **plum,** Flowers, fall color, bark, SP ○ ◐ ▙
Zones: Variable
Height: 20 to 50 feet; 70 feet
Foliage: Simple broad-leaved deciduous
Shape: Spreading globe, some weeping, about as wide as high
Characteristics: Flowering cherries and plums are beautiful, small trees with life spans of 20 to 40 years. They mature fast and are perfect for the new homeowner who needs something to grow quickly.

Most are grown primarily for their flowers, but the Amur chokecherry (*Prunus Maackii*; Zones 2 to 6) and *P. serrula* (Zones 5 to 6) are planted for their shiny, smooth or shaggy brownish bark. They dislike summer heat, but are well suited to the north. Both are native to Asia.

Best known among *Prunus* are the Japanese flowering cherries. They have similar landscape use as the crabapples, but they are more graceful in habit, less hardy and lack showy fall fruit. Cultivated in Japan, they are thought to be native to China. *P. serrulata* (Zones 5 to 8) bears the large, double pink-and-white flowers that are usually associated with the Japanese cherries. *P. serrulata* 'Kwanzan' is the cultivar most often planted. It has large, double pink flowers, but is rather stiff in habit compared with other cultivars. Dull red fall color. Higan cherry (*P. subhirtella;* Zones 4 to 8) has more small, deep pink flowers, and blooms a week or two earlier. *P. subhirtella* 'Pendula' is a beautiful weeping cultivar seen in many suburban neighborhoods. *P. subhirtella* 'Autumnalis' has pale pink flowers, some of which open in autumn. *P.* 'Okame' (Zones 5 to 9) is an excellent early flowering hybrid with rich pink flowers. After the petals drop, the red flower stalks remain showy for another few weeks before the leaves emerge. Fall color is orange-red. Yoshina cherry (*P. yedoensis*; Zones 5 to 8) is believed to be a hybrid of *P. serrulata* and *P. subhirtella*. It grows 40 to 50 feet high and is the most floriferous Japanese cherry. The lightly fragrant flowers are pink or white. *P. y.* 'Akebono' ('Daybreak') is a blush pink cultivar of the Yoshina cherry. This cherry makes up most of the planting in the tidal basin in Washington, D.C.

In northern climates, where the large-flowered Japanese cherries are not hardy, the double sweet cherry (*P. avium* 'Plena'; Zones 3 to 7; N: Europe) is a worthy substitute with clusters of large white flowers. Fall color is yellow.

Purple-leaf plum is a striking small tree with deep purple foliage all summer. Most common is *P. cerasifera* 'Thundercloud', hardy in Zones 3 to 8 and native to eastern Europe and western Asia. The light pink flowers are small and not especially showy. *P. ×blireiana* (Zones 5 to 9) is a hybrid with foliage nearly as purple, and larger double flowers of carmine pink. It is a spectacle when blooming in early spring.

Several evergreen *Prunus* are planted in southern landscapes. Perhaps the most important one is Portuguese cherry laurel (*P. lusitanica*), which has dark green leaves highlighted by reddish petioles (leaf stems) and clusters of white flowers in spring. It grows with one or more trunks, to 20 to 40 feet (the warmer the area, the larger it grows). It is native to Spain and Portugal and is hardy in Zones 7 to 10.
Cultural Information: Plant in well-drained soil, either acid or alkaline, and water in dry spells. Susceptible to many pests and diseases, but these are not normally serious in young, vigorous trees. Older trees should be replaced when they begin to decline. *P. serrula* is especially susceptible to borers. Prune after flowering to remove crossing and undesirable branches.

Prunus serrulata *'Kwanzan'*

Prunus cerasifera

Pseudocydonia sinensis

Pseudolarix Kaempferi

Pseudotsuga Menziesii

Pseudocydonia sinensis (soo-DOH-sy-doh-nee-a sy-NEN-sis) **Chinese quince,** Flowers, fruit, fall color, bark, MSP ○ ◐ ▙

Zones: 6 to 8
Height: 20 feet; 40 feet
Foliage: Simple broad-leaved deciduous
Shape: Rounded, not as wide as high
Characteristics: This tree is also called *Cydonia*. The bark—mottled with shades of brown, tan and olive—and the pale pink flowers are this tree's greatest features. In autumn, the foliage changes to yellow and red, and the tree bears large, fragrant, oval, yellow fruit, the size of grapefruits. These fruits are edible (if cooked with a lot of sugar as for jelly), but they may be a nuisance. Don't let one fall on your head! Native to China.
Cultural Information: Grows best in well-drained, acid soil. Susceptible to fire blight. Train to single trunk and prune undesirable and crossing branches to improve shape.

Pseudolarix Kaempferi (soo-doh-LAR-iks KEMP-fer-eye) **golden larch,** Summer foliage, fall color ○ ◐ ▙

Zones: 4 to 7
Height: 50 feet; over 100 feet
Foliage: Short-needled deciduous
Shape: Broadly pyramidal, about ⅔ as wide as high
Characteristics: A magnificent deciduous conifer named for its golden yellow fall color. Summer foliage is attractive light green. Also called *Pseudolarix amabilis*. Native to China.
Cultural Information: Prefers a deep, acid, light, well-drained soil. Tolerates air pollution. Pest and disease free.

Pseudotsuga Menziesii (soo-doh-SOO-ga men-ZEE-zee-i) **Douglas fir,** Evergreen foliage ○ ◐ ▙

Zones: 4 to 6
Height: 80 feet; more than 200 feet
Foliage: Short-needled evergreen
Shape: Pyramidal, about ¼ as wide as tall
Characteristics: A magnificent conifer, native to western North America. *Pseudotsuga Menziesii* 'Glauca' has blue-green needles and is hardier than those with green foliage.
Cultural Information: Needs a moist, rich, well-drained, acid to neutral soil and prefers climates with high humidity. Subject to wind damage; not suitable for wind breaks.

Purple beech; see ***Fagus***

Purple-leaf plum; see ***Prunus***

Pyrus Calleryana *'Chanticleer'*

Pyrus (PY-rus) **pear,** Flowers, fall color, ESP ○ ◐ ▙

Zones: Variable
Height: 20 to 50 feet
Foliage: Simple broad-leaved deciduous
Shape: Pyramidal, globe or weeping, about ⅔ as wide as high
Characteristics: The callery pear (*Pyrus Calleryana*; Zones 5 to 9; N: China) makes a fine ornamental tree with a profusion of white flowers, clean foliage and yellow to red fall color. The fruit is marble size and insignificant. *P. C.* 'Bradford' has been widely planted, but with age, it forms weak branch crotches that split, ultimately disfiguring or destroying the tree. *P. C.* 'Chanticleer' is one of the best alternatives to 'Bradford' callery pears. Grows to 30 feet, or more. Weeping willow-leaved pear (*P. salicifolia* 'Pendula'; Zones 4 to 7; N: southeastern Europe and western Asia) has silvery gray foliage with a weeping habit and grows to about 20 feet.

Pyrus salicifolia *'Pendula'*

Cultural Information: Adaptable to most soils if well drained and not too alkaline. Tolerates city conditions and some drought. Fire blight is a serious problem of pears (especially *P. salicifolia*) in climates with warm summers so they should only be grown in cool climates. Some cultivars of callery pear, such as *P. C.* 'Bradford' and *P. C.* 'Chanticleer' are resistant. Callery pears generally have few pest and disease problems.

Quercus (KWER-kus) **oak,** Foliage, fall color, evergreen foliage ○ ◐ ■

Zones: Variable

Height: 40 to 80 feet; more than 100 feet

Foliage: Simple or pinnately lobed, broad-leaved, evergreen or deciduous

Shape: Fastigiate to spreading globe, some wider than high

Characteristics: Oaks are strong-wooded, long-lived, quality landscape trees. They are not fast growing and should be planted as part of long-term plans, perhaps in combination with some faster-growing trees. Only deciduous kinds are hardy in the North, but evergreen species are also commonly grown in the South. The acorns provide food for a variety of wildlife.

White oak (*Quercus alba*; Zones 3 to 9; N: eastern North America) must be planted from a container as a small tree, but it is one of the grandest shade trees and can live for hundreds of years. Named for its gray bark. Fall color consists of brownish to reddish tones. Red oak (*Q. rubra*; Zones 4 to 8; N: eastern North America) has blackish bark, deep green leaves and red fall color. Pin oak (*Q. palustris*; Zones 4 to 8; N: eastern United States) is the most commonly planted oak in landscapes because of its compact, easily transplanted root system. It is, however, subject to leaf chlorosis, has poor fall color, and is short-lived. Scarlet oak (*Q. coccinea*; Zones 4 to 9; N: eastern United States) is similar in appearance and more difficult to transplant, but has strikingly beautiful scarlet fall color. Willow oak (*Q. phellos*; Zones 5 to 9; N: eastern United States) is so-called for its smaller, deep green, narrow, willowlike leaves that require less raking. It is a popular landscape tree with a compact, easily transplanted root system. Fastigiate English oak (*Q. robur* 'Fastigiata'; Zones 4 to 8; N: Europe) is narrowly columnar and makes a good substitute for Lombardy poplar. More adaptable to alkaline soil than other oaks.

Evergreen oaks are only hardy in warmer regions. They are long-lived, but grow more slowly and take longer to reach great size than the deciduous oaks. Live oak (*Q. virginiana*; Zones 8 to 10; N: southeastern United States) has deep green leaves and forms a massive rounded tree, broader than high. California live oak (*Q. agrifolia*; Zones 9 to 10) is a useful landscape plant in coastal California. It grows to 80 feet. Canyon live oak (*Q. chrysolepsis*; Zones 8 to 10; N: Oregon to southern California) is hardier and smaller, reaching only about 60 feet. The oaks native to the West Coast are adapted to a dry climate and will not survive repeated summer irrigation. Holm or holly oak (*Q. Ilex*) and cork oak (*Q. Suber*) are both evergreens native to southern Europe, hardy in Zones 8 to 10. They grow slowly to 60 feet. Holm oaks are large spreading, densely foliaged trees, good for coastal plantings. The thick bark of cork oak is the source of cork.

Cultural Information: Most oaks prefer a well-drained, acid soil. Pin oak will tolerate wet, poorly drained soils. Scarlet oak and the evergreen oaks from the West Coast and southern Europe are drought tolerant. Some oaks, notably pin oak, will develop chorosis (pale green leaves) when growing in an alkaline soil. Most will grow in shade when young, but all make the best specimens when in full sun. Many are difficult to transplant except as small trees because they have a deep tap root and a far-reaching root system. Willow, pin and red oaks, with short tap roots and fibrous root systems, are easier to transplant. Oaks can be troubled by many pests and diseases, but these are seldom serious.

Quercus alba

Quercus coccinea

Quince, Chinese; see ***Pseudocydonia***

Redbud, eastern; see ***Cercis canadensis***

Red cedars; see ***Juniperus***

Red maple; see ***Acer***

Red oak; see ***Quercus***

Red-vein maple; see ***Acer***

Redwood, coast; see ***Sequoia***

Redwood, dawn; see ***Metasequoia***

Redwood, giant; see ***Sequoiadendron***

Retinospora; see ***Chamaecyparis***

River birch; see ***Betula***

Robinia Pseudoacacia *'Frisia'*

Robinia Pseudoacacia

'Frisia' (row-BIN-ee-a SOO-doh-a-KAY-see-a free-SEE-a) **golden black locust,** Golden foliage, flowers, LSP ○

Zones: 3 to 8
Height: 40 feet
Foliage: Pinnately compound broad-leaved deciduous
Shape: Narrow upright, about ½ as wide as tall
Characteristics: Robinia pseudoacacia 'Frisia' originated in a nursery in Holland and is the only really garden-worthy form of this species (N: eastern United States). It has remarkable canary yellow foliage that maintains its color all summer. The best color will occur in climates with cool summers. Clusters of fragrant white flowers are borne at the ends of the branches. It has an annoying tendency to sprout from the roots all around the tree, often at some distance from the trunk. This is much more of a nuisance in the South than in the North. *R. P.* 'Frisia' is propagated by grafting, and the best-quality trees are grafted low, just above the roots.
Cultural Information: Adaptable to well-drained, acid or alkaline soil. As with other grafted trees, be sure to remove all sprouts from the roots. Stake young trees. Watch for borers and leaf miners. Borer susceptibility decreases when the bark has thickened, after about 10 years.

Salix alba 'Tristis'

Salix

(SAY-liks) **willow,** Foliage, fall color, colorful winter twigs ○

Zones: Variable
Height: 30 to 70 feet; 80 to 100 feet
Foliage: Simple broad-leaved deciduous
Shape: Weeping or globe, often as wide as tall
Characteristics: Willows are fast growing and weak wooded. They are also messy when planted along walkways because they tend to drop debris continuously. Willows are the quintessential trees for naturalistic, moist areas. They are so easy to grow that a small branch stuck into moist soil is likely to take root and grow. Golden weeping willow (*Salix alba* 'Tristis' or 'Niobe') is perhaps the most beautiful weeping tree, growing to about 60 feet. In winter, the golden branches are striking. Other cultivars of *S. alba* are grown for their upright habits and colorful twigs in winter. They should be cut back severely each spring (they grow 6 feet or more annually), to encourage strong, vigorous shoots, which have the best color. *S. a.* 'Britzensis' has red stems, whereas those of *S. a. vitellina* are yellow. *S. alba* is native to Europe and Asia, and is hardy in Zones 3 to 9. The dragon's claw or contorted willow (*S. Matsudana* 'Tortuosa'; Zones 4 to 8; N: China) is a rounded tree to 30 feet with crooked, twisted trunks and branches. Interesting at any season.
Cultural Information: Prefers deep, moist soils, either acid or alkaline. *S. Matsudana* grows in drier locations. Easy to transplant. Susceptible to a variety of pests and diseases, including various cankers, leaf spots, rust, mildew, aphids, caterpillars, scale and borers, but these are not serious problems in healthy, vigorous trees.

Sarvis-tree; see ***Amelanchier***

Saucer magnolia; see ***Magnolia***

Sawara false cypress; see ***Chamaecyparis***

Scarlet oak; see ***Quercus***

Sciadopitys verticillata

(sy-a-DOP-it-eez ver-ti-si-LAY-ta) **Japanese umbrella pine,** Evergreen foliage, bark, cones ○ ◐

Zones: 4 to 8
Height: 15 to 30 feet; 90 feet
Foliage: Long-needled evergreen
Shape: Pyramidal, about ⅔ as wide as tall
Characteristics: A slow-growing conifer with deep green, lustrous, wide needles. The reddish bark is often hidden by the dense foliage. Older trees bear thick-scaled cones, low enough on the tree to be interesting. Japanese umbrella pines are high-quality but expensive ornamentals. They deserve a special location where they can be enjoyed to their fullest. Native to Japan.
Cultural Information: Grows best in rich moist soil. Best with afternoon shade in hot climates. Pest and disease free.

Scotch pine; see ***Pinus***

Sequoia sempervirens

(se-KWOI-a sem-per-VY-renz) **coast redwood,** Evergreen foliage, bark ○ ◐

Zones: 7 to 9
Height: 60 feet; more than 300 feet
Foliage: Short-needled evergreen
Shape: Pyramidal, ⅓ to ½ as wide as tall
Characteristics: Native to coastal California and Oregon, this large conifer has deep green, glossy, flat needles. Reddish bark is attractive in older trees. This species is one of the tallest-growing trees in the world, reaching 370 feet and living for thousands of years. It is much smaller in the short life of a garden. Only the hardiest forms will grow in Zone 7.
Cultural Information: Grow in rich, moist, well-drained, acid soil. Does best where summers are cool and humid as in coastal California and Europe, but is satisfactory, though smaller, in the Southeast.

Sequoiadendron giganteum

(see-kwoy-a-DEN-dron jy-GAN-te-um) **giant redwood, Wellingtonia,** Evergreen foliage, bark ○ ◐

Zones: 6 to 8
Height: 60 to 100 feet; 275 feet
Foliage: Scalelike needled evergreen
Shape: Pyramidal, ⅓ as wide as tall
Characteristics: A conifer with fine-textured, sharp, scalelike needles, this tree is extraordinary because of its size. It is considered to be the most massive living thing. The reddish bark is curiously thick and spongy. It develops a thicker trunk than the coast redwood, but does not grow as high. The giant redwood may also live for thousands of years. *Sequoiadendron giganteum* 'Hazel Smith' is an especially attractive blue-foliaged cultivar that does well in the East. *S. g.* 'Pendulum' has branches that hang close to the crooked trunk, forming a tall, ghostly-looking tree. Native to California.
Cultural Information: Prefers deep, rich, well-drained soil. Attains the greatest size in western North America and Europe, but grows better than the coast redwood in the East and in areas with low humidity.

Serbian spruce; see ***Picea***

Serviceberry; see ***Amelanchier***

Service tree; see ***Amelanchier***

Sciadopitys verticillata

Shadbush; see ***Amelanchier***

Siberian elm; see ***Ulmus***

Silk tree, hardy; see ***Albizia***

Silver bells; see ***Halesia***

Small-leaved linden; see ***Tilia***

Snowbells; see ***Styrax***

Sequoia sempervirens

Sequoiadendron giganteum

Sophora japonica (so-FOR-ra ja-PON-i-ka) **Japanese pagoda tree,** Flowers, MSU ○ ▮▙

Zones: 4 to 8
Height: 50 to 70 feet; 70 feet
Foliage: Pinnately compound broad-leaved deciduous
Shape: Globe, about as wide as tall
Characteristics: The pagoda tree, native to China, is valued because it is the last large tree to bloom in summer. The creamy white pea-shaped flowers are followed by green pods that ripen to brown in fall. Leaf color is bright green, but no fall color develops. The tree has a desirable, compact rounded shape. *Sophora japonica* 'Princeton Upright' has a narrower upright habit, good for narrow street locations. *S. j.* 'Regent' is a fast-growing cultivar.
Cultural Information: Adaptable but prefers a light soil, either mildly acid or slightly alkaline. Tends to be susceptible to cold injury in northern areas when young, but settles down after a few years. Tolerant of city conditions. Prune in fall. Needs training as young tree to develop trunk and central leader.

Sorbus Aucuparia

Sorbus (SOR-bus) **mountain ash,** Flowers, fruit, fall color, SP ○ ▮▙

Zones: Variable
Height: 20 to 50 feet; 60 feet
Foliage: Simple or pinnately compound broad-leaved deciduous
Shape: Rounded pyramidal, about ½ as wide as high
Characteristics: The mountain ashes may have either simple or compound leaves, and white flowers in flat clusters. European mountain ash (*Sorbus Aucuparia*; Zones 3 to 6; N: Europe and Asia) is the species most often planted. The leaves are pinnately compound. It certainly has one of the most striking autumn fruit displays. The berries, borne in large clusters on the ends of branches, are normally orange-red, but cultivars and hybrids are available with pink, yellow and apricot fruit. Fall color varies from greenish yellow to reddish purple, depending on the cultivar and the climate. In undesirable climates, defoliation may occur before fall color develops. *S. Aucuparia* can only be recommended in northern climates with cool summers. It grows 20 to 40 feet. *S. rufoferruginea* 'Longwood Sunset' (Zones 4 to 7; N: Japan) resembles *S. Aucuparia* and has proven to be an excellent ornamental, despite the hot, humid summers at Longwood Gardens, near Philadelphia. It is heat tolerant, has good foliage through the summer, develops burgundy autumn color and bears beautiful crops of orange fruit that persist into late fall. Korean mountain ash (*S. alnifolia;* Zones 3 to 7; N: eastern Asia) looks very different from the familiar mountain

Sophora japonica

Sorbus alnifolia

ashes. It has simple leaves and a broader shape, becoming as broad as high. The flower clusters are smaller but more profuse, and are followed by small reddish fruit, although the fruit is not abundant in warmer climates. Fall color is yellow and orange. Grows 40 to 50 feet.
Cultural Information: Mountain ashes are northern and high-altitude trees; they resent high summer temperatures, which stress the tree and increase susceptibility to pests and diseases. Prevention of pest and disease problems includes watering in dry spells, and mulching to keep the soil cool. The soil should be well drained and acid. Pests and diseases include fire blight, canker, borers, mites, scab, scale and aphids. In stressful situations, trees usually fall prey to canker and borer after a few years.

Sorrel tree; see ***Oxydendrum***

Sour gum; see ***Nyssa***

Sourwood; see ***Oxydendrum***

Southern catalpa; see ***Catalpa***

Southern magnolia; see ***Magnolia***

Spruces; see ***Picea***

Star magnolia; see ***Magnolia***

Stewartia (stew-AR-tee-a) **stewartia,** Flowers, fall color, bark, LSP-ESU ○ ◐ ▙
Zones: 5 to 7
Height: 20 to 40 feet; 45 to 60 feet
Foliage: Simple broad-leaved deciduous
Shape: Pyramidal, about ½ as wide as tall
Characteristics: The stewartias hold an honored place among small flowering trees. The showy white flowers with golden stamens resemble those of the Franklin tree and camellia. When they fall intact, they carpet the ground with perfectly formed blooms. The bark, mottled with gray, brown and orange, is a yearround feature. Perhaps the Korean stewartia (*S. koreana*) is the most beautiful species, with wide open flowers and yellow and orange fall color. Its small size, to about 20 feet, is ideal for small gardens. The Japanese stewartia (*S. Pseudocamellia*) is very similar but generally grows to 40 feet or more, with more purplish fall color, and cup-shaped flowers.
Cultural Information: Plant in a rich, moist, well-drained, acid soil. Likes to be shaded from hot afternoon sun. A naturally well-shaped tree requiring little pruning, and bothered by few problems.

Stewartia Pseudocamellia

Stone pines; see ***Pinus***

Striped-bark maple; see ***Acer***

Styrax (STY-raks) **snowbell,** Flowers, MSP ○ ◐ ▙
Zones: 5 to 8
Height: 20 to 30 feet; 50 feet
Foliage: Simple broad-leaved deciduous
Shape: Spreading globe, sometimes wider than high
Characteristics: The snowbells are small, spreading trees with fragrant, nodding, usually white flowers. They are fast growing when young and have clean foliage. Japanese snowbell (*Styrax japonicus*; N: Japan and China) has small leaves and slightly fragrant flowers that hang under the branches. The fragrant snowbell (*S. Obassia*; N: Japan) is a much coarser landscape plant with large leaves and more strongly fragrant flowers in dropping clusters at the ends of the branches.
Cultural Information: Plant in rich, acid, well-drained soil. Not very drought tolerant. Locate in light shade in hot climates. Virtually pest and disease free.

Styrax Obassia

Styrax Obassia *(detail of flower)*

Sugar maple; see ***Acer***

Swamp magnolia; see ***Magnolia***

Sweet cherry, double; see ***Prunus***

Sweet gum; see ***Liquidambar***

Swiss stone pine; see ***Pinus***

Tatarian maple; see ***Acer***

Taxodium distichum

(taks-O-dee-um DIS-tee-kum) **bald cypress,** Foliage, fall color ○ ◐

Zones: 4 to 9
Height: 70 feet; more than 150 feet
Foliage: Short-needled deciduous
Shape: Narrowly pyramidal, about 1/4 as wide as tall
Characteristics: This is the tree of the cypress swamps in the southeastern United States (where it is native). In the wild, they grow in very wet soils where their roots are submerged and the trees often form woody projections from their roots called "cypress knees." In gardens, these knees will form only on old trees planted in wet soil. Bald cypress is similar to dawn redwood, but grows into a narrower, more round-topped tree. With age, it develops more spreading, widely branched crowns. Foliage is soft and feathery, with the short needles arranged along short deciduous twigs. Summer foliage color is light green, becoming rusty orange-brown in fall. A stately and magnificent deciduous conifer.
Cultural Information: Prefers sandy, acid conditions but is adaptable to a wide range of soils—wet, dry, well drained or waterlogged. Young specimens are easy to transplant. Seldom seriously bothered by pests and diseases, although bagworms can be very destructive.

Taxodium distichum

Thread-leaf cypresses; see ***Chamaecyparis***

Thuja

(THEW-ya) **arborvitae,** Evergreen foliage ○ ◐

Zones: Variable
Height: 40 to 70 feet; 200 feet
Foliage: Scalelike needled evergreen
Shape: Fastigiate to pyramidal, about 1/3 as wide as tall
Characteristics: Arborvitaes are useful landscape conifers with soft, fanlike foliage. The eastern arborvitae or white cedar (*Thuja occidentalis*; Zones 2 to 8) is native to eastern North America. It is usually a small, narrow tree to 40 feet, and often used for screens and hedges. Many forms have light green foliage and turn a sickly yellow-green during the winter. These should be avoided in favor of deep green cultivars, such as *T. o.* 'Nigra' and *T. o.* 'Emerald' ('Smaragd'), that hold their color all year long. They also have a tendency to form multiple trunks or double leaders subject to breakage and splitting under snow and ice. Avoid buying multiple-trunked trees. The western arborvitae (*T. plicata*; Zones 5 to 7) is a more massive pyramidal tree from the Pacific Northwest. *T. p.* 'Atrovirens' is an especially fine cultivar that retains its deep green color and makes a shapely specimen. In gardens, it reaches 50 to 70 feet.
Cultural Information: Grows best in rich, moist, well-drained, acid soil, but will tolerate poor drainage. Easily transplanted. Bothered by few pests and diseases, but watch for bagworms and mites, particularly in hot, dry locations.

Thuja occidentalis *'Emerald'*

Tilia cordata (TIL-ee-a kor-DAY-ta) **small-leaved linden,** Summer foliage, fragrant flowers, LSP-ESU ○ ▙
Zones: 3 to 7
Height: 60 to 70 feet; 90 feet
Foliage: Simple broad-leaved deciduous
Shape: Pyramidal to globe, about ⅔ as wide as tall
Characteristics: A shapely, medium- to large-size tree with clean, deep green foliage. The yellowish flowers are not showy, but are noticeably fragrant. *Tilia cordata* 'Greenspire' is an especially popular cultivar for its neat, pointed, single-leader habit. Native to Europe.
Cultural Information: An excellent street and city tree that tolerates pollution and a variety of soils. Easily transplanted. Aphids can be a problem because of the honeydew they produce in spring. Japanese beetles can also be a problem.

Tilia cordata

Tsuga canadensis

Tsuga (SOO-ga) **hemlock,** Evergreen foliage ○ ◐ ● ▙
Zones: Variable
Height: 70 feet; 100 to 200 feet
Foliage: Short-needled evergreen
Shape: Pyramidal, about ½ as wide as tall
Characteristics: Hemlocks are widely used landscape plants, particularly useful because they will grow in more shade than any other evergreen conifer. They are widely used for hedges and screening, and as specimen trees. They take clipping very well. Canadian hemlock (*Tsuga canadensis*; Zones 3 to 7) is the most widely used, especially in eastern North America, where it is native. The western hemlock (*T. heterophylla*; Zones 6 to 7) becomes a massive tree to 200 feet in its native habitat along the Pacific coast. It is grown only in the Pacific Northwest where summers are cool.
Cultural Information: Requires a well-drained, moist, acid soil. Avoid hot, dry, windy locations. Best growth occurs in sun or light shade. Easily transplanted. Many pests and diseases may be found on hemlocks, but the worst are scale and woolly adelgid. They can weaken and kill trees in some areas of the Mid-Atlantic states and New England where they are prevalent. Control them with dormant oil spray.

Tulip poplar; see ***Liriodendron***

Tulip tree; see ***Liriodendron***

Turkish filbert; see ***Corylus Colurna***

Turkish hazel; see ***Corylus Colurna***

Tupelo, black; see ***Nyssa***

Ulmus (UL-mus) **elm,** Summer foliage, fall color, bark ○ ▮ ▮

Zones: Variable
Height: 60 feet; 70 to 80 feet
Foliage: Simple broad-leaved deciduous
Shape: Spreading vase, may become as wide as high
Characteristics: The American elm (*Ulmus americana*; Zones 2 to 9; N: eastern and central North America) was one of our best-loved shade and street trees. Its upright, gracefully vase-shaped, spreading habit, to 80 feet tall, dwarfed everything else and provided high shade. The introduction of Dutch elm disease has killed almost all of them, and they are no longer planted. Research and hybridization with other resistant species is ongoing to find resistant trees with the classical elm shape. *U. a.* 'Liberty' was developed by the Elm Research Institute; it is claimed that this cultivar has high resistance to the disease. The lacebark or Chinese elm (*U. parvifolia*; Zones 4 to 9) is very resistant to the disease and is an excellent ornamental tree. It is usually more spreading than American elm and only grows to about 50 feet. The mottled bark is one of its best features, a mixture of gray, green, brown and orange-brown. Its adaptability and beauty make it an excellent landscape tree. It is native to China, Korea and Japan. The lacebark elm should not be confused with the Siberian elm (*U. pumila*; Zones 4 to 9), which is an inferior, messy and weak-wooded tree.
Cultural Information: Adaptable to wet or dry, acid or alkaline soils. Easily transplanted. The only serious pest is Dutch elm disease, which has effectively eliminated the American elm and several other species from the American landscape. Lacebark elm is highly resistant to the disease.

Ulmus parvifolia

Umbrella pine; see ***Pinus***

Umbrella pine, Japanese; see ***Sciadopitys***

Weeping beech; see ***Fagus***

Weeping nootka false cypress; see ***Chamaecyparis***

Weeping willow, golden; see ***Salix***

Weeping willow-leaved pear; see ***Pyrus***

Wellingtonia; see ***Sequoiadendron***

Western arborvitae; see ***Thuja***

Western hemlock; see ***Tsuga***

Western red cedar; see ***Juniperus***

White ash; see ***Fraxinus***

White cedar; see ***Thuja***

White fir; see ***Abies***

White oak; see ***Quercus***

White pine, eastern; see ***Pinus***

White spruce; see ***Picea***

Willows; see ***Salix***

Willow-leaved pear, weeping; see ***Pyrus***

Willow oak; see ***Quercus***

Winter king hawthorn; see ***Crataegus***

Yellowwood; see ***Cladrastis***

Yoshino cherry; see ***Prunus***

Zelkova serrata (zel-KOH-va ser-RA-ta) **Japanese zelkova,** Summer foliage, fall color, bark
○ ◐ ■ ■
Zones: 5 to 8
Height: 60 to 80 feet; 120 feet
Foliage: Simple broad-leaved deciduous
Shape: Spreading vase, as wide as high
Characteristics: Closely related to the elm, zelkova is becoming increasingly popular as a landscape, street, and shade tree. It is often recommended as a substitute for the American elm, but it does not have quite the same grand, high-arching branches. Although its vase shape is somewhat more stiff, the mottled bark and deep green foliage are very handsome. Fall foliage is yellowish brown to reddish purple. *Zelkova serrata* 'Green Vase' is a tall, fast-growing, upright selection. *Z. s.* 'Village Green' is a hardier, fast-growing cultivar with a more spreading habit and richer red fall color. Native to Japan and Korea.
Cultural Information: Adapted to acid or alkaline soils. Drought and wind resistant when established, but grows best in deep, moist soils. Tolerates city conditions. Highly resistant to Dutch elm disease and other problems that trouble elms.

Zelkova serrata *'Village Green'*

5

PESTS AND DISEASES

Every landscape is host to pest and disease organisms, but they are usually not serious. Other organisms prey on them and control these problems naturally. This interaction creates a natural balance, something that is important to preserve as much as possible. Resistance of trees to pests and diseases is important in controlling problems naturally, but even resistant trees may become susceptible to attack when they are stressed and weakened by unsuitable conditions. A tree that is not adapted to its location will always have problems. Drought, soil compaction, poor nutrition, pollution, shade in excess of a species's adaptation and hard winters are just a few factors that contribute to poor health. When new diseases or pests are introduced to an area, they can attack trees that have no natural resistance and had previously been free of serious problems. Examples of such introductions are the gypsy moth, Dutch elm disease and the chestnut blight.

It is important to decide when a pest or disease is truly a problem. A few caterpillars can do little damage on their own, and even provide food for wildlife or become beautiful butterflies. A single spot on a leaf is not going to mar the ornamental value of a tree; but when a leaf disease defoliates a whole tree in midsummer, it is a serious problem, at least from the aesthetic standpoint. Take crabapples, for example: Resistant varieties keep their foliage and fruit to maturity with only insignificant infection. Susceptible varieties, however, are often defoliated or their fruit is severely damaged. Even so, the health of the tree may not be seriously harmed, but it can become an eyesore in the landscape. Tulip trees and lindens are susceptible to aphid attacks for a short period in spring when the new foliage is soft. Aphids secrete a sticky substance called honeydew that falls to the ground in tiny droplets, coating surfaces below, and becoming a nuisance on parked cars and patio furniture. The severity of the attack will vary from year to year. Healthy trees don't require control measures because they are not harmed by aphids, but people find them inconvenient. The best solution is not to plant susceptible trees where the honeydew will be a problem. Simply selecting a different species of linden can be a solution, because some kinds are resistant to aphids.

Once the most common shade tree in much of the eastern United States, the American elm, Ulmus americana, *has now been virtually wiped out of the landscape by Dutch elm disease.*

CONTROLLING PESTS AND DISEASES

When a problem starts, take care of it before it gets big. Pick off obvious insects such as caterpillars and bagworms. Wash off aphids and mites with a forceful stream of water—they soon die when deprived of food. Often these measures are enough to prevent an epidemic.

Disease problems can be reduced by avoiding conditions that favor infection, and by sanitation. Most disease spores need wet foliage to germinate and infect plants. Do any watering that will wet foliage early enough for it to dry before nightfall. Good air movement will help dry foliage, and reduce disease generally. Pruning can increase air circulation. Clean up diseased foliage and don't put it in your compost. An infected branch, as in the case of fire blight, should be pruned off before it spreads down into the whole tree.

Chemical pesticides pose problems because they are also toxic to beneficial insects and people. When using them, there is a risk to yourself, your family and friends from the residues. They upset the natural balance of the environment, and can actually perpetuate or create problems by killing the other organisms that work to control your pests. Also, pests and bacteria can build up immunity to chemical controls, making them ineffective and creating a need for stronger chemicals. There are a few environmentally friendly pesticides that are safe for the homeowner to use. Insecticidal soap and horticultural light oil kill only those insects and mites that they touch, with no toxic residue. They are very effective against a wide range of pests, too. Dormant oil sprays are an especially effective way to kill scale insects and eggs of mites; they are sprayed on the trunks and branches when the plants are dormant, and smother the pests by clogging their pores.

Biological pest control methods are becoming more available and are preferred because they are effective without disrupting the natural balance in your garden and in the environment as a whole. The most successful biological control to date is the bacterial disease of caterpillars called *Bacillus thuringiensis* (BT). Caterpillars and some worms are the only organisms that can be infected by this disease. It comes as a powder that you mix with water and spray on the leaves of plants that the caterpillars are eating. It is widely used to control gypsy moths and tent caterpillars. Experience with gypsy moths has shown that BT is the best long-term control. Conventional chemical insecticides also kill the predators of gypsy moth, a situation that perpetuates the epidemic. BT kills only the caterpillars, leaving plenty of predators to carry on the battle against any remaining gypsy moths, and their offspring, in future years. BT can, therefore, be instrumental in creating a balance of predators and hosts.

You can also purchase lady bugs and other predatory insects (usually through the mail) from garden product firms such as Burpee to release in your garden. These controls are less useful for large trees because of the number of predators required. The best overall strategy for controlling pests and diseases is integrated pest management. It simply means that you take a multifaceted approach. Keep your plants healthy and clean. Maintain the natural predator population by not using sprays and poisons indiscriminately. When you encounter a problem, assess whether it is really serious before you act and, when necessary, use the least disruptive control methods. Check the following individual pests and diseases to see which controls are appropriate for your problems.

Ladybug

METHODS OF CONTROL:
1. Crush pests with fingers or pick off.
2. Wash off with forceful spray of water.
3. Apply *Bacillus thuringiensis* (Bt) to foliage.
4. Spray with insecticidal soap.
5. Spray with light horticultural summer oil.
6. Spray with dormant oil in early spring.
7. Plant resistant varieties.
8. Poke wires into holes in trunk to kill borers.
9. Remove infected parts; for example, pick off leaves or prune branches.
10. Maintain sanitary conditions; rake up and dispose of infected leaves.
11. Catch pests in traps.
12. Fertilize to increase tree vigor.
13. Keep foliage as dry as possible; water only early in day so foliage can dry before nightfall.
14. Increase air circulation by thinning surrounding foliage.
15. Eliminate either of the alternate hosts to fungus disease to break the life cycle of the fungus.
16. Don't plant the same kind of tree or a related kind in the same place where the infected tree was growing.
17. Prune out infected branches below signs of disease where wood is unstained; sterilize pruning equipment in 10% solution of chlorine bleach (1 part household bleach to 9 parts water) after each cut.
18. Spray with neem (Trade name: Margosan).

COMMON PESTS OF TREES

APHIDS: Small green, reddish, white, clear or black insects clustered along soft stems and on undersides of leaves that are often distorted and curled. Usually affect trees only in spring. Secrete honeydew in which grows black sooty mold, harmless to the tree but unsightly. Controls: 1, 2, 4, 5 and 18.

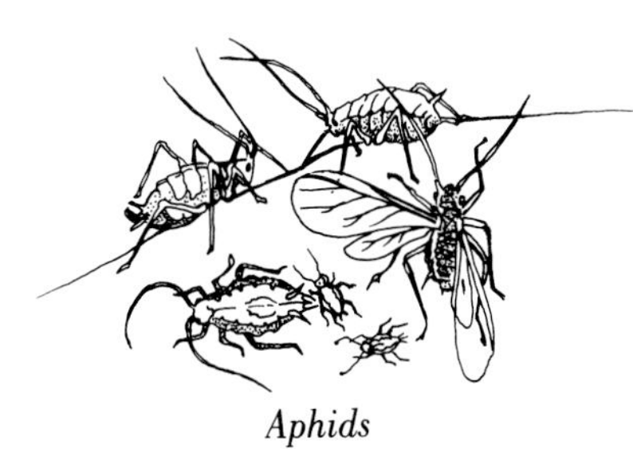

Aphids

MITES: Tiny and difficult to see, they are related to the spider. Often make tiny webs. Leaves become speckled as feeding destroys chlorophyll, then drop off. Common in hot weather. Controls: 2, 4, 5, and 6.

Red spider mite

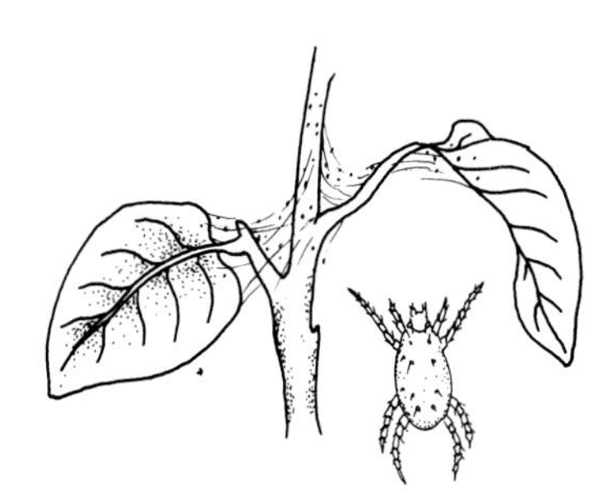

Spider mite

BORERS: Larvae burrow under bark or into trunk and branches. Branches die back. Sawdust evident around holes. Controls: 7, 8 and 9.

LEAF MINERS: Larvae tunnel through leaf, creating visible channels, destroying color and causing defoliation. Controls: 7, 9, 10 and 18.

SCALE: Flat platelike or rounded immobile scales along trunk, branches or on leaves that suck sap and produce honeydew. Crawler stage during growing season is susceptible to controls 4 and 5 if correctly timed, but control 6 is the standard method. Controls: 1, 4, 5, 6, 9 and 18.

CATERPILLARS: Larvae of moths and butterflies that eat leaves. Not serious in small numbers. Many colors, sizes and markings. Tent caterpillars occur in large groups; they build silk tents in tree crotches for protection. Gypsy moths can defoliate whole trees with their great numbers but are not always serious if predators are active. Sawfly larvae eat needles on pine trees. Controls: 1, 3 and 18.

BAGWORMS: Cocoons hang from ends of branches from which they emerge to feed. They colonize and defoliate conifers, killing the tree. Easy to spot, but often mistaken for cones. Controls: 1, 3 and 18.

JAPANESE BEETLES: Shiny beetles with metallic green sheen eat foliage and flowers of wide

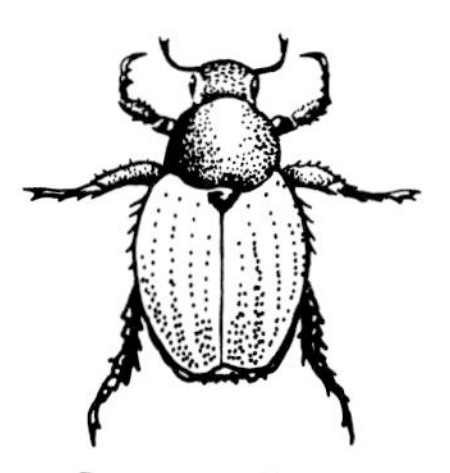

Japanese beetle

range of plants during midsummer. Larvae live in lawns and eat grass roots. Controls: 1, 11 and 18.

MICE AND VOLES: These rodents strip bark and girdle young trees below the snowline or under mulch. Protect with wire or plastic guards specially manufactured for this problem.

RABBITS: Only small trees are in danger from rabbits, which can eat young shoots. They have also been known to strip bark off trunks as high as they can reach when snow covers food supply. Best protection is wire mesh around young plants and around susceptible parts of trunks. Remove or replace wire before it strangles trunk.

DEER: Low branches of trees can be seriously damaged by browsing deer, particularly where deer are overpopulated. Protect by fencing around young trees as high as the deer can reach. Large trees are safe from damage because their branches are out of reach.

Leaves damaged by the following pests, from left; beetles, flea beetles, caterpillars, aphids and leafhoppers.

COMMON TREE DISEASES

ANTHRACNOSE: Particularly serious on sycamore during a wet spring. Trees may be defoliated, but soon grow a new set of foliage. If not defoliated every year, a healthy tree will not be seriously harmed. Controls: 7, 10, 12, 13 and 14.

POWDERY MILDEW: Common on a wide variety of trees and identified by a grayish or whitish coating on the surface of leaves, stems and flower buds. May cause distortion and defoliation. Unless serious, many trees can tolerate moderate infection. Controls: 7, 13 and 14.

CEDAR-APPLE RUST: A fungus disease that alternates in generations between red cedar (juniper) one year and apples, crabapples and hawthorns the next. Cedars develop small round galls among the foliage that produce spores in wet spring weather. A serious infection may cause defoliation on crabapples and hawthorns. Controls: 13, 14 and 15.

FIRE BLIGHT: A bacterial disease that infects crabapples, pears, hawthorns and mountain ashes. Infected branches die back, turning black as if burned. It is spread mostly by bees when pollinating flowers, but also by contaminated pruning equipment. Controls: 7, 9 and 17.

ROOT ROT: Many kinds of fungus can cause root rot in many different trees. Indentification of these requires a specialist. Poor drainage and soil compaction, which weaken a tree, often are contributing factors. Some disease-causing fungi can remain in the soil for many years. Controls: 7 and 16.

SCAB: This fungus infects the fruit and leaves of crabapples, mountain ashes and hawthorns and may cause defoliation. Controls: 7, 10, 13 and 14.

LEAF SPOTS: Many kinds of fungi cause leaf spots on a wide variety of trees. Most trees are only mildly affected and will not be disfigured. Controls: 7, 10, 13 and 14.

DIPLODIA BLIGHT: Die back, beginning with lower branches and working upward on black and Scotch pines. Control: 7.

WILTS: Sudden wilting of a branch or a section of a tree usually indicates the presence of an internal fungus that has cut off sap to the area. Many fungi may cause similar symptoms. Controls: 7 and 16.

DUTCH ELM DISEASE: A serious disease affecting some species of elm, including American elm. Fungus clogs vascular system and inhibits tree's ability to supply water to leaves. Primarily spread by bark beetles. Remove any dead elm trees and infected branches in tree. Controls: 7, 12 and 17.

6

GARDENERS' MOST-ASKED QUESTIONS

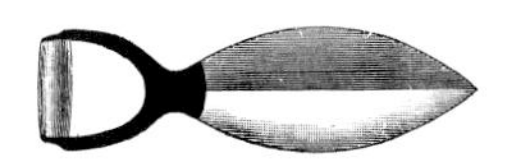

Q: Which flowering trees will bloom in the shade? Which can be used effectively as an understory?
A: Many small flowering trees will grow and bloom well in light shade under tall trees. These include redbuds, dogwood, dove trees, Franklin trees, silver bells, snowbell, stewartias and magnolias. Low branches of large trees that crowd flowering trees beneath should be removed to allow enough light for good bloom.

Q: Which flowering trees make good shade trees?
A: Trees with high spreading branches make the best shade trees. For neatness, they should also drop a minimum of leaves, flowers and fruit through the growing season. Such flowering trees include Japanese pagoda tree, Korean mountain ash and mountain silver bell.

Q: How long does it take for a newly planted flowering tree to flower?
A: This depends on the kind of tree and how it was propagated. Small-growing varieties often flower at a younger age. Most flowering trees are grown from cuttings or by grafting, and usually flower at a younger age than those grown from seed. These trees should flower within two or three years of planting in your yard. Some will flower the first year.

Q: Which trees have the best fall color?
A: Black gums, katsura trees, parrotias and many maples have brilliant red and yellow autumn color. Birches, yellowwoods and ginkgos turn yellow.

Q: Which flowering trees bloom before they produce leaves?
A: Such early flowering trees as Cornelian cherry, flowering dogwood (*Cornus florida*), star and saucer magnolias, callery pear, redbud and many flowering cherries bloom before any leaves have emerged. Crabapples bloom while the leaves are still very small.

Q: Which flowering trees bloom with most tulips? Which with daffodils?
A: The most popular tulips are the Darwin hybrids and the May-flowering varieties such as the single and double lates and lily-flowered types. These bloom along with the redbud, flowering dogwood, horse chestnut and many crabapple varieties. Earlier tulips bloom with daffodils and such trees as saucer magnolia, Japanese flowering cherry and callery pear.

Q: Which bulbs can be planted under flowering trees?

Burpee employees filling orders, 1911.

A: Most spring bulbs need to be planted under deciduous trees, rather than evergreens, so they will receive the early spring sun. Such early blooming bulbs as snowdrops, Siberian squills, and daffodils will grow best. Later-blooming wood hyacinths and camasias will also thrive. They will all last for many years. Tulips usually require more sun and less root competition for best performance and will not last as many years in the garden.

Q: Which flowering trees have four seasons of interest?
A: The following trees are of exceptional interest in the landscape at all four seasons because of a combination of characteristics such as spring or summer flowers, attractive summer foliage, fall color, and fruit, foliage or interesting bark during the winter: crabapple, winter king hawthorn, Chinese quince, Japanese and paperbark maples, sorrel tree, parrotia, mountain ash, stewartia and southern magnolia.

Q: Can I prune flowering trees at any time of the year? Which trees should be pruned when dormant? Which after they bloom?
A: Flowering trees should be pruned only at the proper time or flower buds will be removed, with a decrease in bloom. Spring-flowering trees should be pruned immediately after they flower. Summer-flowering trees can be pruned in the winter or early spring before growth begins.

Q: Do newly planted trees need to be pruned back 1/3 when they are planted:
A: When dormant bareroot trees are planted, new growth will usually be in proportion to the roots, which will begin growing before the top does. Some studies indicate that leaving the terminal buds of the shoots in place actually stimulates faster root growth than when they are removed. Balance the roots and the top by pruning to shape the young tree in other ways, such as removing crowded branches and leaving well-spaced branches with wide crotches, which will form the main trunk and branches. Container-grown trees and balled-and-burlapped trees require even less pruning.

Q: Does pruning improve blooming?
A: When done properly, pruning can improve blooming, but if done incorrectly, it can drastically reduce bloom production. Most trees do not require regular pruning except to correct shape, such as removing crossing branches or preventing narrow crotches from forming. In fact, careless pruning can encourage undesirable suckers and water sprouts. Old trees sometimes form many crowded weak branches that bloom poorly. Thinning these can encourage renewed vigor. Consult a specialized book on pruning for techniques for specific kinds of trees.

Q: Which ornamental trees are the hardiest?
A: Consult the Plant Portraits and The USDA Plant Hardiness Map (page 92) to determine which trees will grow in the coldest climates. Some of the spruces, firs and junipers, as well as eastern arborvitaes, are the hardiest evergreens. The hardiest deciduous trees include maples, larches, crabapples and cherries.

Q: Which trees can be espaliered?
A: Many trees are suitable for training as espaliers, if they are pruned regularly. Those with moderate growth rates are easiest. Some of the easiest to train are crabapples and junipers.

Q: What is the maximum height a tree can be for it to be moved safely? When and how should this be done?
A: The only safe time to move most trees is when they are dormant. Most trees can be moved in the fall, winter or spring, but a few, such as those that are not fully hardy, should be moved only in early spring. If properly done, even very large trees can be successfully moved, but the homeowner is limited by the size of the root ball and soil that can be lifted. Generally, trees under 6 to 8 feet transplant most successfully because they have the vigor to reestablish more rapidly.

Q: Do dogwood really prefer partial shade to full sun? Do they bloom as well in the shade?
A: Dogwood grow best in light shade along the edge of a woods or among tall trees, where they bloom prolifically. Although they will grow in full sun and perhaps bloom even more, they require more water to overcome

the additional heat and drought stress.

Q: What should I do if I see suckers coming from the ground on my cherry trees? Are they from a different tree? Will they develop into trees themselves? Can they replace the main trunk if it dies?

A: Many trees, particularly cherries and crabapples, are propagated by grafting onto a different kind of rootstock. The suckers from below the ground are probably coming from this rootstock. They will be inferior to the rest of the tree and may even grow more strongly and crowd out the more desirable top. They will not provide a suitable replacement for the original trunk. The suckers should be cut to the ground as soon as possible, while still small. Fewer suckers will reoccur if they are cut as close to their origin below ground as possible.

Q: How can I control aphids on my trees when I can't reach the branches to spray them?

A: Aphids are usually more of a concern and inconvenience to homeowners than they are a threat to the health of their trees. Most trees are only susceptible to large aphid populations in the spring when shoots are young and soft. Aphids soon disappear naturally, without damage to healthy trees. Young trees are most easily damaged by aphids and are also most easily treated by the homeowner. If large trees require control, a professional arborist should be consulted.

*Q: Why are the dogwood in my neighborhood dying? Are the newer types of dogwood (*Cornus florida*) stronger and more resistant?*

A: In recent years, the flowering dogwood have been attacked by a fungus disease called anthracnose. Several other stresses, such as drought, add to the problem and gradually weaken and kill the trees, branch by branch. There is no single remedy, but keeping your dogwood healthy by fertilizing and watering them in dry spells helps the trees to resist the disease. Also provide good air circulation by planting them in locations where they have plenty of space and trimming away low branches of other nearby trees. The Chinese dogwood is very resistant to anthracnose in most situations. New hybrids between flowering and Chinese dogwood from Rutgers University are also very resistant.

Q: How can I prevent "lawn mower blight" on my dogwood? Do tree guards work? Do I need them for a mature tree?

A: Many dogwood, young and old, die from injuries to the base of the trunk that allow entry to disease organisms. The trunk is gradually girdled by this infection, which leads to the death of the tree. Lawn mowers bumping and bruising the bark are the most common cause of such injury. The best solution is to create an area free of grass around the base of the tree, with mulch or a groundcover, to eliminate the need to mow close to the trunk. Enclosing the trunks in tree guards is unsightly and not recommended because it may encourage attacks by borers.

Q: How can I prevent or treat fire blight on my ornamental pear tree?

A: Fire blight is most serious in climates with very hot summers. In such climates, it is best not to grow extremely susceptible varieties. Control minor infections by removing blackened infected branches as soon as noticed to prevent the bacteria from moving down the trunk. Prune 12 to 18 inches below any signs of infection and sterilize tools as described on page 81. Avoid heavy fertilization with nitrogen, because the resulting growth is most susceptible to infection. Some varieties of callery pear, such as *Pyrus Calleryana* 'Bradford' are resistant to fire blight.

Please write or call for a free Burpee catalog:

W. Atlee Burpee & Company
300 Park Avenue
Warminster, PA 18974
215-674-9633

APPENDICES

TREES FOR SPECIAL PURPOSES

USUALLY LESS THAN 40 FEET TALL IN LANDSCAPES

Abies koreana
Acer
  A. campestre
  A. ginnala
  A. palmatum
  A. pensylvanicum
  A. rufinerve
  A. tataricum
Albizia Julibrissin
Amelanchier arborea
Carpinus Betulus 'Fastigiata'
Catalpa bignonioides
Cercis canadensis
Chionanthus species
Cladrastis lutea
Cornus species
Crataegus species
Cupressus species
Davidia involucrata
Franklinia Alatamaha
Halesia carolina
Ilex species
Juniperus
  J. chinensis
  J. scopulorum
Koelreuteria paniculata
Laburnum × *Watereri*
Magnolia species
Malus species
Oxydendrum arboreum
Parrotia persica
Pinus
  P. Bungeana
  P. Cembra
  P. koraiensis
  P. muricata
  P. Thunbergiana
Prunus species
Pseudocydonia sinensis
Pyrus species
Robinia Pseudoacacia 'Frisia'
Sciadopitys verticillata
Sorbus
  S. Aucuparia
  S. rufoferruginea
   'Longwood Sunset'
Stewartia species
Styrax species
Thuja occidentalis

MORE THAN 40 FEET TALL

Abies
  A. concolor
  A. homolepsis
Acer
  A. platanoides
  A. rubrum
  A. saccharum
Aesculus Hippocastanum
Araucaria araucana
Betula
  B. nigra 'Heritage'
  B. platyphylla japonica
   'White Spire'
Calocedrus decurrens
Catalpa speciosa
Cedrus species
Cercidiphyllum japonicum
Chamaecyparis species
Corylus Colurna
Cryptomeria japonica
Cunninghamia lanceolata
× *Cupressocyparis Leylandii*
Fagus species
Fraxinus species
Ginkgo biloba
Gleditsia triacanthos
Halesia monticola
Idesia polycarpa
Juniperus virginiana
Larix species
Liquidambar Styraciflua
Liriodendron Tulipifera
Magnolia species
Metasequoia glyptostroboides
Nyssa sylvatica
Picea species
Pinus
  P. canariensis
  P. halapensis
  P. nigra
  P. pinea
  P. Strobus
  P. sylvestris
  P. Taeda
  P. Wallichiana

Platanus ×*acerifolia*
Populus species
Pseudolarix Kaempferi
Pseudotsuga Menziesii
Quercus species
Salix species
Sequoia sempervirens
Sequoiadendron giganteum
Sophora japonica
Sorbus alnifolia
Taxodium distichum
Thuja plicata
Tilia cordata
Tsuga species
Ulmus species
Zelkova serrata

WET LOCATIONS

Acer rubrum
Magnolia virginiana
Nyssa sylvatica
Picea glauca
Quercus palustris
Salix species
Taxodium distichum
Thuja occidentalis

TOLERANT OF SUMMER DROUGHT

Calocedrus decurrens
Catalpa species
Cedrus species
Corylus Colurna
Cupressus species
Fraxinus pennsylvanica
Gleditsia triacanthos
Juniperus species
Koelreuteria paniculata
Oxydendrum arboreum
Pinus
- *P. canariensis*
- *P. halapensis*
- *P. muricata*
- *P. nigra*
- *P. pinea*
- *P. sylvestris*
- *P. Thunbergiana*

Pyrus Calleryana
Quercus
- *Q. agrifolia*
- *Q. chrysolepsis*
- *Q. coccinea*
- *Q. Ilex*
- *Q. Suber*

Robinia Pseudoacacia 'Frisia'
Salix Matsudana 'Tortuosa'
Sequoiadendron giganteum
Zelkova serrata

EVERGREEN CONIFERS

Abies
- *A. concolor*
- *A. homolepsis*
- *A. koreana*

Araucaria araucana
Calocedrus decurrens
Cedrus species
Chamaecyparis species
Cryptomeria japonica
Cunninghamia lanceolata
×*Cupressocyparis Leylandii*
Cupressus species
Juniperus species
Picea species
Pinus species
Pseudotsuga Menziesii
Sciadopitys verticillata
Sequoia sempervirens
Sequoiadendron giganteum
Thuja species
Tsuga species

DECIDUOUS CONIFERS

Larix species
Metasequoia glyptostroboides
Pseudolarix Kaempferi
Taxodium distichum

EVERGREEN BROAD-LEAVED

Ilex species
Magnolia grandiflora
Prunus lusitanica
Quercus
- *Q. agrifolia*
- *Q. chrysolepsis*
- *Q. Ilex*
- *Q. Suber*
- *Q. virginiana*

SPRING FLOWERING

Aesculus Hippocastanum
Amelanchier arborea
Cercis canadensis
Chionanthus species
Cladrastis lutea
Cornus species
Corylus Colurna
Crataegus species
Davidia involucrata
Halesia species
Idesia polycarpa
Laburnum ×*Watereri*
Liriodendron Tulipifera
Magnolia species
Malus species
Parrotia persica
Prunus species
Pseudocydonia sinensis
Pyrus species
Robinia Pseudoacacia 'Frisia'
Sorbus species
Styrax species

SUMMER FLOWERING

Albizia Julibrissin
Catalpa species
Franklinia Alatamaha
Koelreuteria paniculata
Magnolia grandiflora
Oxydendrum arboreum
Sophora japonica
Stewartia species

DECORATIVE FRUIT

Amelanchier arborea
Crataegus viridis 'Winter King'
Idesia polycarpa
Ilex species
Koelreuteria paniculata
Magnolia species
Malus species

Oxydendrum arboreum
Pseudocydonia sinensis
Sorbus species

PARTICULARLY ATTRACTIVE BARK

Acer
 A. griseum
 A. palmatum 'Senkaki'
 A. pensylvanicum
 A. rufinerve
Betula
 B. nigra 'Heritage'
 B. platyphylla japonica 'White Spire'
Cladrastis lutea
Cornus
 C. Kousa
 C. officinalis
Davidia involucrata
Fagus species
Parrotia persica
Pinus
 P. Bungeana
 P. nigra
Platanus × *acerifolia*
Prunus
 P. Maackii
 P. serrula
Pseudocydonia sinensis
Stewartia species
Ulmus parvifolia
Zelkova serrata

TWISTED OR PICTURESQUE BRANCHES

Acer palmatum 'Dissectum'
Fagus sylvatica 'Pendula'
Juniperus chinensis 'Kiazuka'
Salix Matsudana 'Tortuosa'

NARROW, UPRIGHT OR COLUMNAR HABIT

Calocedrus decurrens
Carpinus Betulus 'Fastigiata'
×*Cupressocyparis Leylandii*
Cupressus sempervirens
Ginkgo biloba 'Sentry'
Juniperus
 J. chinensis 'Mountbatten'
 J. scopulorum 'Skyrocket'
Liriodendron Tulipifera 'Fastigiatum'
Magnolia grandiflora 'Hasse'
Picea Omorika
Pinus Strobus 'Fastigiata'
Populus nigra 'Italica'
Quercus robur 'Fastigiata'
Sophora japonica 'Princeton Upright'
Taxodium distichum

WEEPING OR PENDULOUS HABIT

Chamaecyparis nootkatensis 'Pendula'
Fagus sylvatica 'Pendula'
Juniperus scopulorum 'Tolleson's Weeping'
Malus species, some
Prunus subhirtella 'Pendula'
Pyrus salicifolia 'Pendula'
Salix alba tristis
Sequoiadendron giganteum 'Pendulum'

VARIEGATED FOLIAGE

Acer platanoides 'Drummondii'
×*Cupressocyparis Leylandii* 'Silver Dust'
Ilex species, some cultivars
Liriodendron Tulipifera 'Aureo-marginatum'
Pinus
 P. Thunbergiana 'Oculus-draconis'
 P. Wallichiana 'Zebrina'

PURPLE FOLIAGE

Acer
 A. palmatum, several cultivars
 A. platanoides 'Crimson King'
Cercis canadensis 'Forest Pansy'
Cryptomeria japonica 'Elegans'
Fagus sylvatica 'Atropunicea'
Gleditsia triacanthos 'Ruby Lace'
Malus species, some
Prunus
 P. × *blireiana*
 P. cerasifera 'Thundercloud'

GOLDEN FOLIAGE

Chamaecyparis
 C. obtusa 'Crippsii'
 C. pisifera 'Filifera Aurea'
Cryptomeria japonica 'Sekkan'
 ×*Cupressocyparis*
 ×*C. Leylandii* 'Castlewellan'
 ×*C. Leylandii* 'Robinson's Gold'
Gleditsia triacanthos 'Sunburst'
Picea orientalis 'Aurea'
Pinus Thunbergiana 'Oculus-draconis'
Robinia Pseudoacacia 'Frisia'

BLUE OR GRAYISH FOLIAGE

Abies concolor
Cedrus atlantica 'Glauca'
Chamaecyparis
 C. pisifera 'Boulevard'
 C. pisifera 'Squarrosa'
Cunninghamia lanceolata 'Glauca'
Juniperus
 J. chinensis 'Mountbatten'
 J. scopulorum 'Tolleson's Weeping'
 J. virginiana 'Manhattan Blue'
Picea
 P. glauca
 P. pungens 'Glauca'
Pinus
 P. Cembra
 P. koraiensis
 P. Strobus
 P. Wallichiana
Pseudotsuga Menziesii 'Glauca'
Pyrus salicifolia 'Pendula'

Sequoiadendron giganteum 'Hazel Smith'

TREES FOR SEASHORE

Acer platanoides
Acer rubrum
Aesculus Hippocastanum
Cryptomeria japonica
×*Cupressocyparis Leylandii*
Cupressus macrocarpa
Ilex opaca
Juniperus virginiana
Magnolia grandiflora
Nyssa sylvatica
Picea pungens 'Glauca'
Pinus halapensis
Pinus nigra
Pinus sylvestris
Pinus Thunbergiana
Platanus ×*acerifolia*
Quercus agrifolia
Quercus alba
Quercus Ilex
Quercus virginiana
Sophora japonica
Thuja occidentalis
Tilia cordata
Ulmus parviflora

THE USDA PLANT HARDINESS MAP OF THE UNITED STATES

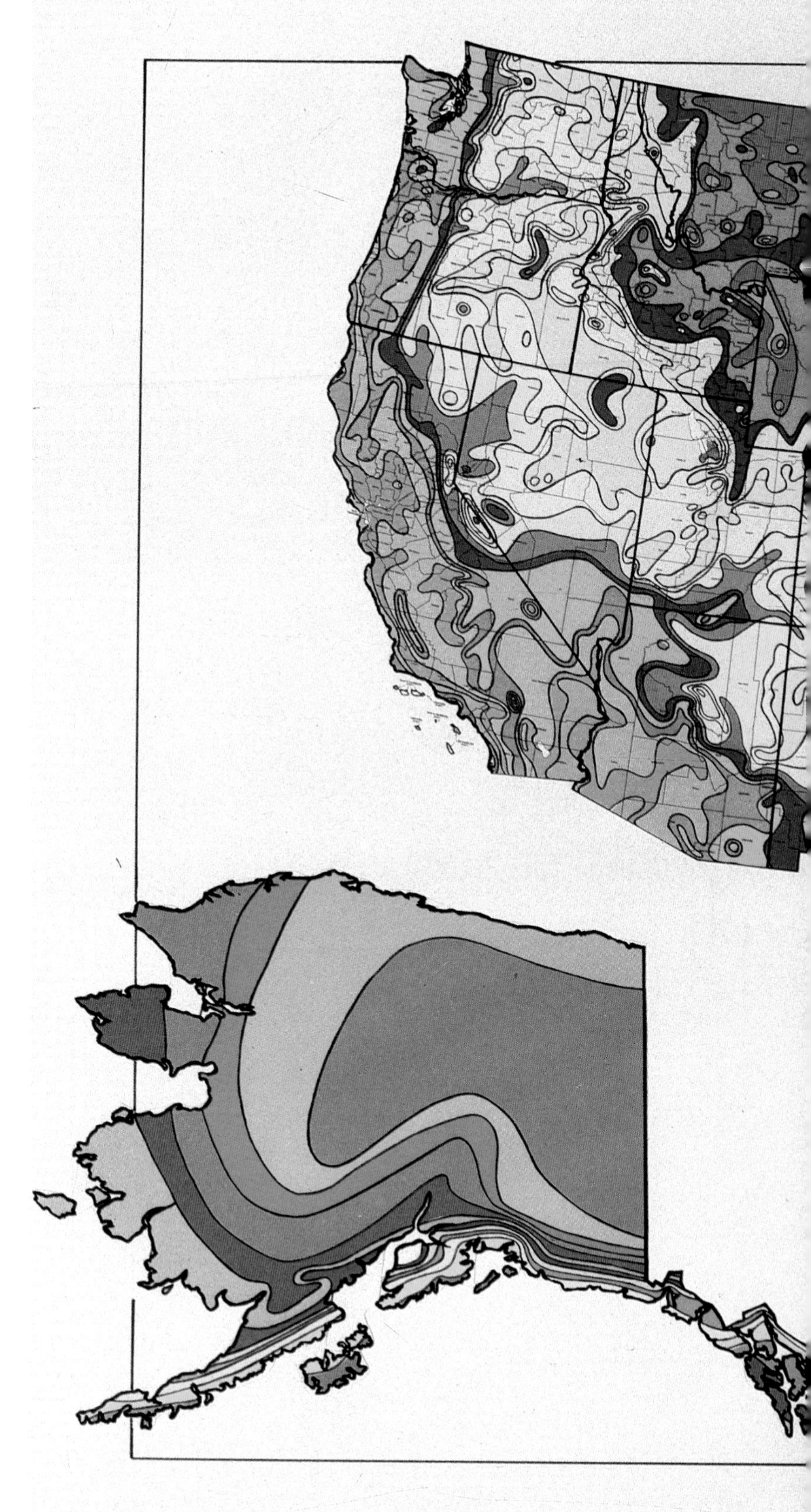

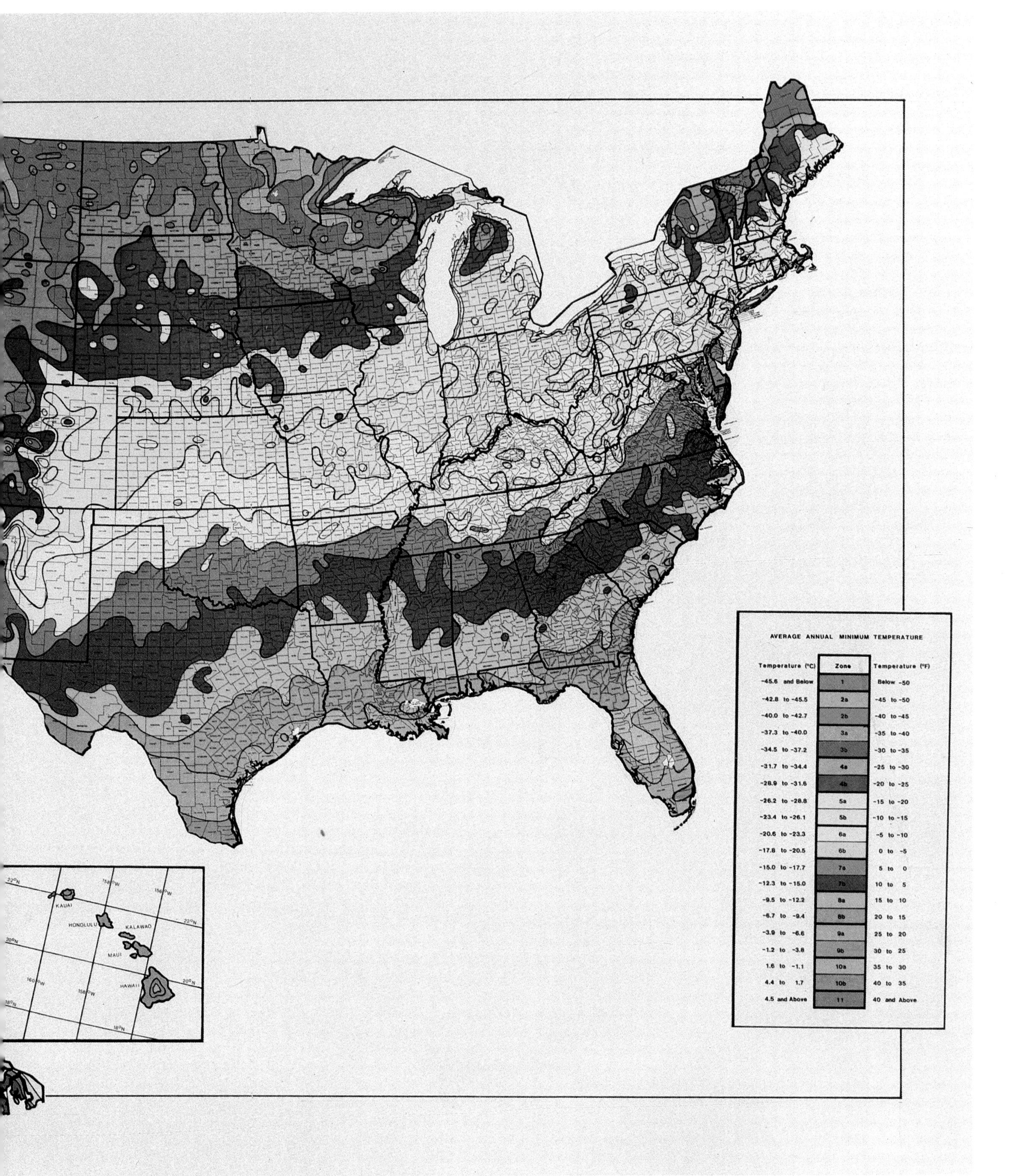
AVERAGE ANNUAL MINIMUM TEMPERATURE
Temperature (°C)
Zone
Temperature (°F)
-45.6 and Below
1
Below -50
-42.8 to -45.5
2a
-45 to -50
-40.0 to -42.7
2b
-40 to -45
-37.3 to -40.0
3a
-35 to -40
-34.5 to -37.2
3b
-30 to -35
-31.7 to -34.4
4a
-25 to -30
-28.9 to -31.6
4b
-20 to -25
-26.2 to -28.8
5a
-15 to -20
-23.4 to -26.1
5b
-10 to -15
-20.6 to -23.3
6a
-5 to -10
-17.8 to -20.5
6b
0 to -5
-15.0 to -17.7
7a
5 to 0
-12.3 to -15.0
7b
10 to 5
-9.5 to -12.2
8a
15 to 10
-6.7 to -9.4
8b
20 to 15
-3.9 to -6.6
9a
25 to 20
-1.2 to -3.8
9b
30 to 25
1.6 to -1.1
10a
35 to 30
4.4 to 1.7
10b
40 to 35
4.5 and Above
11
40 and Above
22°N
158°W
156°W
KAUAI
HONOLULU
KALAWAO
22°N
20°N
MAUI
160°W
158°W
HAWAII
20°N
18°N
18°N

INDEX

C

Centaurea
cyanus, 136-137, 136
moschata, 137
plant portrait, 136-137

Pot marigold. See Calendula officinalis
Praire gentian. See Eustoma grandiflorum

Q

R

S

PHOTOGRAPHIC CREDITS

Flowering Shrubs

Bales, Suzanne Frutig
Cresson, Charles O.
Dirr, Michael A.
Druse, Ken

Drawings by Michael Gale (pages 83 and 85) and
Frederick J. Latasa (page 36)

Cutting Gardens

Armitage, Allan: page 147 top; ***Ball Seed Co.:*** page 145 top; ***Dirr, Michael:*** page 151 top; ***Druse, Ken:*** pages 154, 161 bottom; ***Floranova Ltd:*** page 144 bottom; ***Gitts, Nicholas, of Swan Island Dahlias:*** page 167 middle; ***Horticultural Photography, Corvallis, OR:*** 162 left; ***Mohonk Mountain House Archives:*** page 112, ***Netherlands Flower Bulb Information Center:*** pages 165 bottom, 166 bottom, 167, bottom; ***Pan American Seed Co.:*** page 142 right; ***Rokach, Allen:*** page 150 bottom; ***Sakata Seed America, Inc.:*** page 139 bottom; ***Viette, Andre:*** page 157 bottom; ***W. Atlee Burpee & Co.:*** pages 134 top left and bottom, 135 both, 136 both, 137 top, 138 top, 140 bottom, 141 both, 142 left, 146 both, 147 bottom, 148 middle and bottom, 151 bottom, 155 bottom left, 156 top and middle, 159 top and middle, 163, 164 left, 165 top, 168 top, 168 both, 170 both.

Illustrations on pages 100, 103, 107, 109, 113 , 114 and 120 by Elayne Sears
Illustrations on page 110 by Michael Gale

Ornamental Trees

All photographs by Michael Dirr except as noted. Agricultural Research Service, USDA pages 268-269; Charles Cresson pages 220 bottom right, 226 upper left, 230 right, 235 bottom, 247 bottom, 248 top; W. Atlee Burpee & Co. page 260.

Illustrations on pages 186, 187, 198, 208, 210, 212 by Elayne Sears
Illustrations on pages 256-258 by Michael Gale
Horticultural editor: Suzanne Frutig Bales